D1491057

STOP!

This is the back of the book.
You wouldn't want to spoil a great ending

This book is printed "manga-style," in the authentic Japanese right-to-le format. Since none of the artwork has been flipped or altered, readers get to experience the story just as the creator intended. You've been asking for it, so TOKYOPOP® delivered: authentic, hot-off-the-press, and far more fun!

DIRECTIONS

If this is your first time reading manga-style, here's a quick guide to help you understand how it works.

It's easy... just start in the top right panel and follow the numbers. Have fun, and look fo more 100% authentic manga from TOKYOPOP®!

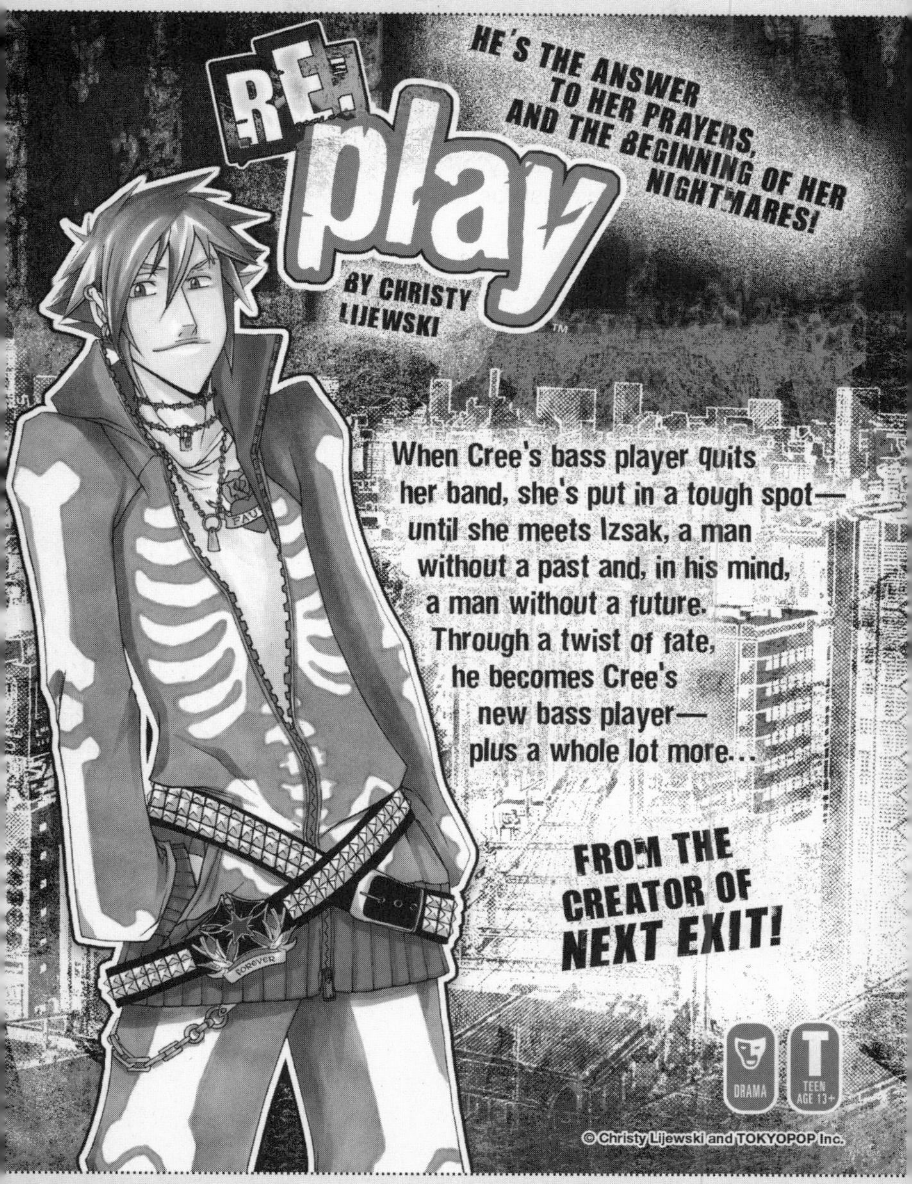
RE: play
BY CHRISTY LIJEWSKI
HE'S THE ANSWER TO HER PRAYERS, AND THE BEGINNING OF HER NIGHTMARES!
When Cree's bass player quits her band, she's put in a tough spot—until she meets Izsak, a man without a past and, in his mind, a man without a future. Through a twist of fate, he becomes Cree's new bass player—plus a whole lot more...
FROM THE CREATOR OF NEXT EXIT!
DRAMA
T
TEEN AGE 13+
© Christy Lijewski and TOKYOPOP Inc.

ARE YOU TRULY ALIVE?

In the collapsing world of the afterlife, two guardians face the ultimate question: Thaddeus yearns for answers, while Mercutio seeks his true love. Will they be able to find it all before it's too late?

ART BY ROB STEEN AND STORY BY STORMCROW HAYES

A MEDITATIVE AND BROODING EXPLORATION INTO THE ENDLESS POSSIBILITIES OF THE AFTERLIFE.

© Sam Hayes, Rob Steen and TOKYOPOP Inc.

GRENADIER

CREATED BY: SOUSUKE KAISE

TWO BIG GUNS CAN BRING PEACE TO THE WORLD...

Rushuna is a golden-haired Senshi—a gunslinger who travels the land with one purpose: to make the world a peaceful place with her high-caliber revolver and enchanting smile. However, her journey of nonviolence won't be easy and she may have to display her amazing gun skills and talent for reloading on the bounce.

THE MANGA THAT SPARKED THE POPULAR ANIME!

ACTION

OT OLDER TEEN AGE 16+

SATISFACTION GUARANTEED

VOLUME 1 BY RYO SAENAGI

HAMBURG // LONDON // LOS ANGELES // TOKYO

Satisfaction Guaranteed Vol. 1
Created by Ryo Saenagi

Translation - Monica Seya
English Adaptation - Matt Yamashita
Copy Editor - Hope Donovan
Retouch and Lettering - Alyson Stetz
Production Artist - Jennifer Carbajal
Cover Design - Louis Csontos

Editor - Elizabeth Hurchalla
Digital Imaging Manager - Chris Buford
Production Managers - Elisabeth Brizzi
Managing Editor - Lindsey Johnston
VP of Production - Ron Klamert
Editor-in-Chief - Rob Tokar
Publisher - Mike Kiley
President and C.O.O. - John Parker
C.E.O. and Chief Creative Officer - Stuart Levy

A  Manga

TOKYOPOP Inc.
5900 Wilshire Blvd. Suite 2000
Los Angeles, CA 90036

E-mail: info@TOKYOPOP.com
Come visit us online at www.TOKYOPOP.com

ISBN:1-59816-532-1

First TOKYOPOP printing: July 2006
10 9 8 7 6 5 4 3 2 1
Printed in the USA

CONTENTS

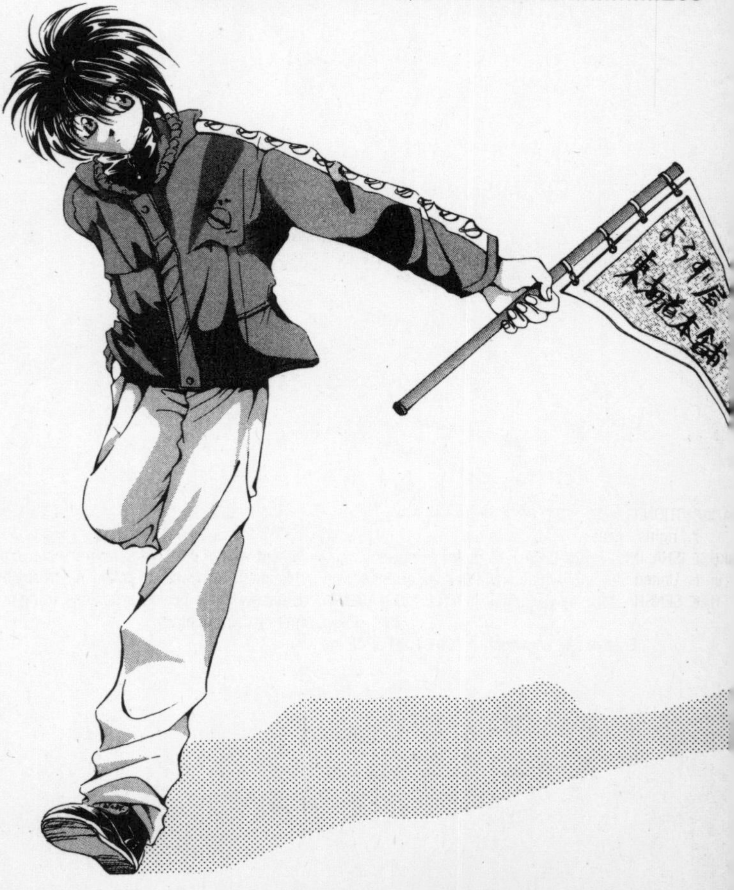

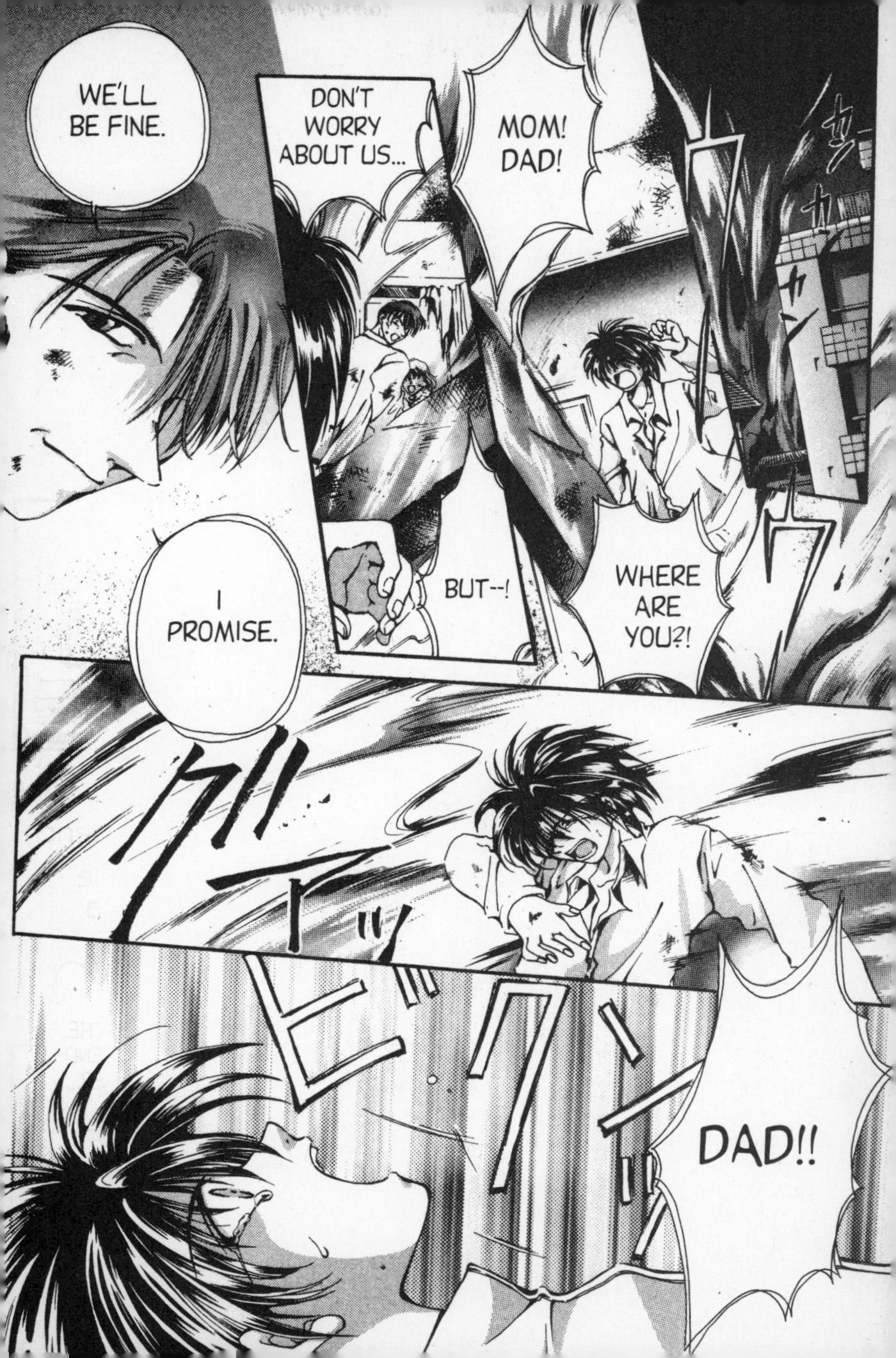
MOM! DAD!
WHERE ARE YOU?!
DON'T WORRY ABOUT US...
BUT--!
WE'LL BE FINE.
I PROMISE.
DAD!!

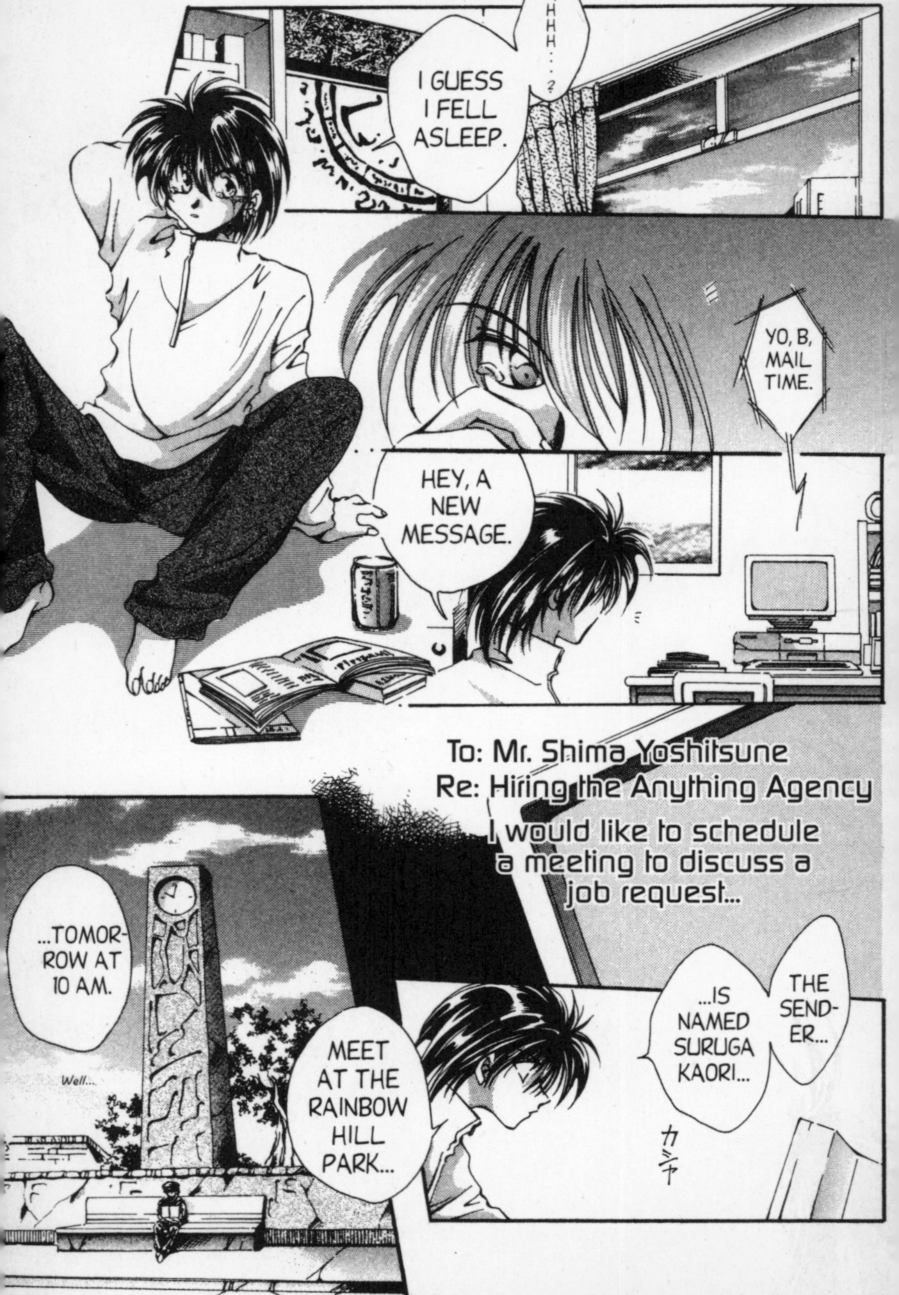
AHHH...?
I GUESS I FELL ASLEEP.
YO, B, MAIL TIME.
HEY, A NEW MESSAGE.
To: Mr. Shima Yoshitsune
Re: Hiring the Anything Agency
I would like to schedule a meeting to discuss a job request...
THE SENDER...
...IS NAMED SURUGA KAORI...
カシャ
MEET AT THE RAINBOW HILL PARK...
...TOMORROW AT 10 AM.
Well...

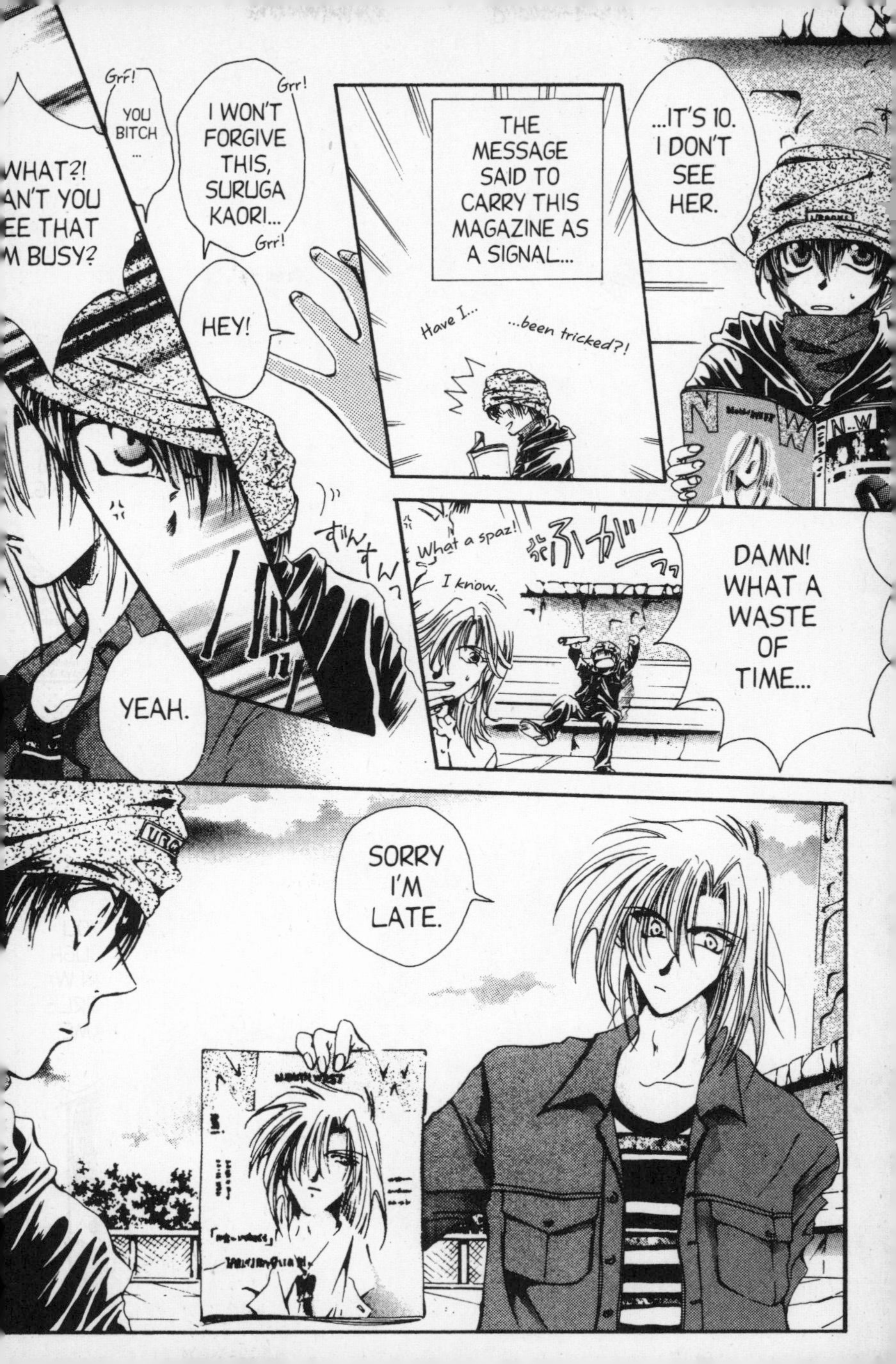

...IT'S 10. I DON'T SEE HER.
THE MESSAGE SAID TO CARRY THIS MAGAZINE AS A SIGNAL...
Have I...
...been tricked?!
Grr!
I WON'T FORGIVE THIS, SURUGA KAORI...
Grr!
Grr!
YOU BITCH ...
DAMN! WHAT A WASTE OF TIME...
What a spaz!
I know.
HEY!
WHAT?! AN'T YOU EE THAT M BUSY?
YEAH.
SORRY I'M LATE.

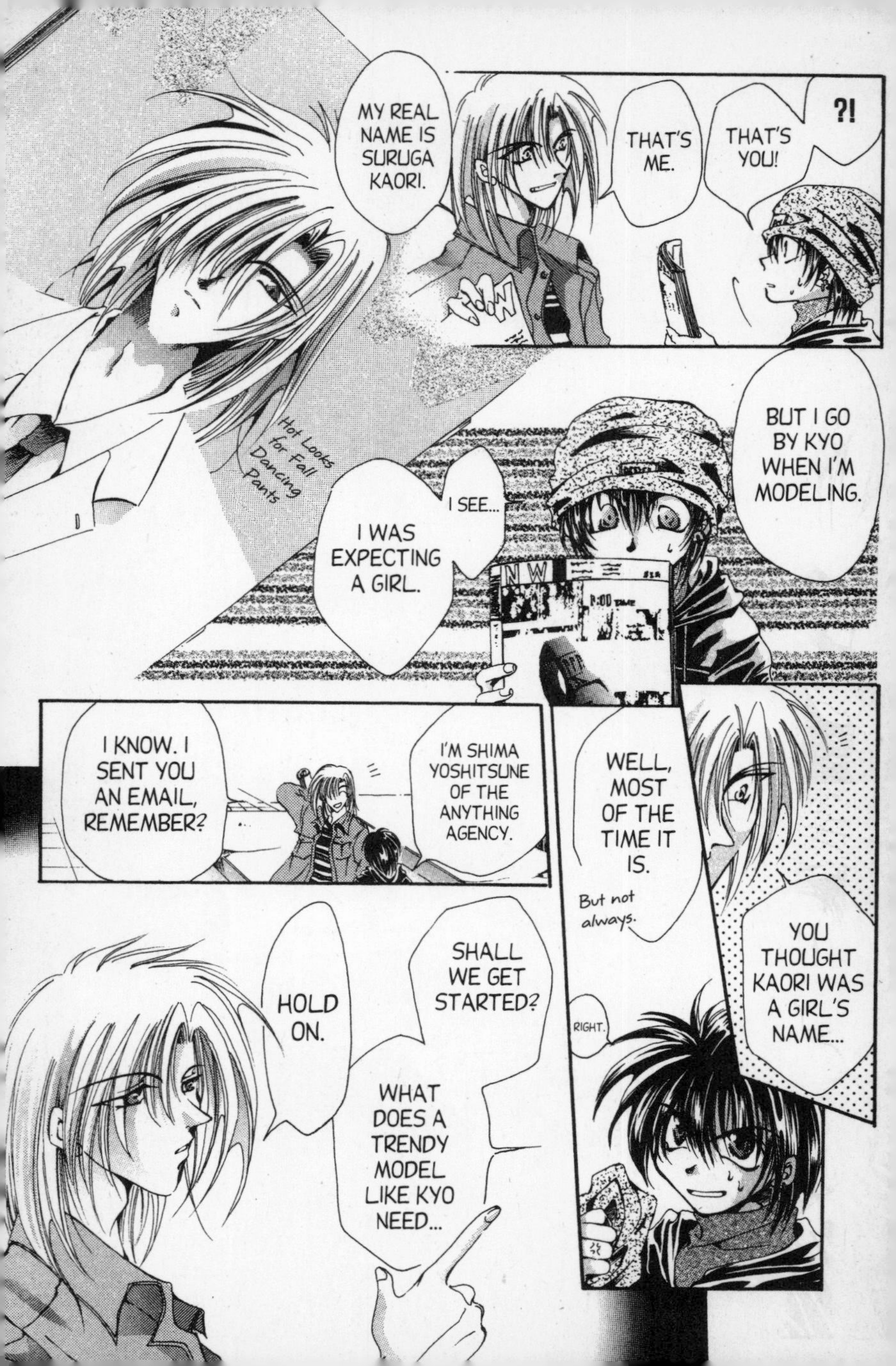

?!
THAT'S YOU!
THAT'S ME.
MY REAL NAME IS SURUGA KAORI.
Hot Looks for Fall Dancing Pants
BUT I GO BY KYO WHEN I'M MODELING.
I SEE...
I WAS EXPECTING A GIRL.
YOU THOUGHT KAORI WAS A GIRL'S NAME...
RIGHT.
WELL, MOST OF THE TIME IT IS.
But not always.
I'M SHIMA YOSHITSUNE OF THE ANYTHING AGENCY.
I KNOW. I SENT YOU AN EMAIL, REMEMBER?
SHALL WE GET STARTED?
HOLD ON.
WHAT DOES A TRENDY MODEL LIKE KYO NEED...

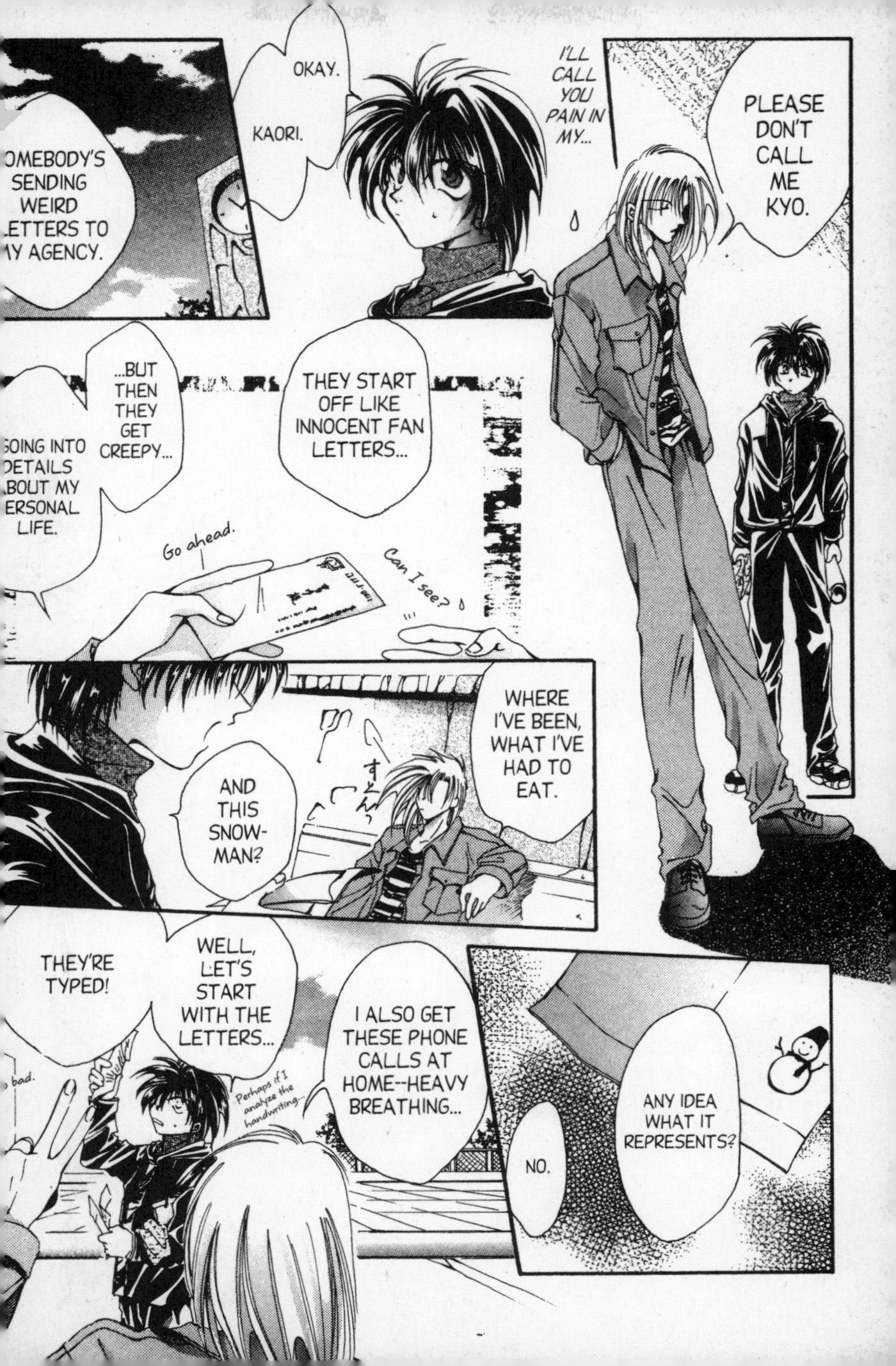
I'LL CALL YOU PAIN IN MY...
PLEASE DON'T CALL ME KYO.
OKAY.
KAORI.
OMEBODY'S SENDING WEIRD ETTERS TO IY AGENCY.
THEY START OFF LIKE INNOCENT FAN LETTERS...
...BUT THEN THEY GET CREEPY...
OING INTO ETAILS BOUT MY ERSONAL LIFE.
Can I see?
Go ahead.
WHERE I'VE BEEN, WHAT I'VE HAD TO EAT.
すとん
AND THIS SNOW-MAN?
ANY IDEA WHAT IT REPRESENTS?
NO.
I ALSO GET THESE PHONE CALLS AT HOME--HEAVY BREATHING...
WELL, LET'S START WITH THE LETTERS...
Perhaps if I analyze the handwriting...
THEY'RE TYPED!

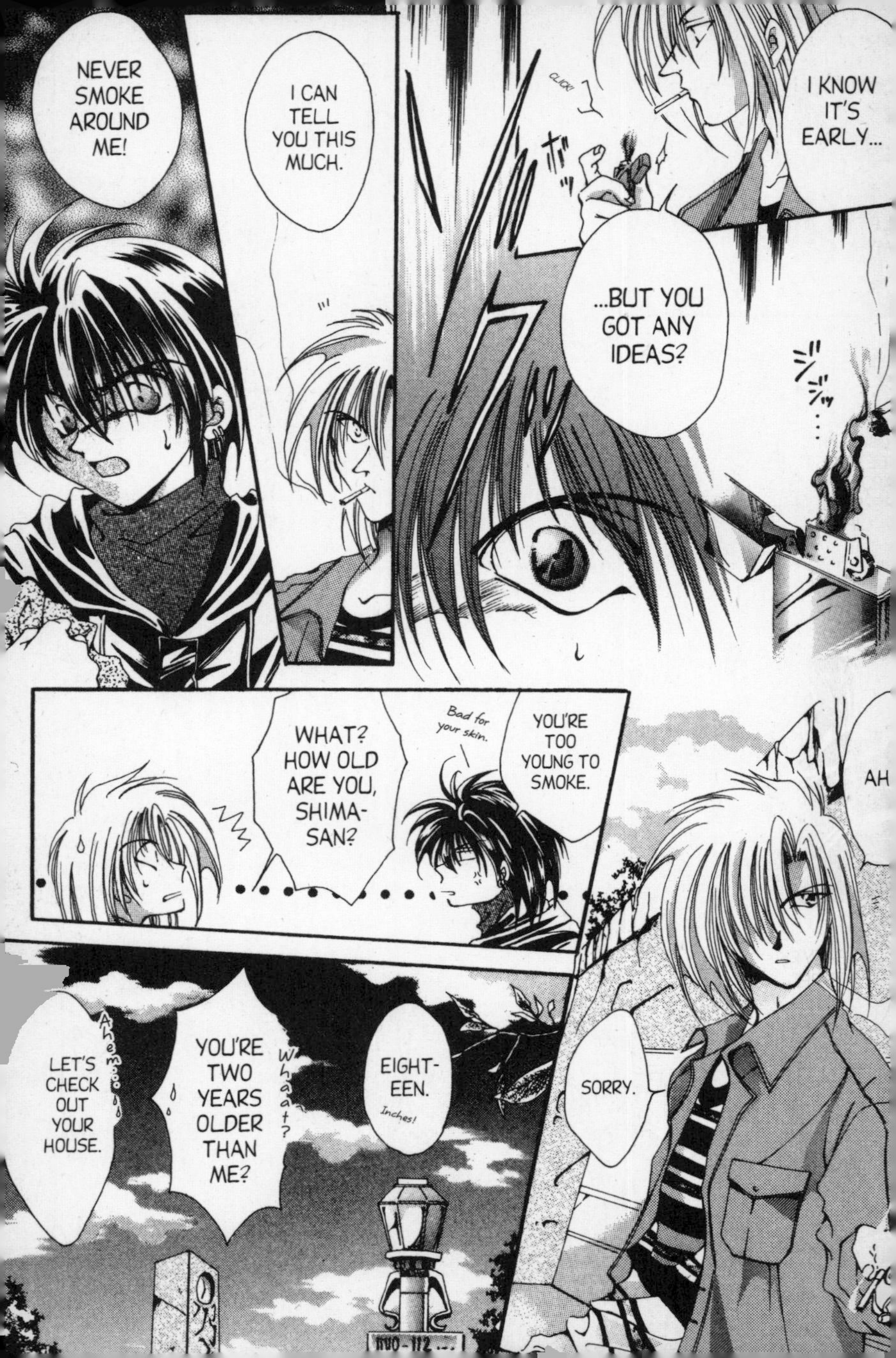
I KNOW IT'S EARLY...
CLICK!
...BUT YOU GOT ANY IDEAS?
I CAN TELL YOU THIS MUCH.
NEVER SMOKE AROUND ME!
AH
SORRY.
YOU'RE TOO YOUNG TO SMOKE.
Bad for your skin.
WHAT? HOW OLD ARE YOU, SHIMA-SAN?
EIGHTEEN.
Inches!
YOU'RE TWO YEARS OLDER THAN ME?
Whaaat?
LET'S CHECK OUT YOUR HOUSE.
Ahem...

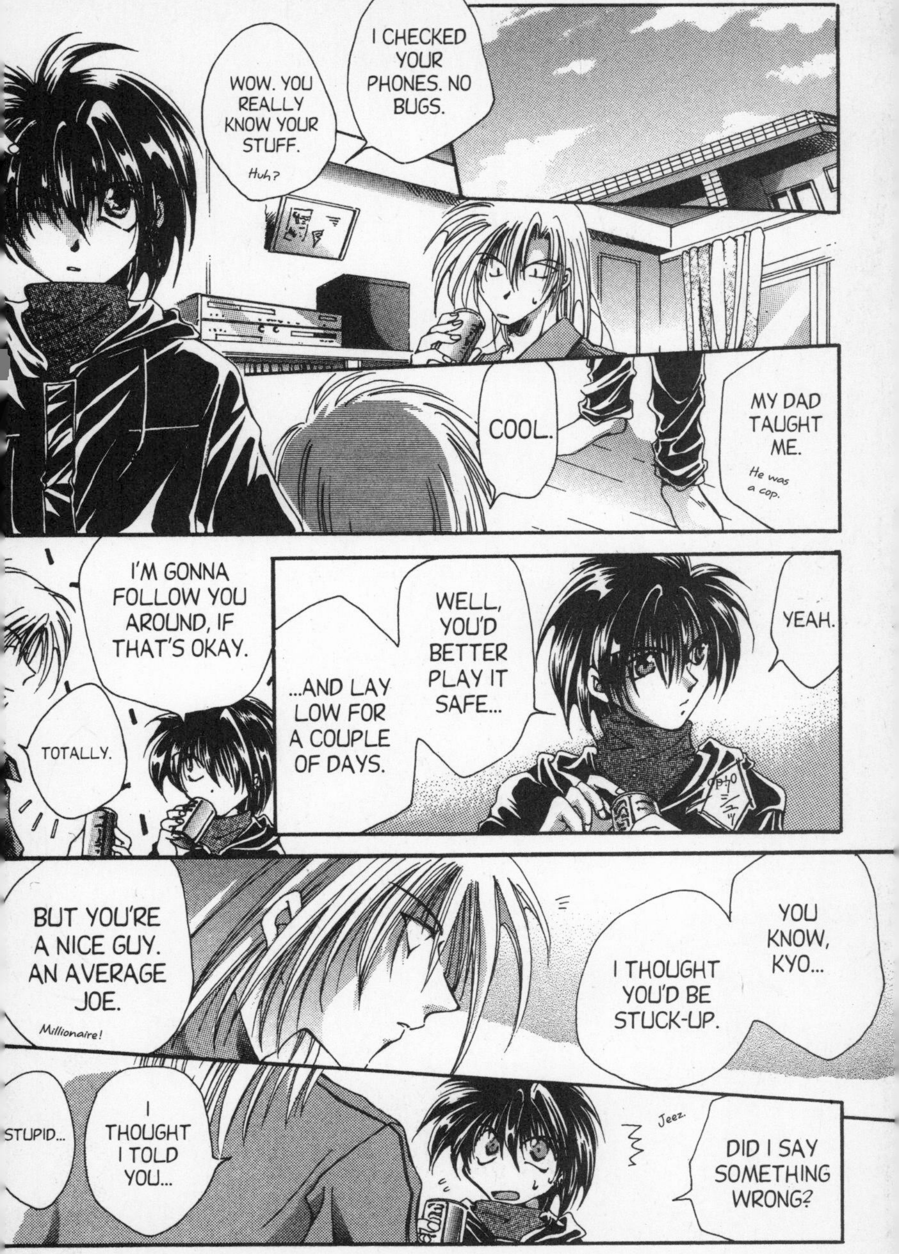
I CHECKED YOUR PHONES. NO BUGS.
WOW. YOU REALLY KNOW YOUR STUFF.
Huh?
MY DAD TAUGHT ME.
He was a cop.
COOL.
YEAH.
WELL, YOU'D BETTER PLAY IT SAFE...
...AND LAY LOW FOR A COUPLE OF DAYS.
I'M GONNA FOLLOW YOU AROUND, IF THAT'S OKAY.
TOTALLY.
YOU KNOW, KYO...
I THOUGHT YOU'D BE STUCK-UP.
BUT YOU'RE A NICE GUY. AN AVERAGE JOE.
Millionaire!
DID I SAY SOMETHING WRONG?
Jeez.
I THOUGHT I TOLD YOU...
STUPID...

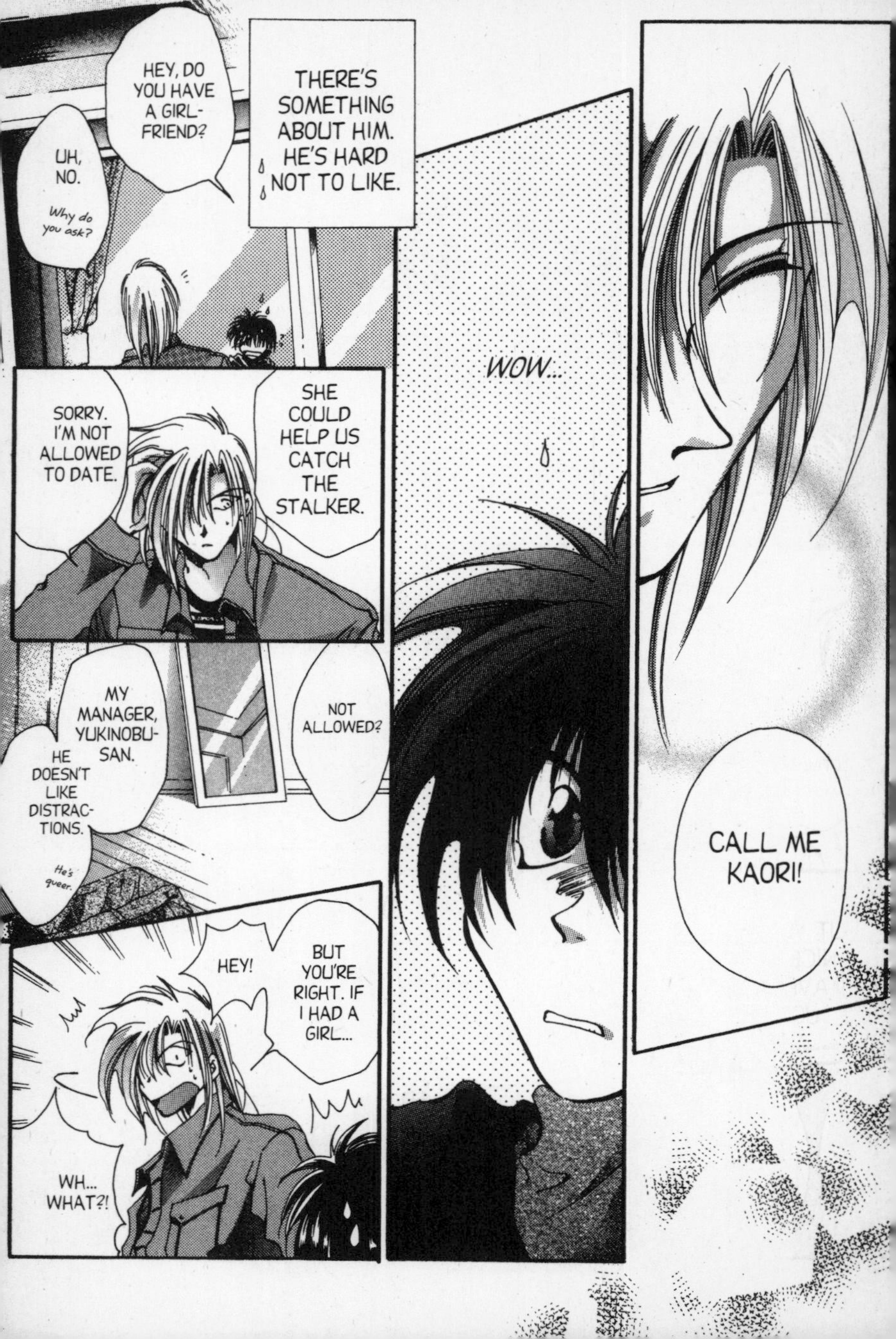
CALL ME KAORI!
WOW...
THERE'S SOMETHING ABOUT HIM. HE'S HARD NOT TO LIKE.
HEY, DO YOU HAVE A GIRL-FRIEND?
UH, NO.
Why do you ask?
SHE COULD HELP US CATCH THE STALKER.
SORRY. I'M NOT ALLOWED TO DATE.
NOT ALLOWED?
MY MANAGER, YUKINOBU-SAN.
HE DOESN'T LIKE DISTRAC-TIONS.
He's queer.
BUT YOU'RE RIGHT. IF I HAD A GIRL...
HEY!
WH... WHAT?!

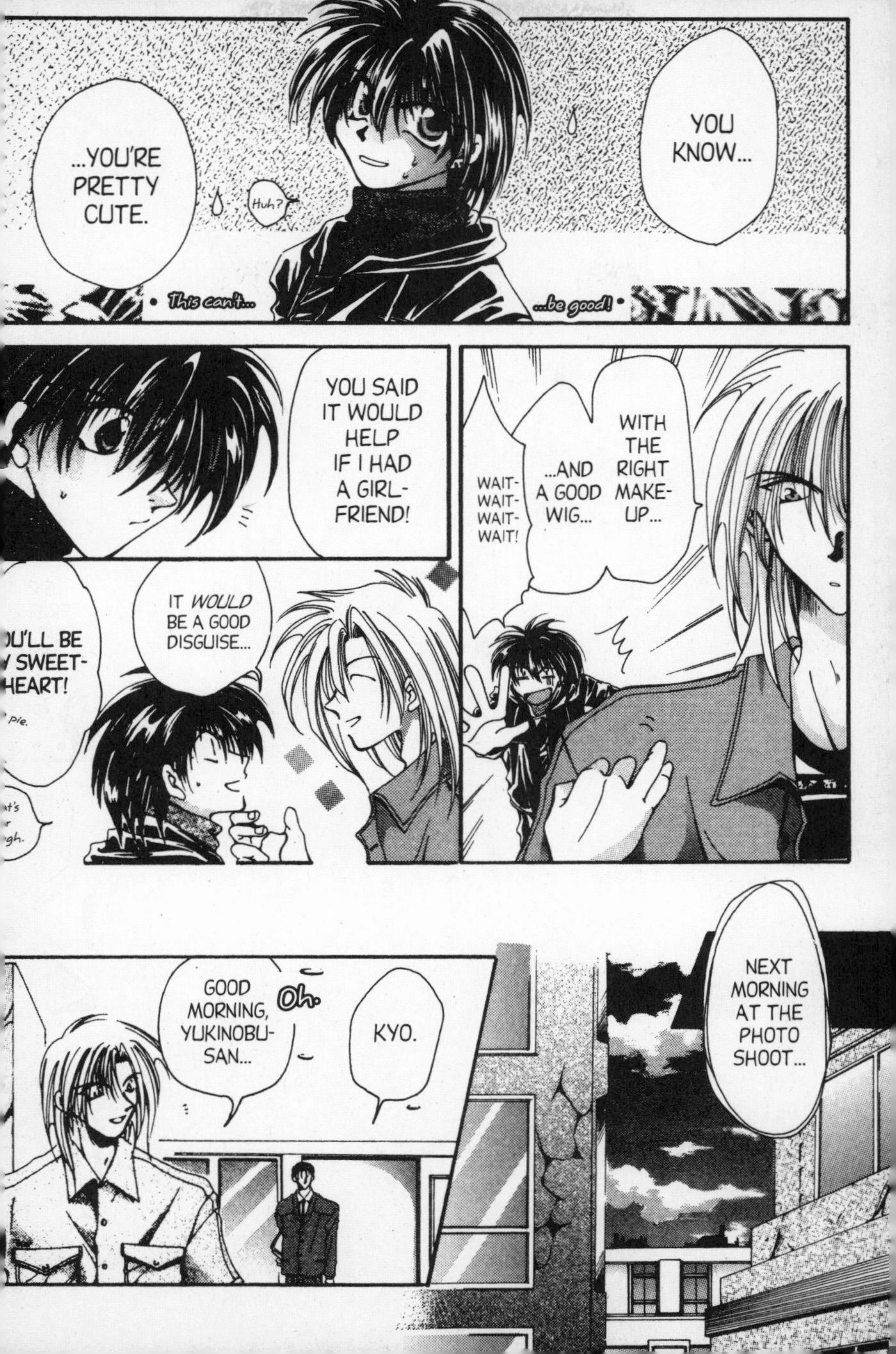
YOU KNOW...
...YOU'RE PRETTY CUTE.
Huh?
This can't...
...be good!
WITH THE RIGHT MAKE-UP...
...AND A GOOD WIG...
WAIT-WAIT-WAIT-WAIT!
YOU SAID IT WOULD HELP IF I HAD A GIRL-FRIEND!
IT WOULD BE A GOOD DISGUISE...
OU'LL BE Y SWEET-HEART!
pie.
NEXT MORNING AT THE PHOTO SHOOT...
KYO.
Oh.
GOOD MORNING, YUKINOBU-SAN...

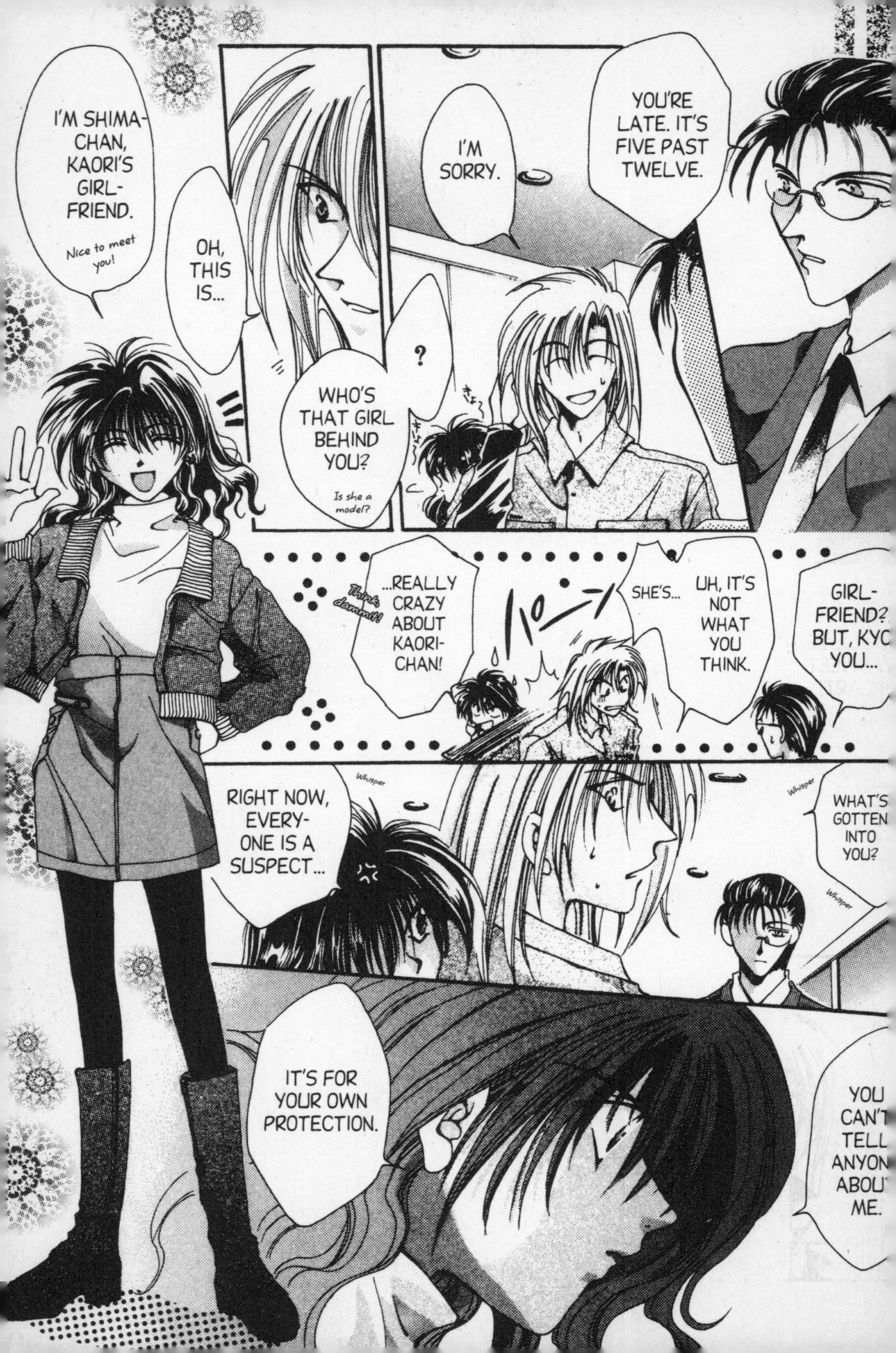
YOU'RE LATE. IT'S FIVE PAST TWELVE.
I'M SORRY.
?
WHO'S THAT GIRL BEHIND YOU?
Is she a model?
OH, THIS IS...
I'M SHIMA-CHAN, KAORI'S GIRL-FRIEND.
Nice to meet you!
GIRL-FRIEND? BUT, KYO YOU...
UH, IT'S NOT WHAT YOU THINK.
SHE'S...
...REALLY CRAZY ABOUT KAORI-CHAN!
Think, dammit!
Whisper
WHAT'S GOTTEN INTO YOU?
Whisper
Whisper
RIGHT NOW, EVERY-ONE IS A SUSPECT...
YOU CAN'T TELL ANYON ABOUT ME.
IT'S FOR YOUR OWN PROTECTION.

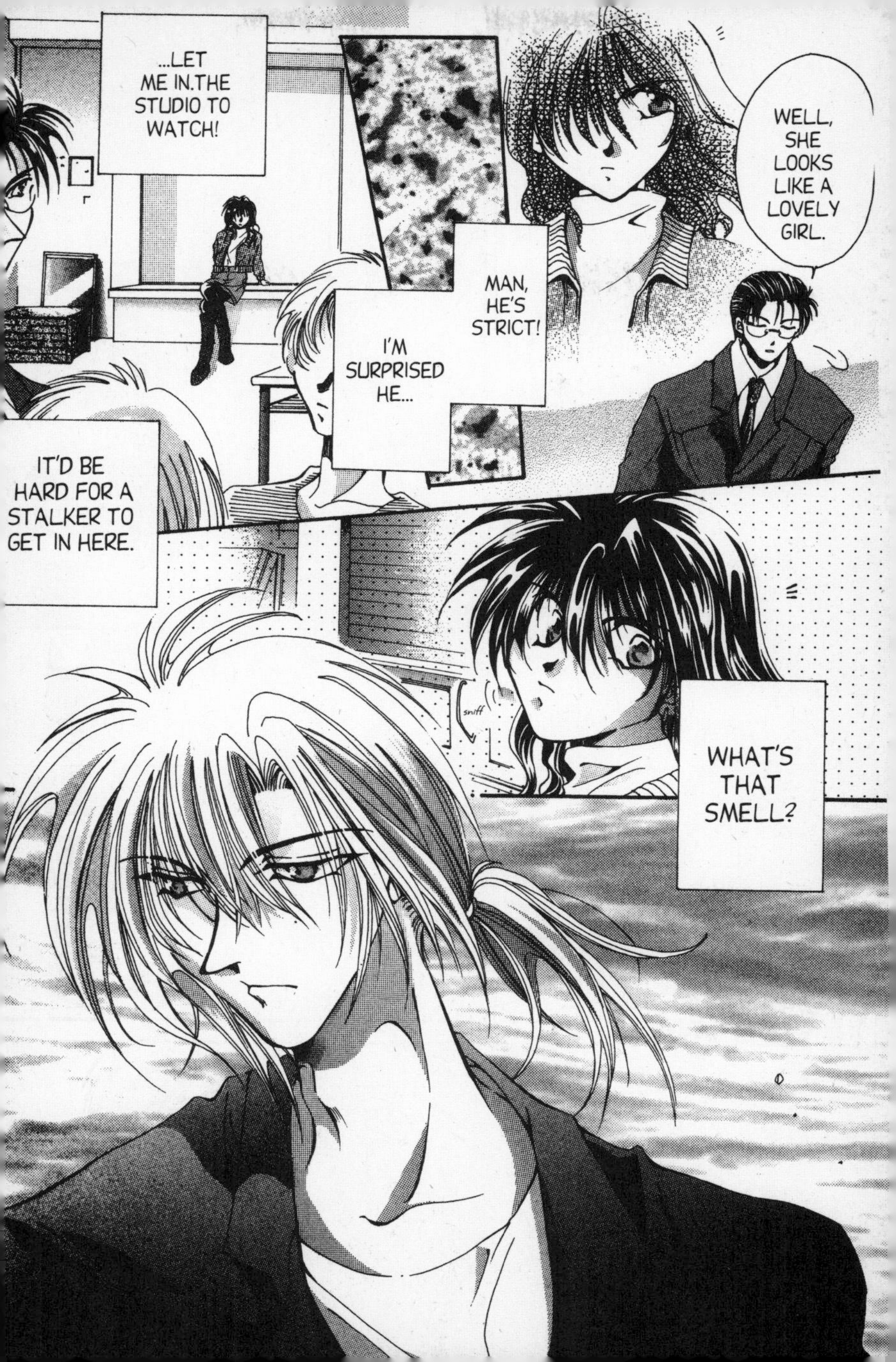
WELL, SHE LOOKS LIKE A LOVELY GIRL.
MAN, HE'S STRICT!
I'M SURPRISED HE...
...LET ME IN.THE STUDIO TO WATCH!
IT'D BE HARD FOR A STALKER TO GET IN HERE.
sniff
WHAT'S THAT SMELL?

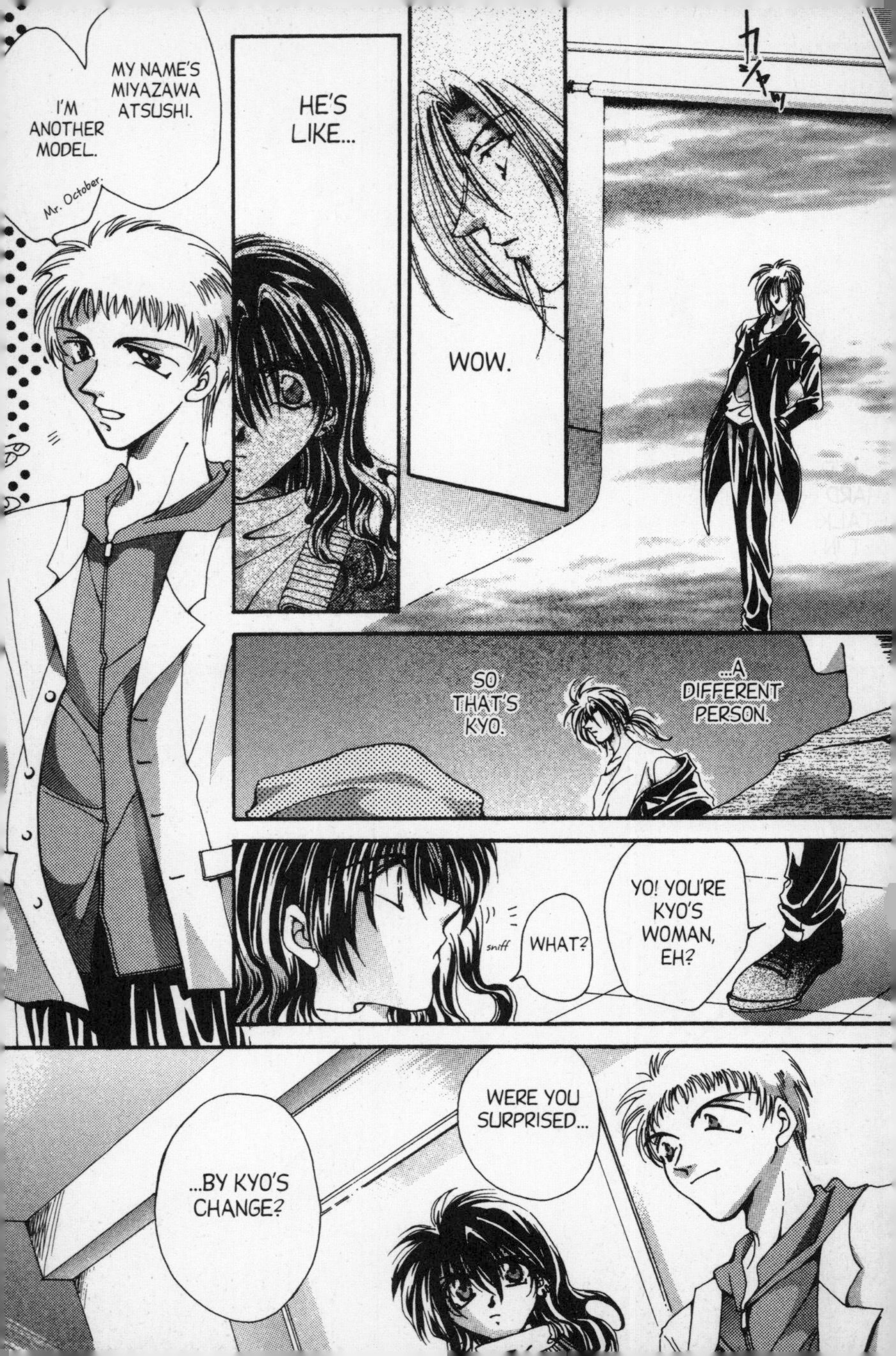
WOW.
HE'S LIKE...
...A DIFFERENT PERSON.
SO THAT'S KYO.
YO! YOU'RE KYO'S WOMAN, EH?
WHAT?
sniff
MY NAME'S MIYAZAWA ATSUSHI.
I'M ANOTHER MODEL.
Mr. October.
WERE YOU SURPRISED...
...BY KYO'S CHANGE?

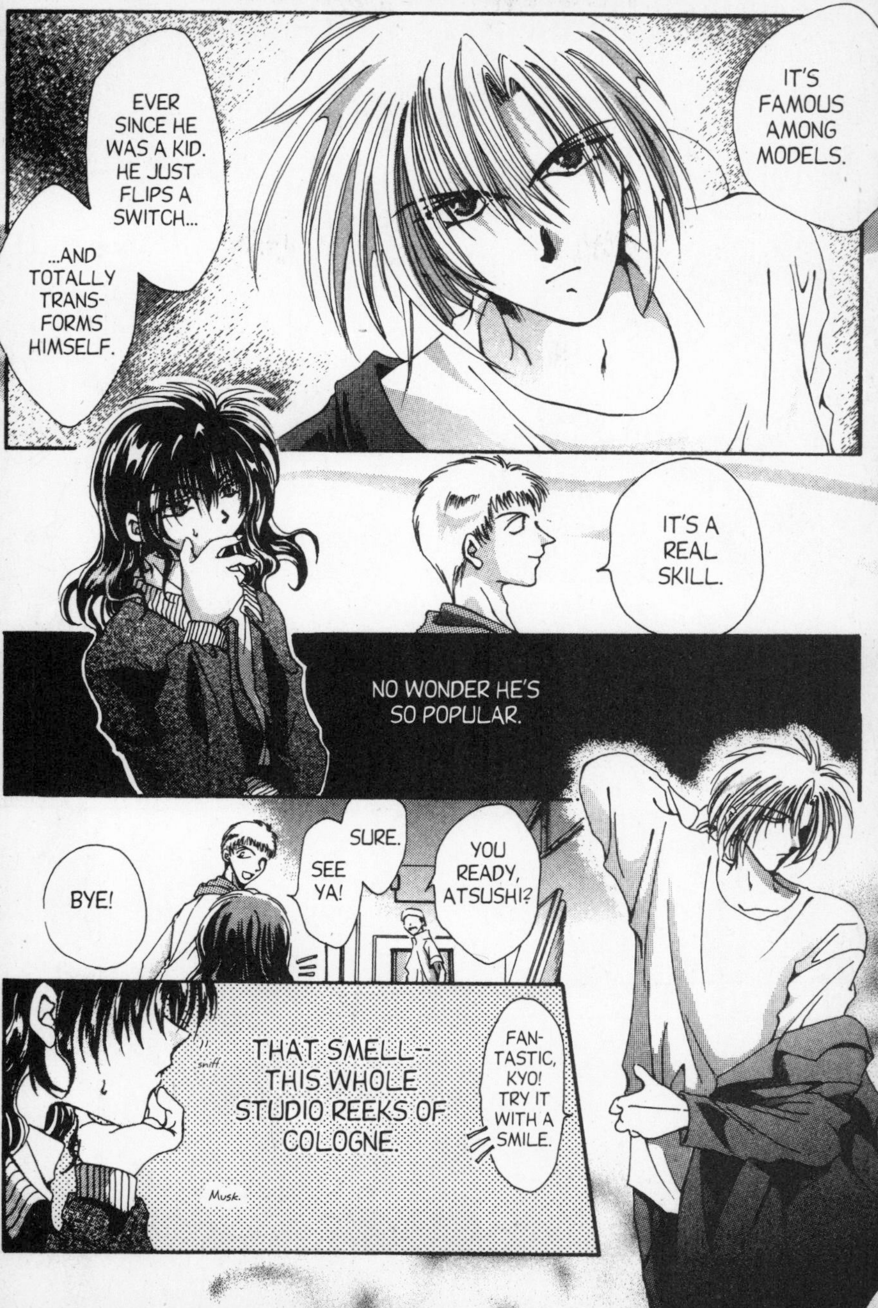
IT'S FAMOUS AMONG MODELS.
EVER SINCE HE WAS A KID. HE JUST FLIPS A SWITCH...
...AND TOTALLY TRANS-FORMS HIMSELF.
IT'S A REAL SKILL.
NO WONDER HE'S SO POPULAR.
YOU READY, ATSUSHI?
SURE.
SEE YA!
BYE!
FAN-TASTIC, KYO! TRY IT WITH A SMILE.
sniff
THAT SMELL-- THIS WHOLE STUDIO REEKS OF COLOGNE.
Musk.

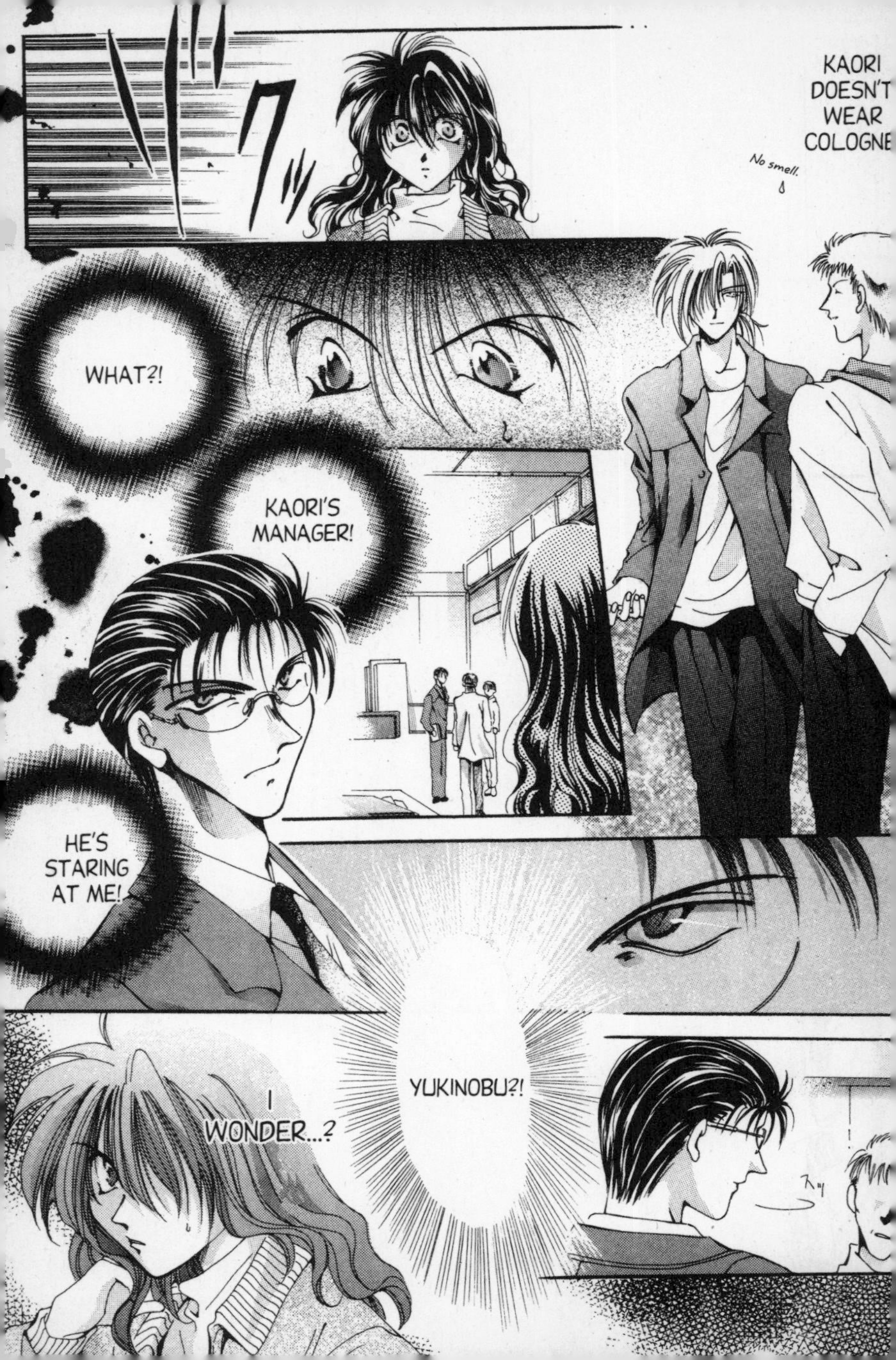
KAORI DOESN'T WEAR COLOGNE
No smell.
WHAT?!
KAORI'S MANAGER!
HE'S STARING AT ME!
YUKINOBU?!
I WONDER...?

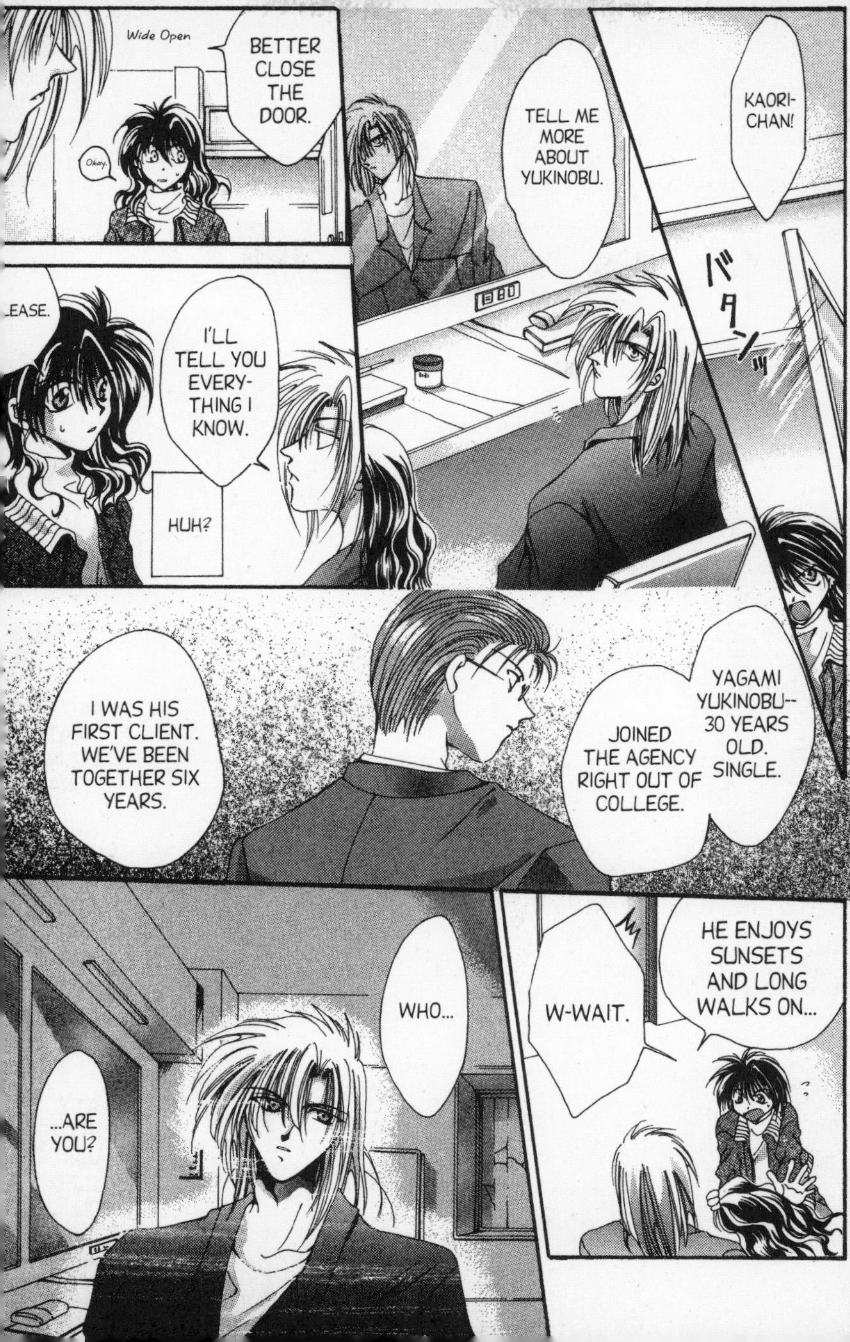
KAORI-CHAN!
バタンッ
TELL ME MORE ABOUT YUKINOBU.
Wide Open
BETTER CLOSE THE DOOR.
Okay.
LEASE.
I'LL TELL YOU EVERY-THING I KNOW.
HUH?
YAGAMI YUKINOBU--30 YEARS OLD. SINGLE.
JOINED THE AGENCY RIGHT OUT OF COLLEGE.
I WAS HIS FIRST CLIENT. WE'VE BEEN TOGETHER SIX YEARS.
HE ENJOYS SUNSETS AND LONG WALKS ON...
W-WAIT.
WHO...
...ARE YOU?

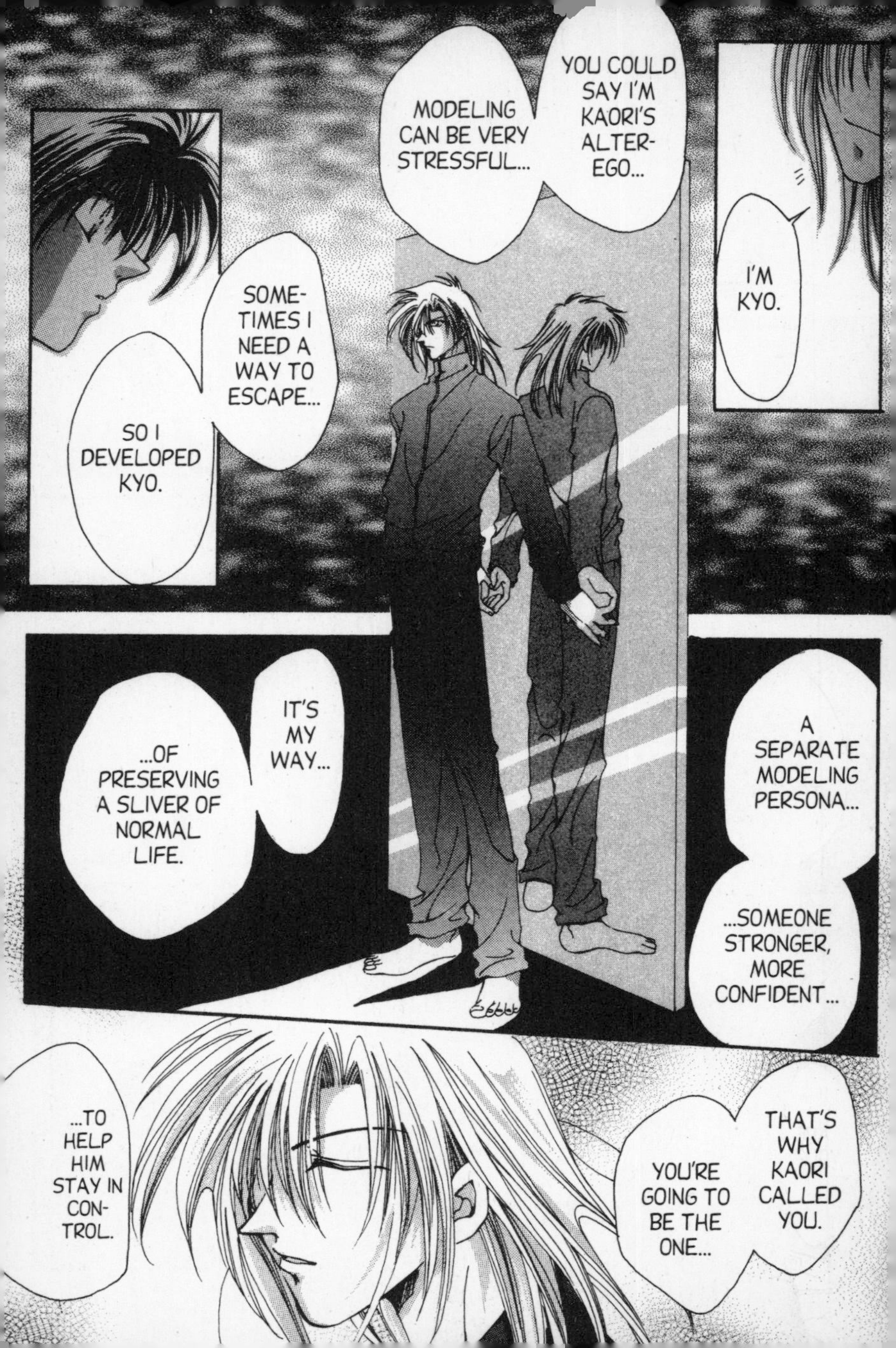
I'M KYO.
YOU COULD SAY I'M KAORI'S ALTER-EGO...
MODELING CAN BE VERY STRESSFUL...
SOME-TIMES I NEED A WAY TO ESCAPE...
SO I DEVELOPED KYO.
A SEPARATE MODELING PERSONA...
...SOMEONE STRONGER, MORE CONFIDENT...
IT'S MY WAY...
...OF PRESERVING A SLIVER OF NORMAL LIFE.
THAT'S WHY KAORI CALLED YOU.
YOU'RE GOING TO BE THE ONE...
...TO HELP HIM STAY IN CON-TROL.

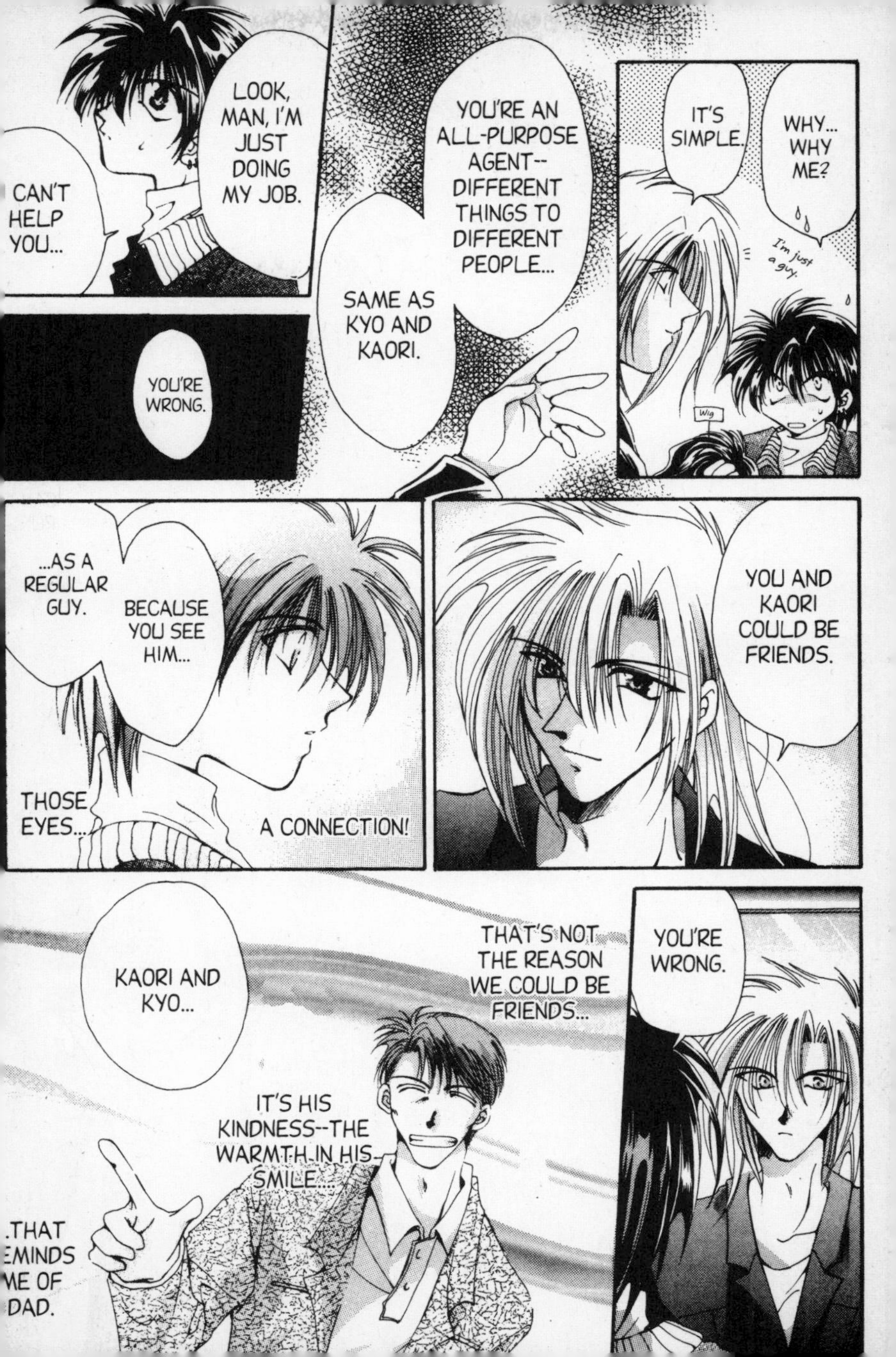

WHY... WHY ME?
IT'S SIMPLE.
I'm just a guy.
Wig
YOU'RE AN ALL-PURPOSE AGENT-- DIFFERENT THINGS TO DIFFERENT PEOPLE...
SAME AS KYO AND KAORI.
LOOK, MAN, I'M JUST DOING MY JOB.
CAN'T HELP YOU...
YOU'RE WRONG.
YOU AND KAORI COULD BE FRIENDS.
BECAUSE YOU SEE HIM...
...AS A REGULAR GUY.
A CONNECTION!
THOSE EYES...
YOU'RE WRONG.
THAT'S NOT THE REASON WE COULD BE FRIENDS...
KAORI AND KYO...
IT'S HIS KINDNESS--THE WARMTH IN HIS SMILE...
.THAT EMINDS ME OF DAD.

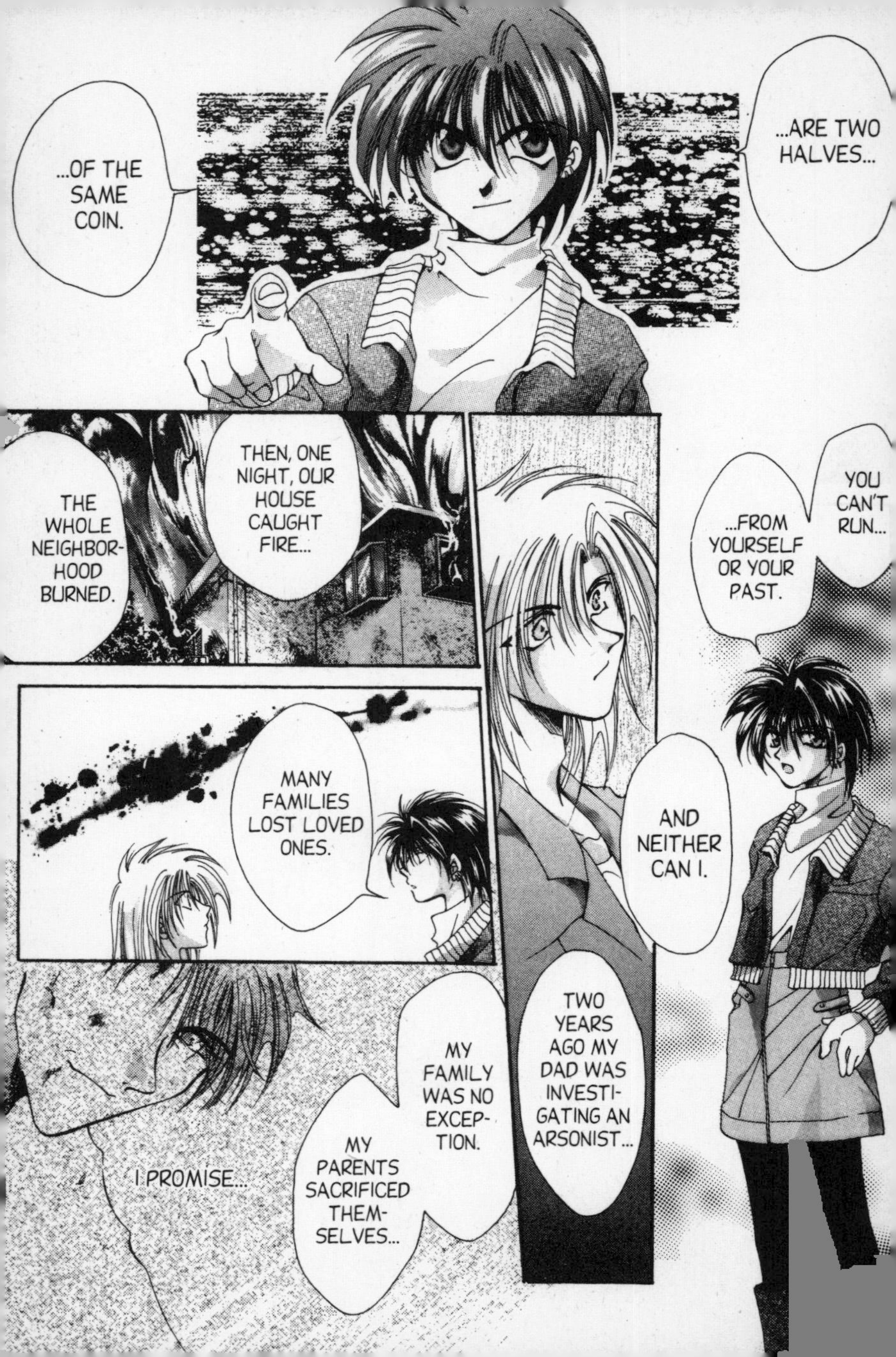

...ARE TWO HALVES...
...OF THE SAME COIN.
YOU CAN'T RUN...
...FROM YOURSELF OR YOUR PAST.
AND NEITHER CAN I.
TWO YEARS AGO MY DAD WAS INVESTI-GATING AN ARSONIST...
THEN, ONE NIGHT, OUR HOUSE CAUGHT FIRE...
THE WHOLE NEIGHBOR-HOOD BURNED.
MANY FAMILIES LOST LOVED ONES.
MY FAMILY WAS NO EXCEP-TION.
MY PARENTS SACRIFICED THEM-SELVES...
I PROMISE...

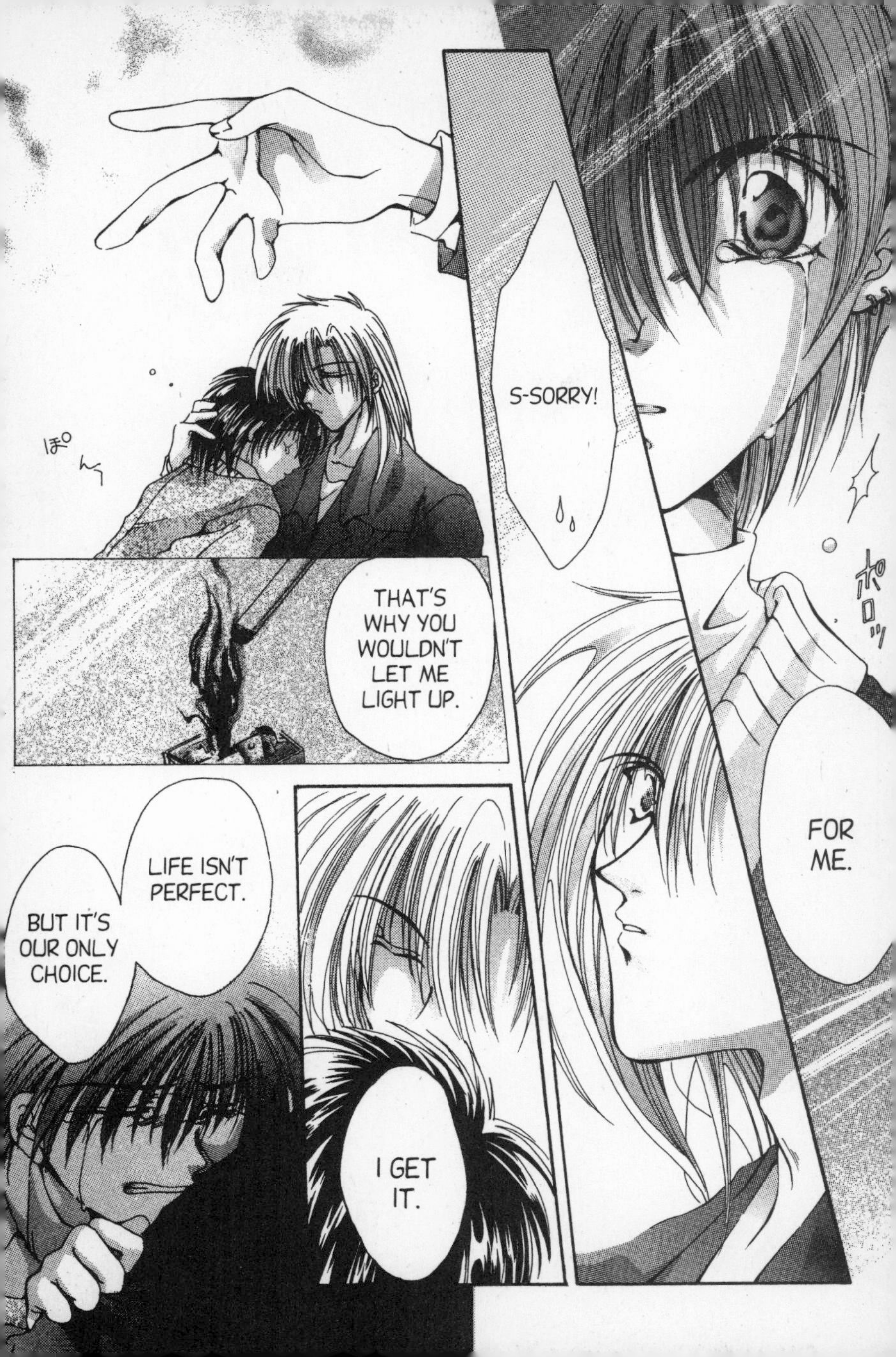

ポロッ
S-SORRY!
ぽん
FOR ME.
THAT'S WHY YOU WOULDN'T LET ME LIGHT UP.
I GET IT.
LIFE ISN'T PERFECT.
BUT IT'S OUR ONLY CHOICE.

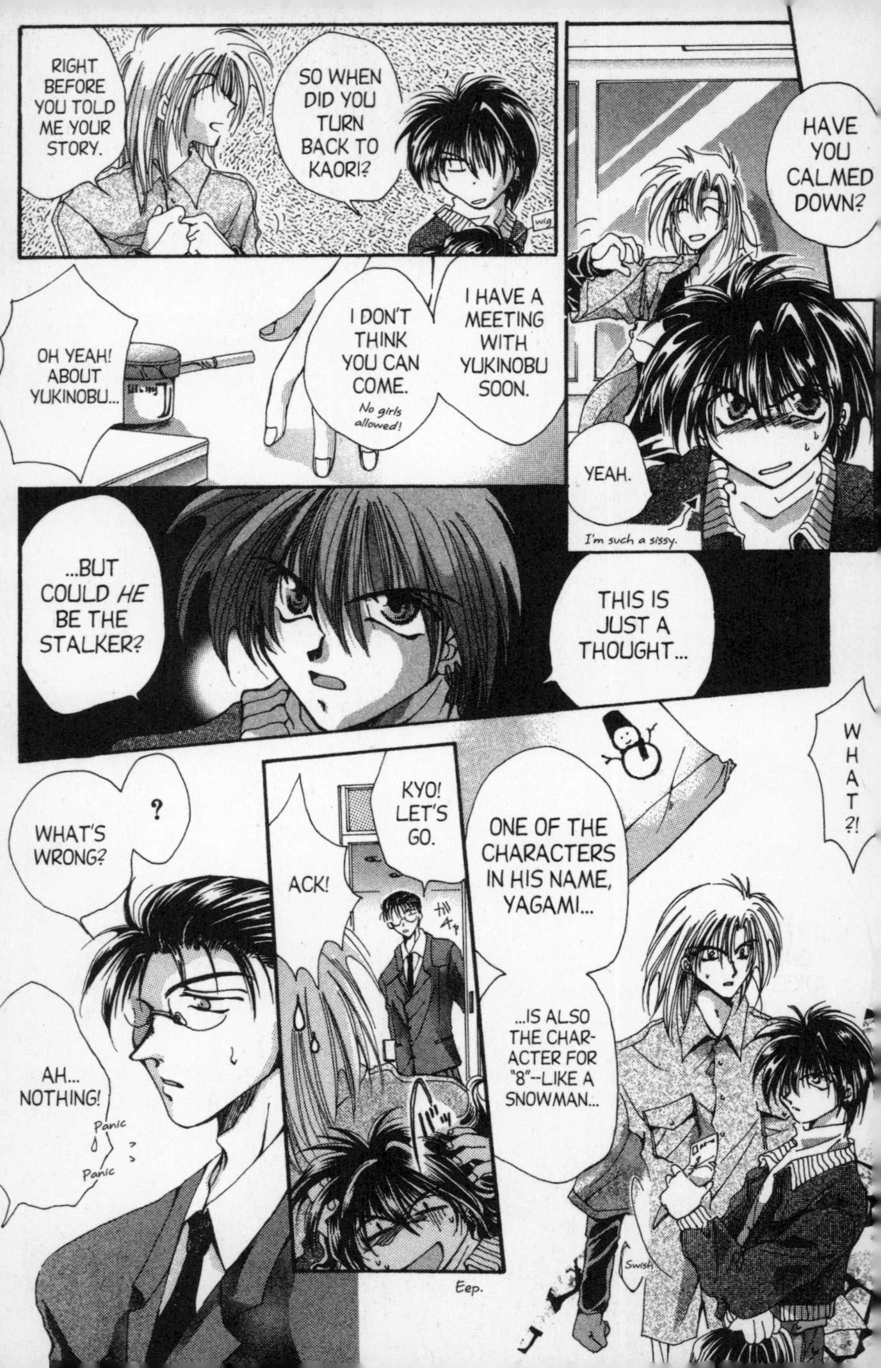
HAVE YOU CALMED DOWN?
YEAH.
I'm such a sissy.
SO WHEN DID YOU TURN BACK TO KAORI?
RIGHT BEFORE YOU TOLD ME YOUR STORY.
wig
I HAVE A MEETING WITH YUKINOBU SOON.
I DON'T THINK YOU CAN COME.
No girls allowed!
OH YEAH! ABOUT YUKINOBU...
THIS IS JUST A THOUGHT...
...BUT COULD *HE* BE THE STALKER?
WHAT?!
ONE OF THE CHARACTERS IN HIS NAME, YAGAMI...
...IS ALSO THE CHARACTER FOR "8"--LIKE A SNOWMAN...
Swish
KYO! LET'S GO.
ACK!
Eep.
?
WHAT'S WRONG?
AH... NOTHING!
Panic
Panic

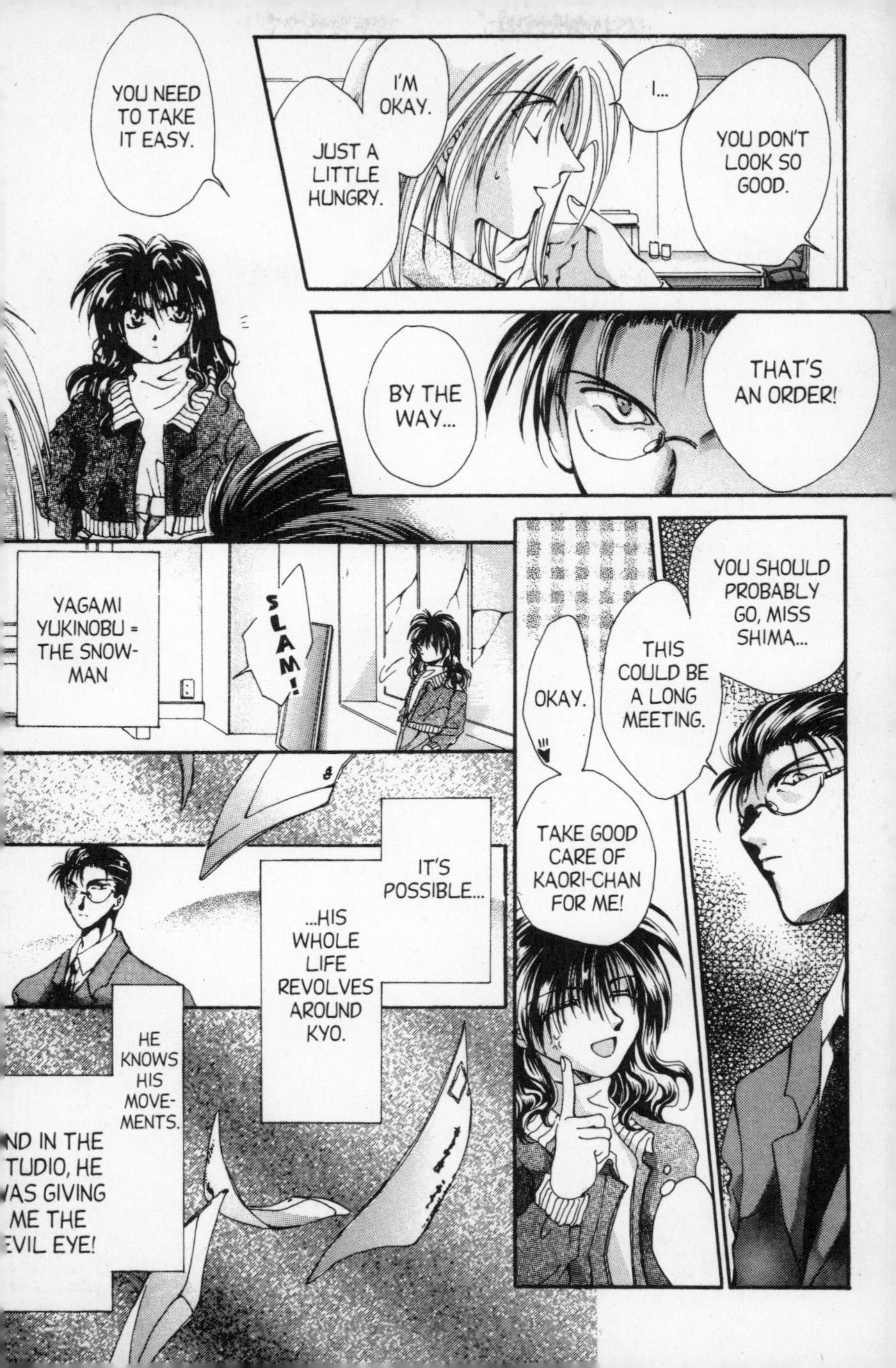
YOU DON'T LOOK SO GOOD.
I...
I'M OKAY.
JUST A LITTLE HUNGRY.
YOU NEED TO TAKE IT EASY.
THAT'S AN ORDER!
BY THE WAY...
YOU SHOULD PROBABLY GO, MISS SHIMA...
THIS COULD BE A LONG MEETING.
OKAY.
TAKE GOOD CARE OF KAORI-CHAN FOR ME!
SLAM!
YAGAMI YUKINOBU = THE SNOW-MAN
IT'S POSSIBLE...
...HIS WHOLE LIFE REVOLVES AROUND KYO.
HE KNOWS HIS MOVE-MENTS.
ND IN THE TUDIO, HE AS GIVING ME THE EVIL EYE!

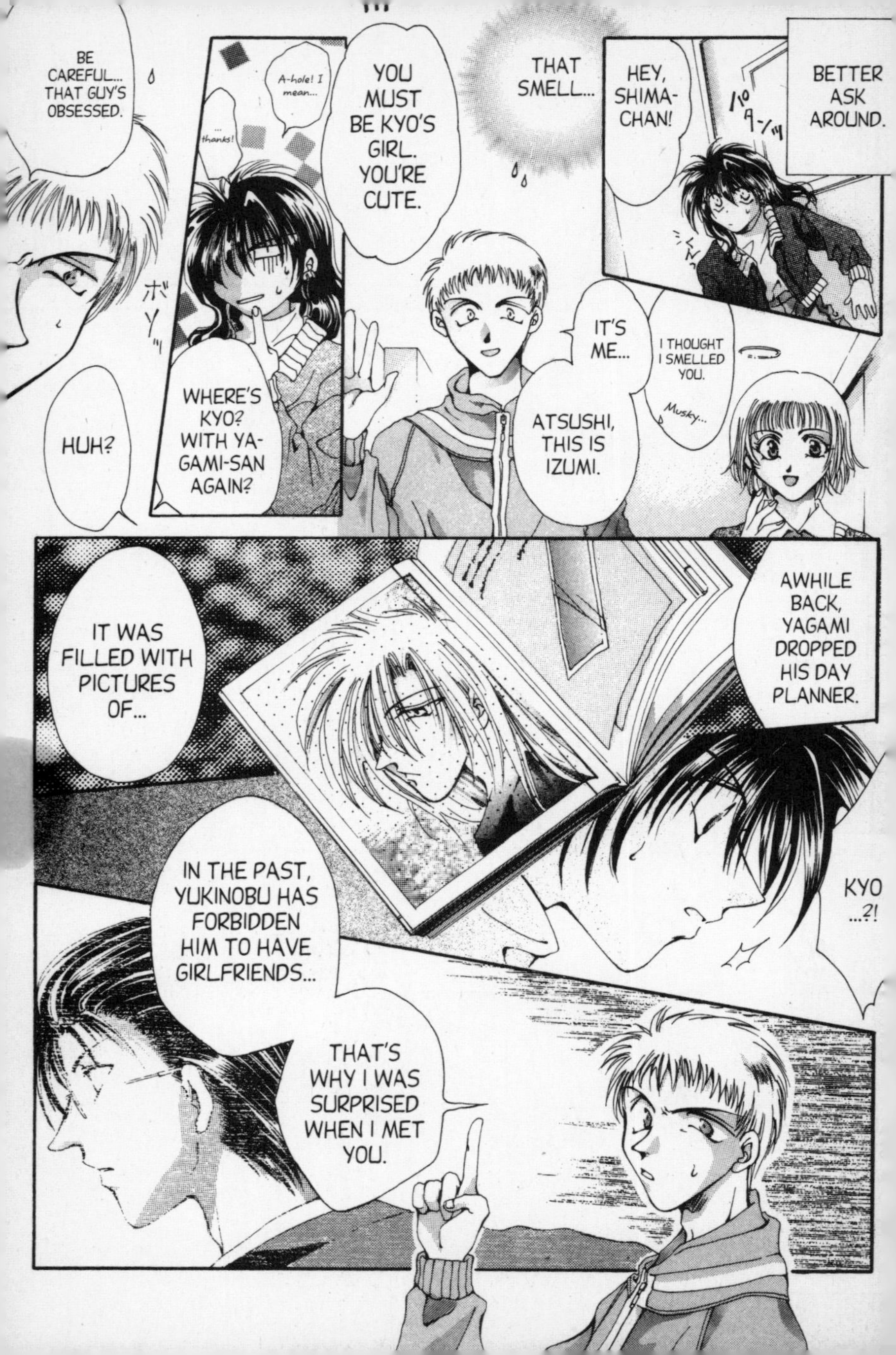
BETTER ASK AROUND.
HEY, SHIMA-CHAN!
THAT SMELL...
I THOUGHT I SMELLED YOU.
Musky...
IT'S ME...
ATSUSHI, THIS IS IZUMI.
YOU MUST BE KYO'S GIRL. YOU'RE CUTE.
A-hole! I mean...
...thanks!
WHERE'S KYO? WITH YA-GAMI-SAN AGAIN?
BE CAREFUL... THAT GUY'S OBSESSED.
HUH?
AWHILE BACK, YAGAMI DROPPED HIS DAY PLANNER.
IT WAS FILLED WITH PICTURES OF...
KYO ...?!
IN THE PAST, YUKINOBU HAS FORBIDDEN HIM TO HAVE GIRLFRIENDS...
THAT'S WHY I WAS SURPRISED WHEN I MET YOU.

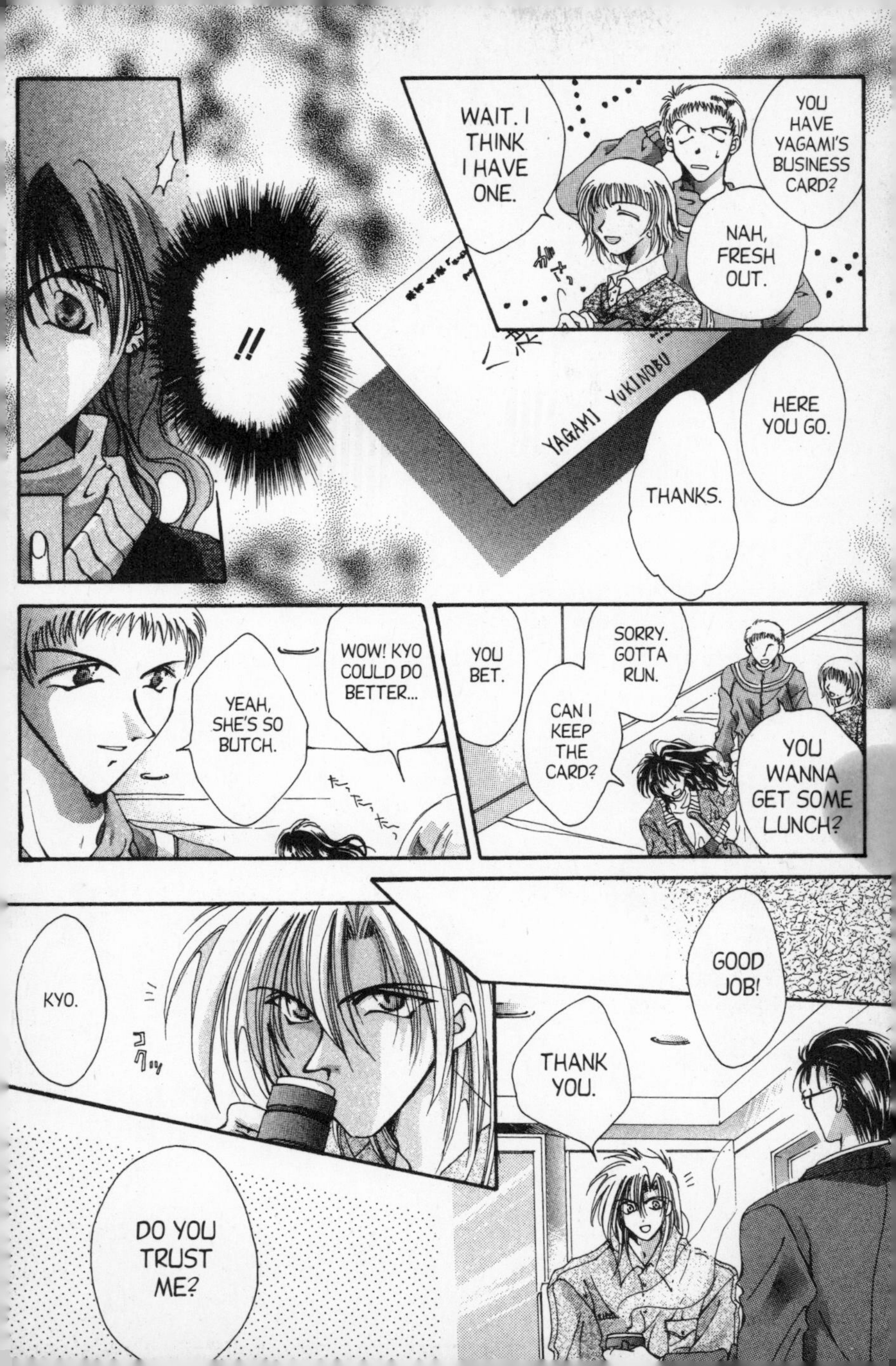
YOU HAVE YAGAMI'S BUSINESS CARD?
NAH, FRESH OUT.
WAIT. I THINK I HAVE ONE.
YAGAMI YUKINOBU
HERE YOU GO.
THANKS.
!!
YOU WANNA GET SOME LUNCH?
SORRY. GOTTA RUN.
CAN I KEEP THE CARD?
YOU BET.
WOW! KYO COULD DO BETTER...
YEAH, SHE'S SO BUTCH.
GOOD JOB!
THANK YOU.
KYO.
DO YOU TRUST ME?

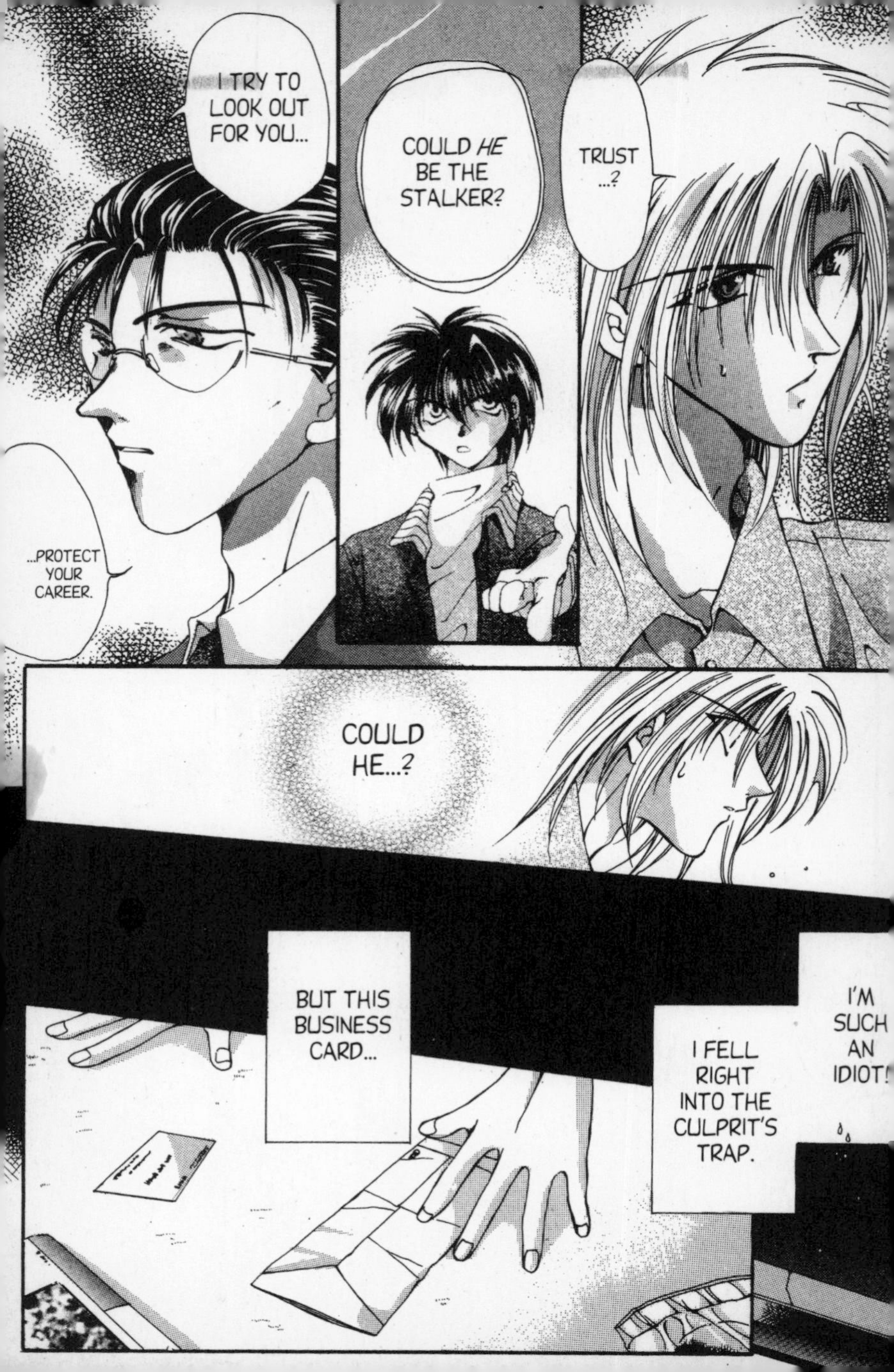
TRUST ...?
COULD *HE* BE THE STALKER?
I TRY TO LOOK OUT FOR YOU...
...PROTECT YOUR CAREER.
COULD HE...?
I'M SUCH AN IDIOT!
I FELL RIGHT INTO THE CULPRIT'S TRAP.
BUT THIS BUSINESS CARD...

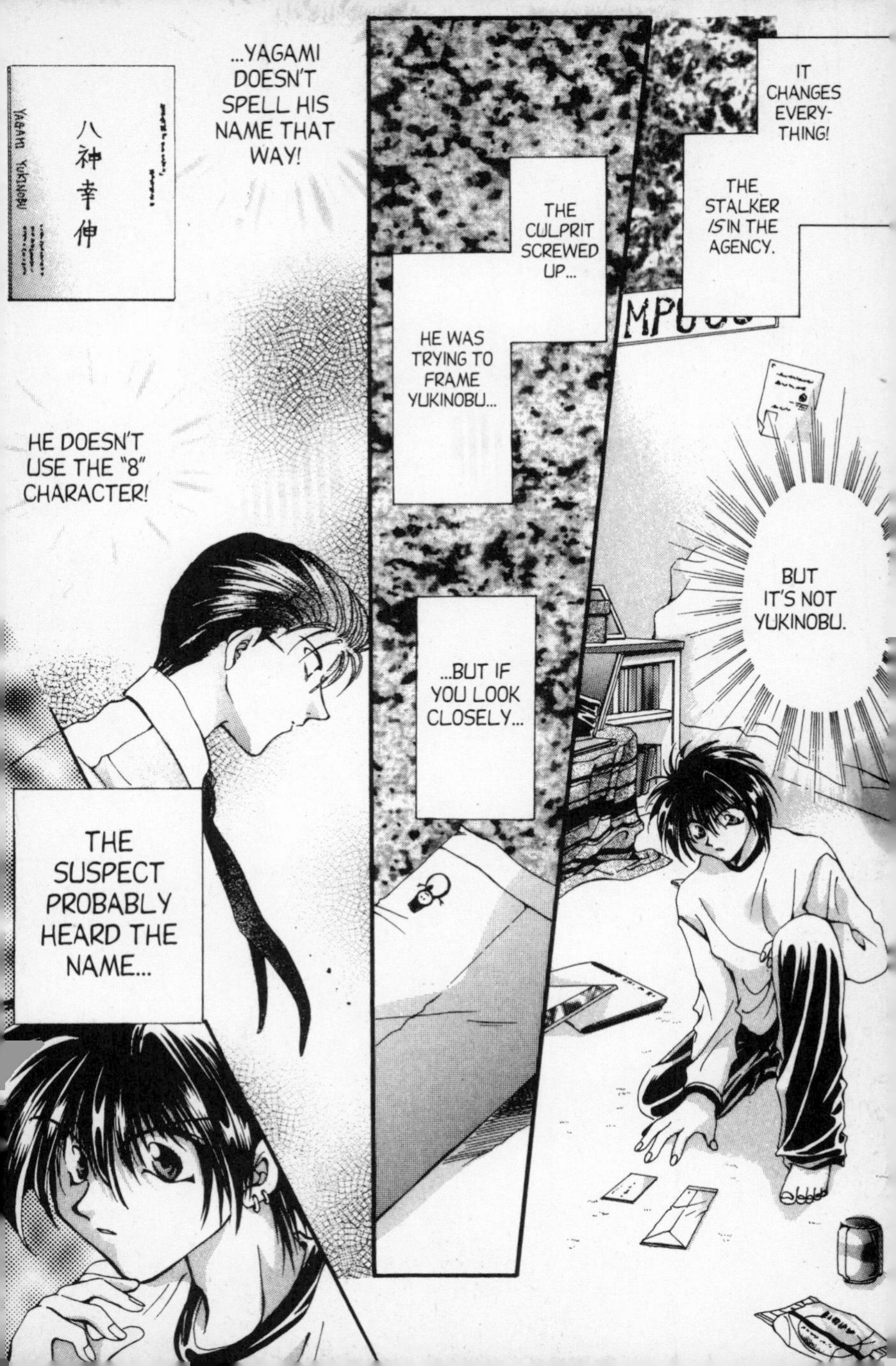

IT CHANGES EVERY-THING!
THE STALKER IS IN THE AGENCY.
BUT IT'S NOT YUKINOBU.
THE CULPRIT SCREWED UP...
HE WAS TRYING TO FRAME YUKINOBU...
...BUT IF YOU LOOK CLOSELY...
...YAGAMI DOESN'T SPELL HIS NAME THAT WAY!
八神幸伸
YAGAMI YUKINOBU
HE DOESN'T USE THE "8" CHARACTER!
THE SUSPECT PROBABLY HEARD THE NAME...

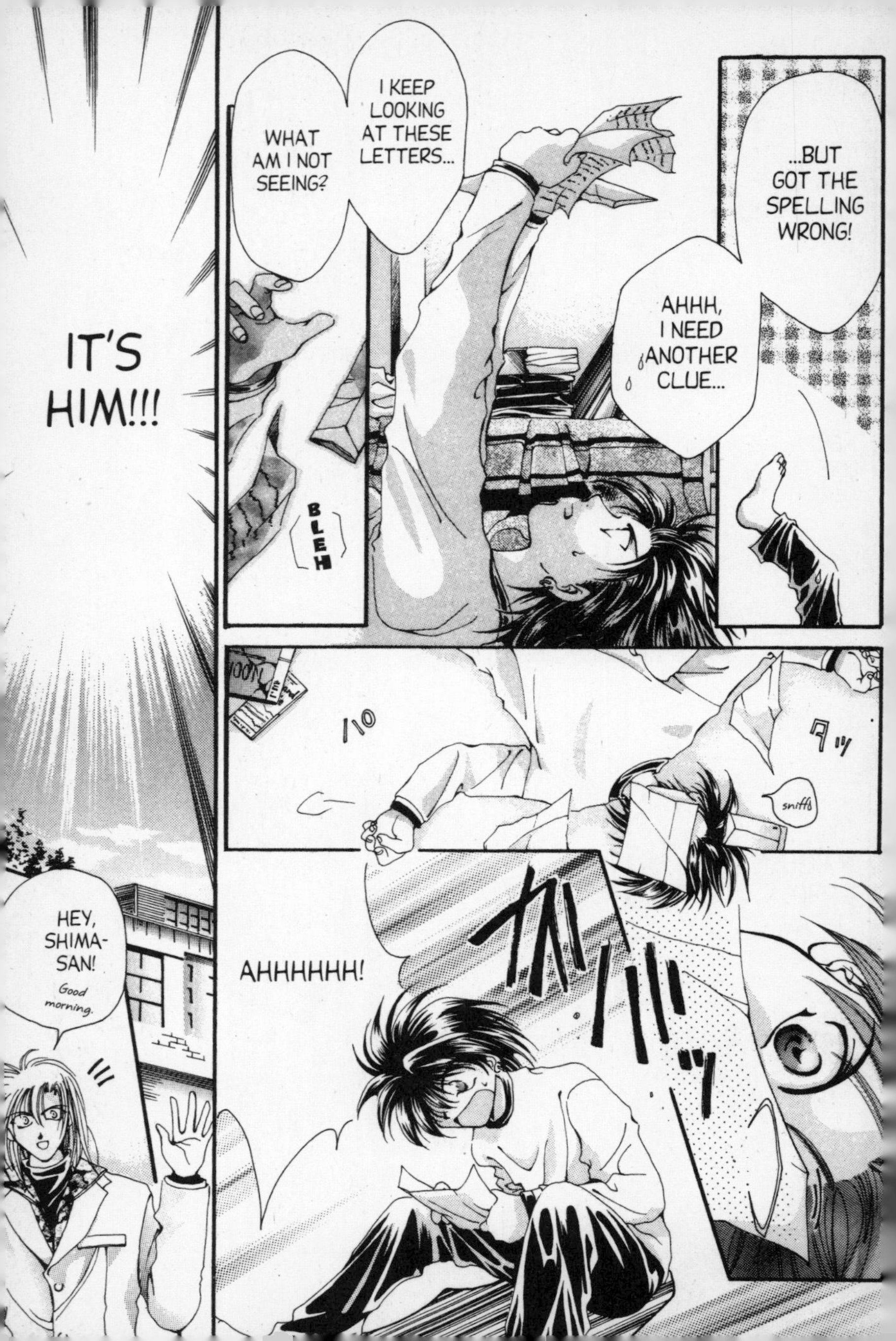
...BUT GOT THE SPELLING WRONG!
AHHH, I NEED ANOTHER CLUE...
I KEEP LOOKING AT THESE LETTERS...
WHAT AM I NOT SEEING?
BLEH
タッ
sniff
ガバッ
AHHHHHH!
IT'S HIM!!!
HEY, SHIMA-SAN!
Good morning.

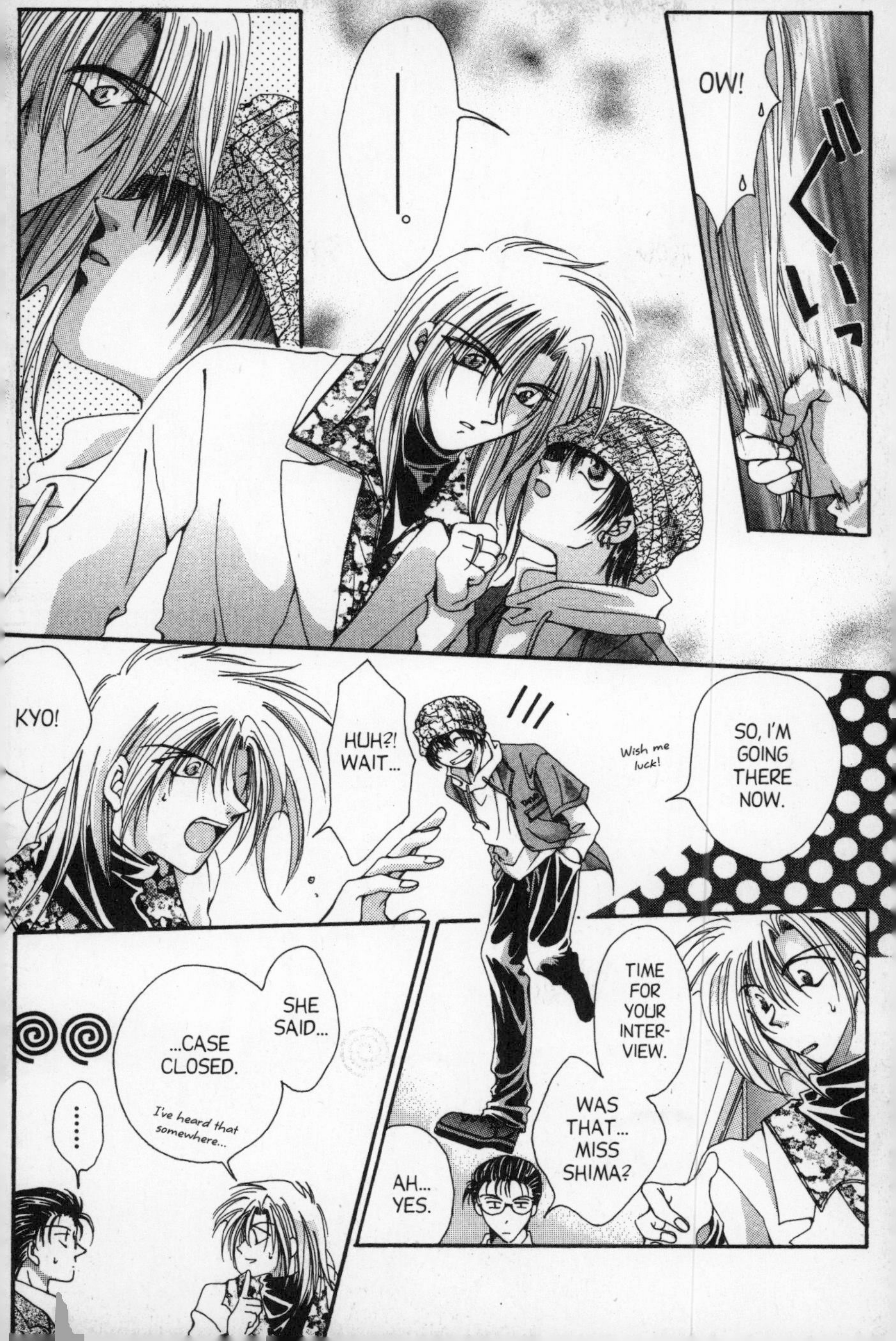

OW!
!
SO, I'M GOING THERE NOW.
Wish me luck!
HUH?! WAIT...
KYO!
TIME FOR YOUR INTER-VIEW.
WAS THAT... MISS SHIMA?
AH... YES.
SHE SAID...
...CASE CLOSED.
I've heard that somewhere...
......

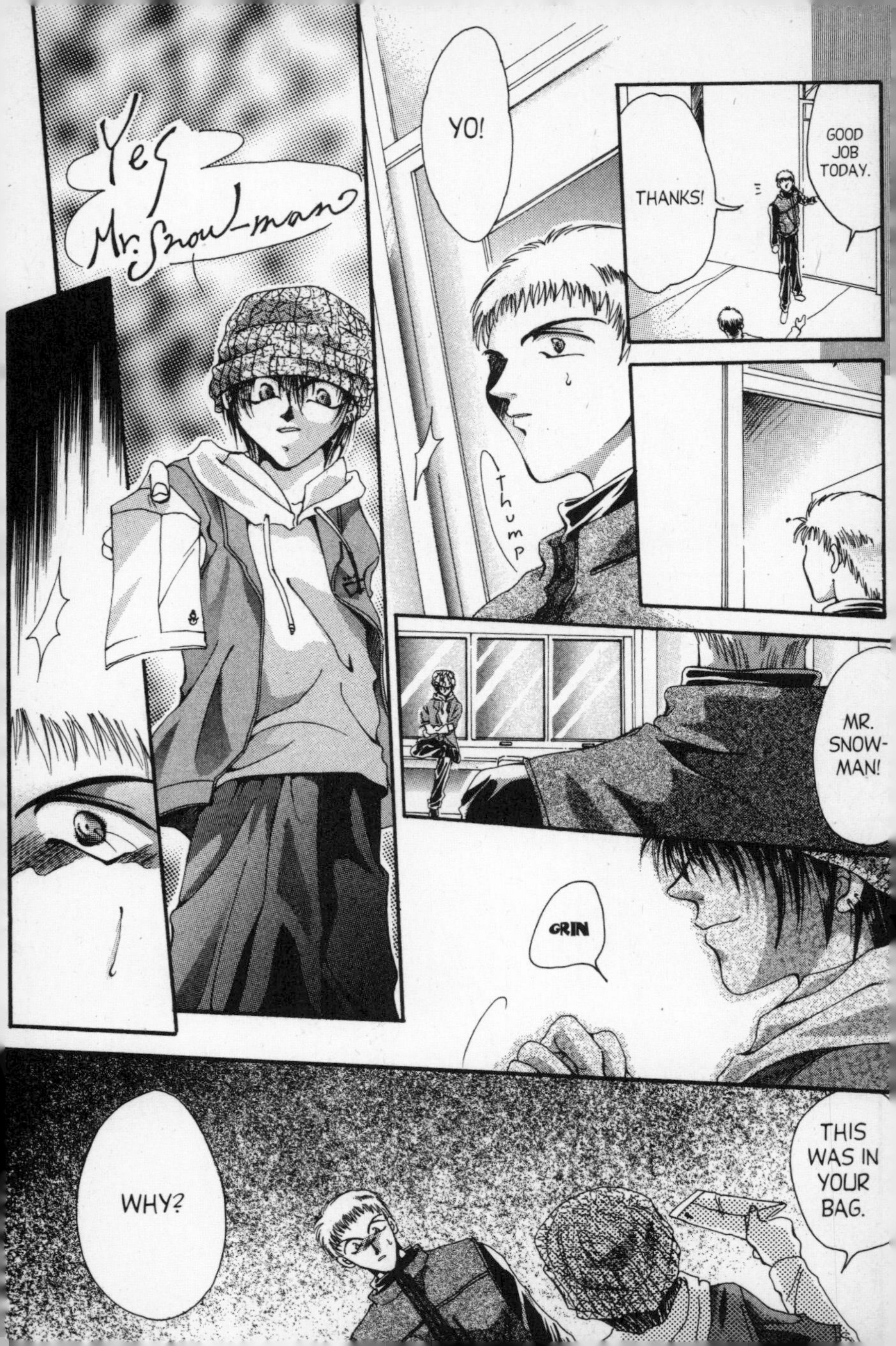
GOOD JOB TODAY.
THANKS!
YO!
THUMP
MR. SNOW-MAN!
GRIN
Yes Mr. Snow-man
THIS WAS IN YOUR BAG.
WHY?

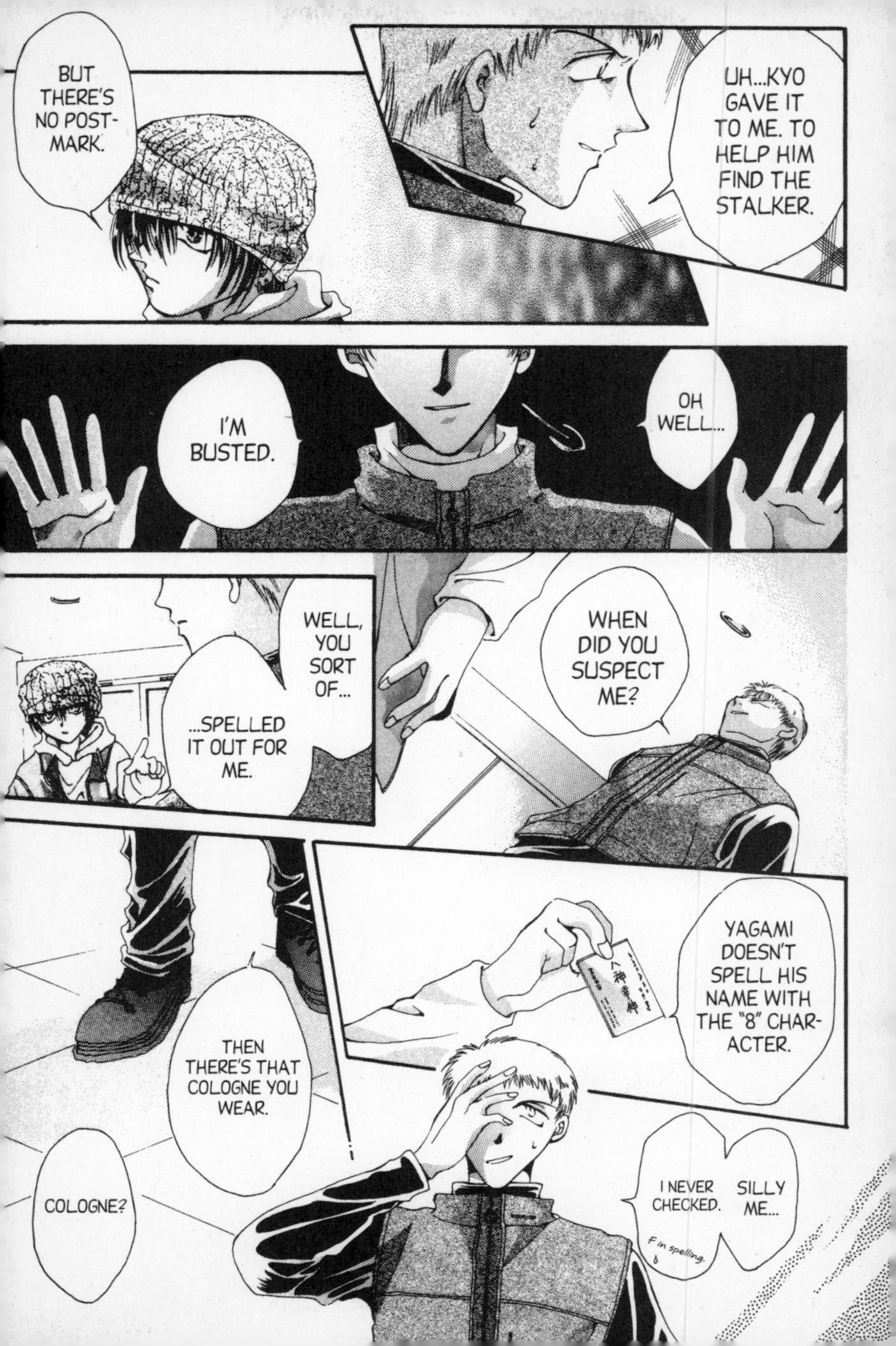
UH...KYO GAVE IT TO ME. TO HELP HIM FIND THE STALKER.
BUT THERE'S NO POST-MARK.
OH WELL...
I'M BUSTED.
WHEN DID YOU SUSPECT ME?
WELL, YOU SORT OF...
...SPELLED IT OUT FOR ME.
YAGAMI DOESN'T SPELL HIS NAME WITH THE "8" CHAR-ACTER.
SILLY ME...
I NEVER CHECKED.
F in spelling.
THEN THERE'S THAT COLOGNE YOU WEAR.
COLOGNE?

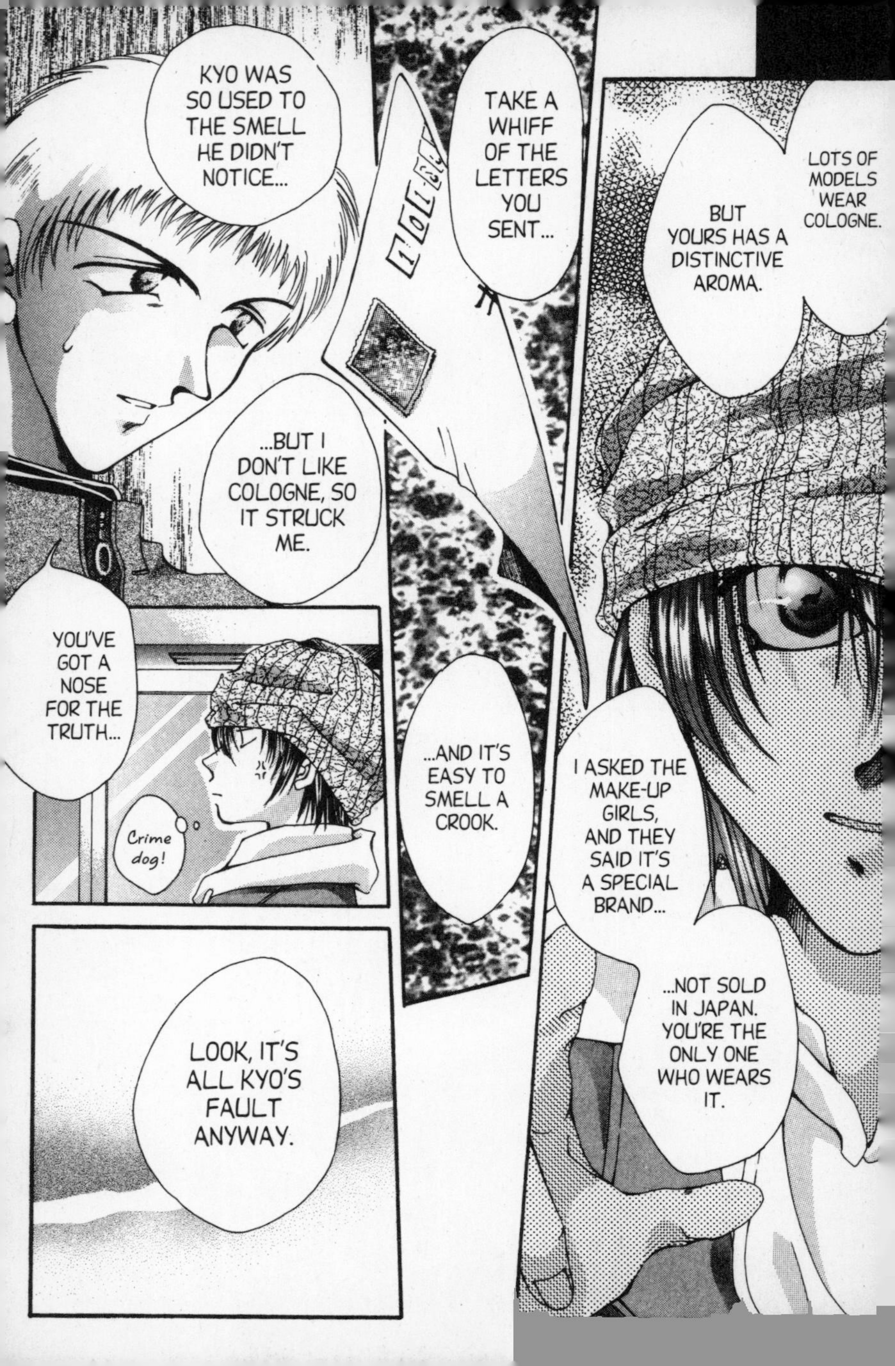
LOTS OF MODELS WEAR COLOGNE.
BUT YOURS HAS A DISTINCTIVE AROMA.
I ASKED THE MAKE-UP GIRLS, AND THEY SAID IT'S A SPECIAL BRAND...
...NOT SOLD IN JAPAN. YOU'RE THE ONLY ONE WHO WEARS IT.
TAKE A WHIFF OF THE LETTERS YOU SENT...
...AND IT'S EASY TO SMELL A CROOK.
KYO WAS SO USED TO THE SMELL HE DIDN'T NOTICE...
...BUT I DON'T LIKE COLOGNE, SO IT STRUCK ME.
YOU'VE GOT A NOSE FOR THE TRUTH...
Crime dog!
LOOK, IT'S ALL KYO'S FAULT ANYWAY.

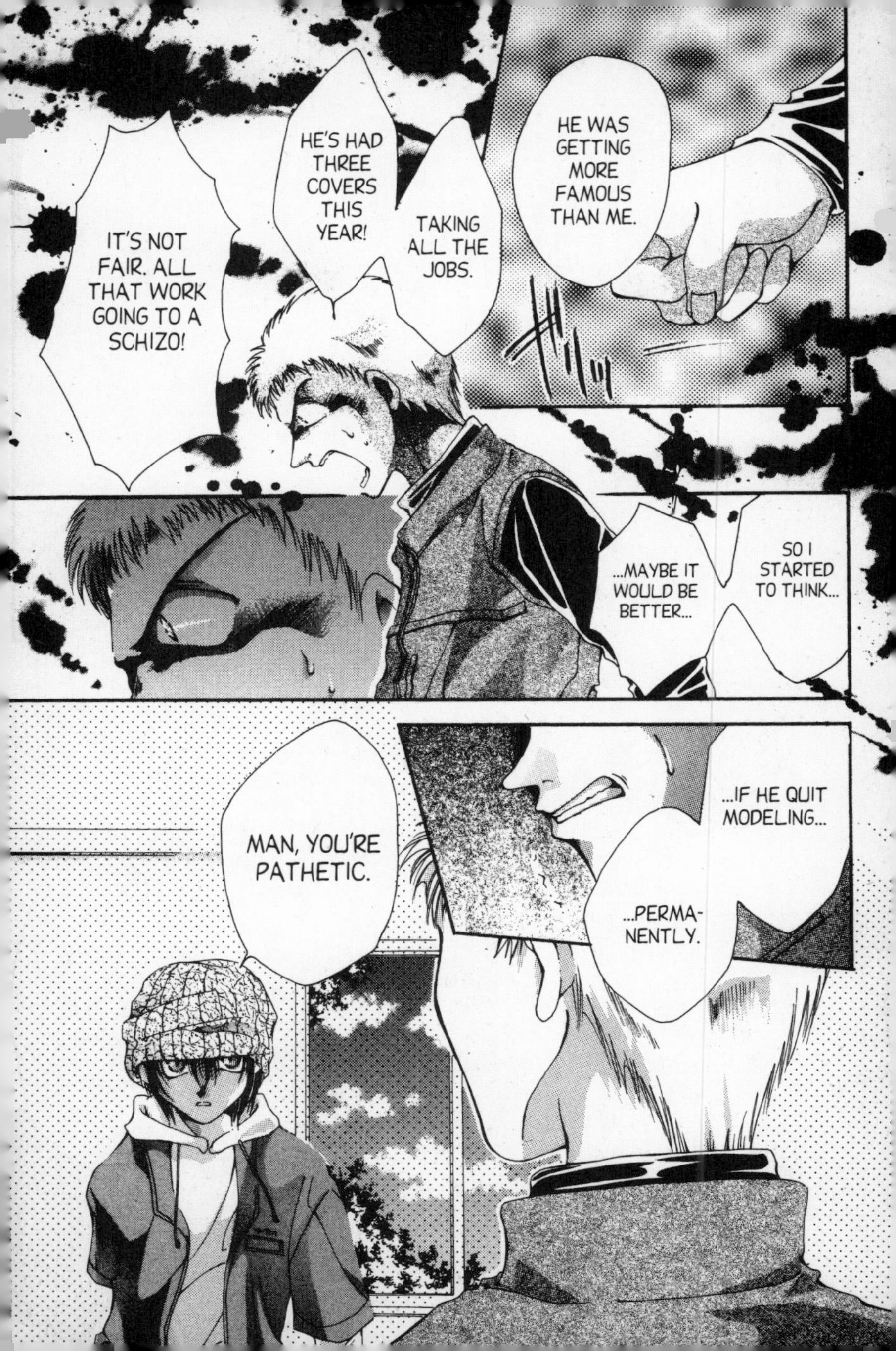
HE WAS GETTING MORE FAMOUS THAN ME.
TAKING ALL THE JOBS.
HE'S HAD THREE COVERS THIS YEAR!
IT'S NOT FAIR. ALL THAT WORK GOING TO A SCHIZO!
SO I STARTED TO THINK...
...MAYBE IT WOULD BE BETTER...
...IF HE QUIT MODELING...
...PERMA-NENTLY.
MAN, YOU'RE PATHETIC.

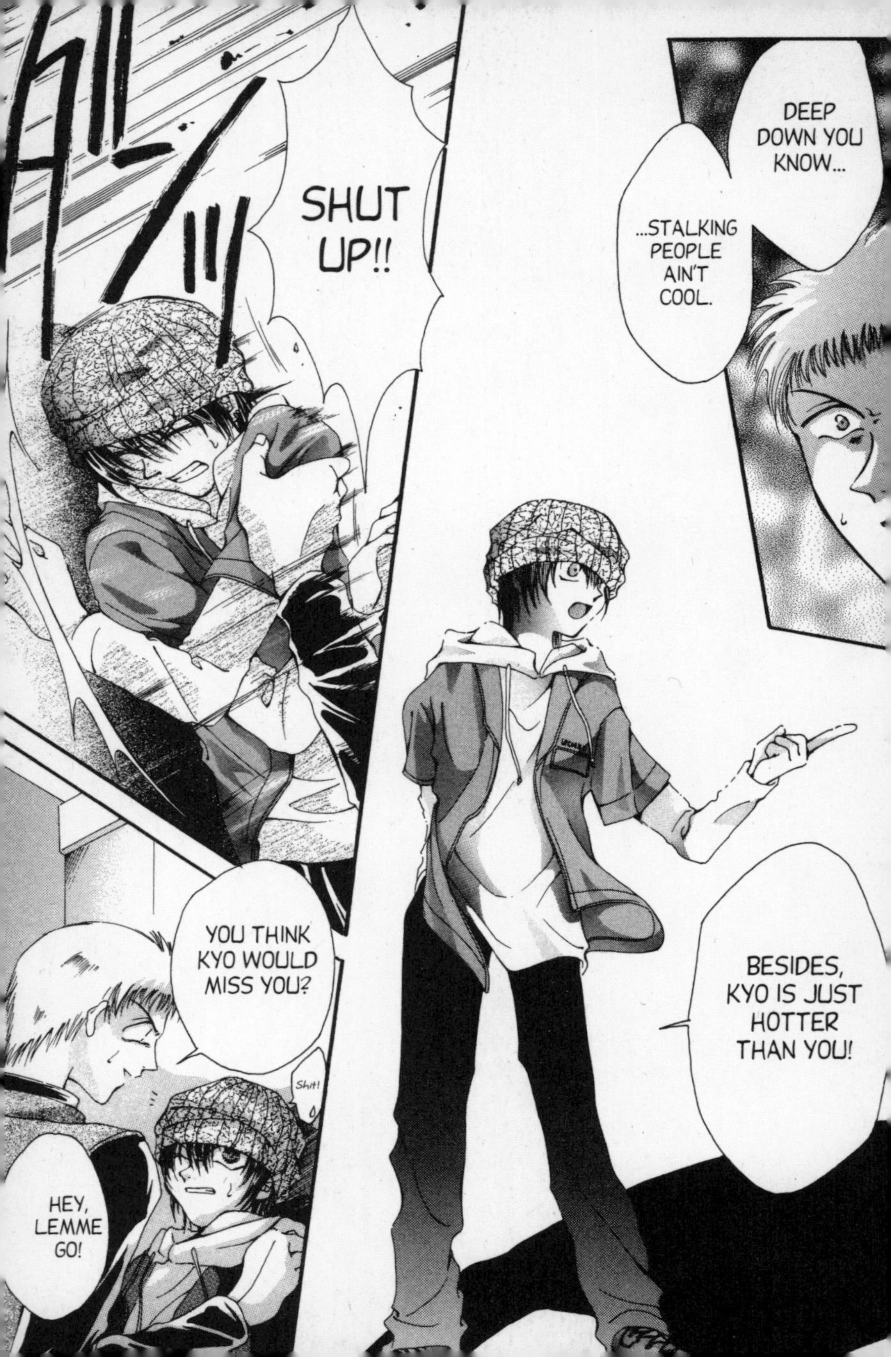
DEEP DOWN YOU KNOW...
...STALKING PEOPLE AIN'T COOL.
BESIDES, KYO IS JUST HOTTER THAN YOU!
SHUT UP!!
YOU THINK KYO WOULD MISS YOU?
Shit!
HEY, LEMME GO!

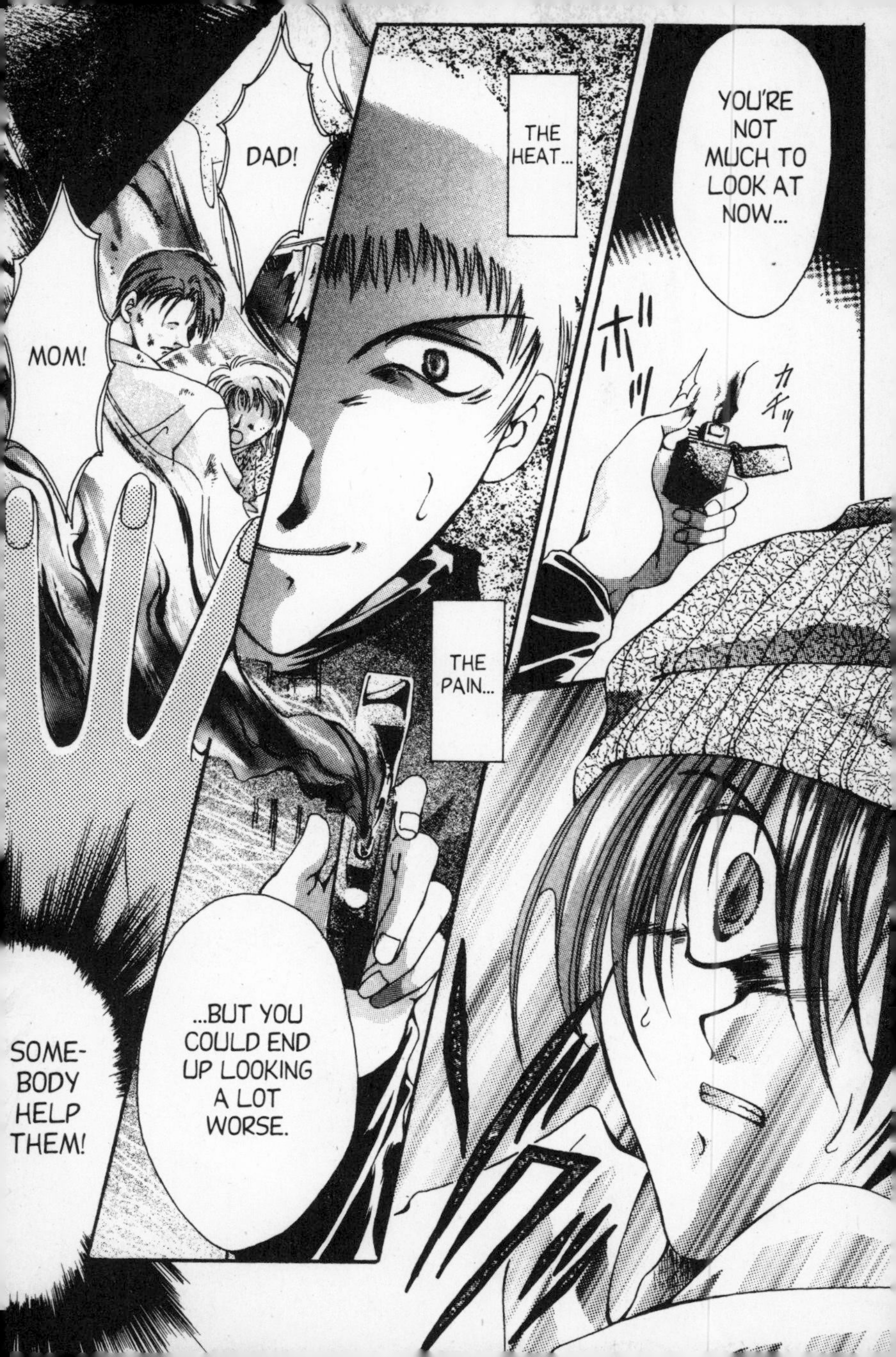

YOU'RE NOT MUCH TO LOOK AT NOW...
ボッ
カチッ
THE HEAT...
THE PAIN...
...BUT YOU COULD END UP LOOKING A LOT WORSE.
DAD!
MOM!
SOME-BODY HELP THEM!

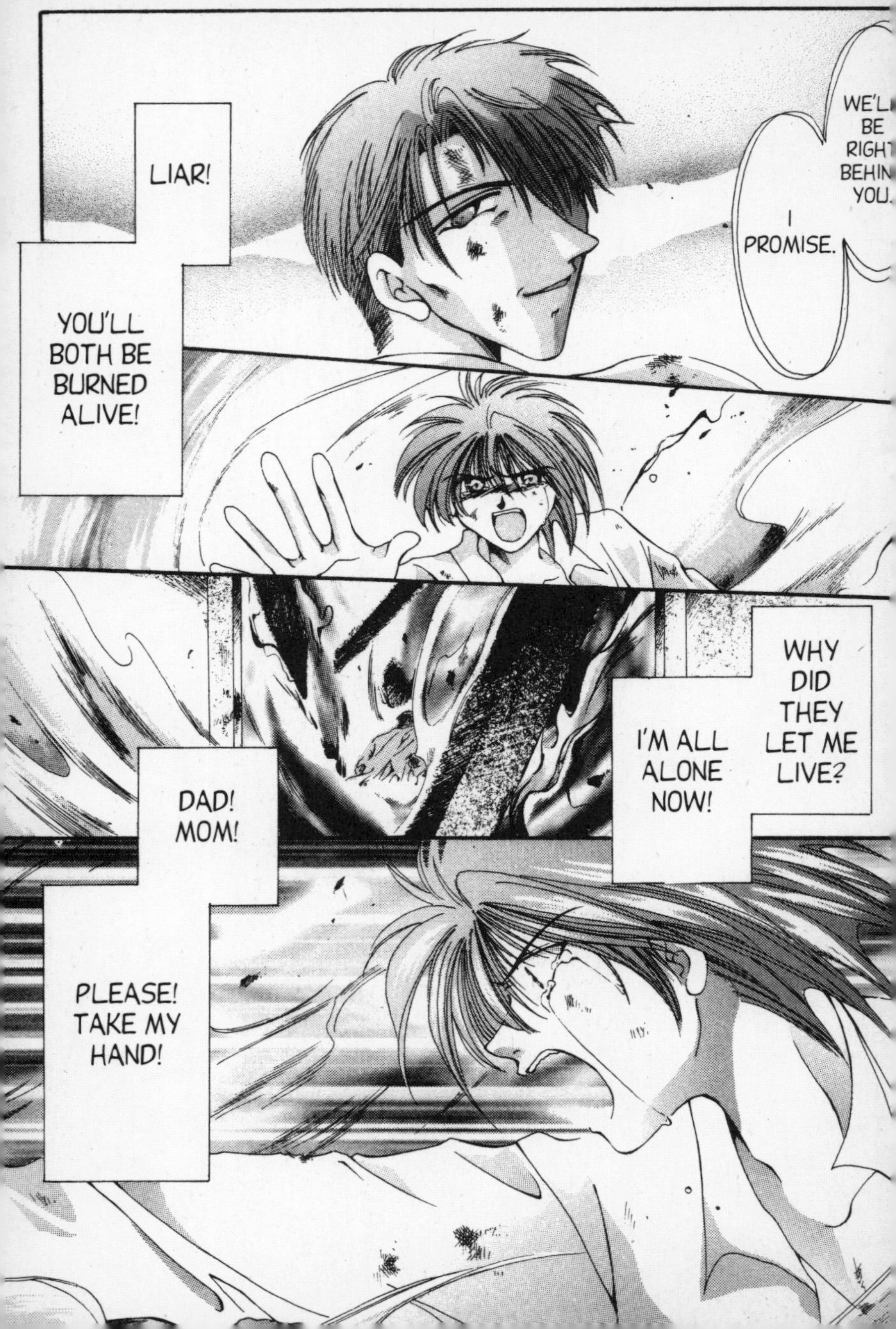
WE'L BE RIGHT BEHIN YOU.
I PROMISE.
LIAR!
YOU'LL BOTH BE BURNED ALIVE!
WHY DID THEY LET ME LIVE?
I'M ALL ALONE NOW!
DAD! MOM!
PLEASE! TAKE MY HAND!

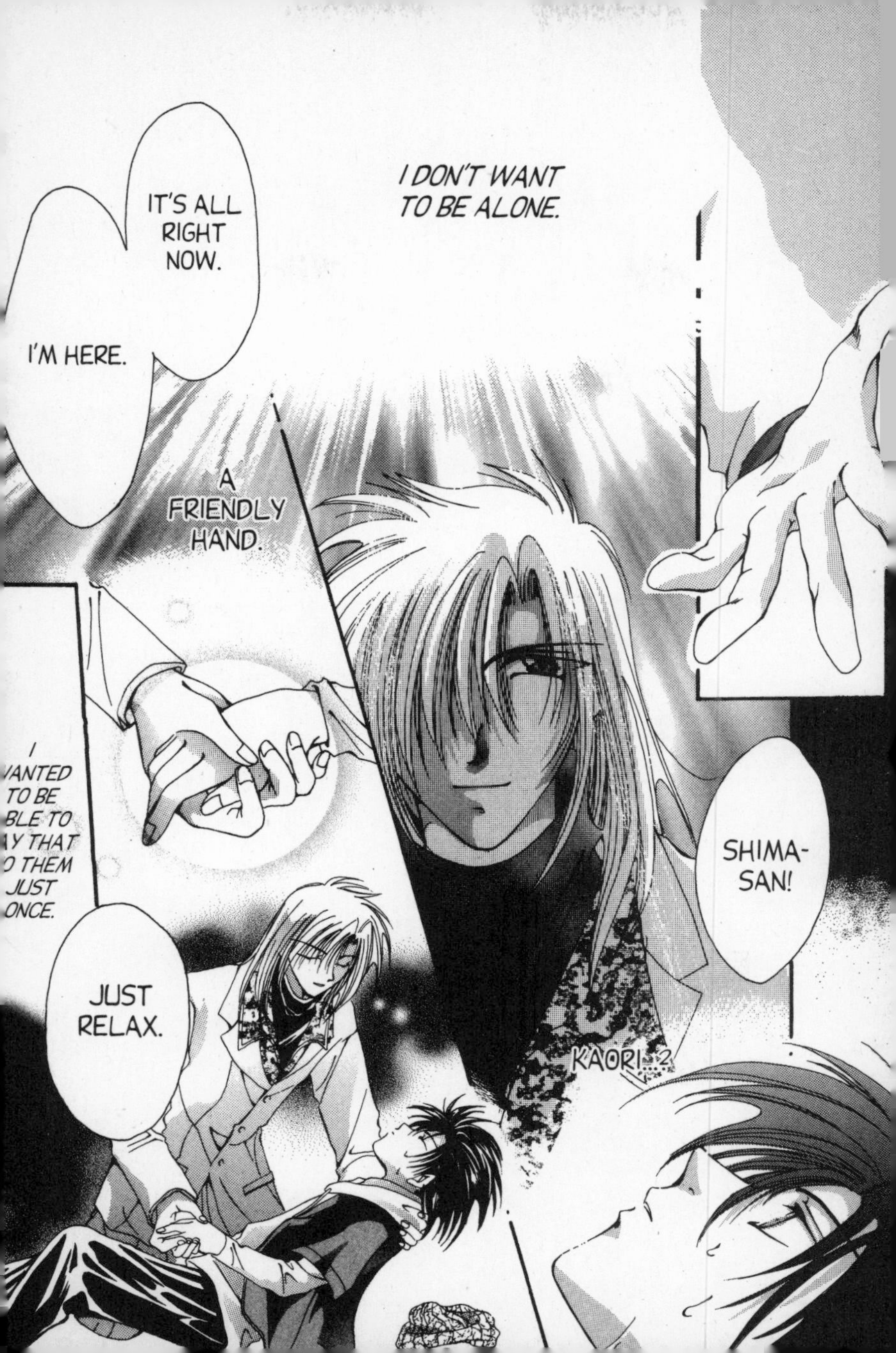
I DON'T WANT TO BE ALONE.
IT'S ALL RIGHT NOW.
I'M HERE.
A FRIENDLY HAND.
SHIMA-SAN!
KAORI...?
JUST RELAX.
I VANTED TO BE BLE TO AY THAT O THEM JUST ONCE.

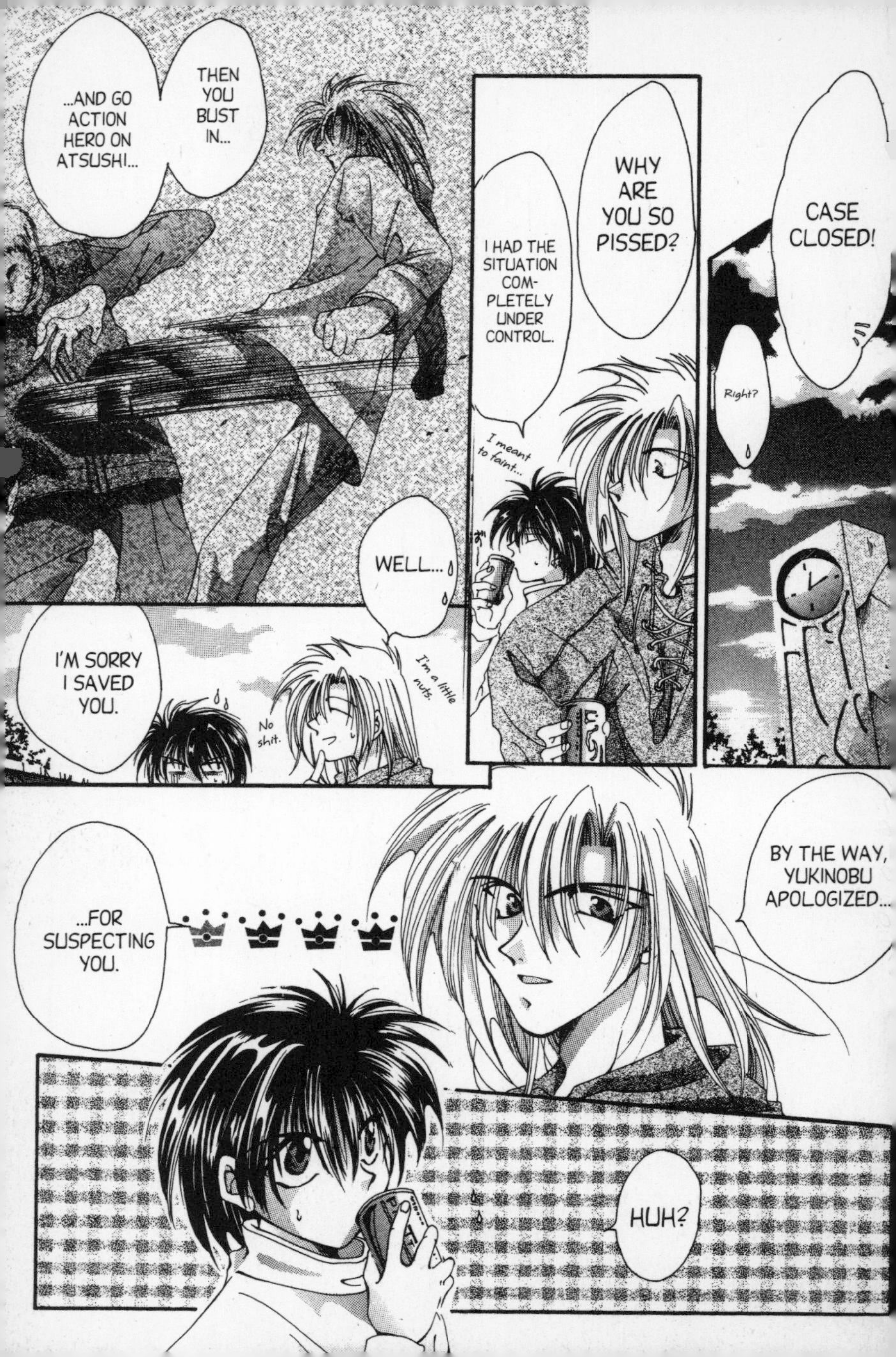
CASE CLOSED!
Right?
WHY ARE YOU SO PISSED?
I HAD THE SITUATION COM-PLETELY UNDER CONTROL.
I meant to faint...
THEN YOU BUST IN...
...AND GO ACTION HERO ON ATSUSHI...
WELL...
I'm a little nuts.
No shit.
I'M SORRY I SAVED YOU.
BY THE WAY, YUKINOBU APOLOGIZED...
...FOR SUSPECTING YOU.
HUH?

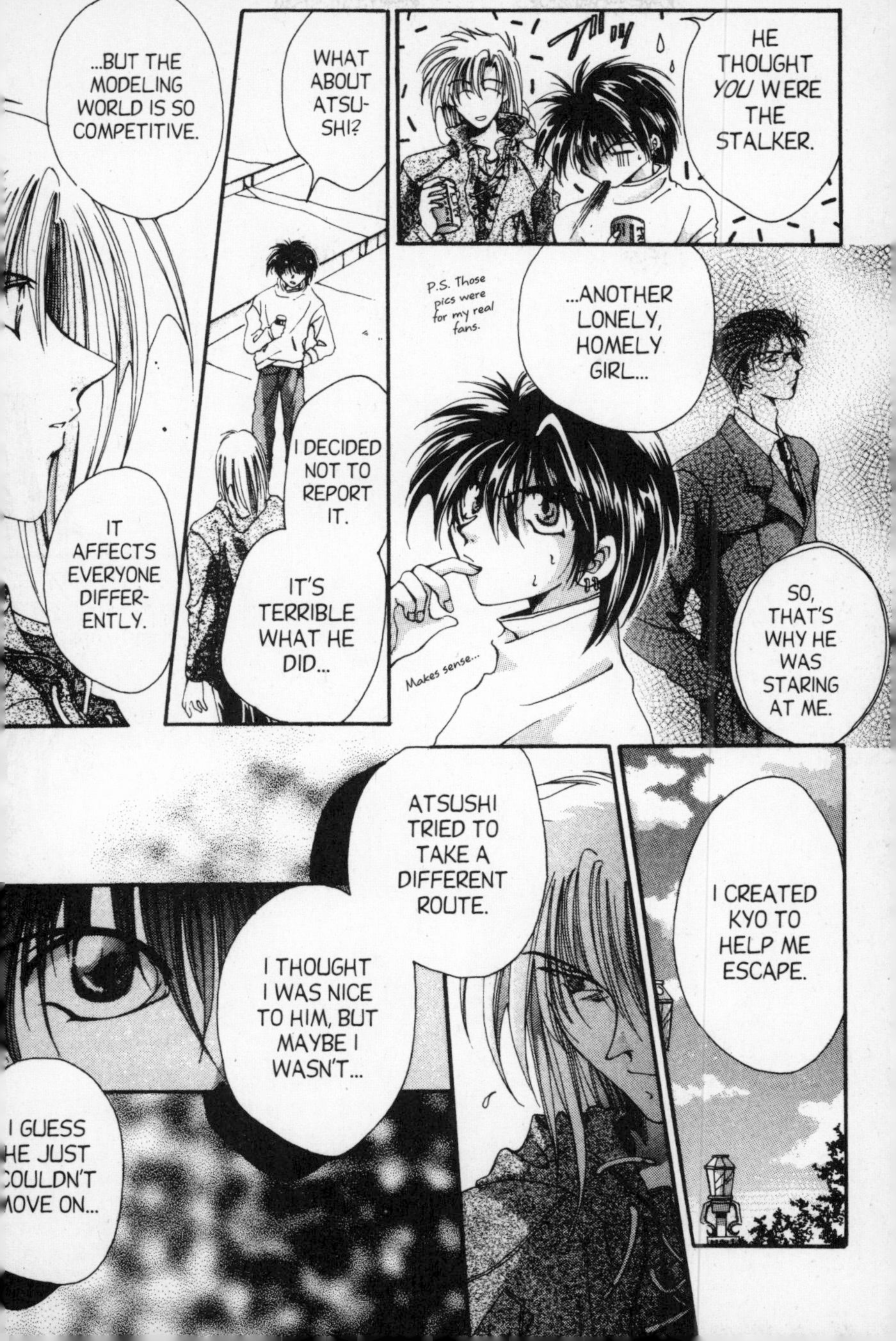
HE THOUGHT YOU WERE THE STALKER.
...ANOTHER LONELY, HOMELY GIRL...
P.S. Those pics were for my real fans.
SO, THAT'S WHY HE WAS STARING AT ME.
Makes sense...
WHAT ABOUT ATSUSHI?
I DECIDED NOT TO REPORT IT.
IT'S TERRIBLE WHAT HE DID...
...BUT THE MODELING WORLD IS SO COMPETITIVE.
IT AFFECTS EVERYONE DIFFERENTLY.
I CREATED KYO TO HELP ME ESCAPE.
ATSUSHI TRIED TO TAKE A DIFFERENT ROUTE.
I THOUGHT I WAS NICE TO HIM, BUT MAYBE I WASN'T...
I GUESS HE JUST COULDN'T MOVE ON...

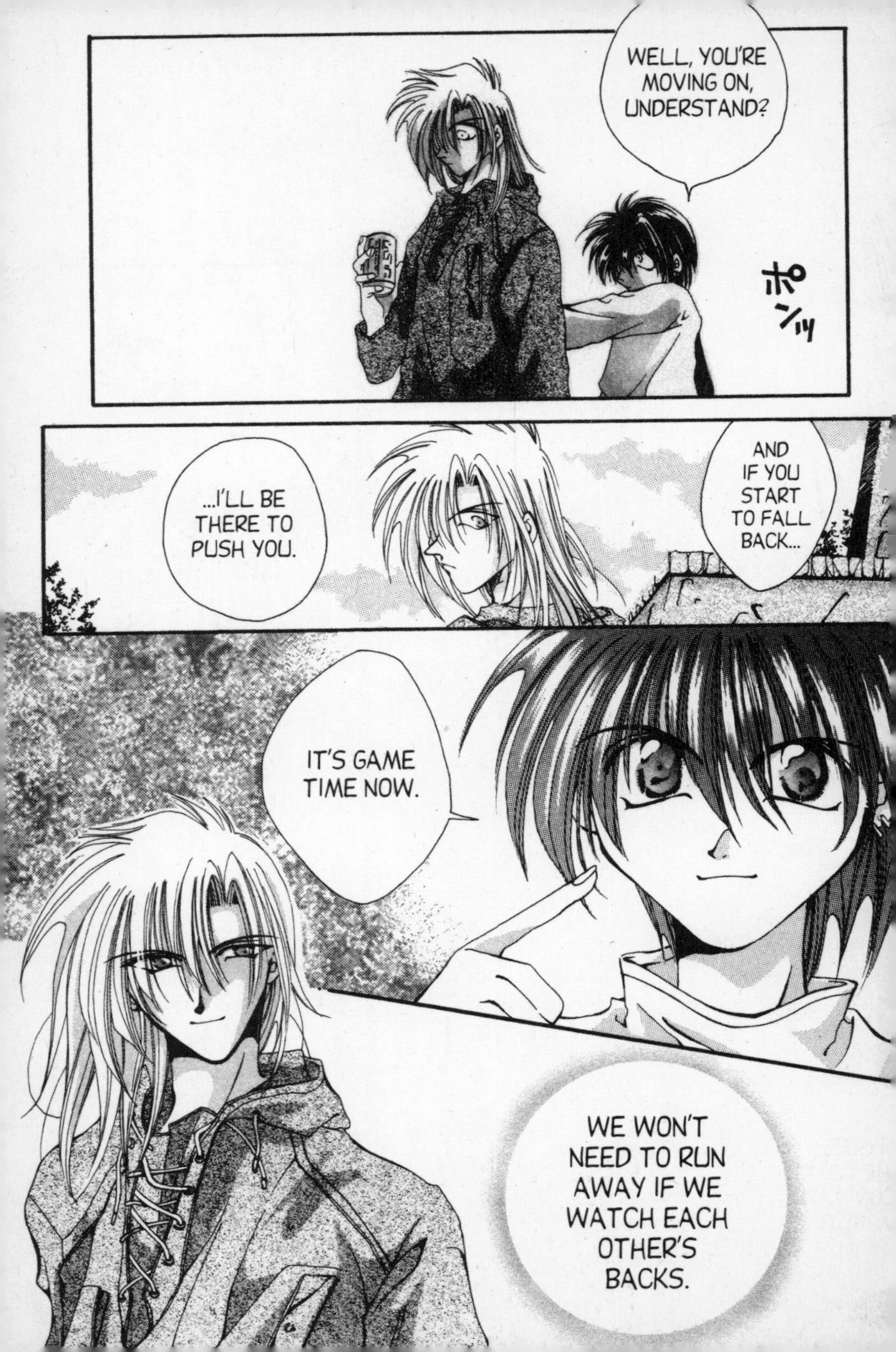
WELL, YOU'RE MOVING ON, UNDERSTAND?
ポンッ
AND IF YOU START TO FALL BACK...
...I'LL BE THERE TO PUSH YOU.
IT'S GAME TIME NOW.
WE WON'T NEED TO RUN AWAY IF WE WATCH EACH OTHER'S BACKS.

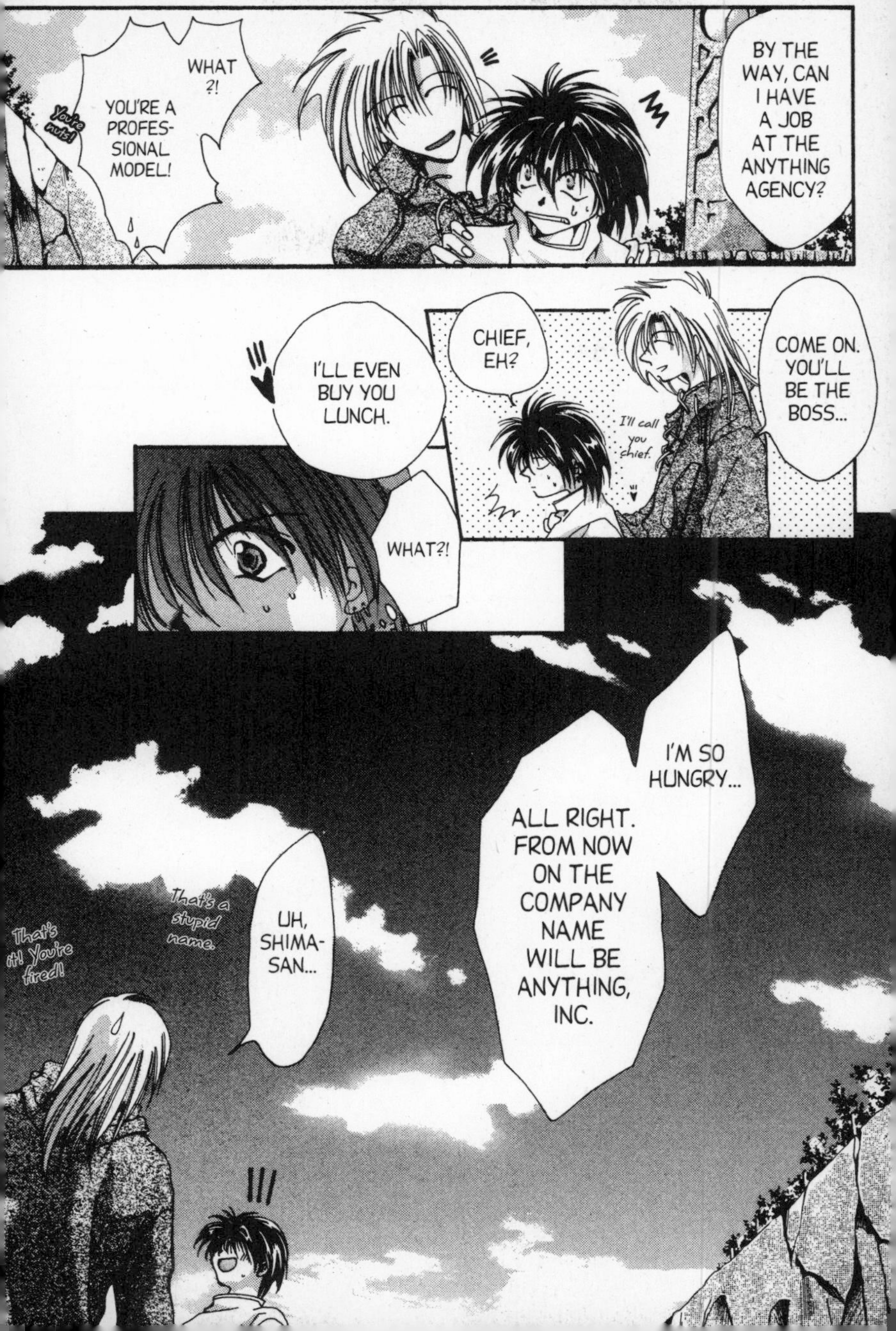
BY THE WAY, CAN I HAVE A JOB AT THE ANYTHING AGENCY?
WHAT?!
YOU'RE A PROFES-SIONAL MODEL!
You're nuts!
COME ON. YOU'LL BE THE BOSS...
I'll call you chief.
CHIEF, EH?
I'LL EVEN BUY YOU LUNCH.
WHAT?!
I'M SO HUNGRY...
ALL RIGHT. FROM NOW ON THE COMPANY NAME WILL BE ANYTHING, INC.
UH, SHIMA-SAN...
That's a stupid name.
That's it! You're fired!

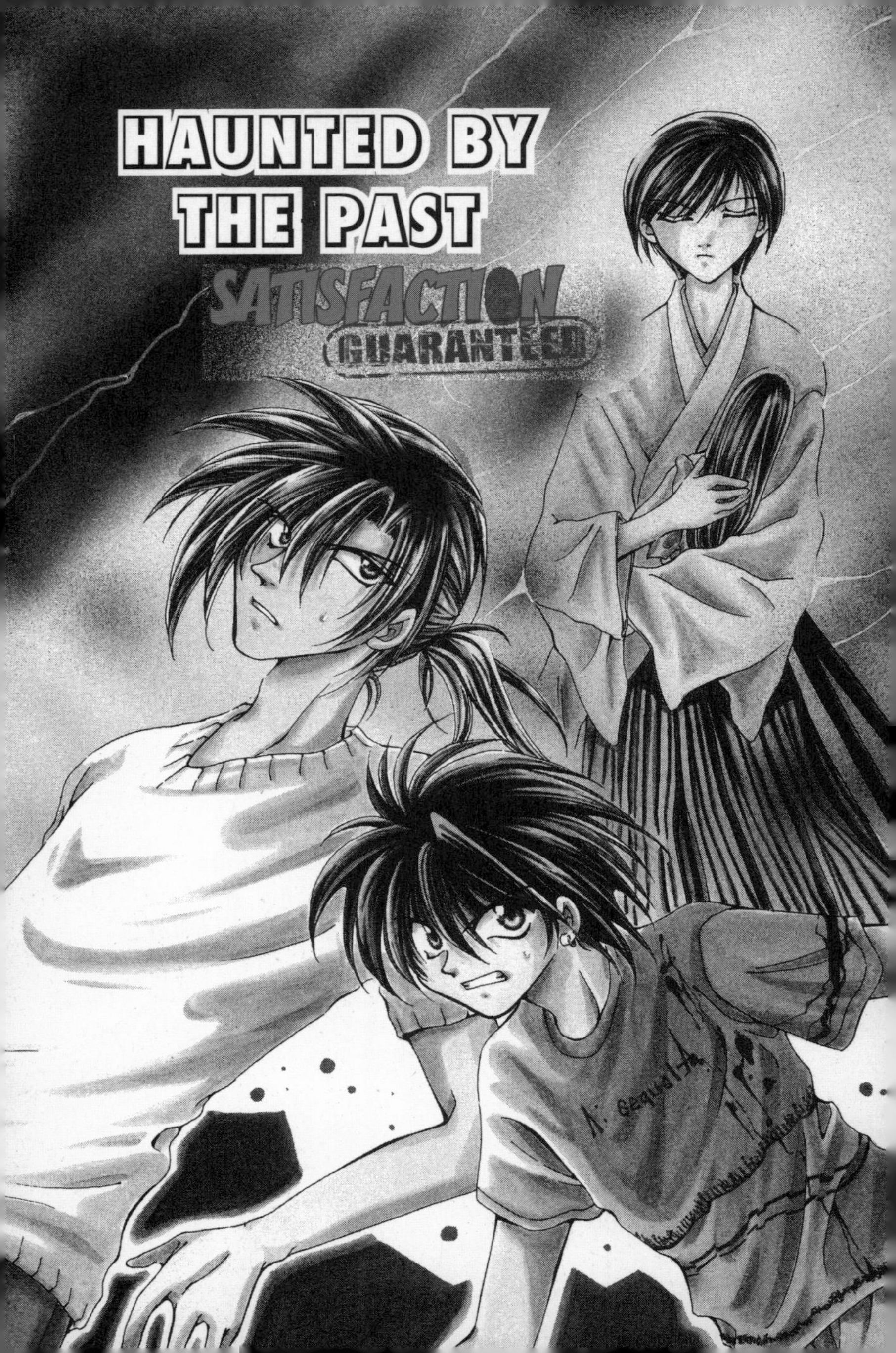
HAUNTED BY THE PAST
SATISFACTION GUARANTEED

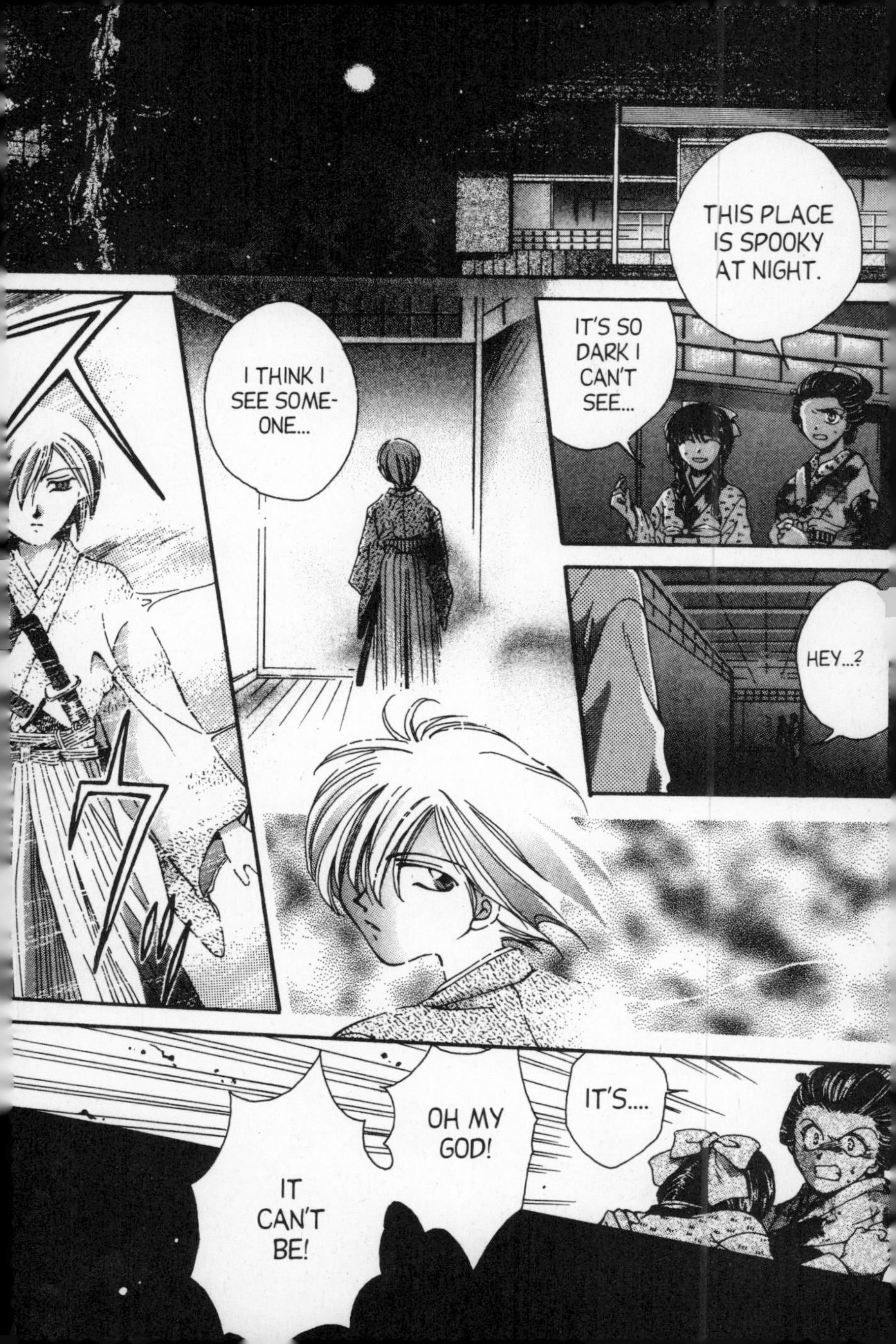
THIS PLACE IS SPOOKY AT NIGHT.
IT'S SO DARK I CAN'T SEE...
HEY...?
I THINK I SEE SOME-ONE...
IT'S....
OH MY GOD!
IT CAN'T BE!

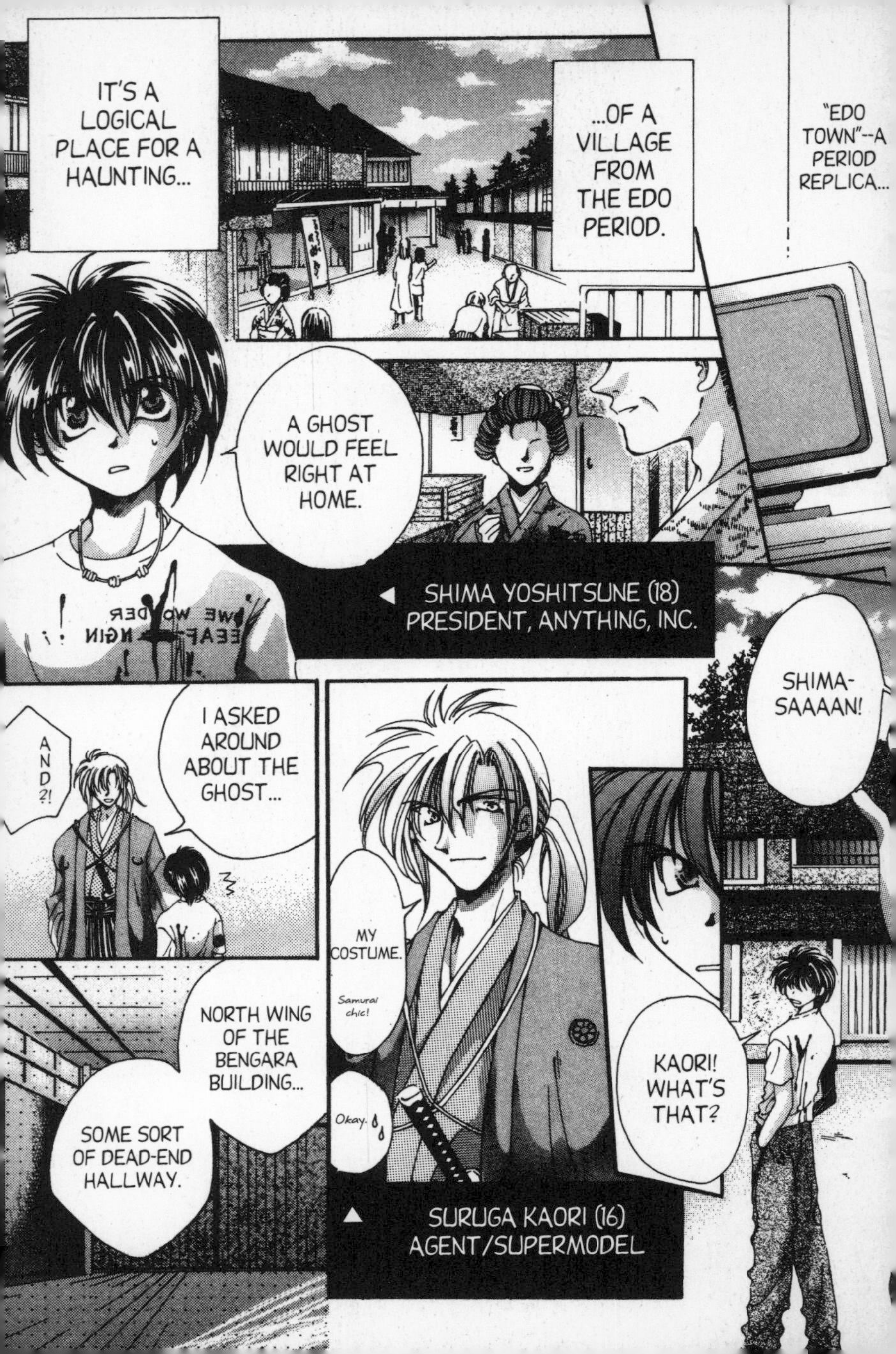
"EDO TOWN"--A PERIOD REPLICA...
...OF A VILLAGE FROM THE EDO PERIOD.
IT'S A LOGICAL PLACE FOR A HAUNTING...
A GHOST WOULD FEEL RIGHT AT HOME.
SHIMA YOSHITSUNE (18)
PRESIDENT, ANYTHING, INC.
SHIMA-SAAAAN!
KAORI! WHAT'S THAT?
MY COSTUME.
Samurai chic!
Okay.
SURUGA KAORI (16)
AGENT/SUPERMODEL
I ASKED AROUND ABOUT THE GHOST...
AND?!
NORTH WING OF THE BENGARA BUILDING...
SOME SORT OF DEAD-END HALLWAY.

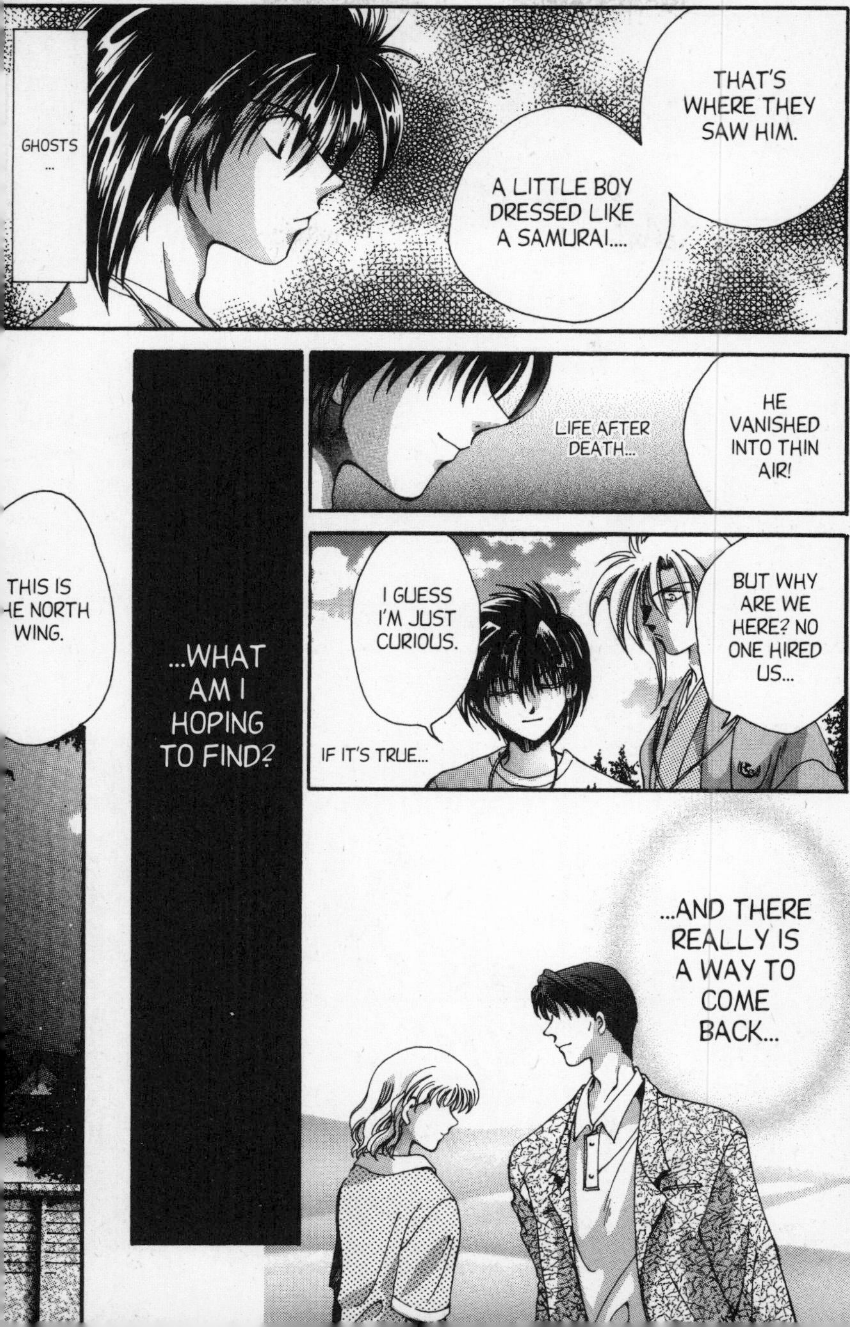
THAT'S WHERE THEY SAW HIM.
A LITTLE BOY DRESSED LIKE A SAMURAI....
GHOSTS ...
HE VANISHED INTO THIN AIR!
LIFE AFTER DEATH...
BUT WHY ARE WE HERE? NO ONE HIRED US...
I GUESS I'M JUST CURIOUS.
IF IT'S TRUE...
...AND THERE REALLY IS A WAY TO COME BACK...
...WHAT AM I HOPING TO FIND?
THIS IS HE NORTH WING.

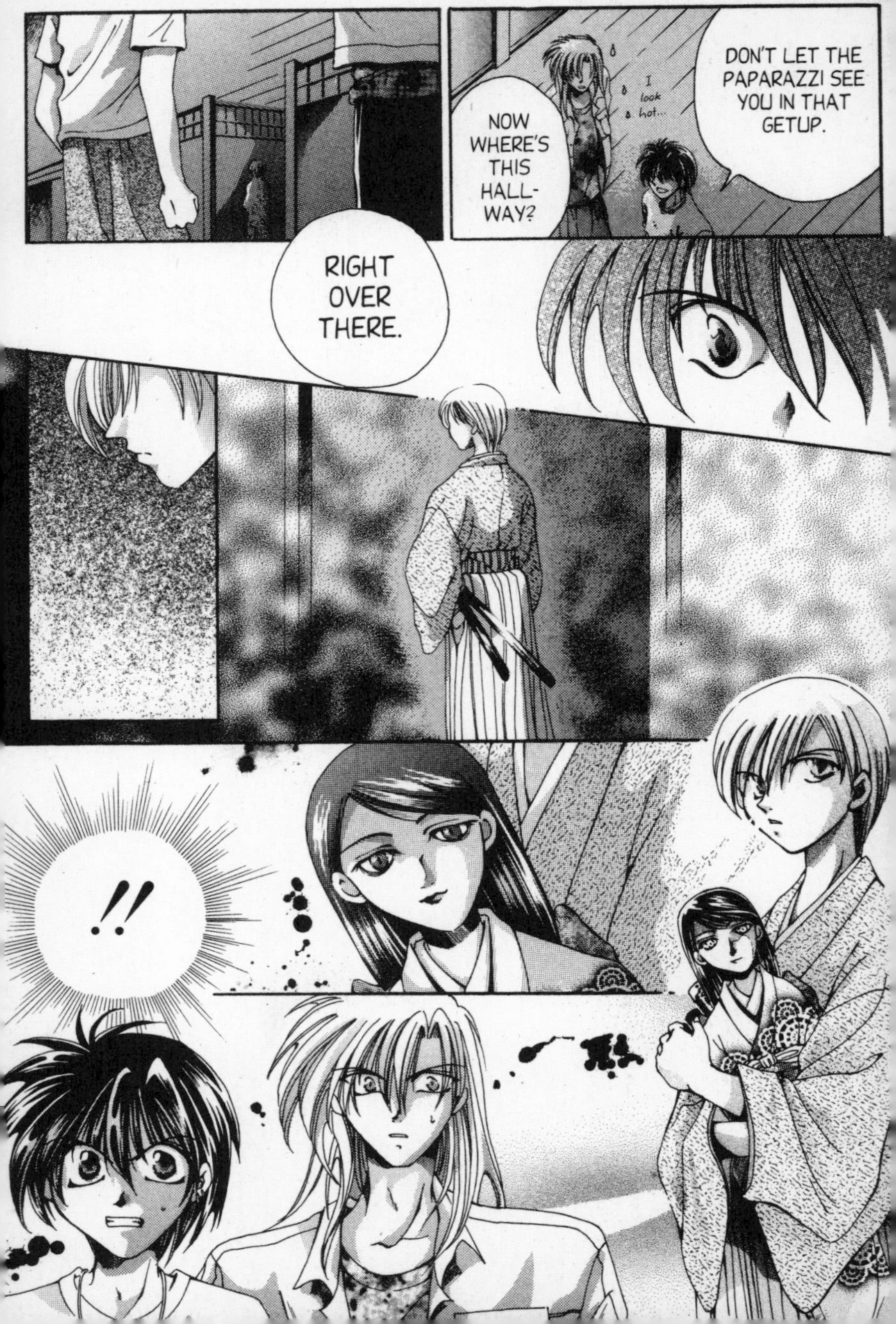
DON'T LET THE PAPARAZZI SEE YOU IN THAT GETUP.
I look hot...
NOW WHERE'S THIS HALL-WAY?
RIGHT OVER THERE.
!!

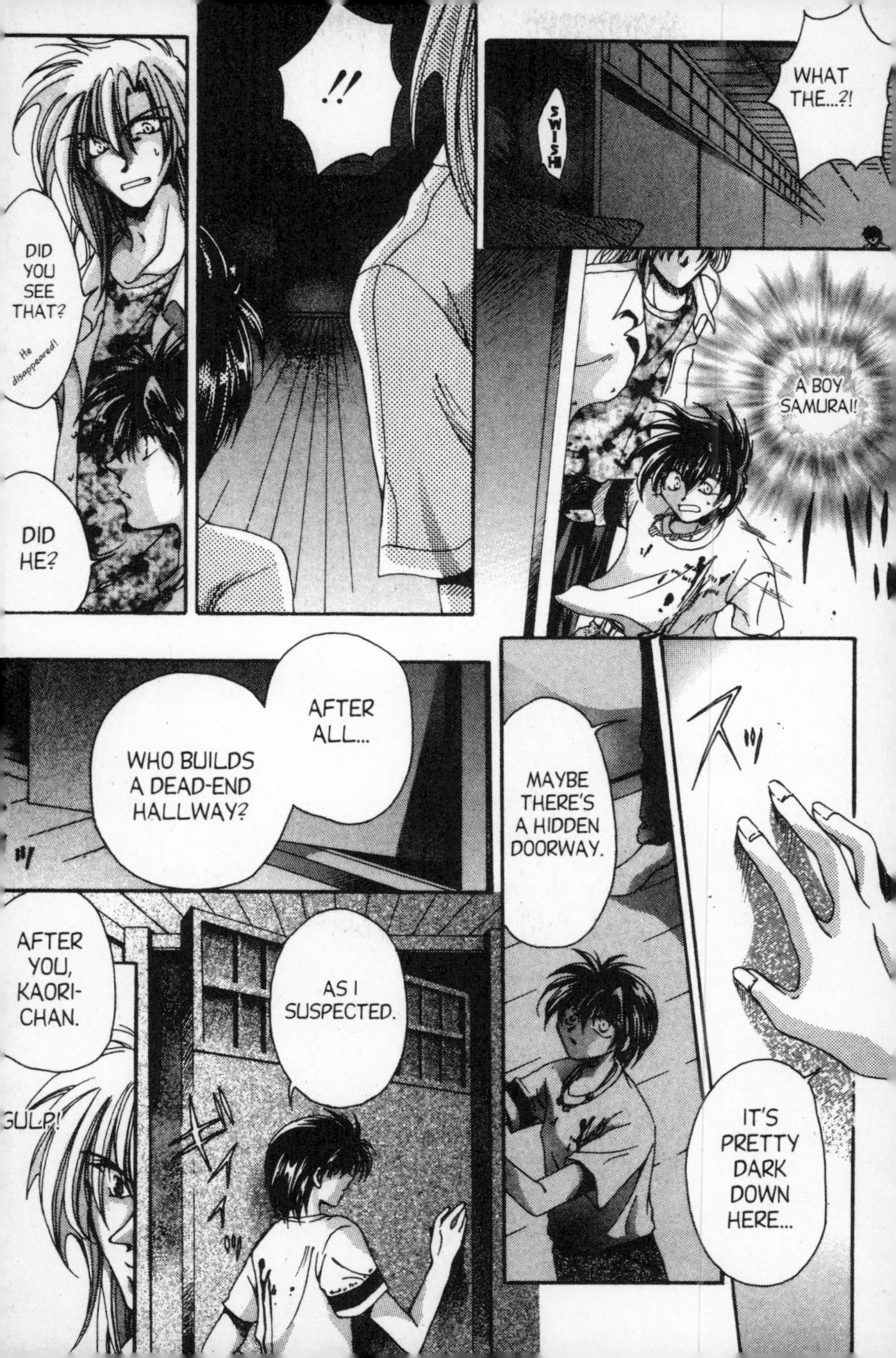
WHAT THE...?!
SWISH
A BOY SAMURAI!
!!
DID YOU SEE THAT?
He disappeared!
DID HE?
MAYBE THERE'S A HIDDEN DOORWAY.
AFTER ALL...
WHO BUILDS A DEAD-END HALLWAY?
AS I SUSPECTED.
AFTER YOU, KAORI-CHAN.
GULP!
IT'S PRETTY DARK DOWN HERE...

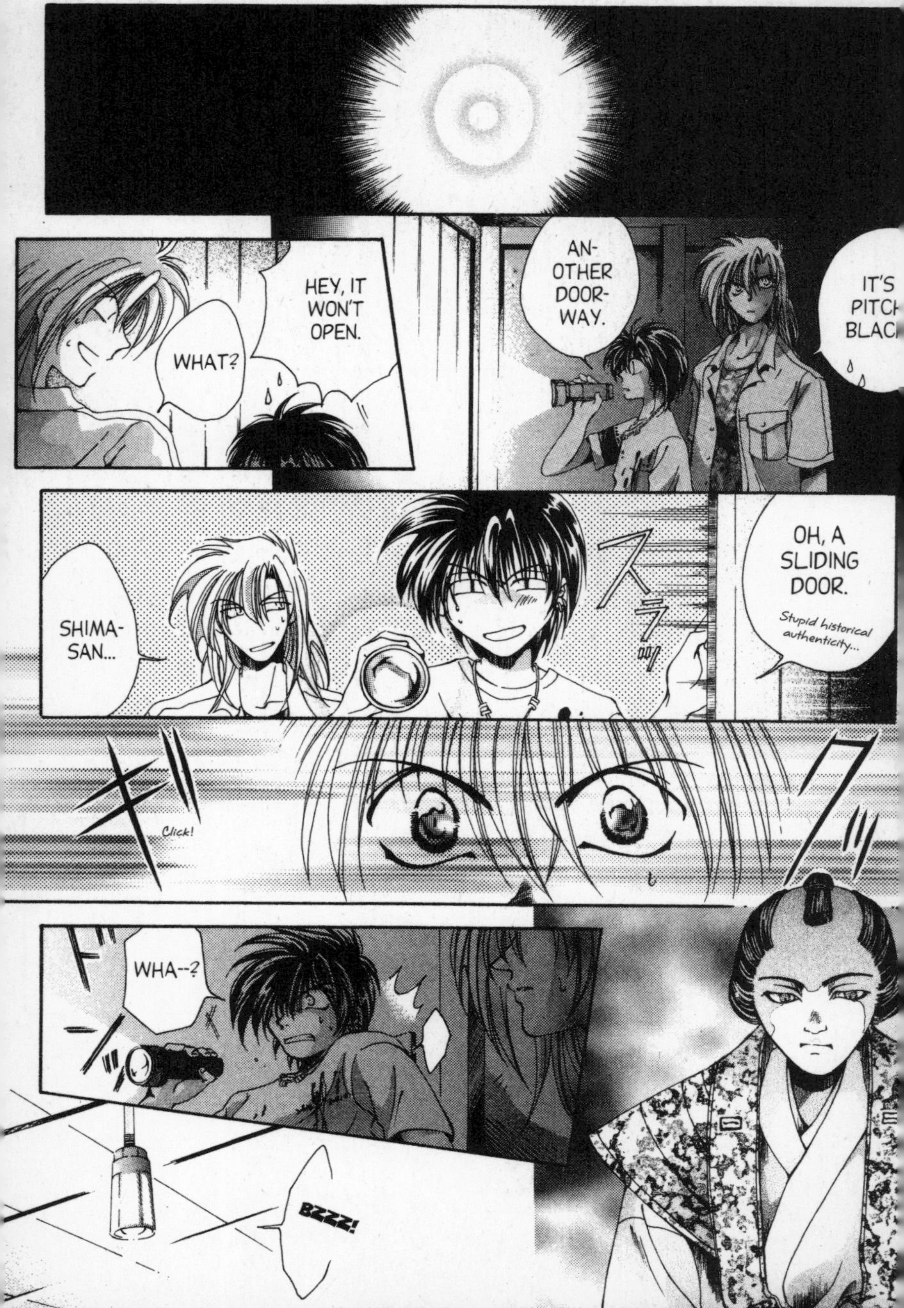
IT'S PITCH BLAC
AN-OTHER DOOR-WAY.
HEY, IT WON'T OPEN.
WHAT?
OH, A SLIDING DOOR.
Stupid historical authenticity...
SHIMA-SAN...
Click!
WHA--?
BZZZ!

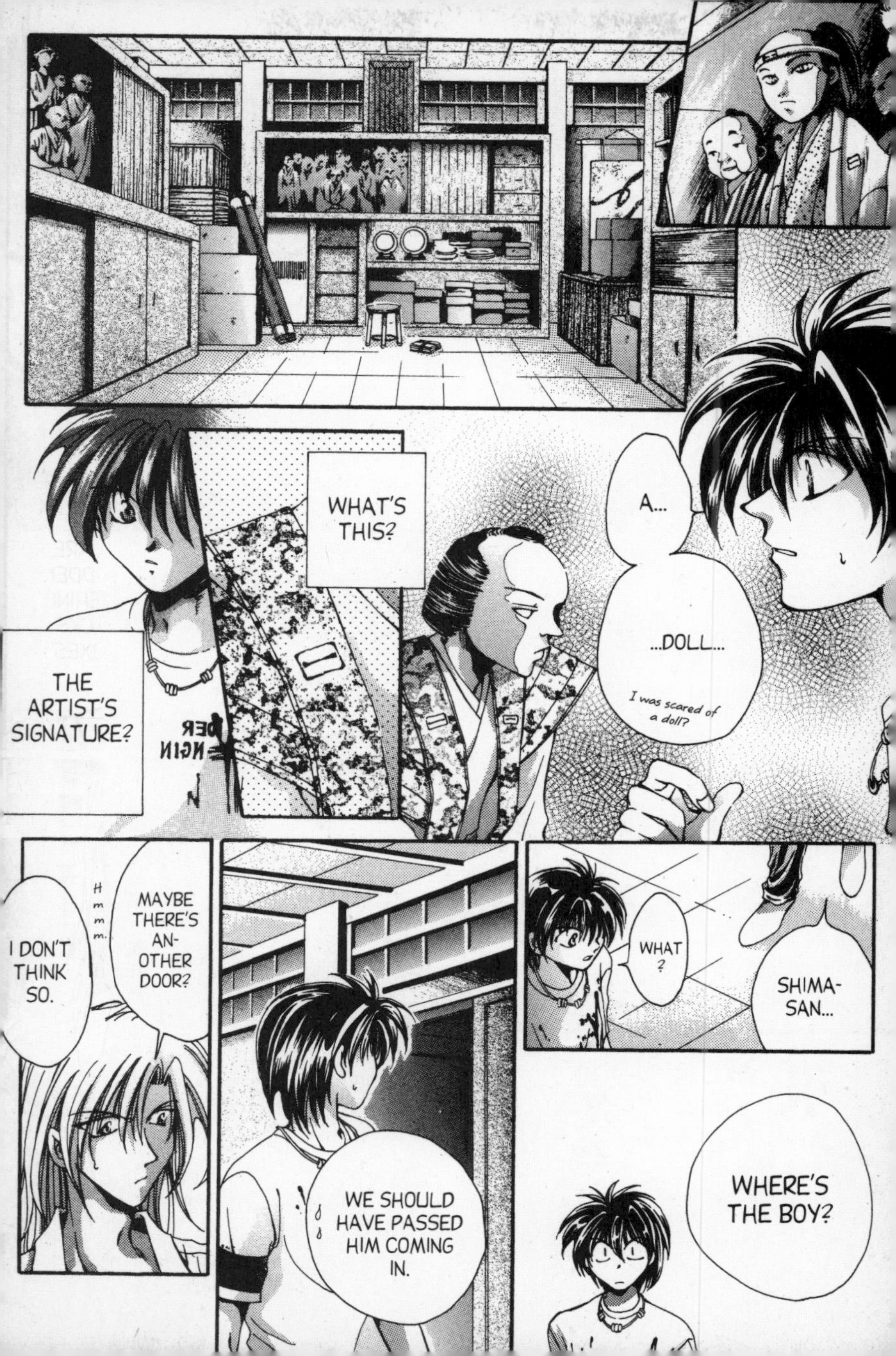
A...
...DOLL...
I was scared of a doll?
WHAT'S THIS?
THE ARTIST'S SIGNATURE?
SHIMA-SAN...
WHAT?
WHERE'S THE BOY?
WE SHOULD HAVE PASSED HIM COMING IN.
MAYBE THERE'S AN-OTHER DOOR?
Hmmm.
I DON'T THINK SO.

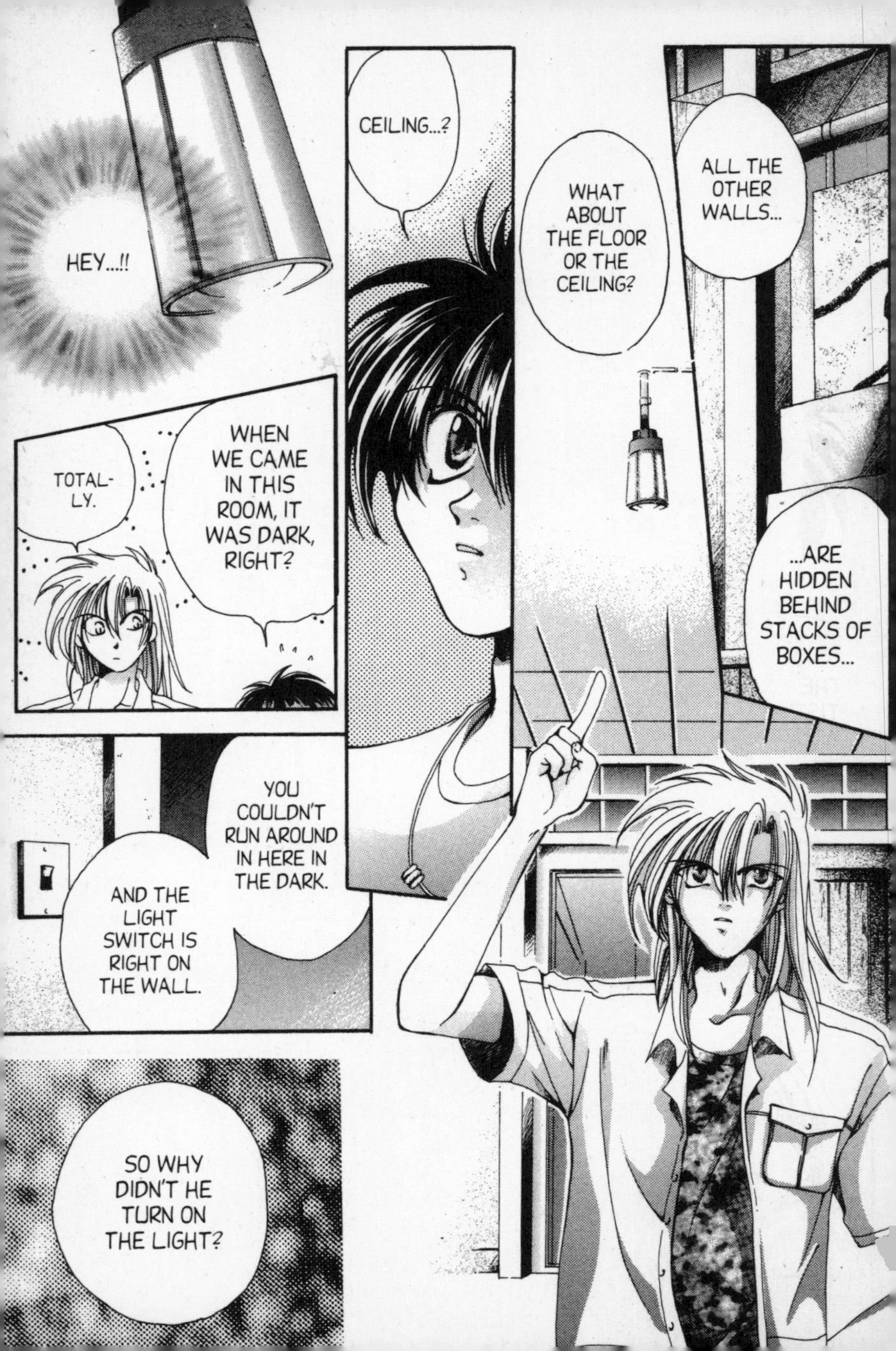

ALL THE OTHER WALLS...
...ARE HIDDEN BEHIND STACKS OF BOXES...
WHAT ABOUT THE FLOOR OR THE CEILING?
CEILING...?
HEY...!!
WHEN WE CAME IN THIS ROOM, IT WAS DARK, RIGHT?
TOTAL-LY.
YOU COULDN'T RUN AROUND IN HERE IN THE DARK.
AND THE LIGHT SWITCH IS RIGHT ON THE WALL.
SO WHY DIDN'T HE TURN ON THE LIGHT?

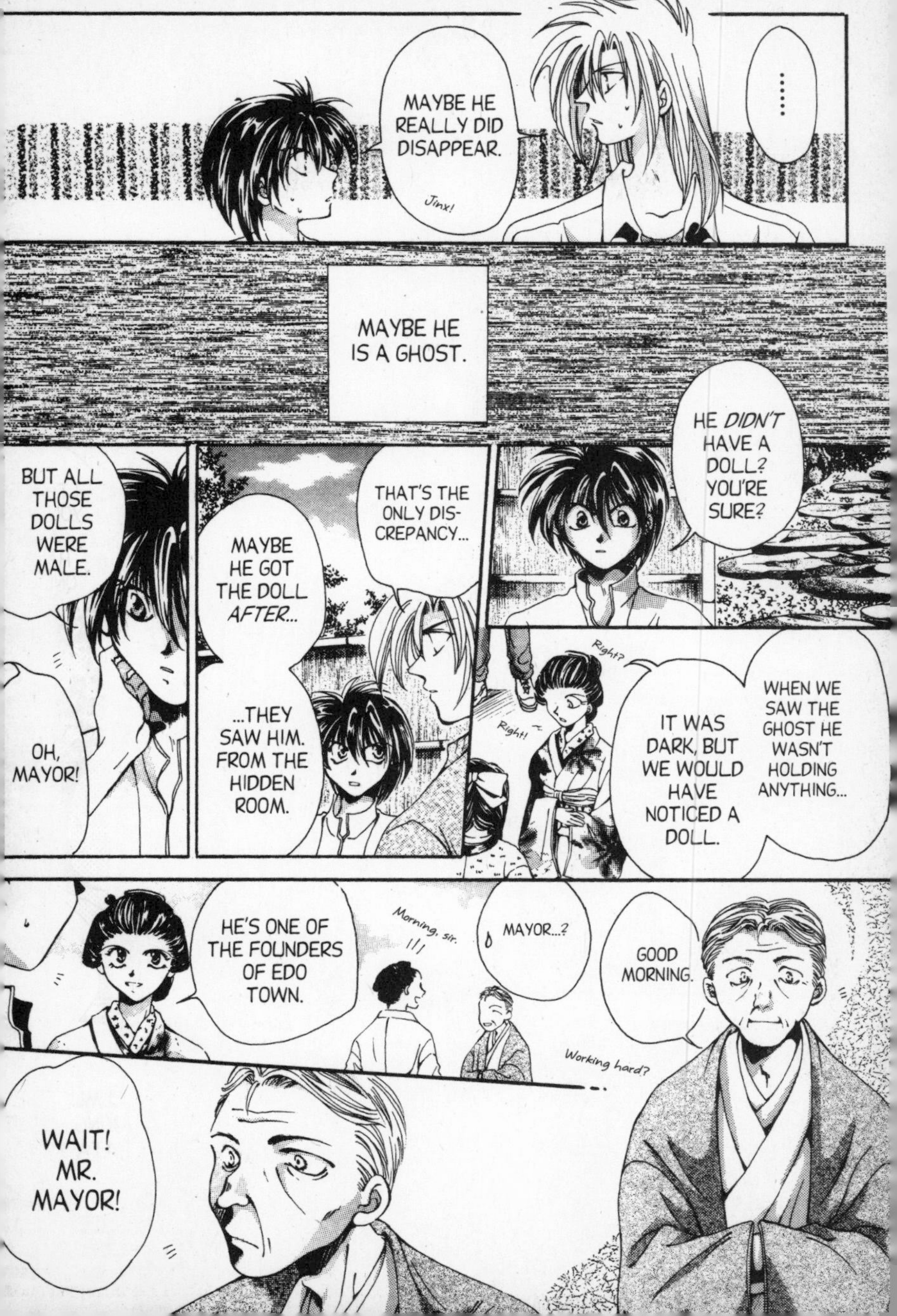

......
MAYBE HE REALLY DID DISAPPEAR.
Jinx!
MAYBE HE IS A GHOST.
HE *DIDN'T* HAVE A DOLL? YOU'RE SURE?
WHEN WE SAW THE GHOST HE WASN'T HOLDING ANYTHING...
IT WAS DARK, BUT WE WOULD HAVE NOTICED A DOLL.
Right?
Right!
THAT'S THE ONLY DIS-CREPANCY...
MAYBE HE GOT THE DOLL *AFTER*...
...THEY SAW HIM. FROM THE HIDDEN ROOM.
BUT ALL THOSE DOLLS WERE MALE.
OH, MAYOR!
GOOD MORNING.
Working hard?
MAYOR...?
Morning, sir.
HE'S ONE OF THE FOUNDERS OF EDO TOWN.
WAIT! MR. MAYOR!

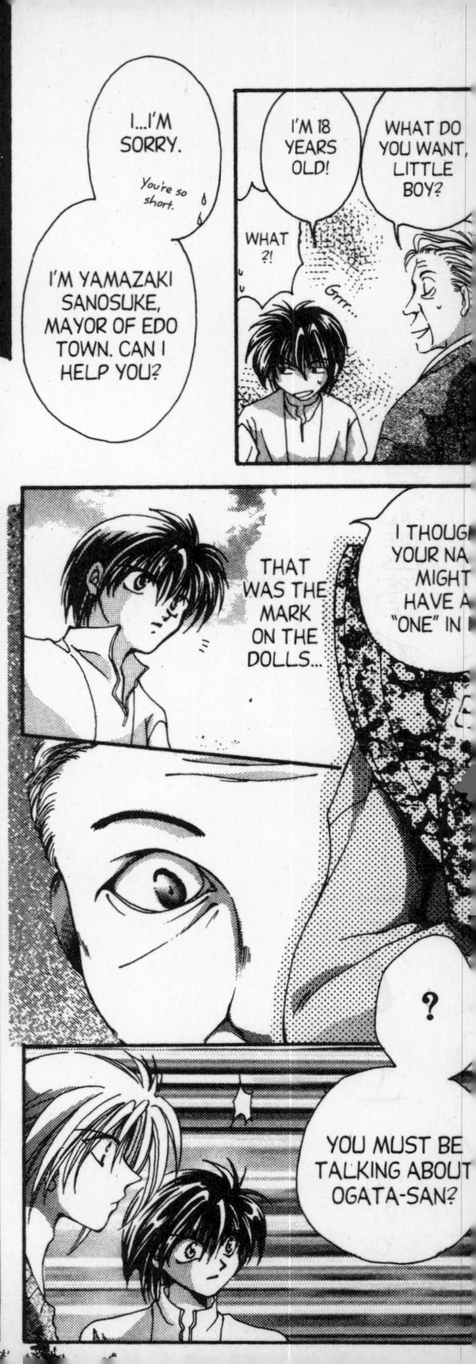
WHAT DO YOU WANT, LITTLE BOY?
I'M 18 YEARS OLD!
WHAT ?!
Grrr...
I...I'M SORRY.
You're so short.
I'M YAMAZAKI SANOSUKE, MAYOR OF EDO TOWN. CAN I HELP YOU?
I THOUG YOUR NA MIGHT HAVE A "ONE" IN
THAT WAS THE MARK ON THE DOLLS...
?
YOU MUST BE TALKING ABOUT OGATA-SAN?
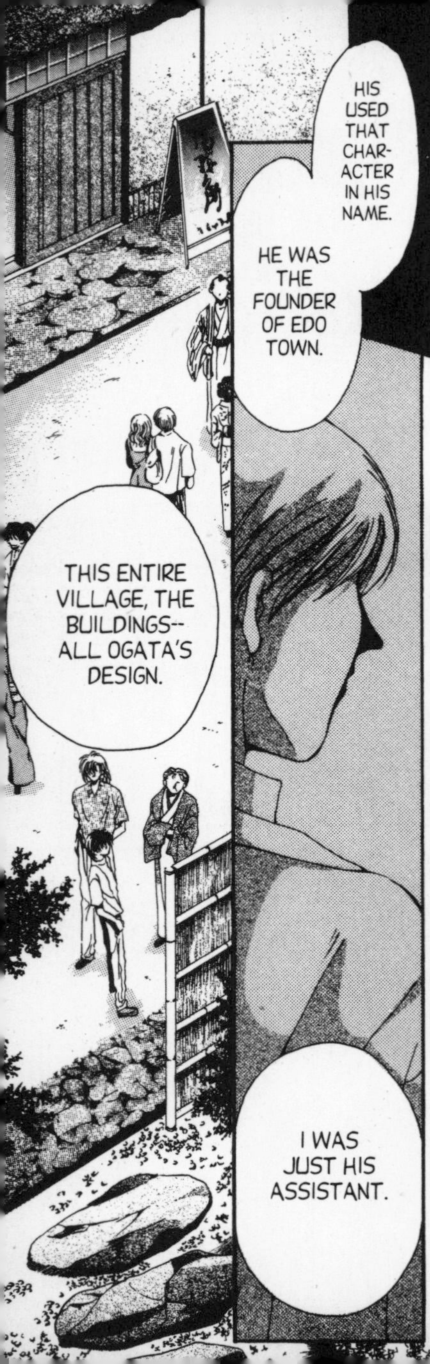
HIS USED THAT CHARACTER IN HIS NAME.
HE WAS THE FOUNDER OF EDO TOWN.
I WAS JUST HIS ASSISTANT.
THIS ENTIRE VILLAGE, THE BUILDINGS--ALL OGATA'S DESIGN.

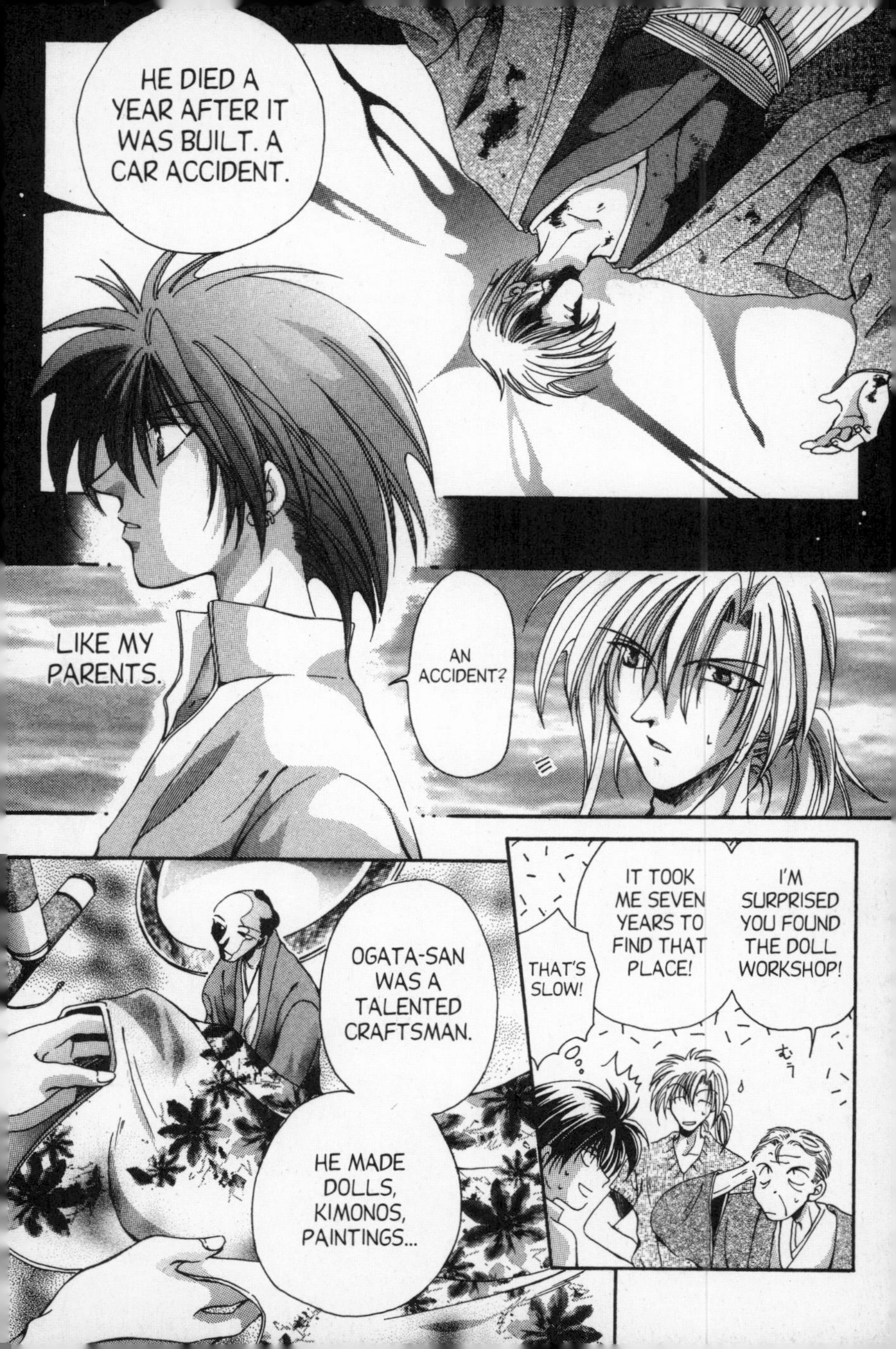
HE DIED A YEAR AFTER IT WAS BUILT. A CAR ACCIDENT.
AN ACCIDENT?
LIKE MY PARENTS.
I'M SURPRISED YOU FOUND THE DOLL WORKSHOP!
IT TOOK ME SEVEN YEARS TO FIND THAT PLACE!
THAT'S SLOW!
OGATA-SAN WAS A TALENTED CRAFTSMAN.
HE MADE DOLLS, KIMONOS, PAINTINGS...

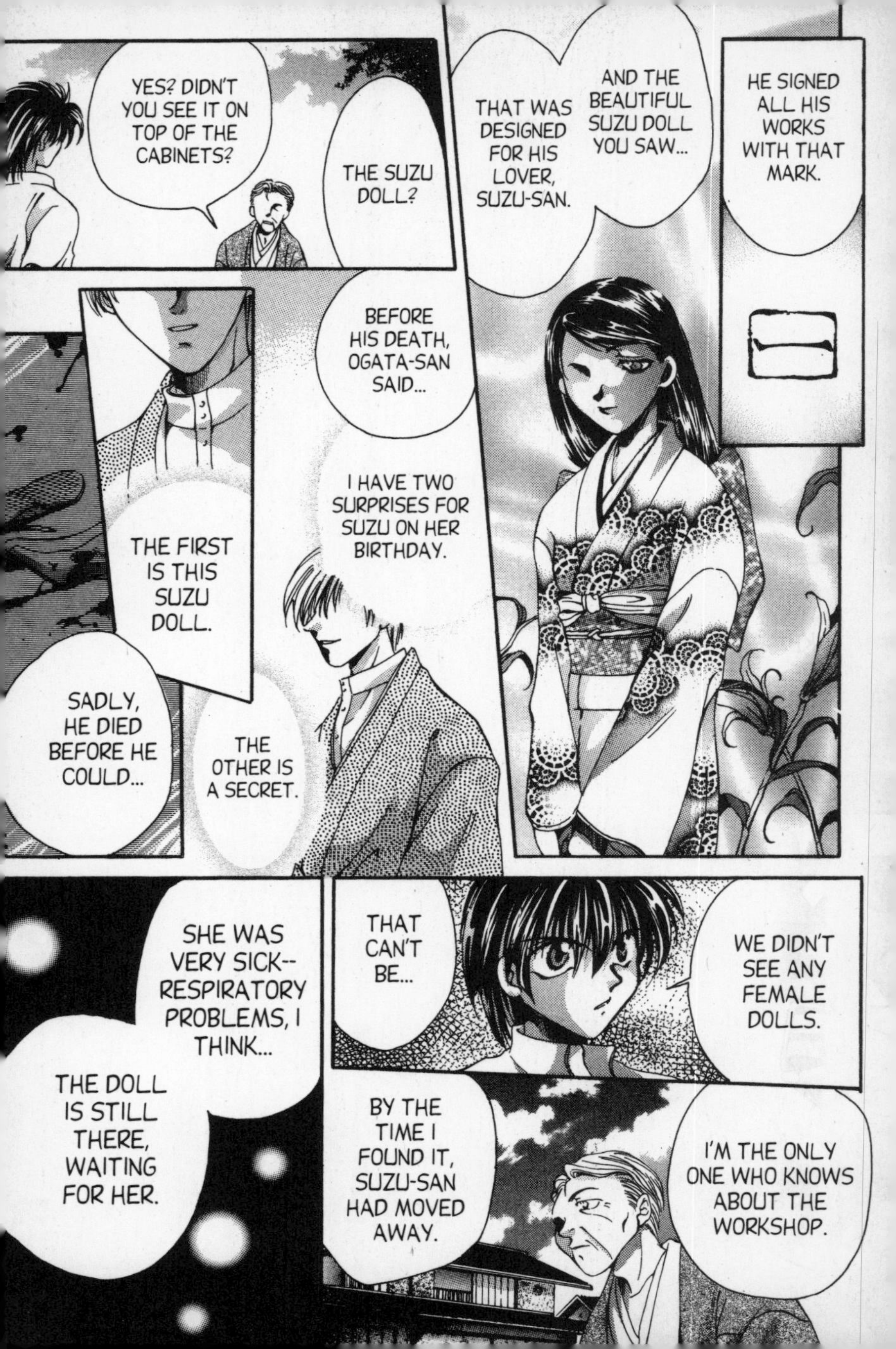
HE SIGNED ALL HIS WORKS WITH THAT MARK.
AND THE BEAUTIFUL SUZU DOLL YOU SAW...
THAT WAS DESIGNED FOR HIS LOVER, SUZU-SAN.
THE SUZU DOLL?
YES? DIDN'T YOU SEE IT ON TOP OF THE CABINETS?
BEFORE HIS DEATH, OGATA-SAN SAID...
I HAVE TWO SURPRISES FOR SUZU ON HER BIRTHDAY.
THE FIRST IS THIS SUZU DOLL.
THE OTHER IS A SECRET.
SADLY, HE DIED BEFORE HE COULD...
WE DIDN'T SEE ANY FEMALE DOLLS.
THAT CAN'T BE...
I'M THE ONLY ONE WHO KNOWS ABOUT THE WORKSHOP.
BY THE TIME I FOUND IT, SUZU-SAN HAD MOVED AWAY.
SHE WAS VERY SICK-- RESPIRATORY PROBLEMS, I THINK...
THE DOLL IS STILL THERE, WAITING FOR HER.

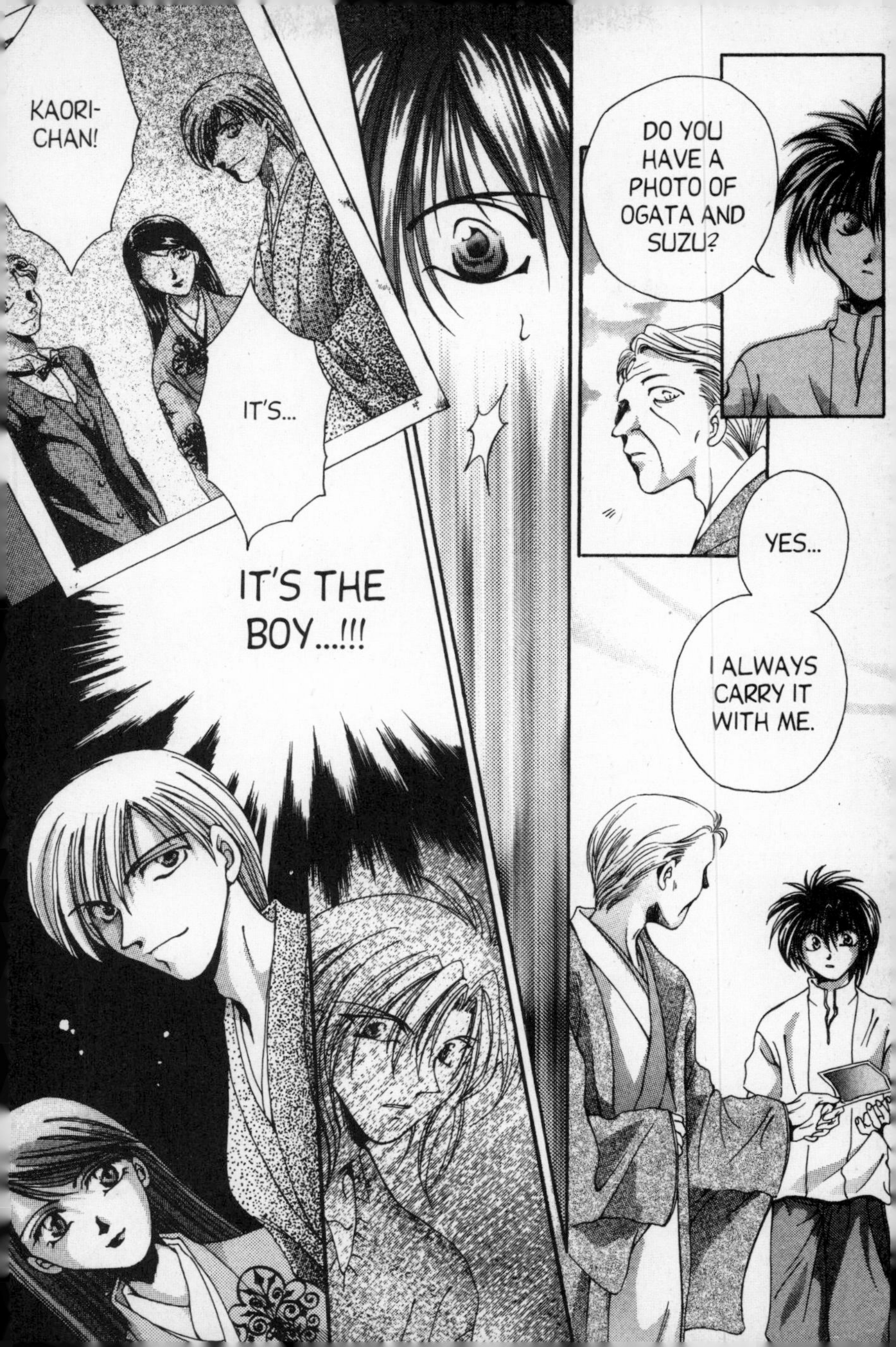
DO YOU HAVE A PHOTO OF OGATA AND SUZU?
YES...
I ALWAYS CARRY IT WITH ME.
KAORI-CHAN!
IT'S...
IT'S THE BOY...!!!

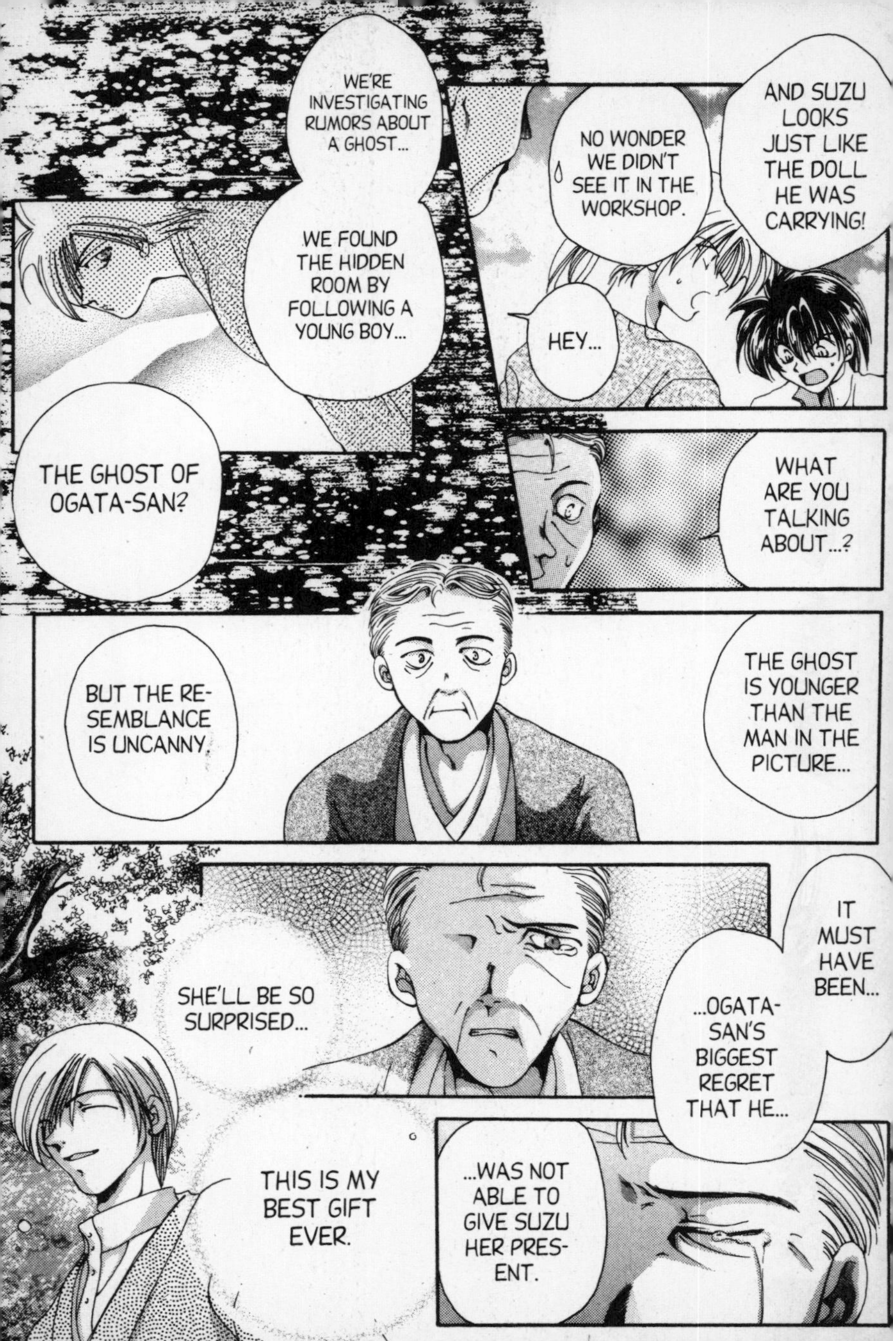
AND SUZU LOOKS JUST LIKE THE DOLL HE WAS CARRYING!
NO WONDER WE DIDN'T SEE IT IN THE WORKSHOP.
HEY...
WE'RE INVESTIGATING RUMORS ABOUT A GHOST...
WE FOUND THE HIDDEN ROOM BY FOLLOWING A YOUNG BOY...
WHAT ARE YOU TALKING ABOUT...?
THE GHOST OF OGATA-SAN?
THE GHOST IS YOUNGER THAN THE MAN IN THE PICTURE...
BUT THE RE-SEMBLANCE IS UNCANNY.
IT MUST HAVE BEEN...
...OGATA-SAN'S BIGGEST REGRET THAT HE...
SHE'LL BE SO SURPRISED...
...WAS NOT ABLE TO GIVE SUZU HER PRES-ENT.
THIS IS MY BEST GIFT EVER.

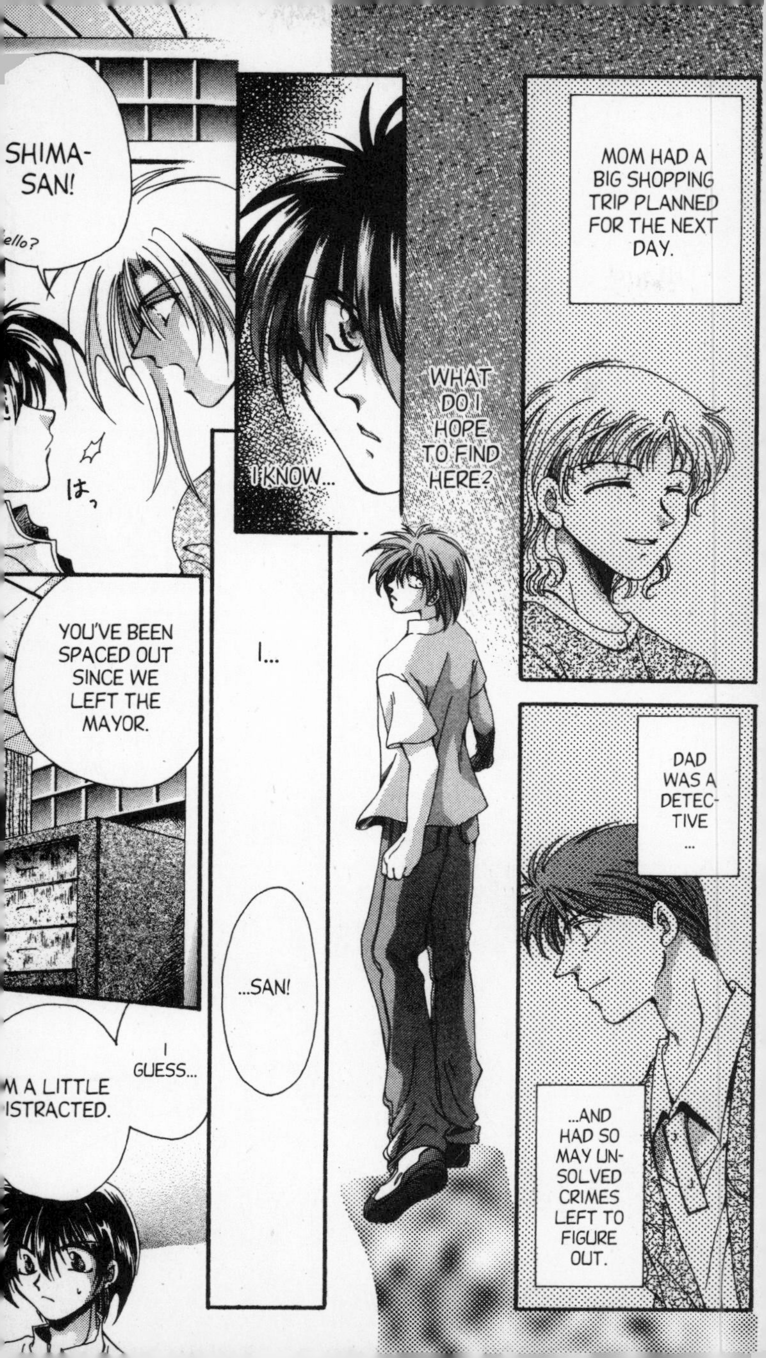
MOM HAD A BIG SHOPPING TRIP PLANNED FOR THE NEXT DAY.
DAD WAS A DETECTIVE...
...AND HAD SO MAY UNSOLVED CRIMES LEFT TO FIGURE OUT.
WHAT DO I HOPE TO FIND HERE?
I KNOW...
I...
...SAN!
SHIMA-SAN!
ello?
はっ
YOU'VE BEEN SPACED OUT SINCE WE LEFT THE MAYOR.
I GUESS...
M A LITTLE
ISTRACTED.

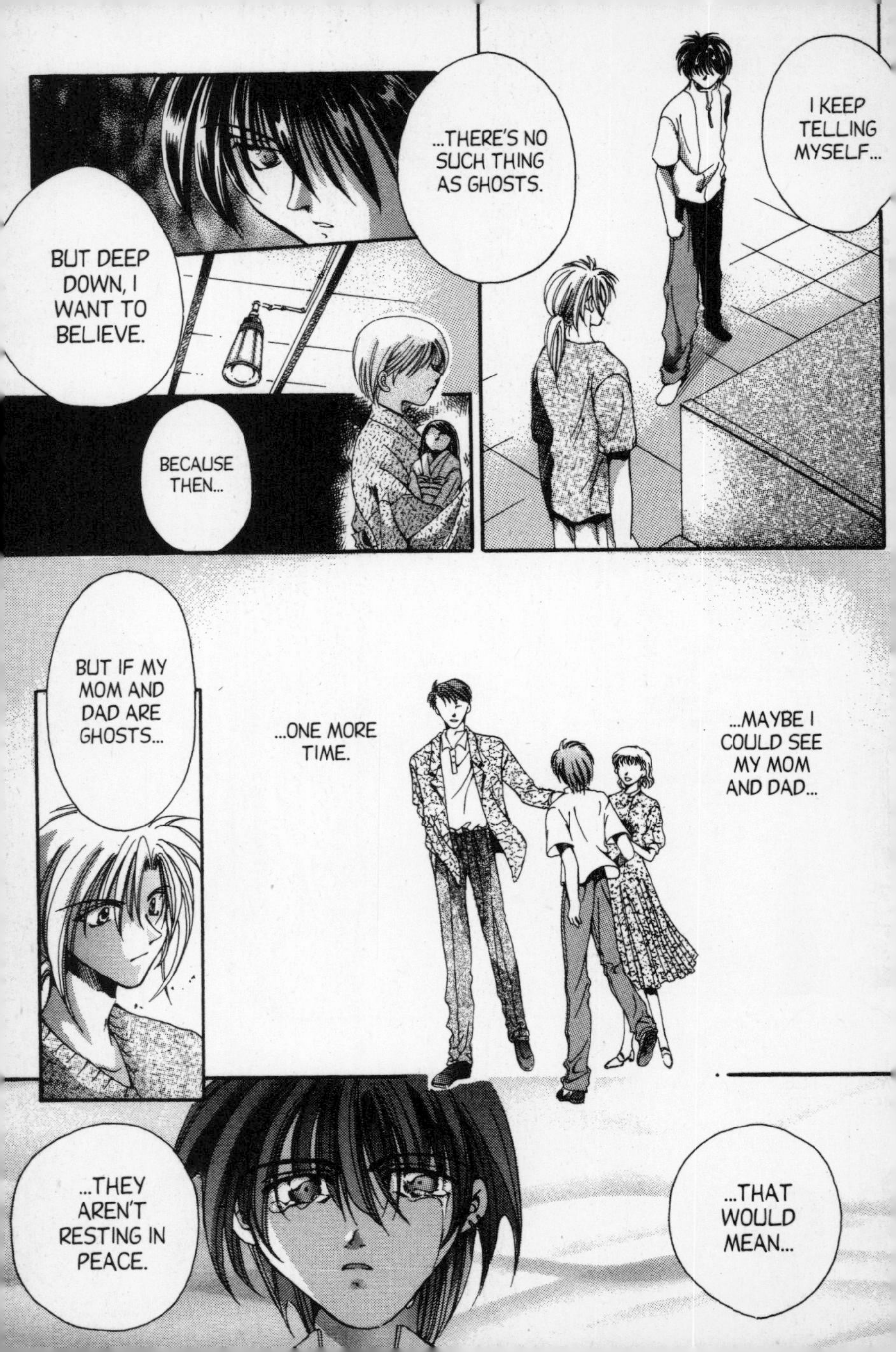
I KEEP TELLING MYSELF...
...THERE'S NO SUCH THING AS GHOSTS.
BUT DEEP DOWN, I WANT TO BELIEVE.
BECAUSE THEN...
...MAYBE I COULD SEE MY MOM AND DAD...
...ONE MORE TIME.
BUT IF MY MOM AND DAD ARE GHOSTS...
...THAT WOULD MEAN...
...THEY AREN'T RESTING IN PEACE.

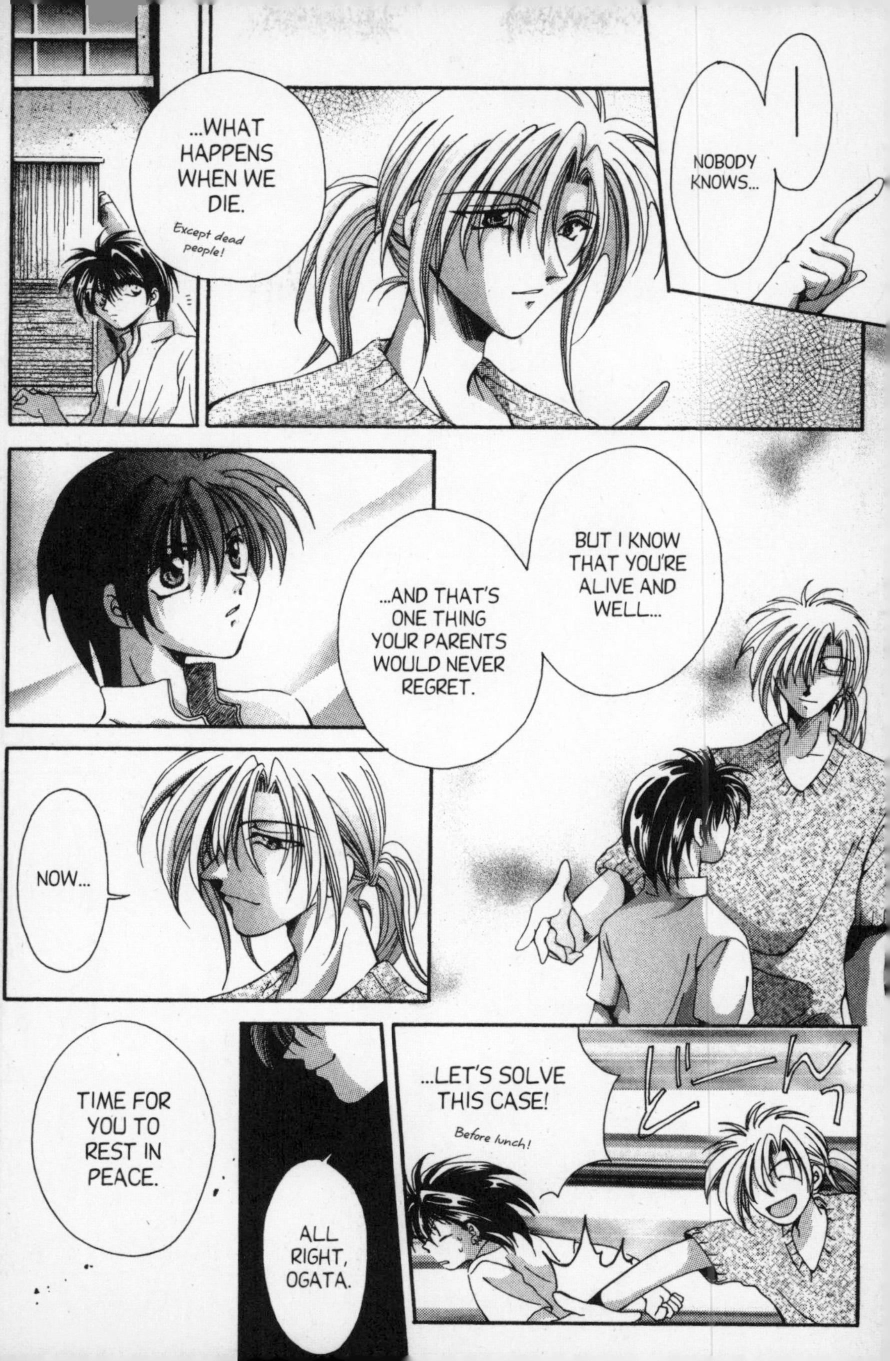
NOBODY KNOWS...
...WHAT HAPPENS WHEN WE DIE.
Except dead people!
BUT I KNOW THAT YOU'RE ALIVE AND WELL...
...AND THAT'S ONE THING YOUR PARENTS WOULD NEVER REGRET.
NOW...
...LET'S SOLVE THIS CASE!
Before lunch!
ALL RIGHT, OGATA.
TIME FOR YOU TO REST IN PEACE.

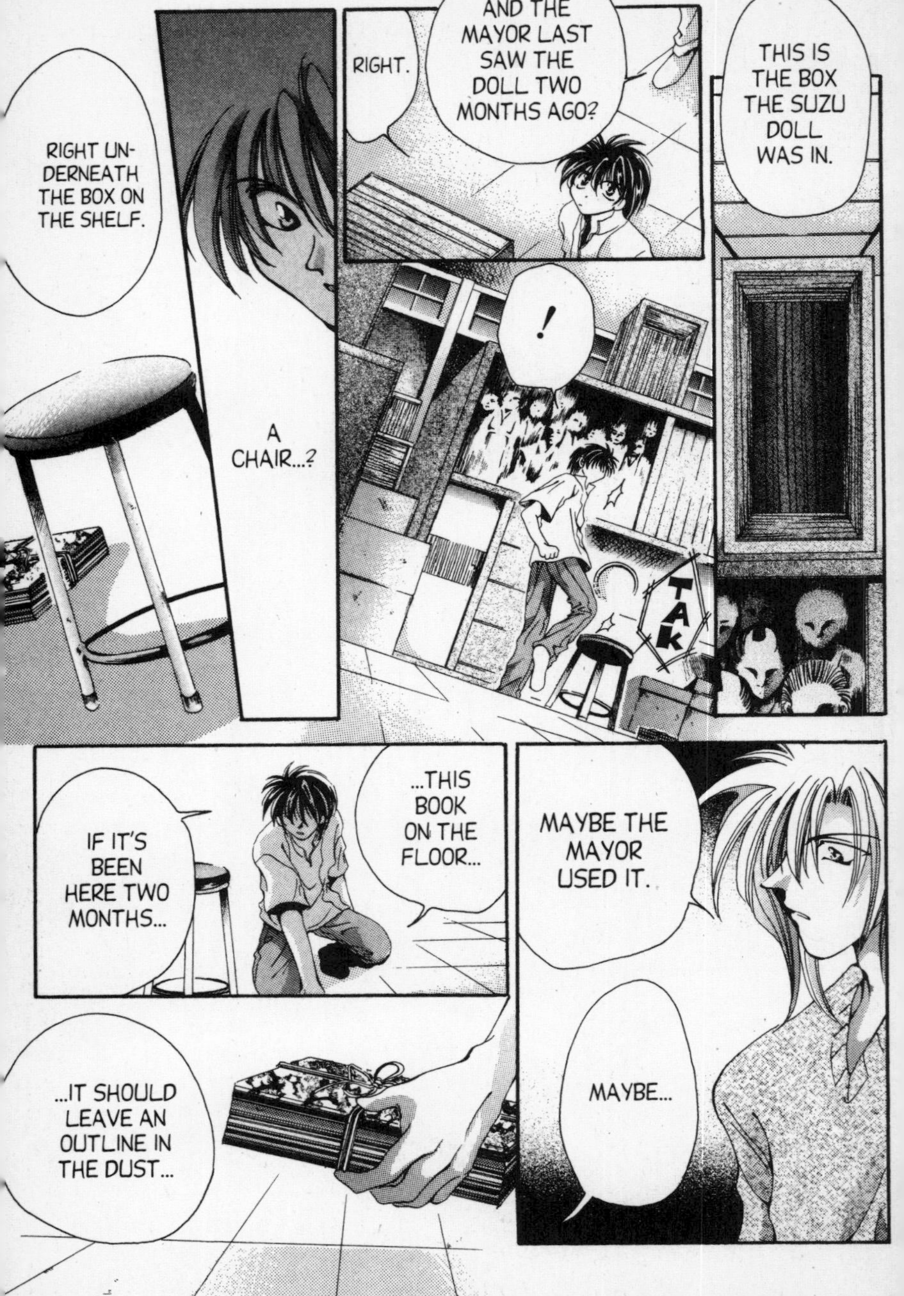
THIS IS THE BOX THE SUZU DOLL WAS IN.
AND THE MAYOR LAST SAW THE DOLL TWO MONTHS AGO?
RIGHT.
!
TAK
RIGHT UN-DERNEATH THE BOX ON THE SHELF.
A CHAIR...?
MAYBE THE MAYOR USED IT.
MAYBE...
...THIS BOOK ON THE FLOOR...
IF IT'S BEEN HERE TWO MONTHS...
...IT SHOULD LEAVE AN OUTLINE IN THE DUST...

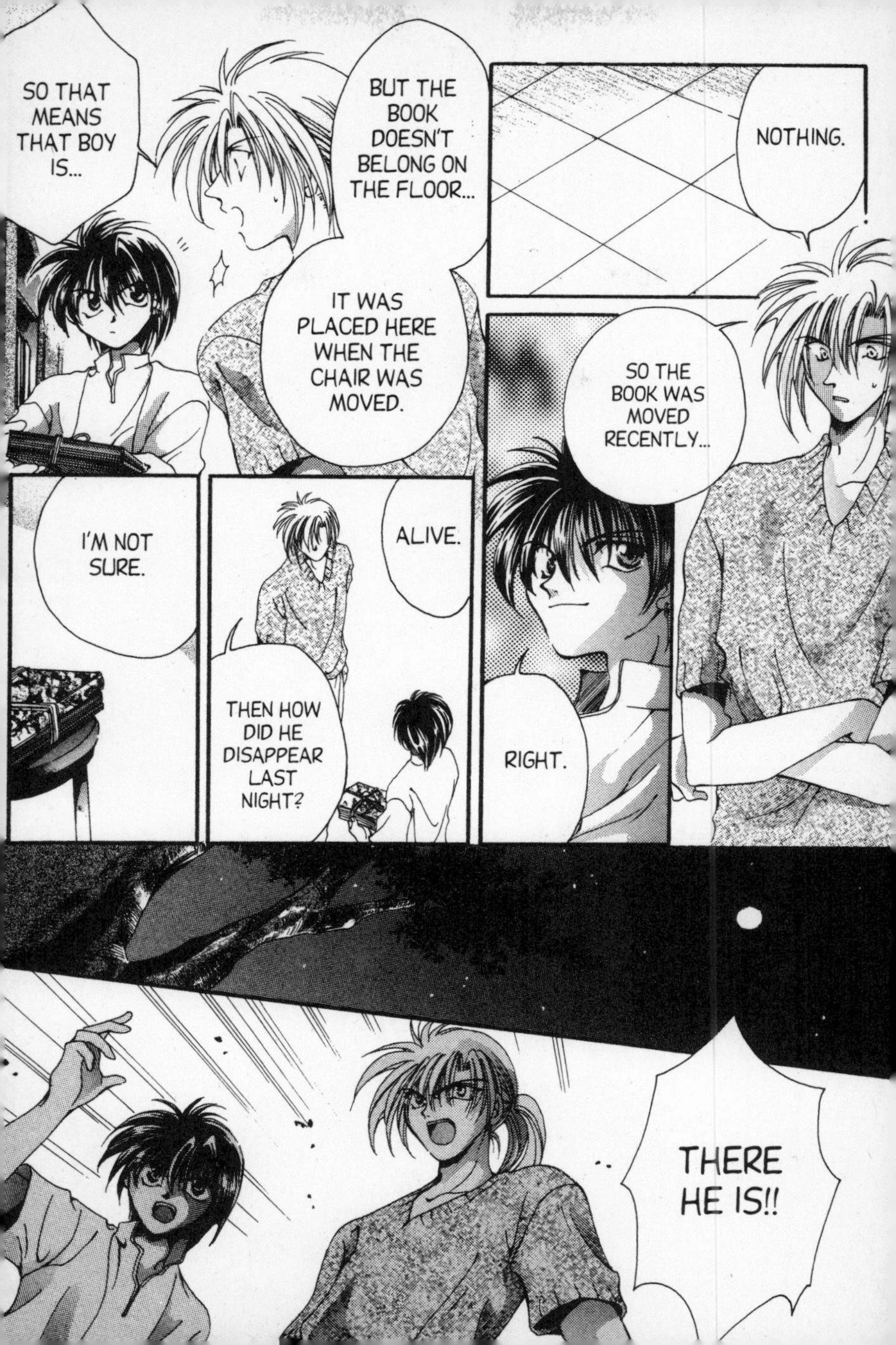
NOTHING.
SO THE BOOK WAS MOVED RECENTLY...
RIGHT.
BUT THE BOOK DOESN'T BELONG ON THE FLOOR...
IT WAS PLACED HERE WHEN THE CHAIR WAS MOVED.
SO THAT MEANS THAT BOY IS...
ALIVE.
THEN HOW DID HE DISAPPEAR LAST NIGHT?
I'M NOT SURE.
THERE HE IS!!

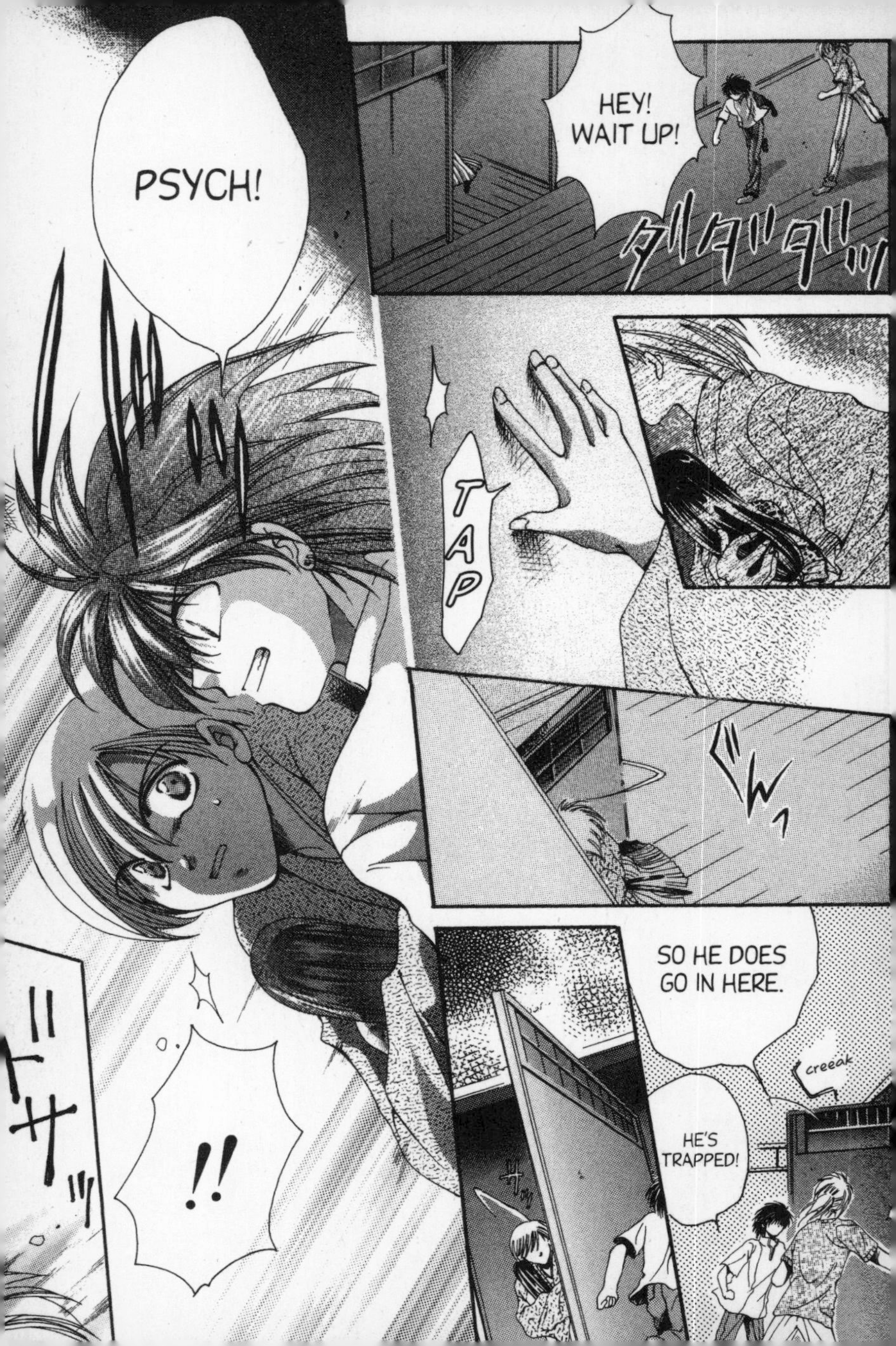
HEY! WAIT UP!
タッタッタッ
TAP
SO HE DOES GO IN HERE.
creeak
HE'S TRAPPED!
PSYCH!
!!

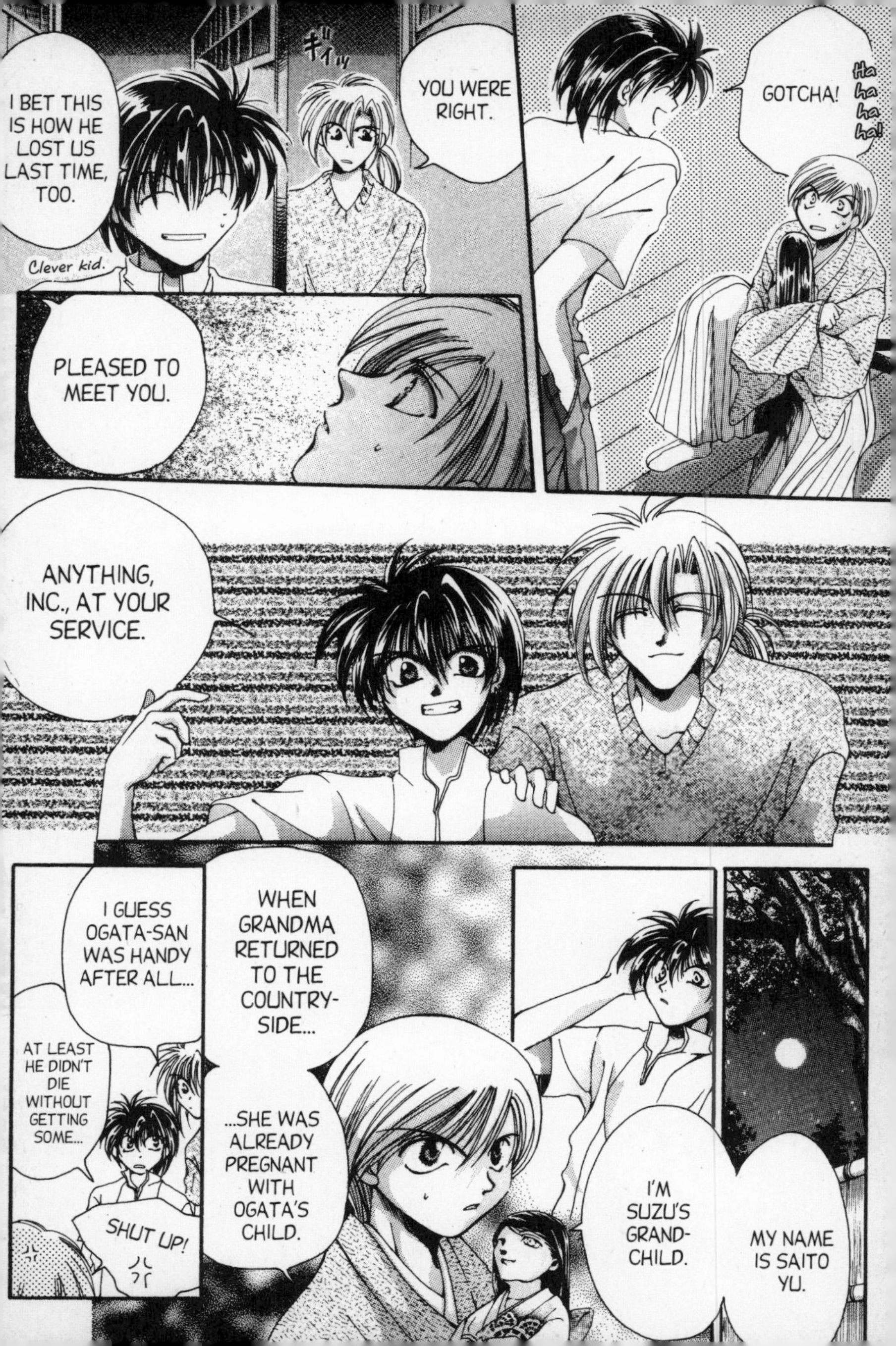
GOTCHA!
Ha ha ha ha!
ギィッ
YOU WERE RIGHT.
I BET THIS IS HOW HE LOST US LAST TIME, TOO.
Clever kid.
PLEASED TO MEET YOU.
ANYTHING, INC., AT YOUR SERVICE.
MY NAME IS SAITO YU.
I'M SUZU'S GRANDCHILD.
WHEN GRANDMA RETURNED TO THE COUNTRYSIDE...
...SHE WAS ALREADY PREGNANT WITH OGATA'S CHILD.
I GUESS OGATA-SAN WAS HANDY AFTER ALL...
AT LEAST HE DIDN'T DIE WITHOUT GETTING SOME...
SHUT UP!

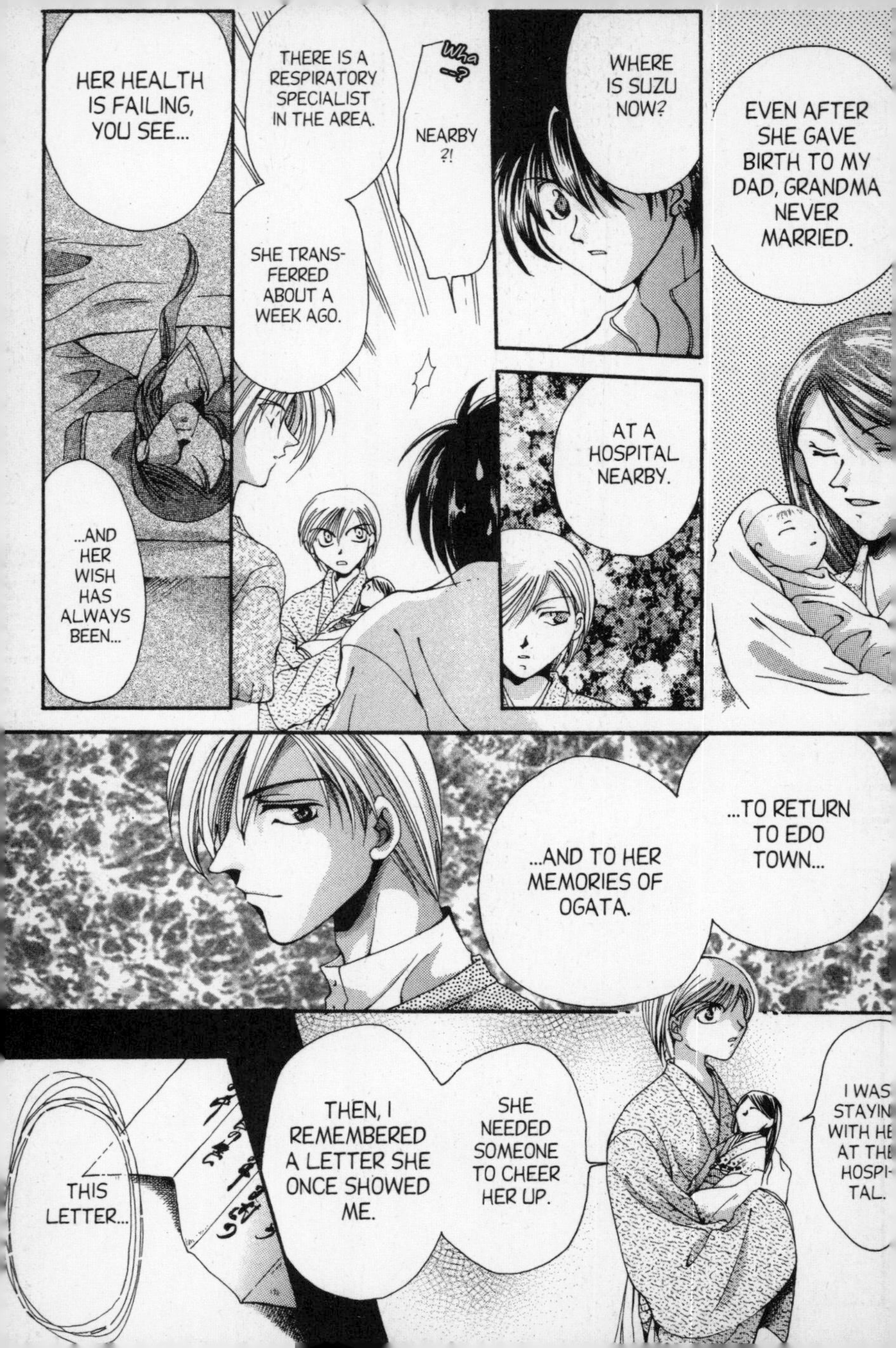

EVEN AFTER SHE GAVE BIRTH TO MY DAD, GRANDMA NEVER MARRIED.
WHERE IS SUZU NOW?
AT A HOSPITAL NEARBY.
Wha--?
NEARBY?!
THERE IS A RESPIRATORY SPECIALIST IN THE AREA.
SHE TRANS-FERRED ABOUT A WEEK AGO.
HER HEALTH IS FAILING, YOU SEE...
...AND HER WISH HAS ALWAYS BEEN...
...TO RETURN TO EDO TOWN...
...AND TO HER MEMORIES OF OGATA.
I WAS STAYIN WITH HE AT THE HOSPI-TAL.
SHE NEEDED SOMEONE TO CHEER HER UP.
THEN, I REMEMBERED A LETTER SHE ONCE SHOWED ME.
THIS LETTER...

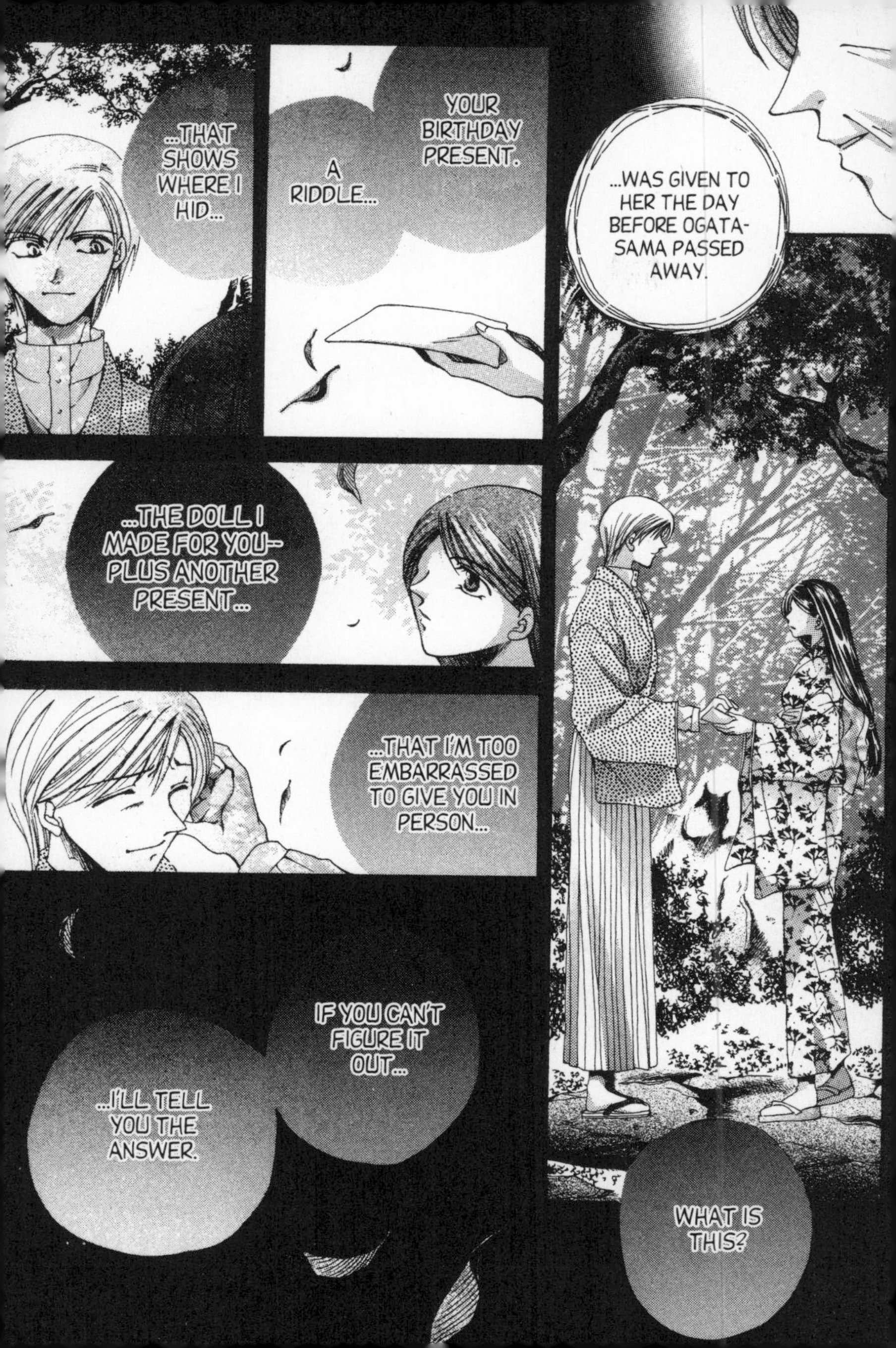
...WAS GIVEN TO HER THE DAY BEFORE OGATA-SAMA PASSED AWAY.
WHAT IS THIS?
YOUR BIRTHDAY PRESENT.
A RIDDLE...
...THAT SHOWS WHERE I HID...
...THE DOLL I MADE FOR YOU-PLUS ANOTHER PRESENT...
...THAT I'M TOO EMBARRASSED TO GIVE YOU IN PERSON...
IF YOU CAN'T FIGURE IT OUT...
...I'LL TELL YOU THE ANSWER.

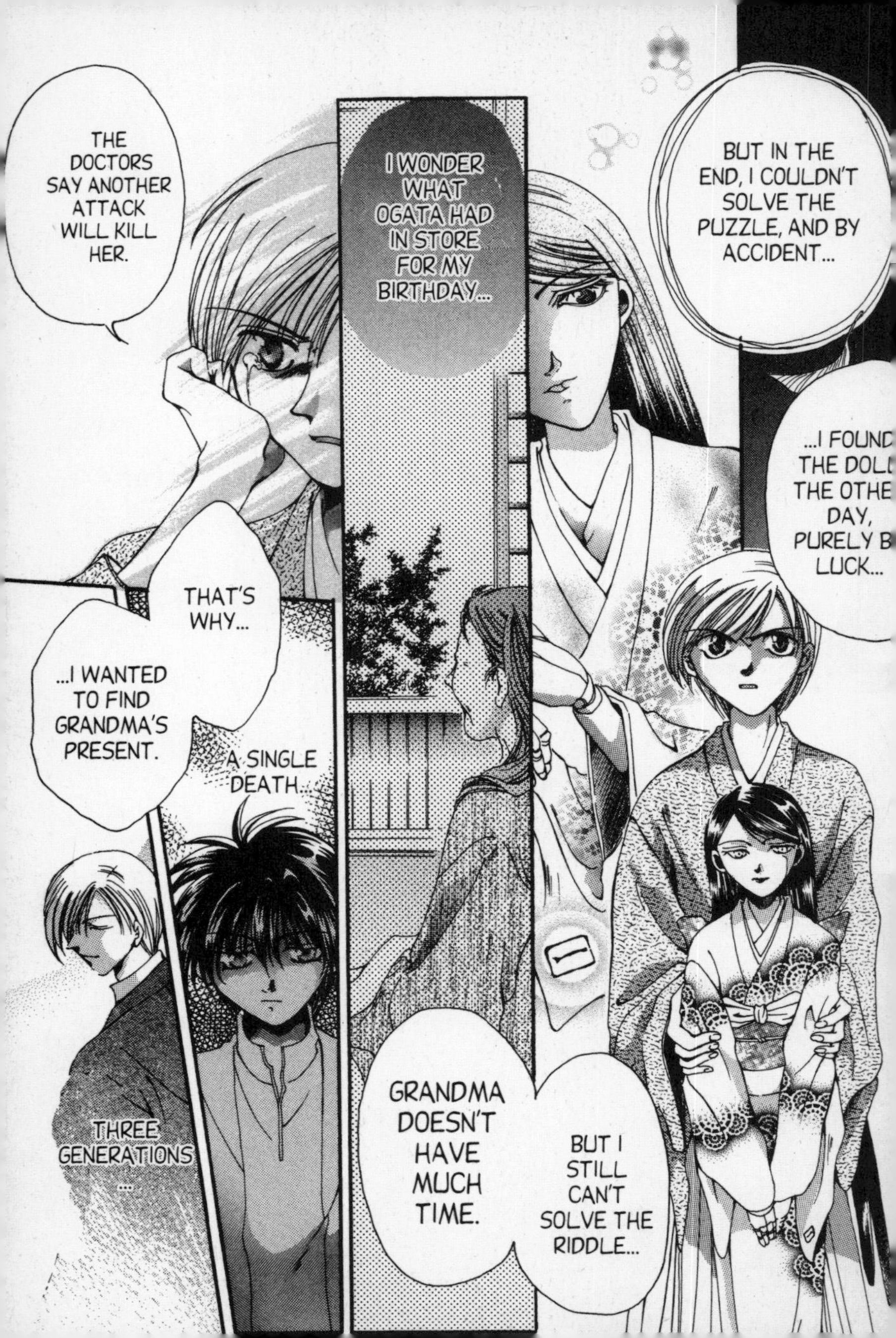
BUT IN THE END, I COULDN'T SOLVE THE PUZZLE, AND BY ACCIDENT...
...I FOUND THE DOLL THE OTHE DAY, PURELY B LUCK...
I WONDER WHAT OGATA HAD IN STORE FOR MY BIRTHDAY...
GRANDMA DOESN'T HAVE MUCH TIME.
BUT I STILL CAN'T SOLVE THE RIDDLE...
THE DOCTORS SAY ANOTHER ATTACK WILL KILL HER.
THAT'S WHY...
...I WANTED TO FIND GRANDMA'S PRESENT.
A SINGLE DEATH...
THREE GENERATIONS ...

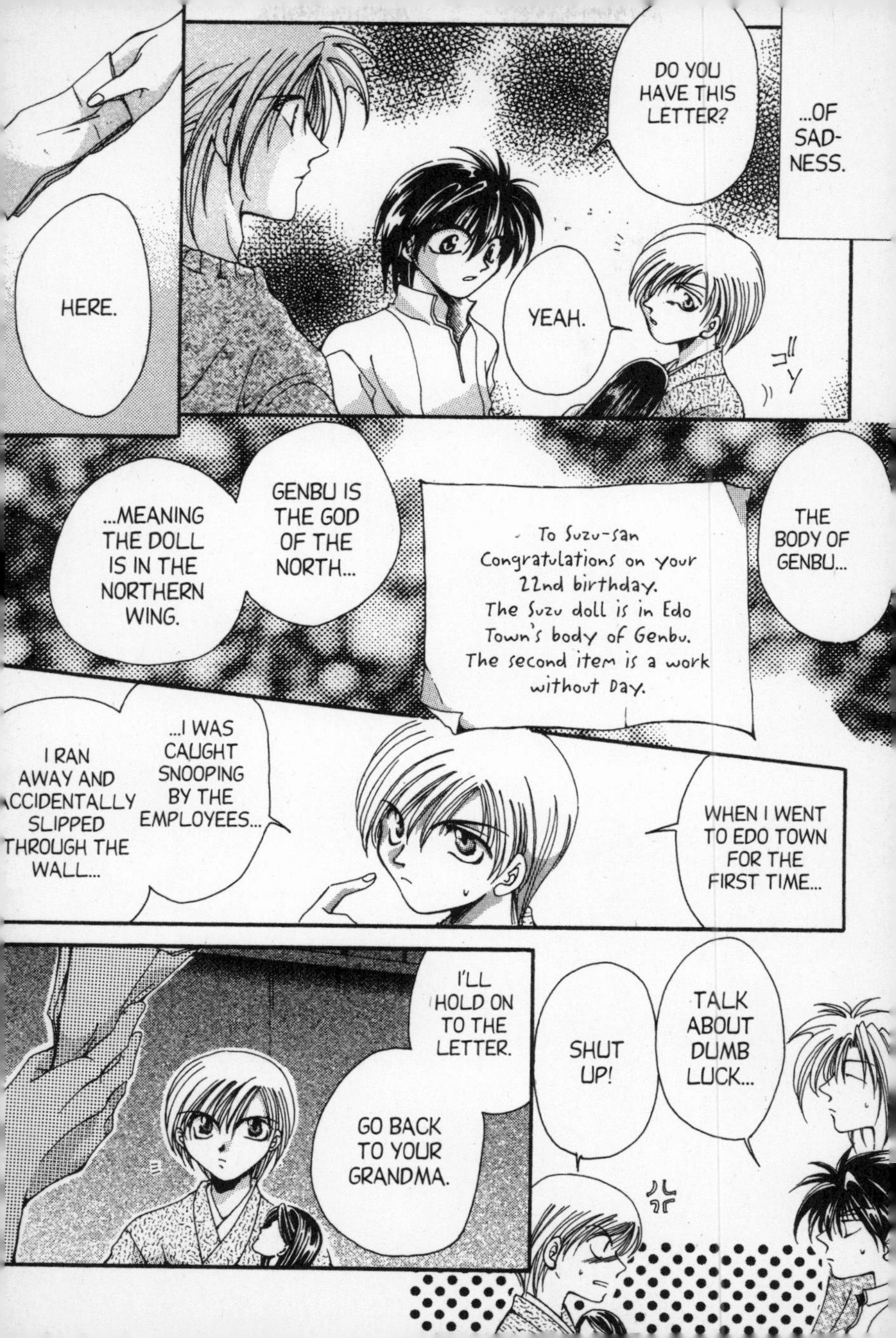
...OF SADNESS.
DO YOU HAVE THIS LETTER?
YEAH.
HERE.
THE BODY OF GENBU...
To Suzu-san
Congratulations on your 22nd birthday.
The Suzu doll is in Edo Town's body of Genbu.
The second item is a work without Day.
GENBU IS THE GOD OF THE NORTH...
...MEANING THE DOLL IS IN THE NORTHERN WING.
WHEN I WENT TO EDO TOWN FOR THE FIRST TIME...
...I WAS CAUGHT SNOOPING BY THE EMPLOYEES...
I RAN AWAY AND CCIDENTALLY SLIPPED THROUGH THE WALL...
TALK ABOUT DUMB LUCK...
SHUT UP!
I'LL HOLD ON TO THE LETTER.
GO BACK TO YOUR GRANDMA.

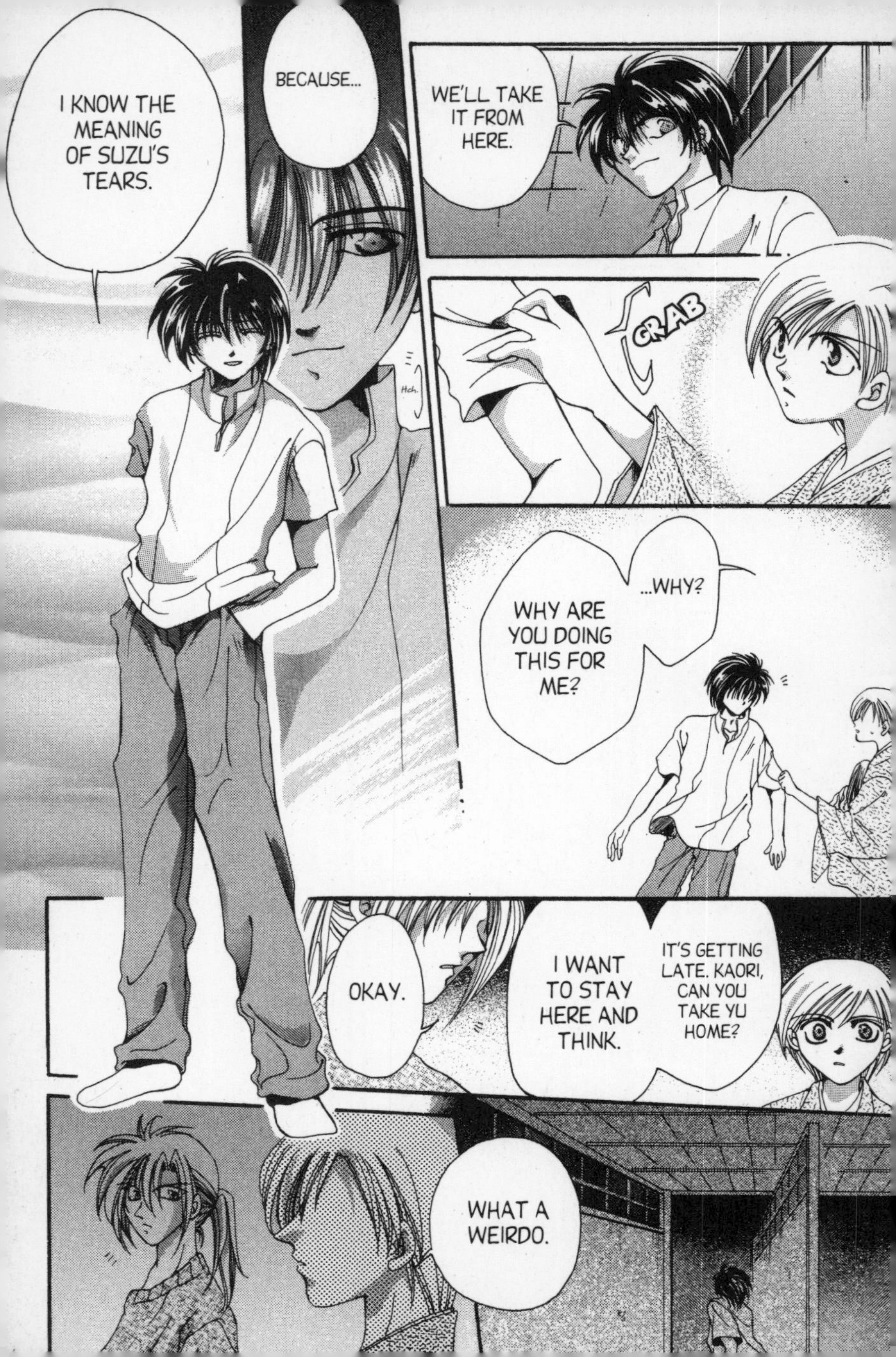

WE'LL TAKE IT FROM HERE.
GRAB
...WHY?
WHY ARE YOU DOING THIS FOR ME?
Hch.
BECAUSE...
I KNOW THE MEANING OF SUZU'S TEARS.
IT'S GETTING LATE. KAORI, CAN YOU TAKE YU HOME?
I WANT TO STAY HERE AND THINK.
OKAY.
WHAT A WEIRDO.

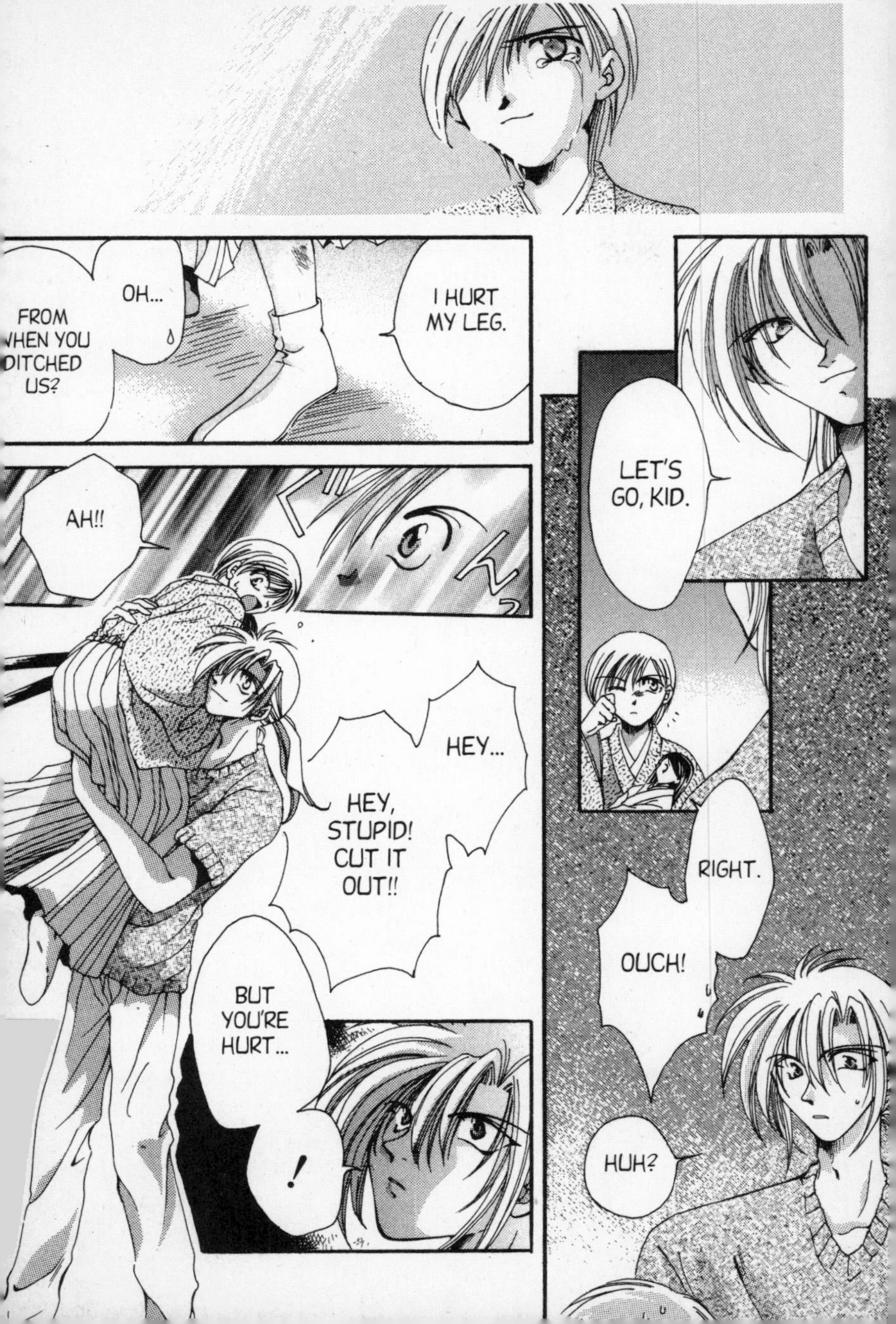
LET'S GO, KID.
RIGHT.
OUCH!
HUH?
I HURT MY LEG.
OH...
FROM WHEN YOU DITCHED US?
AH!!
HEY...
HEY, STUPID! CUT IT OUT!!
BUT YOU'RE HURT...
!

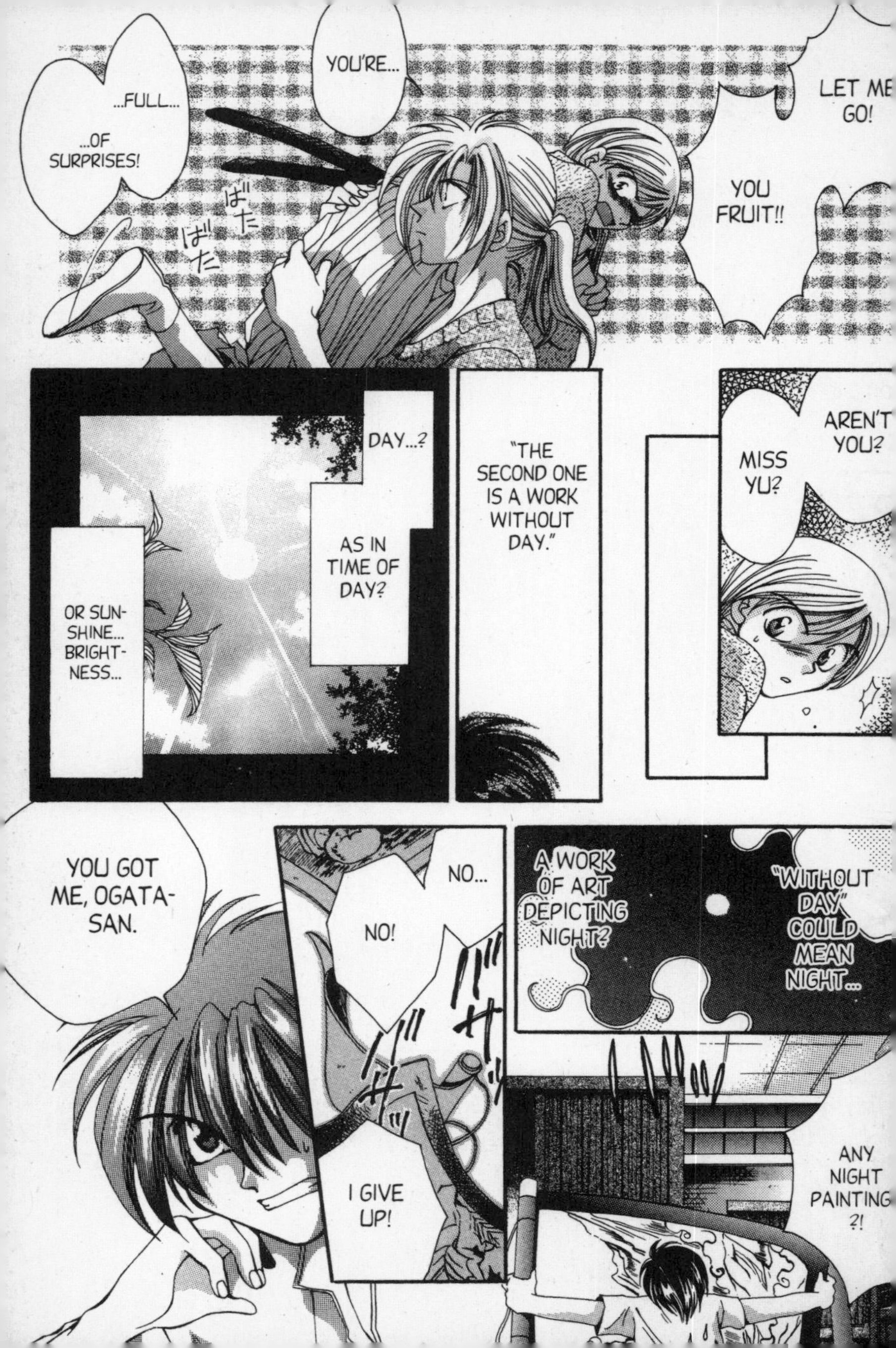
LET ME GO!
YOU FRUIT!!
YOU'RE...
...FULL...
...OF SURPRISES!
ばた ばた
AREN'T YOU?
MISS YU?
"THE SECOND ONE IS A WORK WITHOUT DAY."
DAY...?
AS IN TIME OF DAY?
OR SUN-SHINE... BRIGHT-NESS...
"WITHOUT DAY" COULD MEAN NIGHT...
A WORK OF ART DEPICTING NIGHT?
ANY NIGHT PAINTING?!
NO...
NO!
I GIVE UP!
YOU GOT ME, OGATA-SAN.

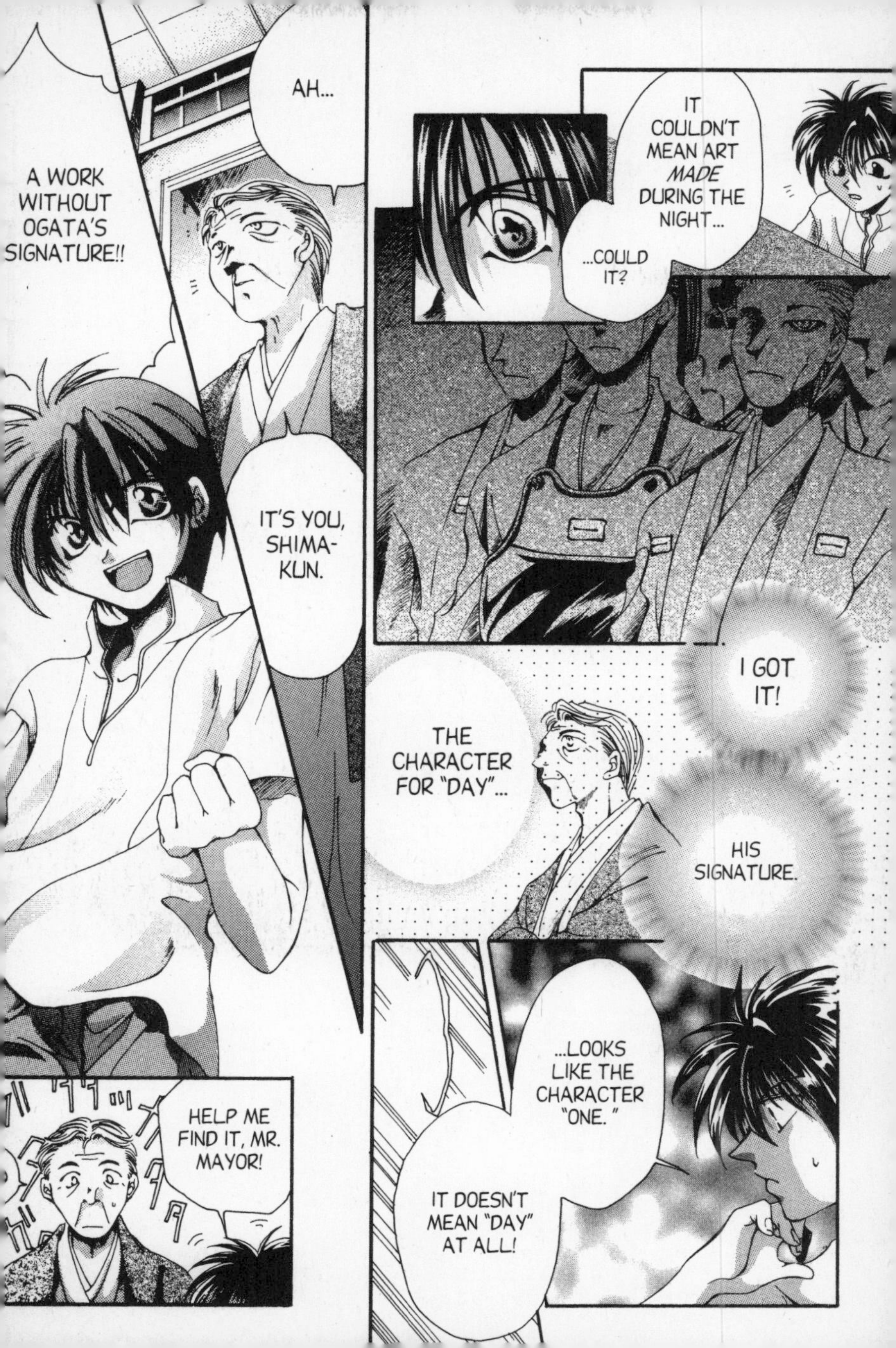
IT COULDN'T MEAN ART *MADE* DURING THE NIGHT...
...COULD IT?
I GOT IT!
HIS SIGNATURE.
THE CHARACTER FOR "DAY"...
...LOOKS LIKE THE CHARACTER "ONE."
IT DOESN'T MEAN "DAY" AT ALL!
AH...
A WORK WITHOUT OGATA'S SIGNATURE!!
IT'S YOU, SHIMA-KUN.
HELP ME FIND IT, MR. MAYOR!

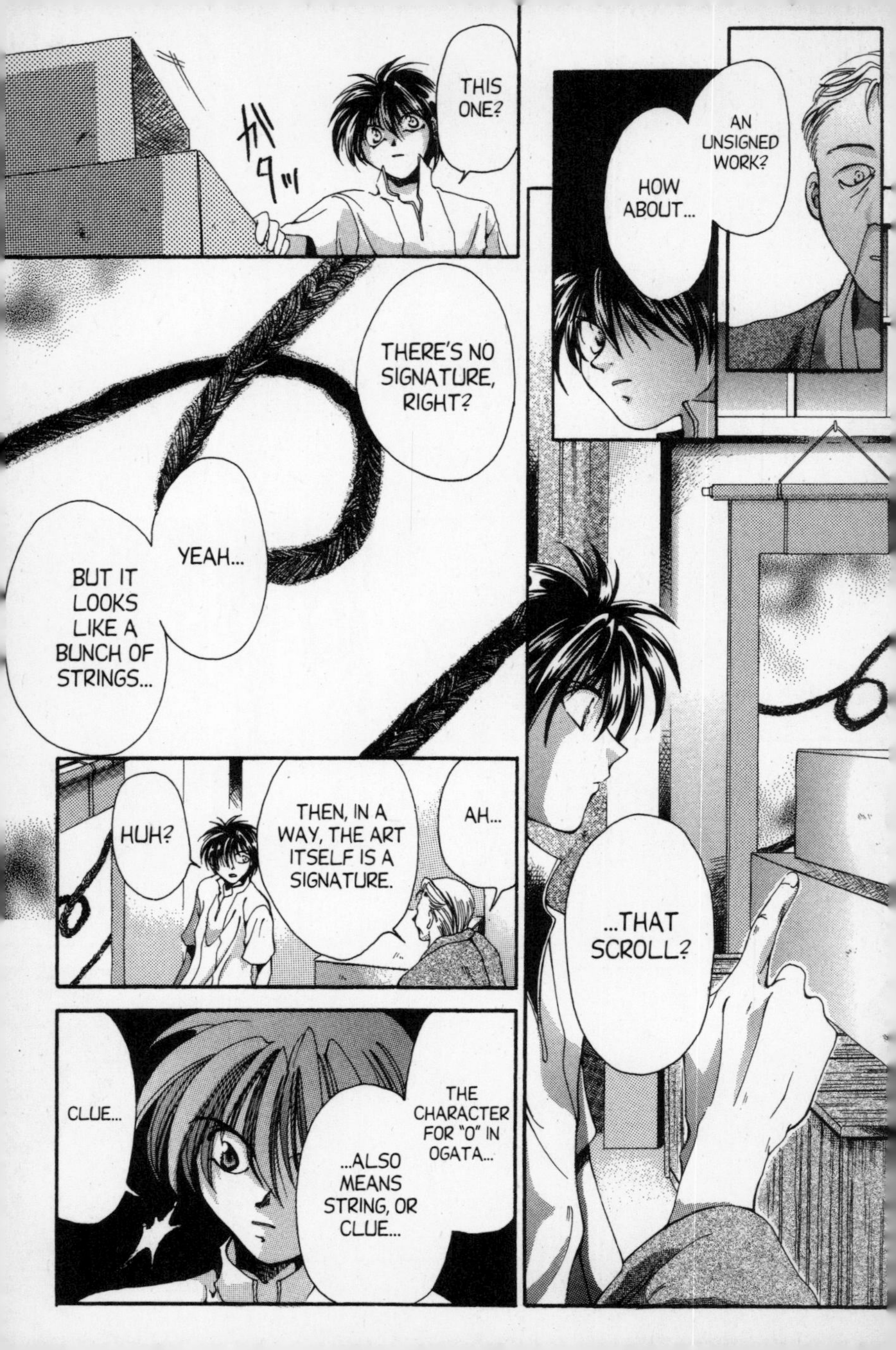
AN UNSIGNED WORK?
HOW ABOUT...
...THAT SCROLL?
ガタッ
THIS ONE?
THERE'S NO SIGNATURE, RIGHT?
YEAH...
BUT IT LOOKS LIKE A BUNCH OF STRINGS...
AH...
THEN, IN A WAY, THE ART ITSELF IS A SIGNATURE.
HUH?
THE CHARACTER FOR "O" IN OGATA...
...ALSO MEANS STRING, OR CLUE...
CLUE...

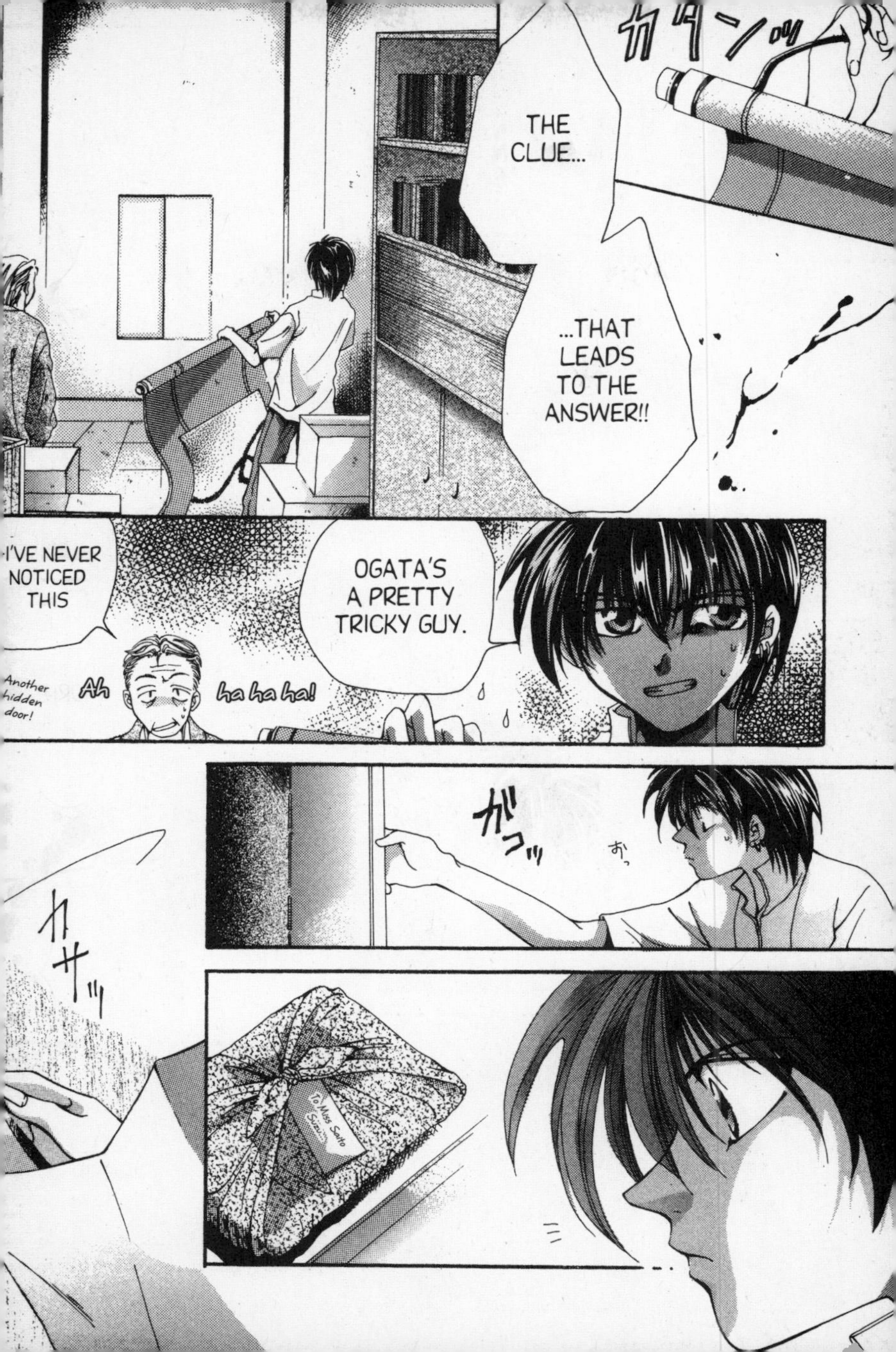
カターンッ
THE CLUE...
...THAT LEADS TO THE ANSWER!!
OGATA'S A PRETTY TRICKY GUY.
I'VE NEVER NOTICED THIS
Ah ha ha ha!
Another hidden door!
ガコッ
おっ
カサッ
To Miss Saito Suzu...

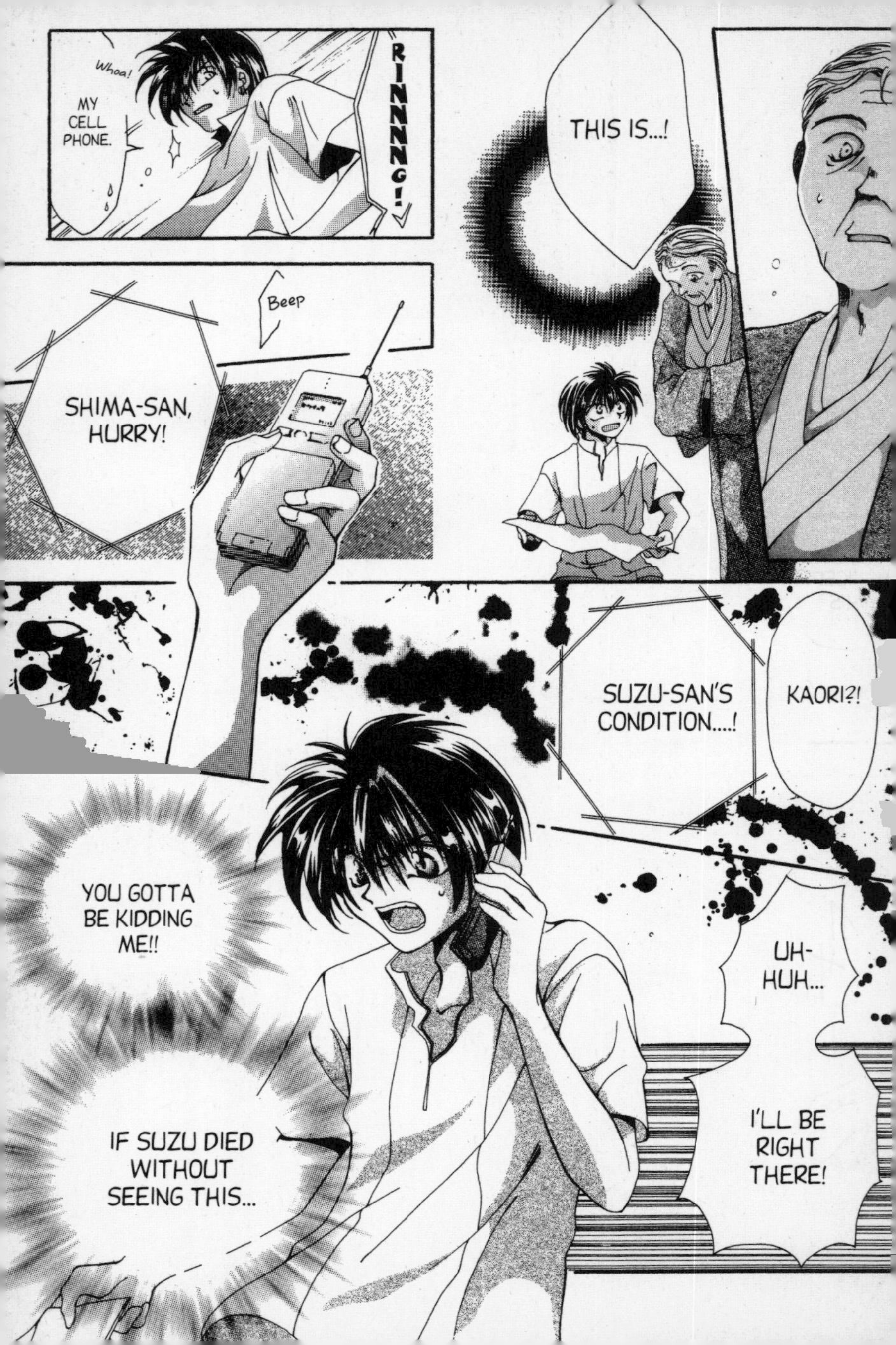
THIS IS...!
Whoa!
MY CELL PHONE.
RINNNNG!
Beep
SHIMA-SAN, HURRY!
KAORI?!
SUZU-SAN'S CONDITION.....!
UH-HUH...
I'LL BE RIGHT THERE!
YOU GOTTA BE KIDDING ME!!
IF SUZU DIED WITHOUT SEEING THIS...

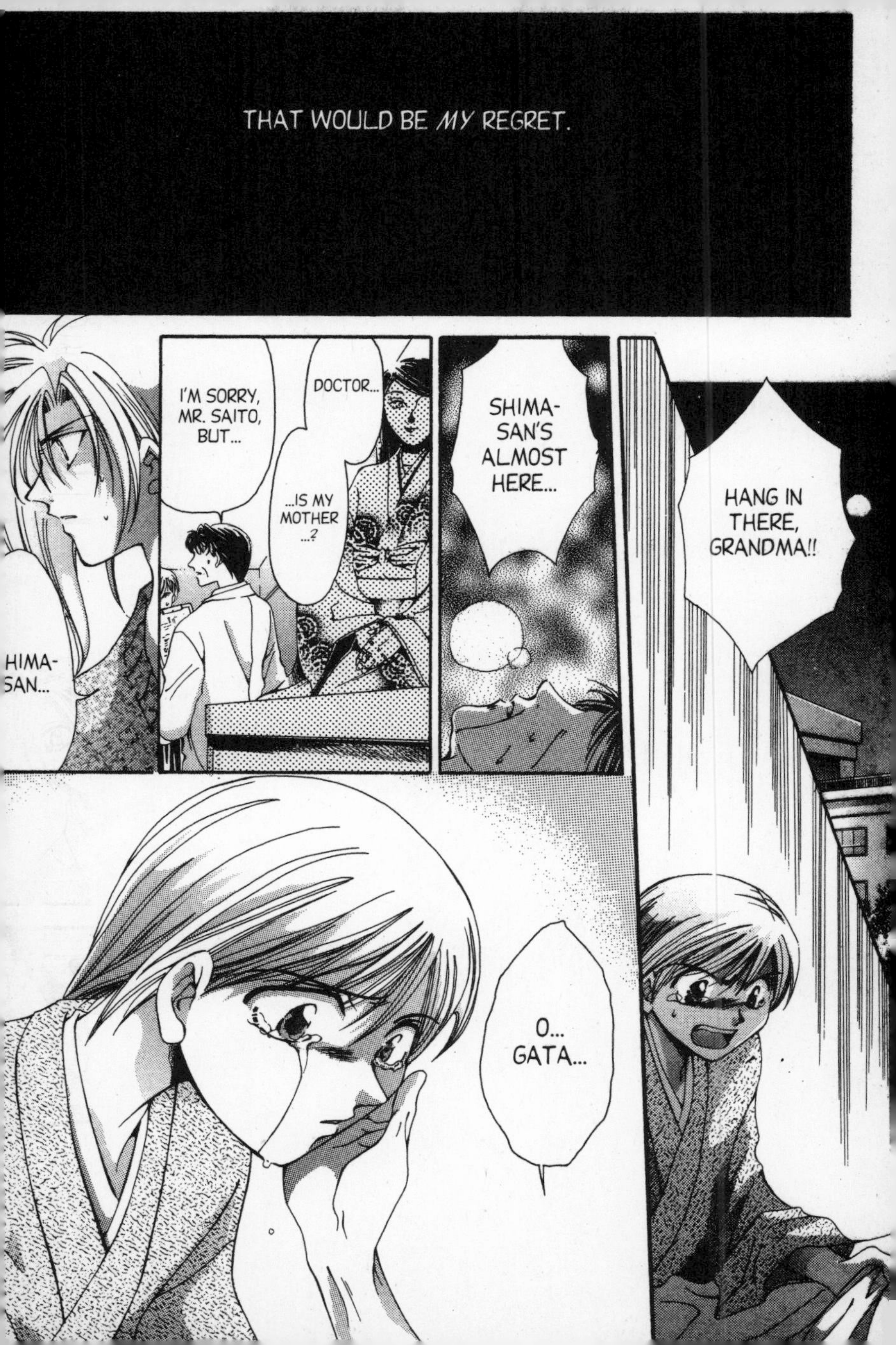
THAT WOULD BE *MY* REGRET.
HANG IN THERE, GRANDMA!!
SHIMA-SAN'S ALMOST HERE...
DOCTOR...
...IS MY MOTHER ...?
I'M SORRY, MR. SAITO, BUT...
HIMA-SAN...
O... GATA...

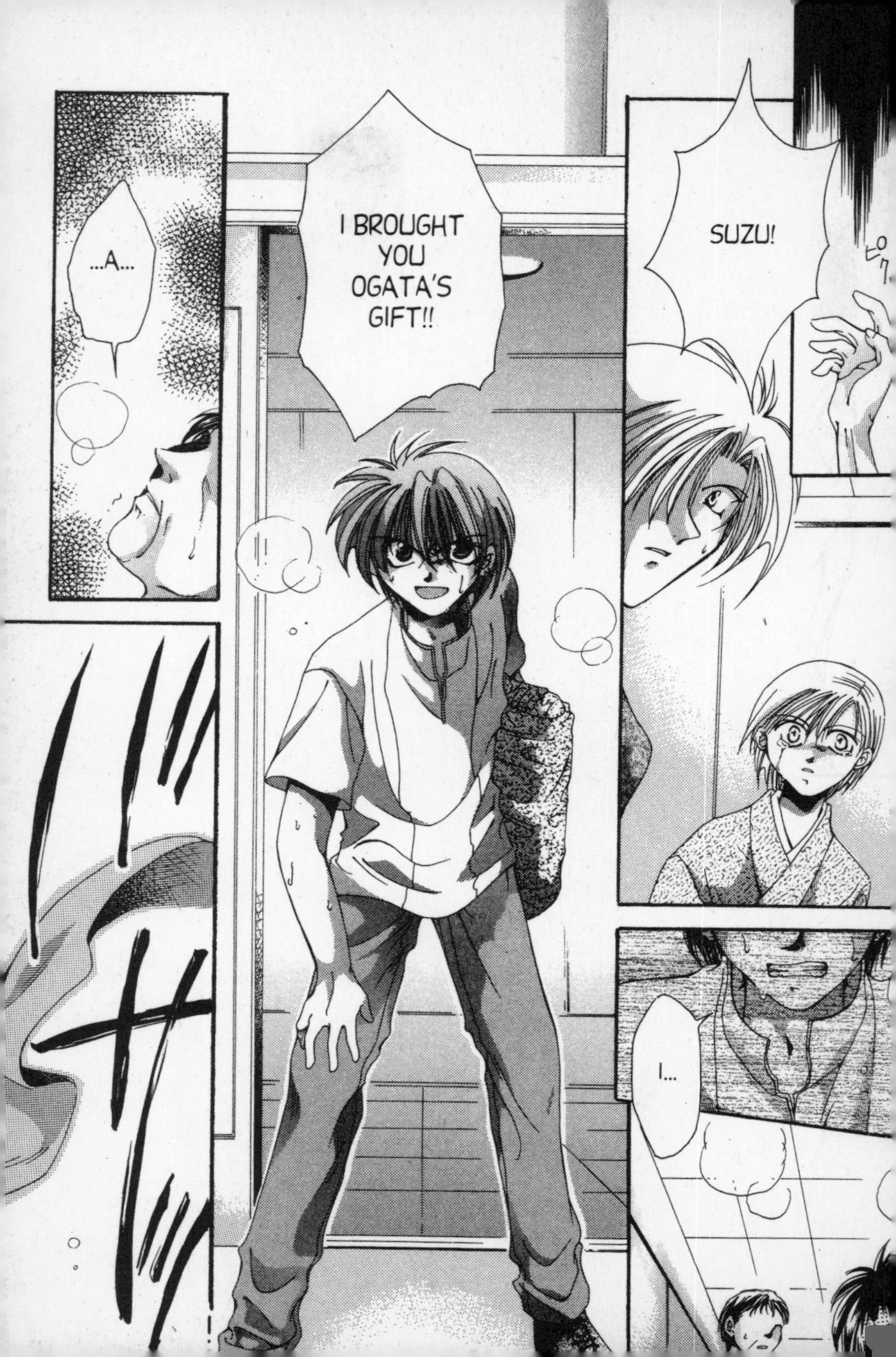
SUZU!
I...
I BROUGHT YOU OGATA'S GIFT!!
...A...

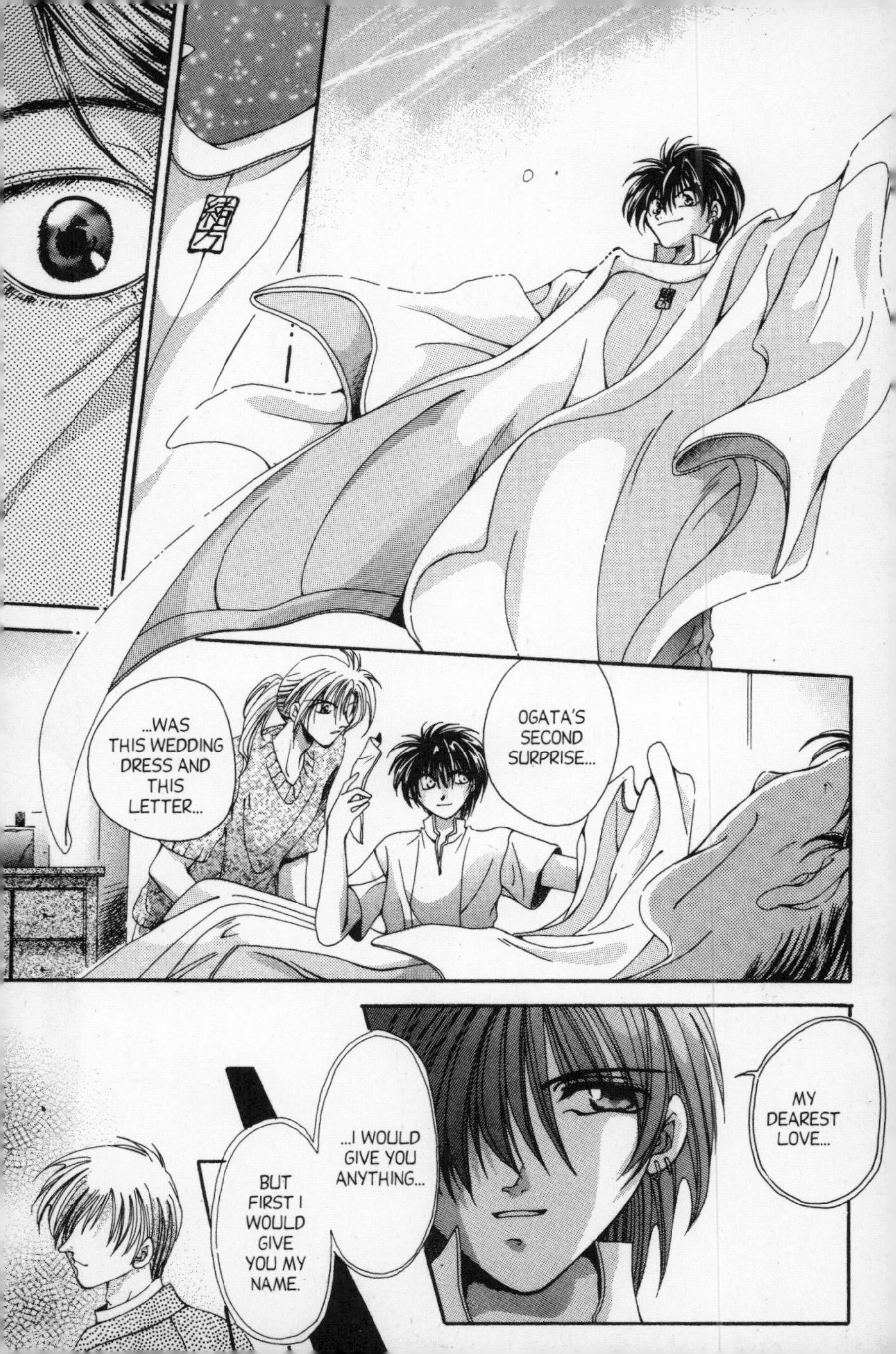
OGATA'S SECOND SURPRISE...
...WAS THIS WEDDING DRESS AND THIS LETTER...
MY DEAREST LOVE...
...I WOULD GIVE YOU ANYTHING...
BUT FIRST I WOULD GIVE YOU MY NAME.

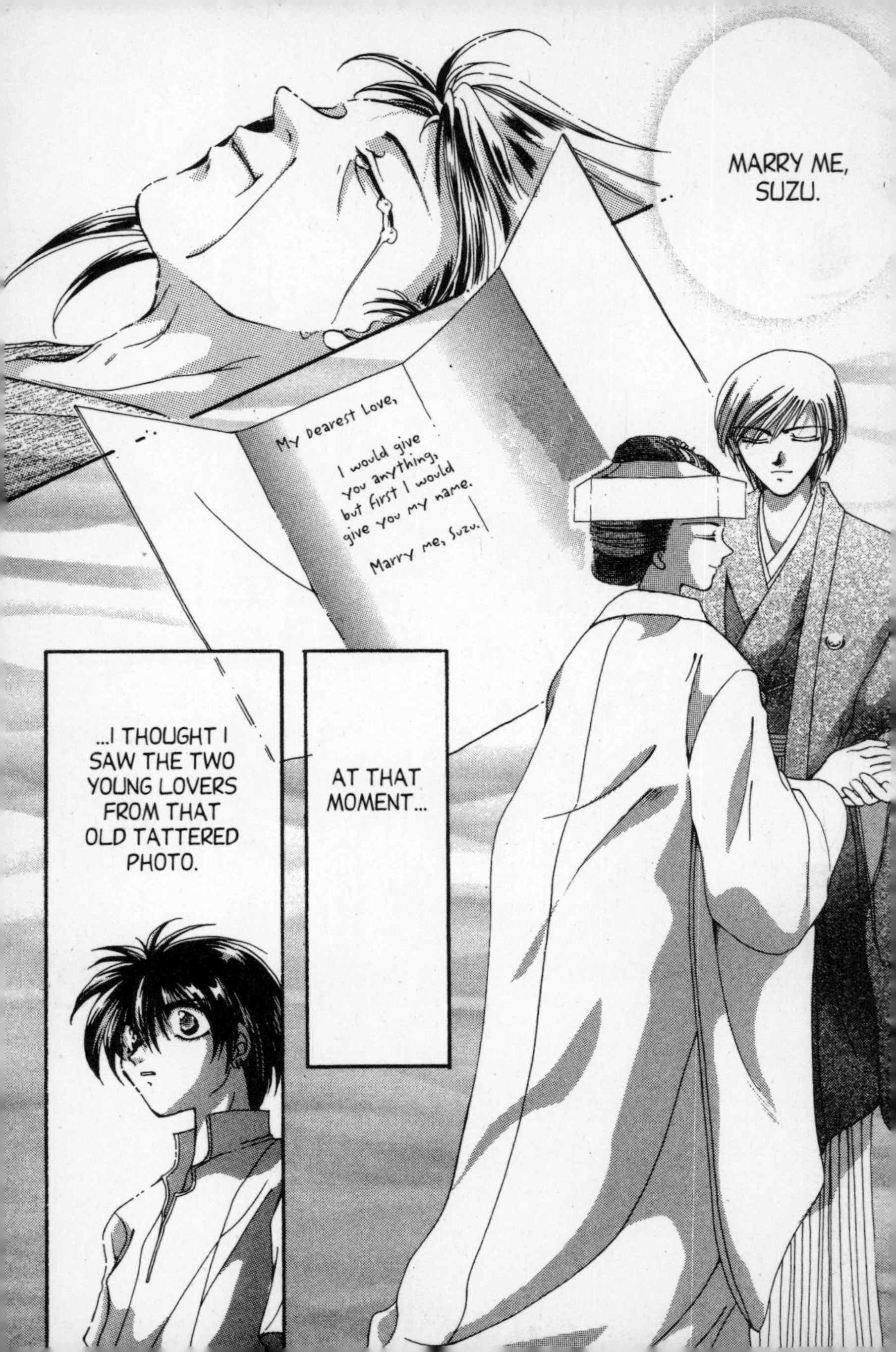
MARRY ME, SUZU.
My Dearest Love,
I would give you anything, but first I would give you my name.
Marry me, Suzu.
AT THAT MOMENT...
...I THOUGHT I SAW THE TWO YOUNG LOVERS FROM THAT OLD TATTERED PHOTO.

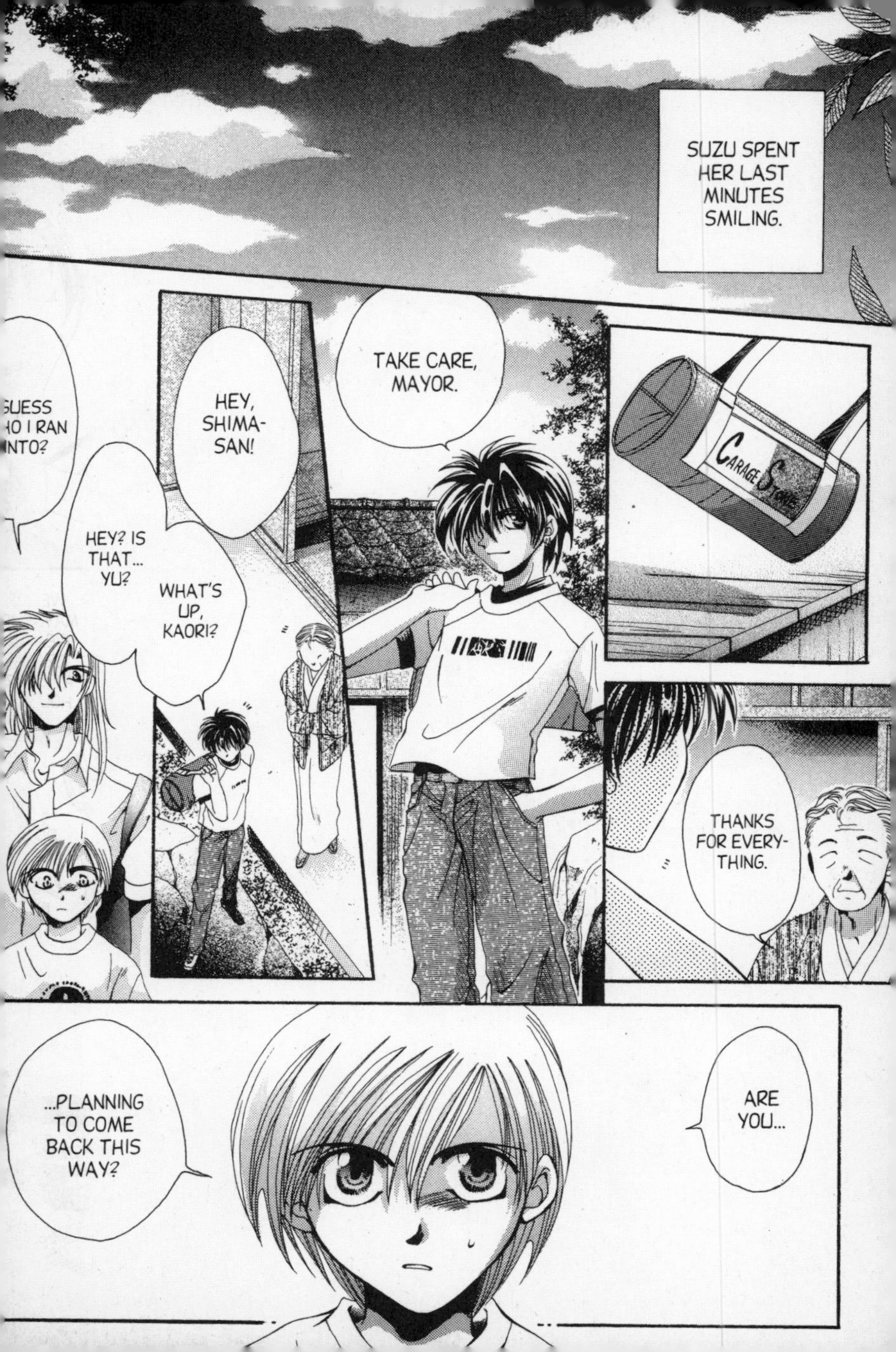
SUZU SPENT HER LAST MINUTES SMILING.
THANKS FOR EVERY-THING.
TAKE CARE, MAYOR.
HEY, SHIMA-SAN!
WHAT'S UP, KAORI?
GUESS HO I RAN NTO?
HEY? IS THAT... YU?
ARE YOU...
...PLANNING TO COME BACK THIS WAY?

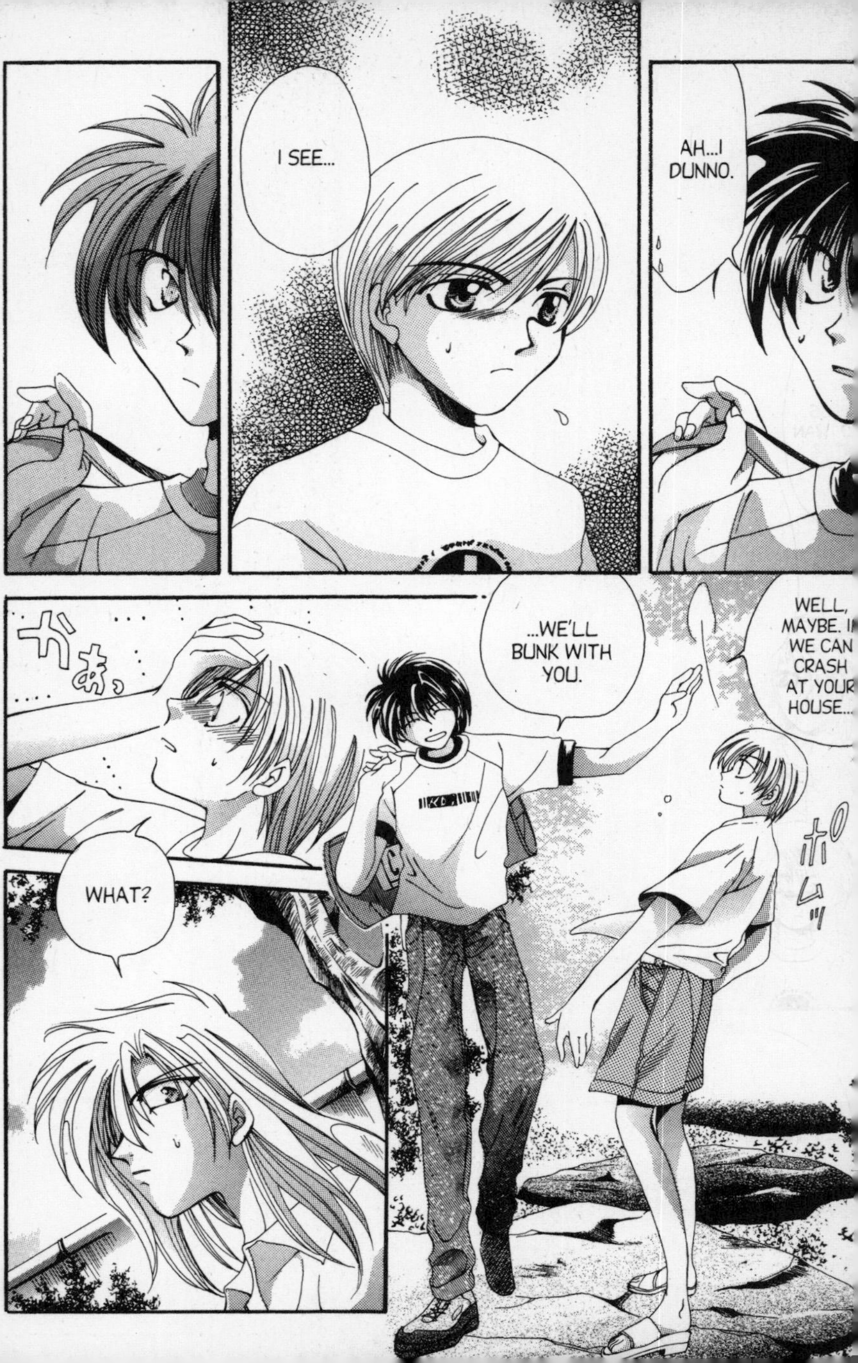
AH...I DUNNO.
I SEE...
WELL, MAYBE. I WE CAN CRASH AT YOUR HOUSE...
...WE'LL BUNK WITH YOU.
ポムッ
かあっ
WHAT?

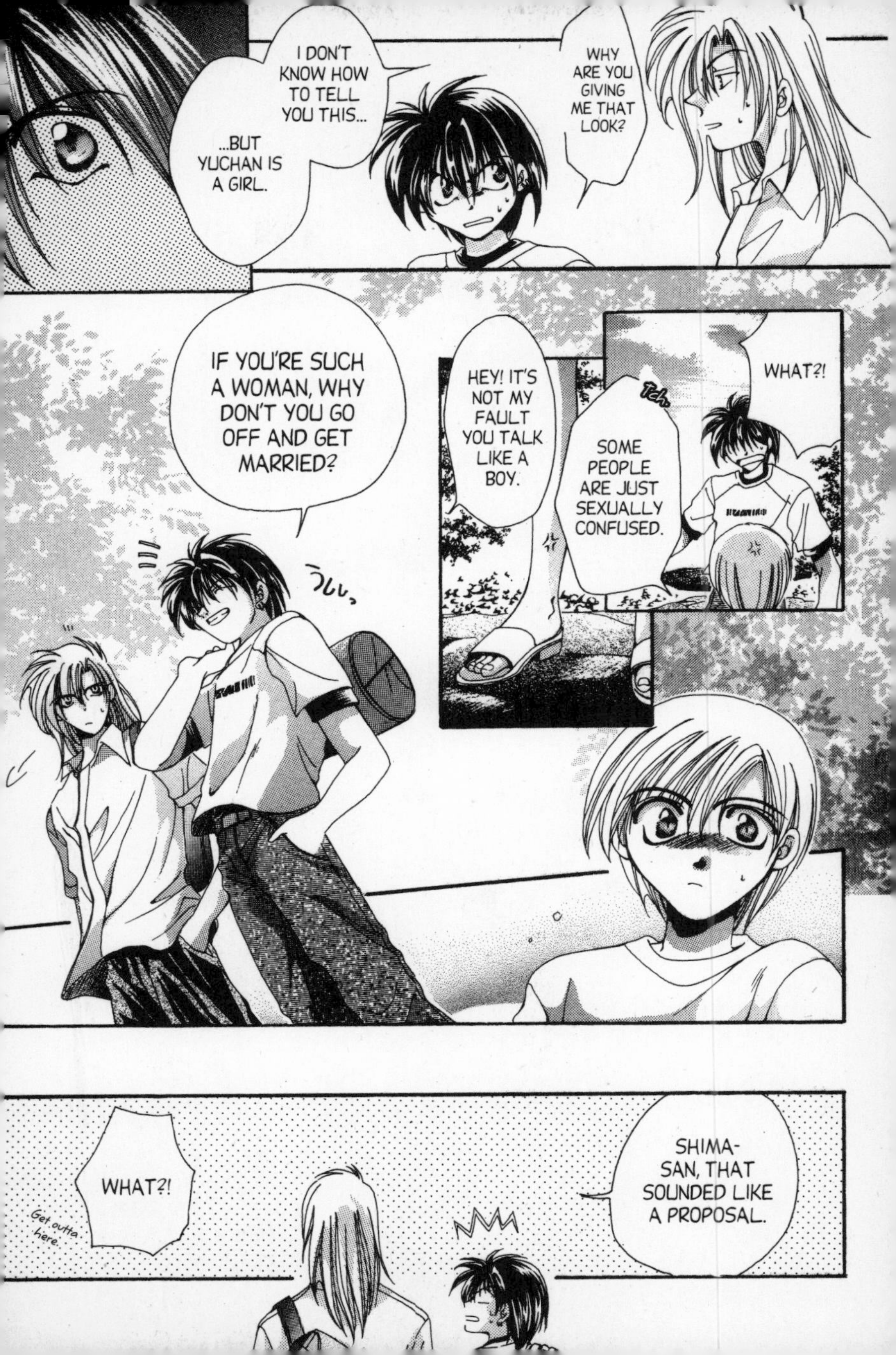
WHY ARE YOU GIVING ME THAT LOOK?
I DON'T KNOW HOW TO TELL YOU THIS...
...BUT YUCHAN IS A GIRL.
WHAT?!
Tch.
SOME PEOPLE ARE JUST SEXUALLY CONFUSED.
HEY! IT'S NOT MY FAULT YOU TALK LIKE A BOY.
IF YOU'RE SUCH A WOMAN, WHY DON'T YOU GO OFF AND GET MARRIED?
SHIMA-SAN, THAT SOUNDED LIKE A PROPOSAL.
WHAT?!
Get outta here.

ACTING ON IMPULSE

SATISFACTION GUARANTEED

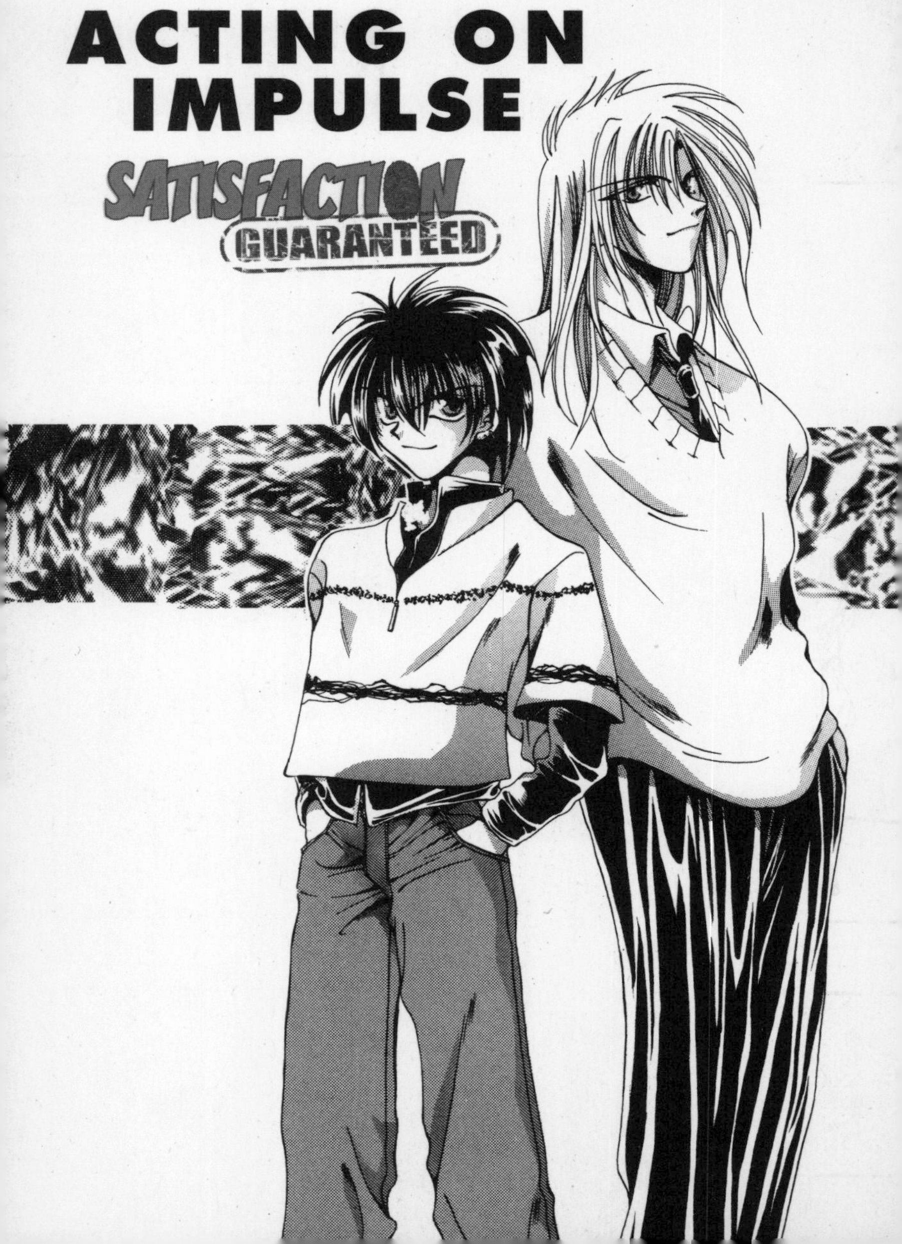

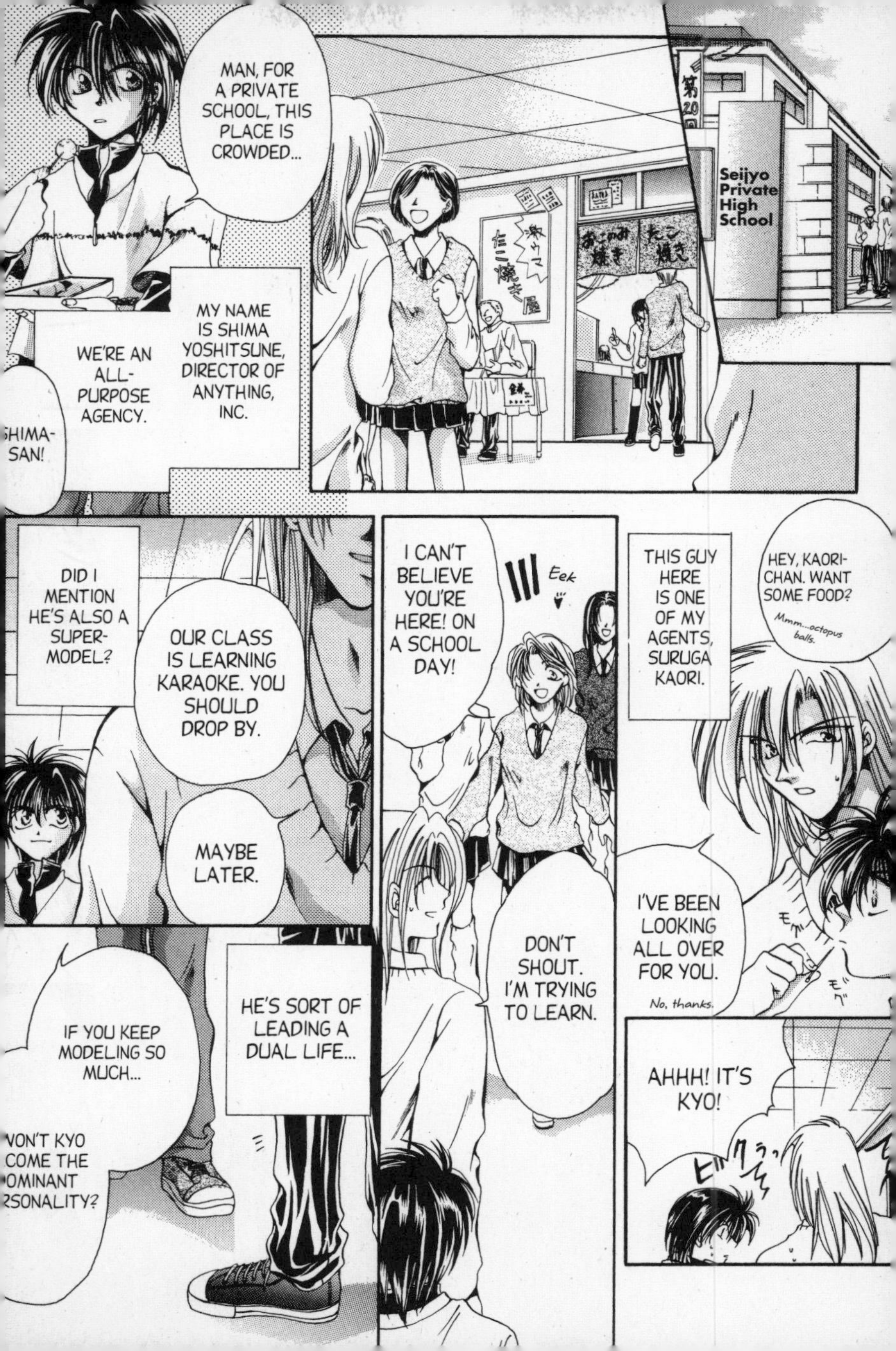
Seijyo Private High School
MAN, FOR A PRIVATE SCHOOL, THIS PLACE IS CROWDED...
MY NAME IS SHIMA YOSHITSUNE, DIRECTOR OF ANYTHING, INC.
WE'RE AN ALL-PURPOSE AGENCY.
SHIMA-SAN!
HEY, KAORI-CHAN. WANT SOME FOOD?
Mmm...octopus balls.
THIS GUY HERE IS ONE OF MY AGENTS, SURUGA KAORI.
I'VE BEEN LOOKING ALL OVER FOR YOU.
No, thanks.
AHHH! IT'S KYO!
I CAN'T BELIEVE YOU'RE HERE! ON A SCHOOL DAY!
Eek
DON'T SHOUT. I'M TRYING TO LEARN.
DID I MENTION HE'S ALSO A SUPER-MODEL?
OUR CLASS IS LEARNING KARAOKE. YOU SHOULD DROP BY.
MAYBE LATER.
HE'S SORT OF LEADING A DUAL LIFE...
IF YOU KEEP MODELING SO MUCH...
WON'T KYO COME THE OMINANT RSONALITY?

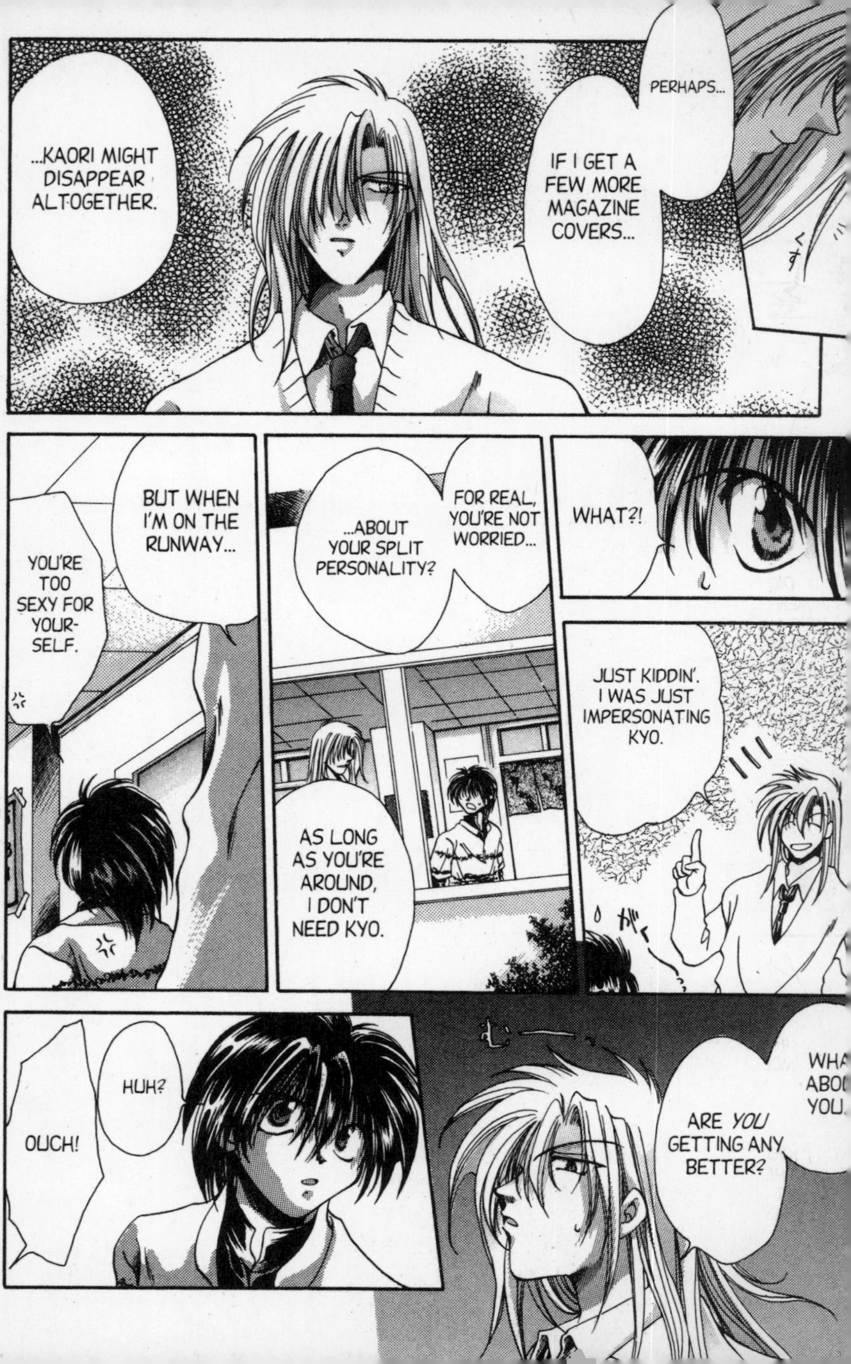
PERHAPS...
IF I GET A FEW MORE MAGAZINE COVERS...
...KAORI MIGHT DISAPPEAR ALTOGETHER.
WHAT?!
JUST KIDDIN'. I WAS JUST IMPERSONATING KYO.
FOR REAL, YOU'RE NOT WORRIED...
...ABOUT YOUR SPLIT PERSONALITY?
AS LONG AS YOU'RE AROUND, I DON'T NEED KYO.
BUT WHEN I'M ON THE RUNWAY...
YOU'RE TOO SEXY FOR YOURSELF.
WHA ABOU YOU.
ARE *YOU* GETTING ANY BETTER?
HUH?
OUCH!

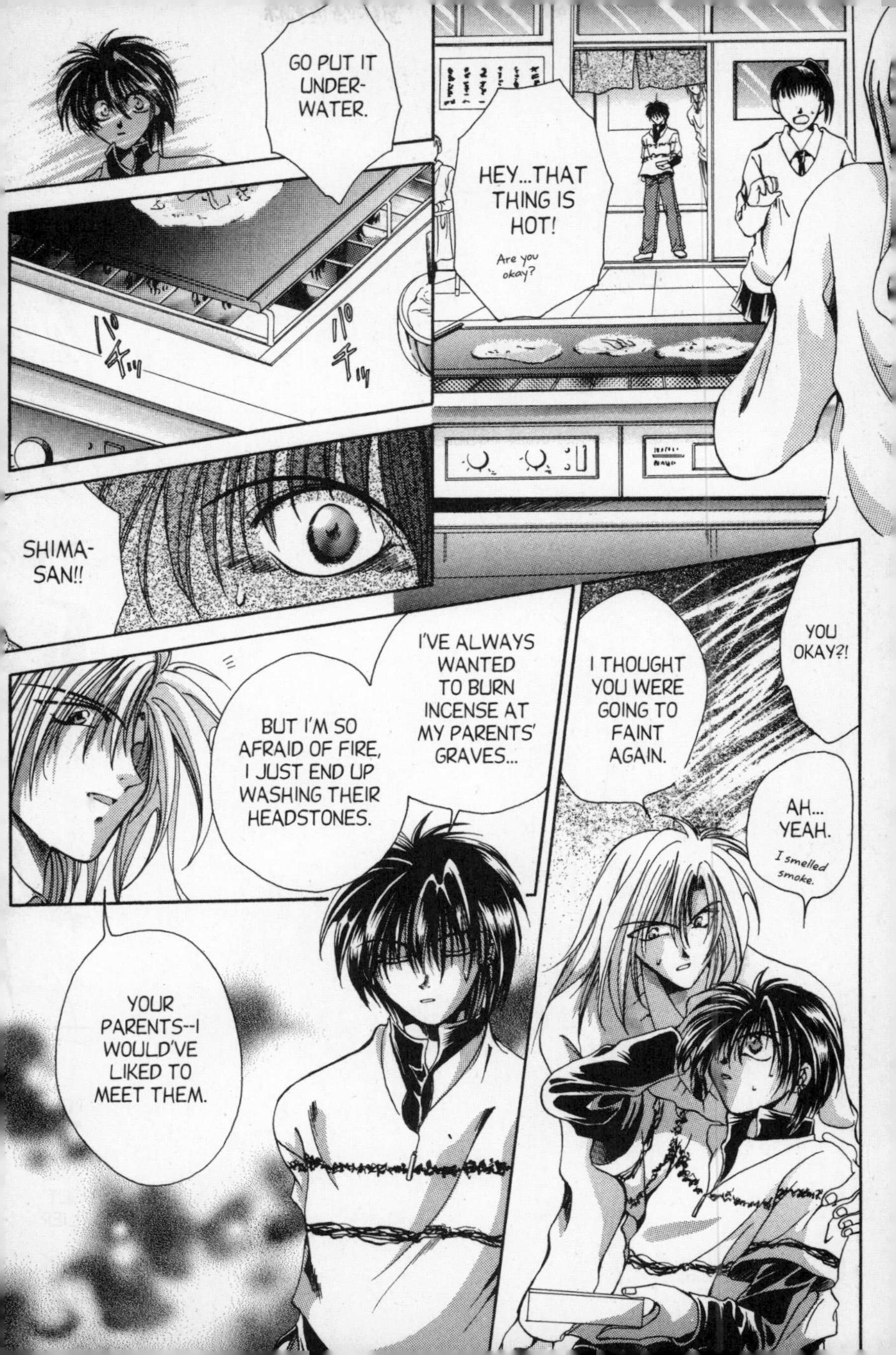
HEY...THAT THING IS HOT!
Are you okay?
GO PUT IT UNDER-WATER.
パチッ
パチッ
SHIMA-SAN!!
YOU OKAY?!
I THOUGHT YOU WERE GOING TO FAINT AGAIN.
AH... YEAH.
I smelled smoke.
I'VE ALWAYS WANTED TO BURN INCENSE AT MY PARENTS' GRAVES...
BUT I'M SO AFRAID OF FIRE, I JUST END UP WASHING THEIR HEADSTONES.
YOUR PARENTS--I WOULD'VE LIKED TO MEET THEM.

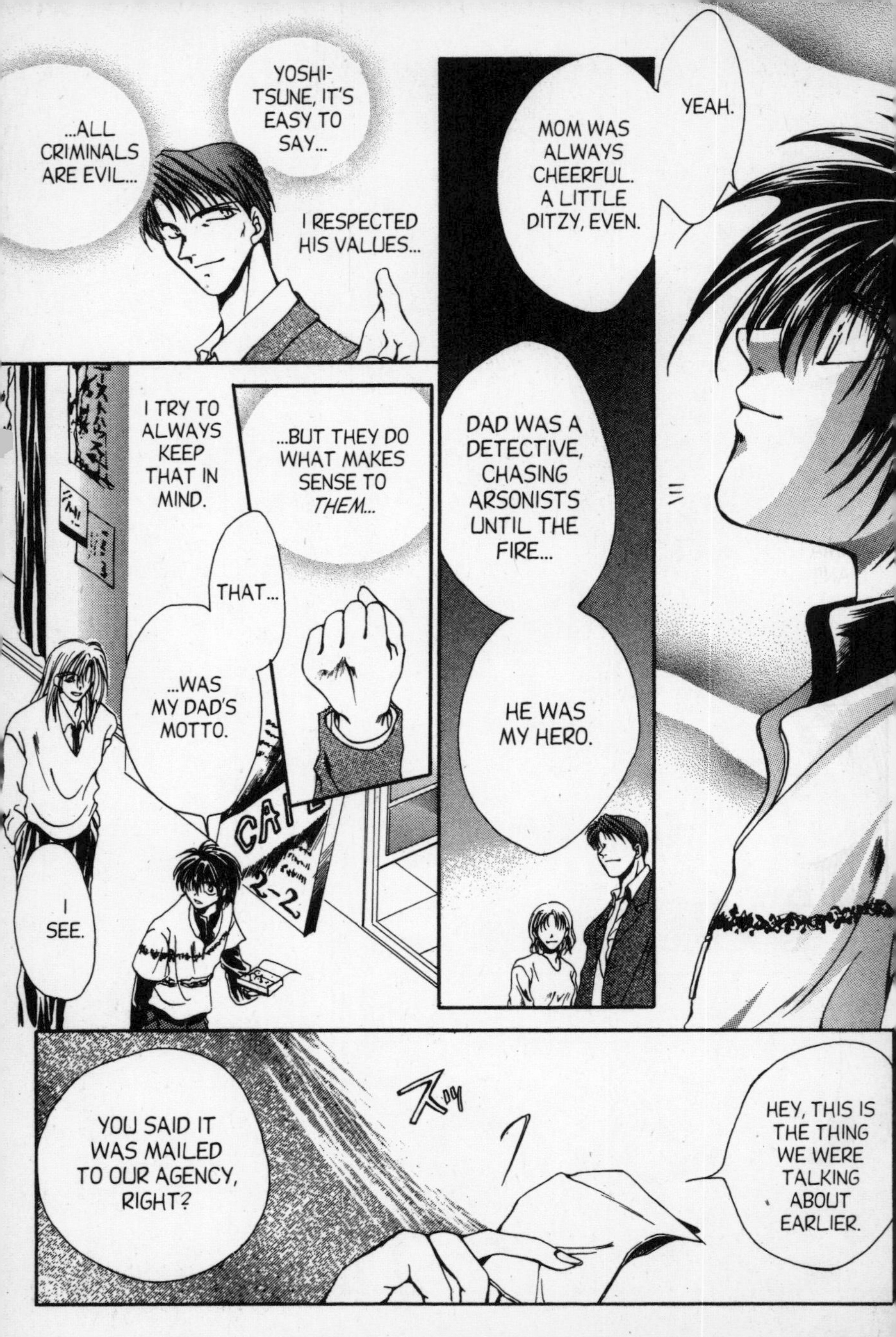
YEAH.
MOM WAS ALWAYS CHEERFUL. A LITTLE DITZY, EVEN.
DAD WAS A DETECTIVE, CHASING ARSONISTS UNTIL THE FIRE...
HE WAS MY HERO.
YOSHI-TSUNE, IT'S EASY TO SAY...
...ALL CRIMINALS ARE EVIL...
I RESPECTED HIS VALUES...
...BUT THEY DO WHAT MAKES SENSE TO *THEM*...
I TRY TO ALWAYS KEEP THAT IN MIND.
THAT...
...WAS MY DAD'S MOTTO.
I SEE.
HEY, THIS IS THE THING WE WERE TALKING ABOUT EARLIER.
YOU SAID IT WAS MAILED TO OUR AGENCY, RIGHT?

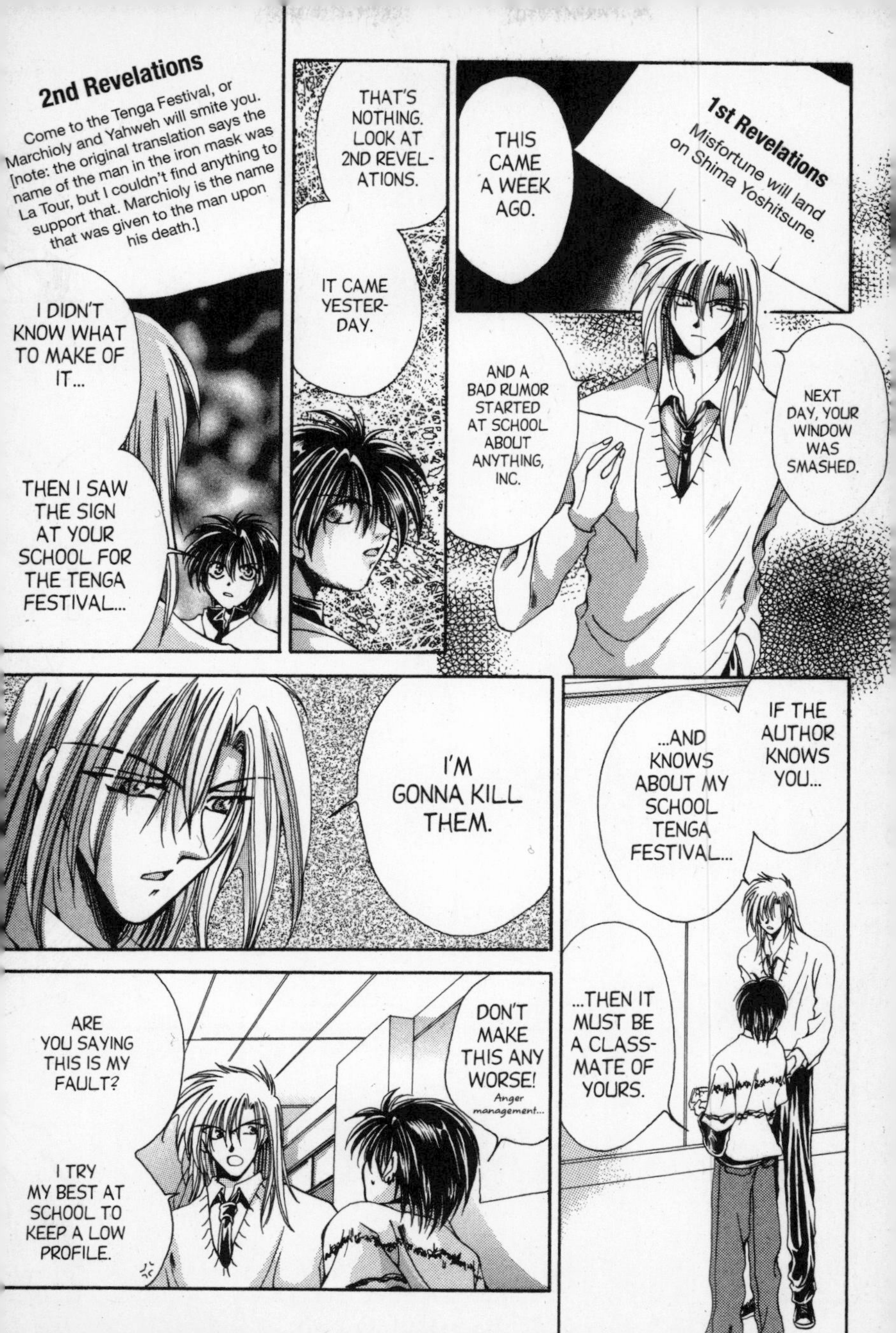
1st Revelations
Misfortune will land on Shima Yoshitsune.
THIS CAME A WEEK AGO.
NEXT DAY, YOUR WINDOW WAS SMASHED.
AND A BAD RUMOR STARTED AT SCHOOL ABOUT ANYTHING, INC.
THAT'S NOTHING. LOOK AT 2ND REVELATIONS.
IT CAME YESTERDAY.
2nd Revelations
Come to the Tenga Festival, or Marchioly and Yahweh will smite you. [note: the original translation says the name of the man in the iron mask was La Tour, but I couldn't find anything to support that. Marchioly is the name that was given to the man upon his death.]
I DIDN'T KNOW WHAT TO MAKE OF IT...
THEN I SAW THE SIGN AT YOUR SCHOOL FOR THE TENGA FESTIVAL...
IF THE AUTHOR KNOWS YOU...
...AND KNOWS ABOUT MY SCHOOL TENGA FESTIVAL...
...THEN IT MUST BE A CLASSMATE OF YOURS.
I'M GONNA KILL THEM.
DON'T MAKE THIS ANY WORSE!
Anger management...
ARE YOU SAYING THIS IS MY FAULT?
I TRY MY BEST AT SCHOOL TO KEEP A LOW PROFILE.

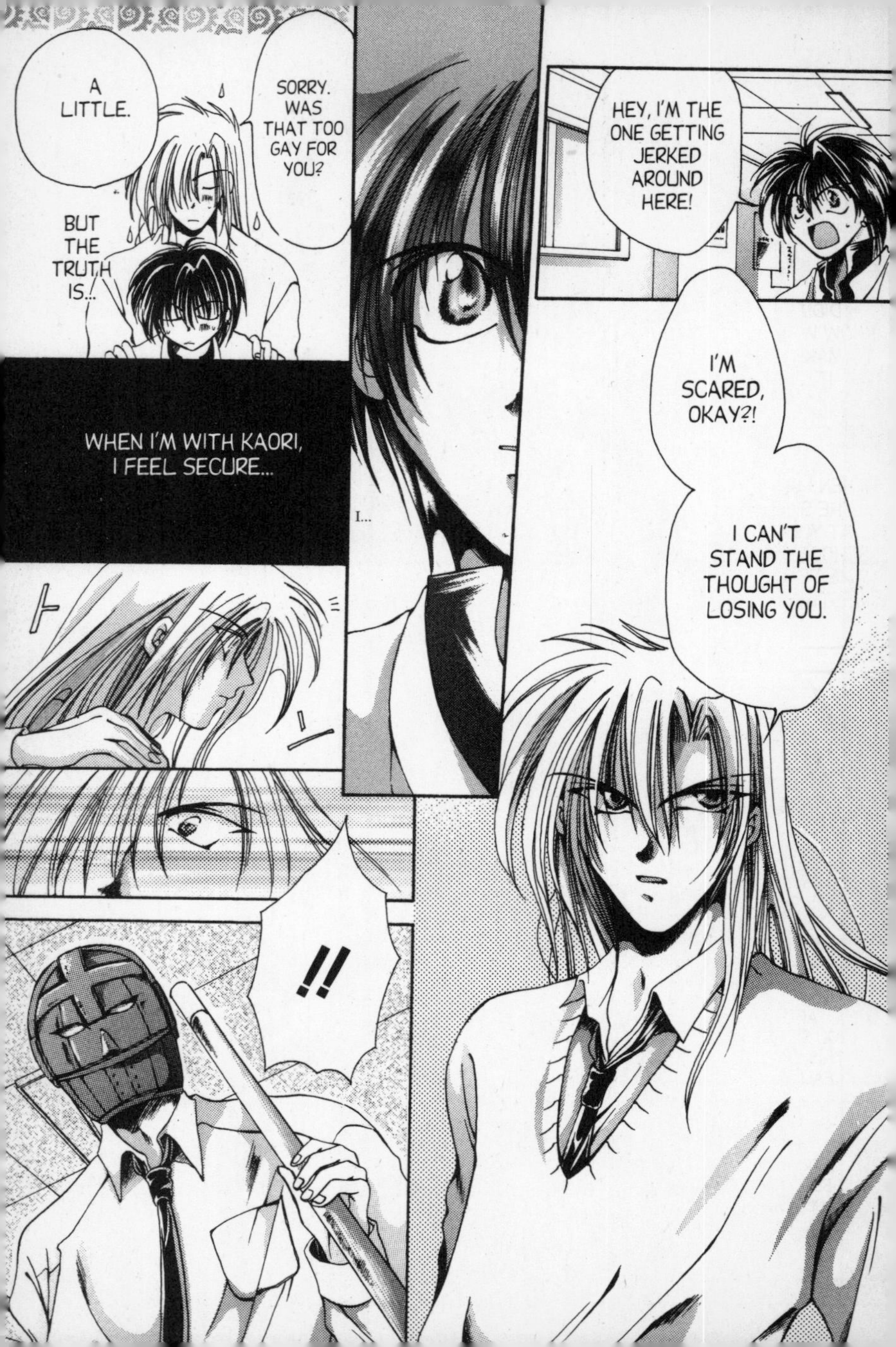
HEY, I'M THE ONE GETTING JERKED AROUND HERE!
I'M SCARED, OKAY?!
I CAN'T STAND THE THOUGHT OF LOSING YOU.
I...
SORRY. WAS THAT TOO GAY FOR YOU?
A LITTLE.
BUT THE TRUTH IS...
WHEN I'M WITH KAORI, I FEEL SECURE...
!!

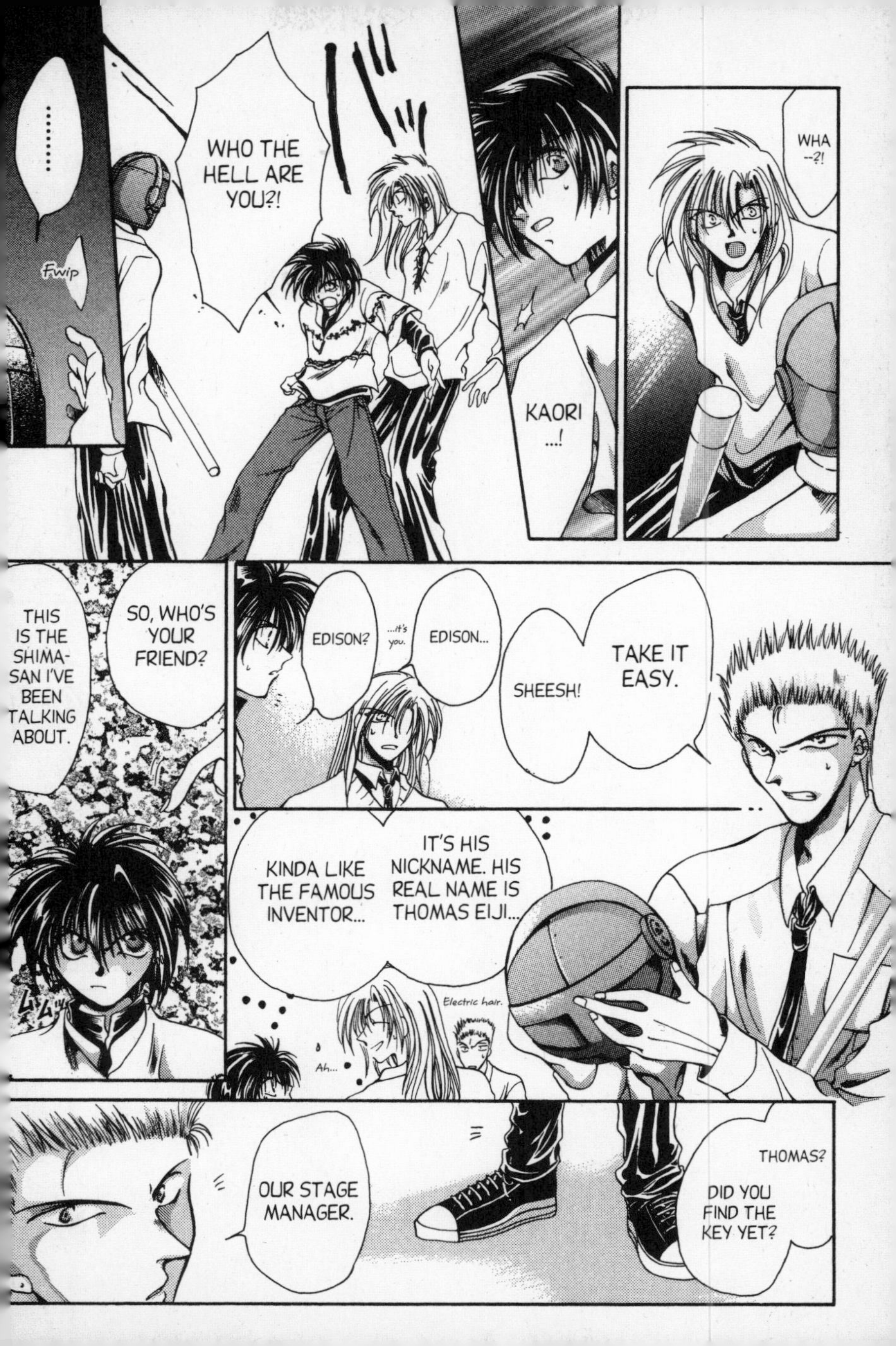
WHA --?!
KAORI ...!
WHO THE HELL ARE YOU?!
......
Fwip
TAKE IT EASY.
SHEESH!
EDISON...
...it's you.
EDISON?
IT'S HIS NICKNAME. HIS REAL NAME IS THOMAS EIJI...
KINDA LIKE THE FAMOUS INVENTOR...
Electric hair.
Ah...
SO, WHO'S YOUR FRIEND?
THIS IS THE SHIMA-SAN I'VE BEEN TALKING ABOUT.
THOMAS?
DID YOU FIND THE KEY YET?
OUR STAGE MANAGER.

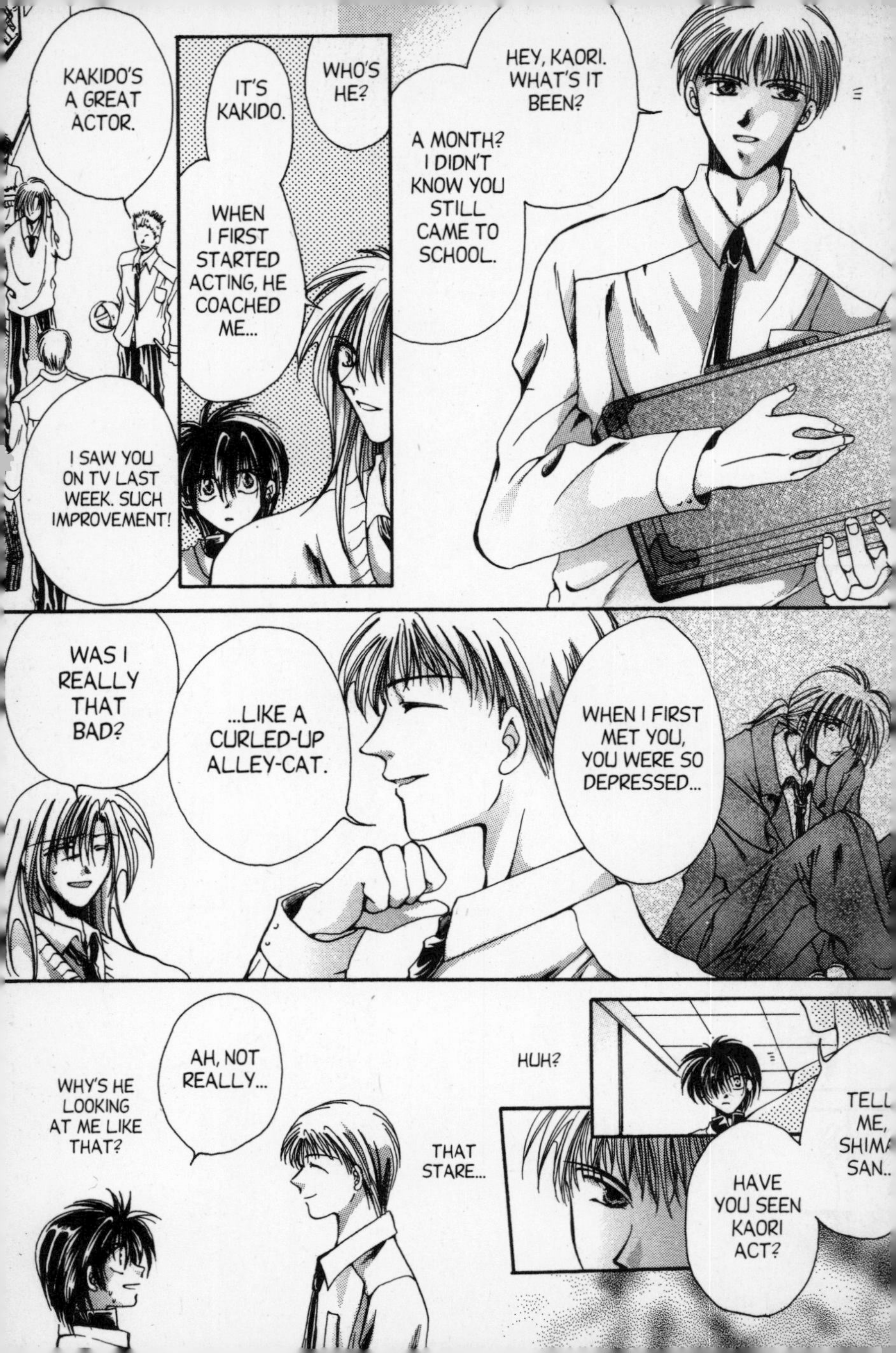
HEY, KAORI. WHAT'S IT BEEN?
A MONTH? I DIDN'T KNOW YOU STILL CAME TO SCHOOL.
WHO'S HE?
IT'S KAKIDO.
WHEN I FIRST STARTED ACTING, HE COACHED ME...
KAKIDO'S A GREAT ACTOR.
I SAW YOU ON TV LAST WEEK. SUCH IMPROVEMENT!
WHEN I FIRST MET YOU, YOU WERE SO DEPRESSED...
...LIKE A CURLED-UP ALLEY-CAT.
WAS I REALLY THAT BAD?
TELL ME, SHIMA SAN..
HAVE YOU SEEN KAORI ACT?
HUH?
THAT STARE...
AH, NOT REALLY...
WHY'S HE LOOKING AT ME LIKE THAT?

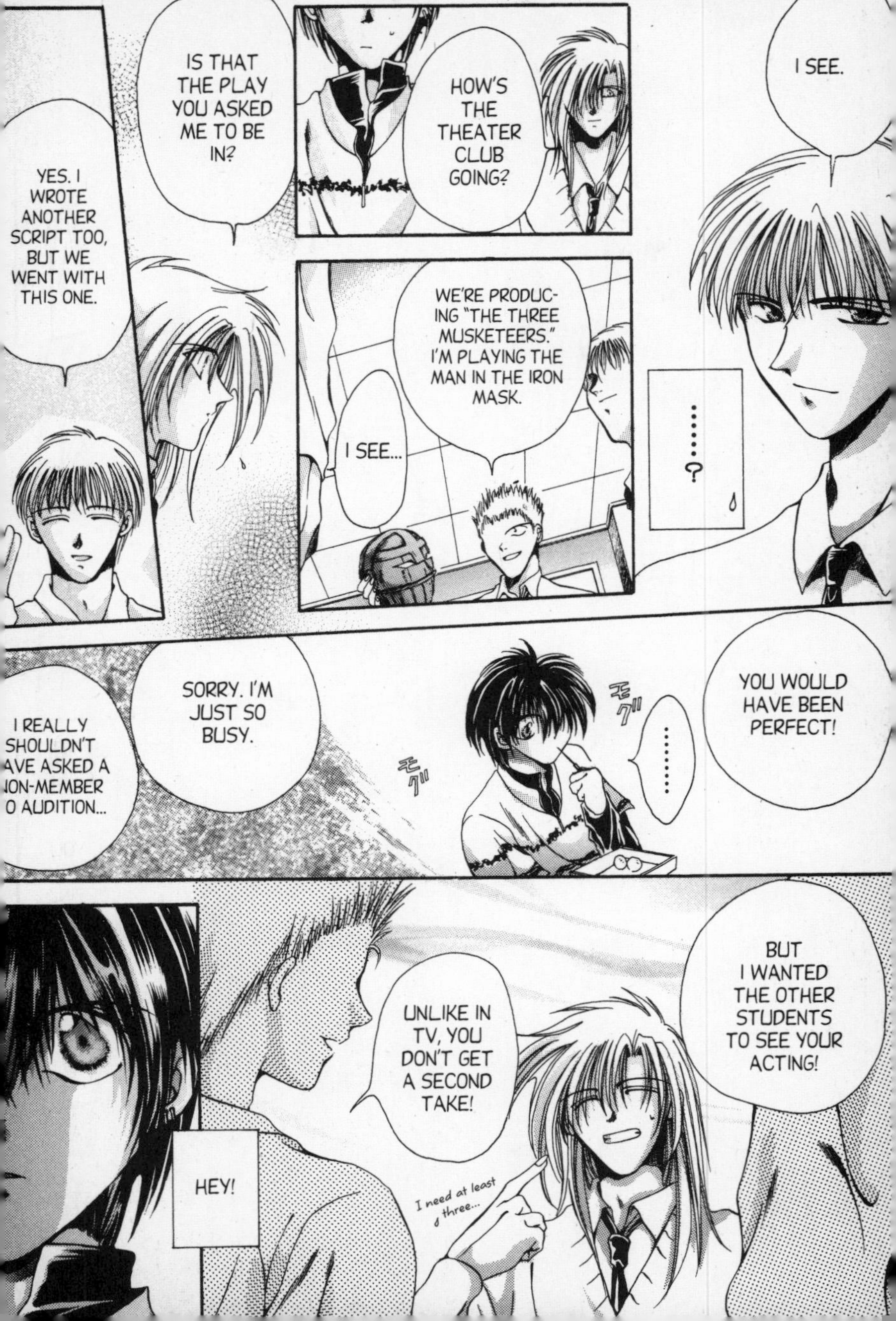

I SEE.
......?
HOW'S THE THEATER CLUB GOING?
WE'RE PRODUCING "THE THREE MUSKETEERS." I'M PLAYING THE MAN IN THE IRON MASK.
I SEE...
IS THAT THE PLAY YOU ASKED ME TO BE IN?
YES. I WROTE ANOTHER SCRIPT TOO, BUT WE WENT WITH THIS ONE.
YOU WOULD HAVE BEEN PERFECT!
....
モグ
モグ
SORRY. I'M JUST SO BUSY.
I REALLY SHOULDN'T AVE ASKED A ION-MEMBER O AUDITION...
BUT I WANTED THE OTHER STUDENTS TO SEE YOUR ACTING!
UNLIKE IN TV, YOU DON'T GET A SECOND TAKE!
I need at least three...
HEY!

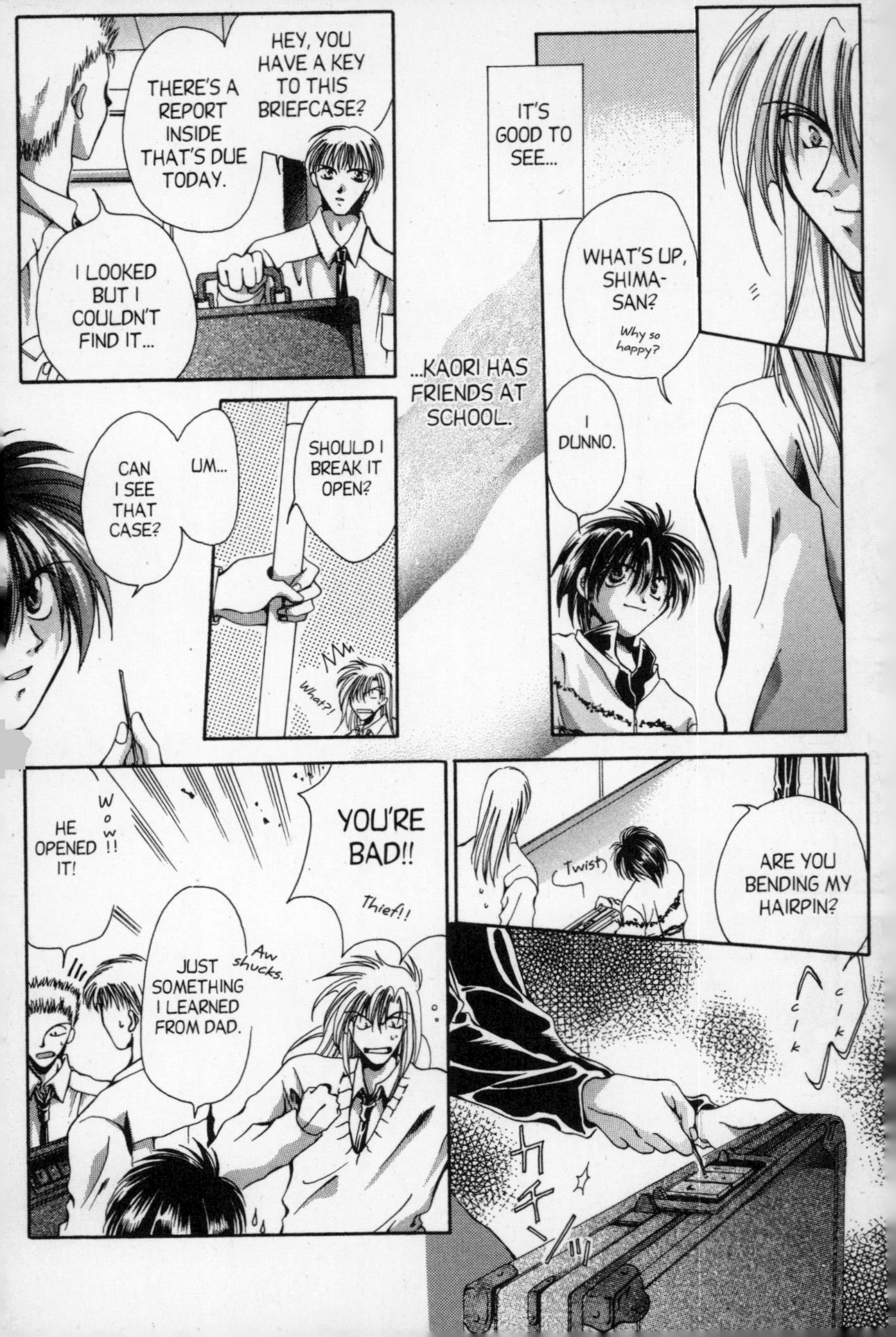
IT'S GOOD TO SEE...
...KAORI HAS FRIENDS AT SCHOOL.
WHAT'S UP, SHIMA-SAN?
Why so happy?
I DUNNO.
HEY, YOU HAVE A KEY TO THIS BRIEFCASE?
THERE'S A REPORT INSIDE THAT'S DUE TODAY.
I LOOKED BUT I COULDN'T FIND IT...
SHOULD I BREAK IT OPEN?
UM...
CAN I SEE THAT CASE?
What?!
ARE YOU BENDING MY HAIRPIN?
Twist
clik clik
カチー!!
YOU'RE BAD!!
Thief!!
HE OPENED IT!
Wow!!
Aw shucks.
JUST SOMETHING I LEARNED FROM DAD.

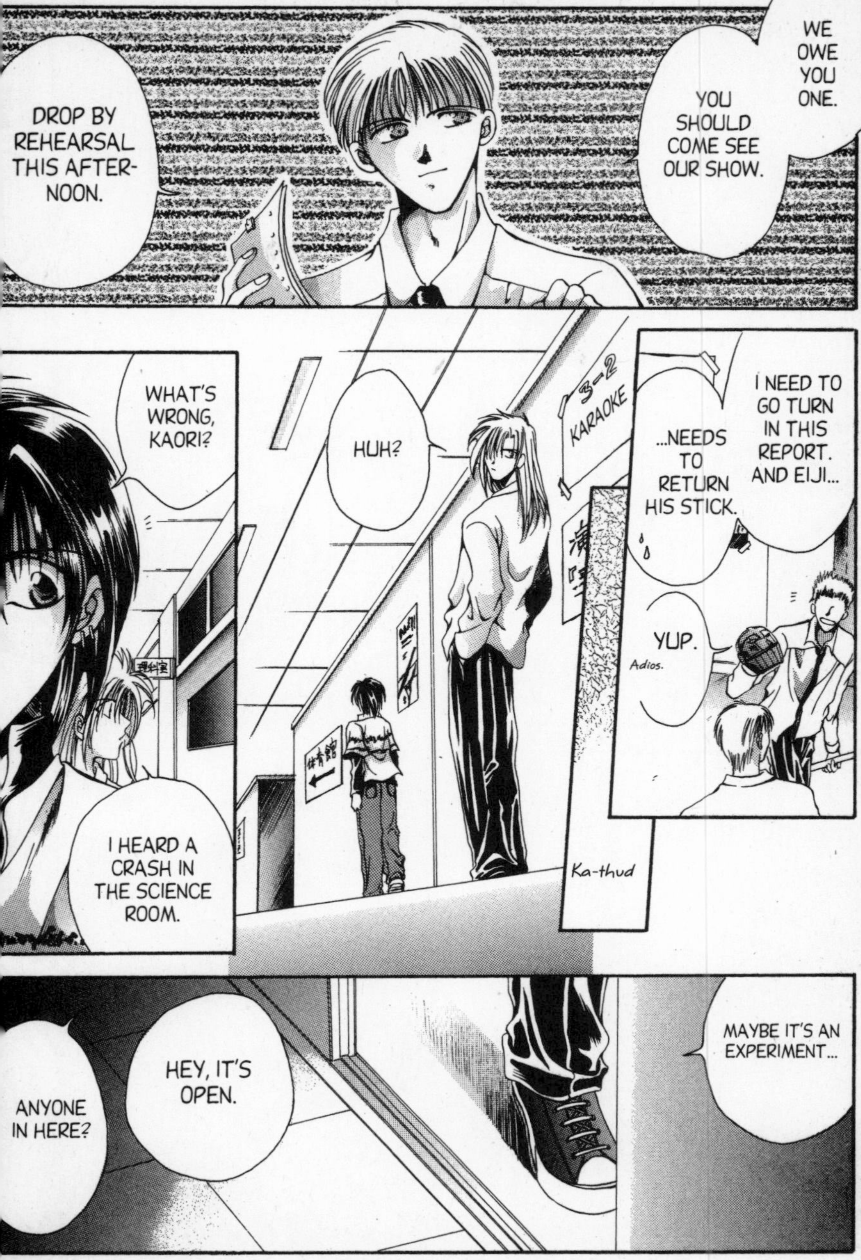
WE OWE YOU ONE.
YOU SHOULD COME SEE OUR SHOW.
DROP BY REHEARSAL THIS AFTER-NOON.
I NEED TO GO TURN IN THIS REPORT. AND EIJI...
...NEEDS TO RETURN HIS STICK.
YUP.
Adios.
3-2 KARAOKE
HUH?
Ka-thud
WHAT'S WRONG, KAORI?
I HEARD A CRASH IN THE SCIENCE ROOM.
MAYBE IT'S AN EXPERIMENT...
HEY, IT'S OPEN.
ANYONE IN HERE?

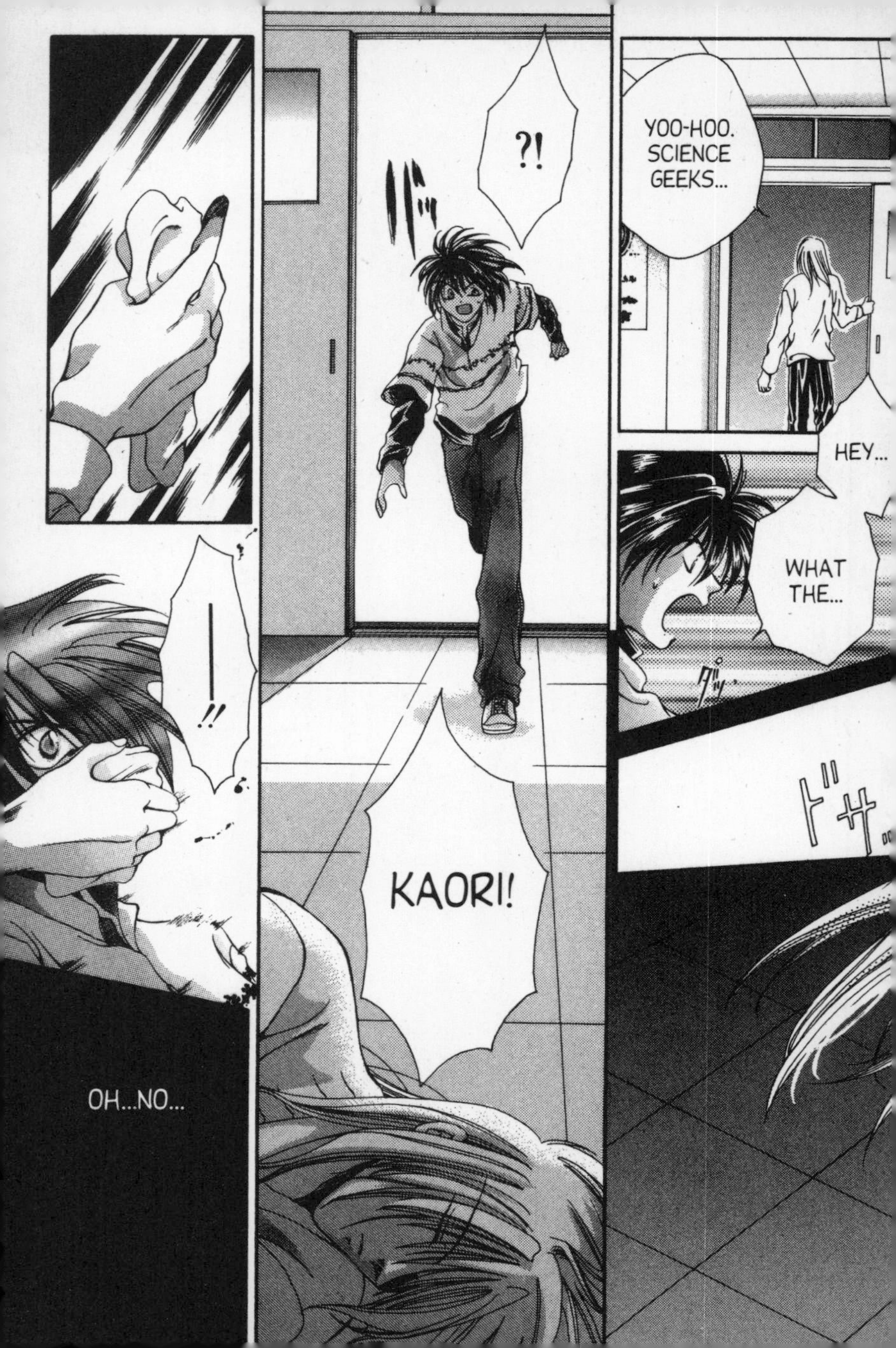
YOO-HOO. SCIENCE GEEKS...
HEY...
WHAT THE...
?!
KAORI!
—!!
OH...NO...

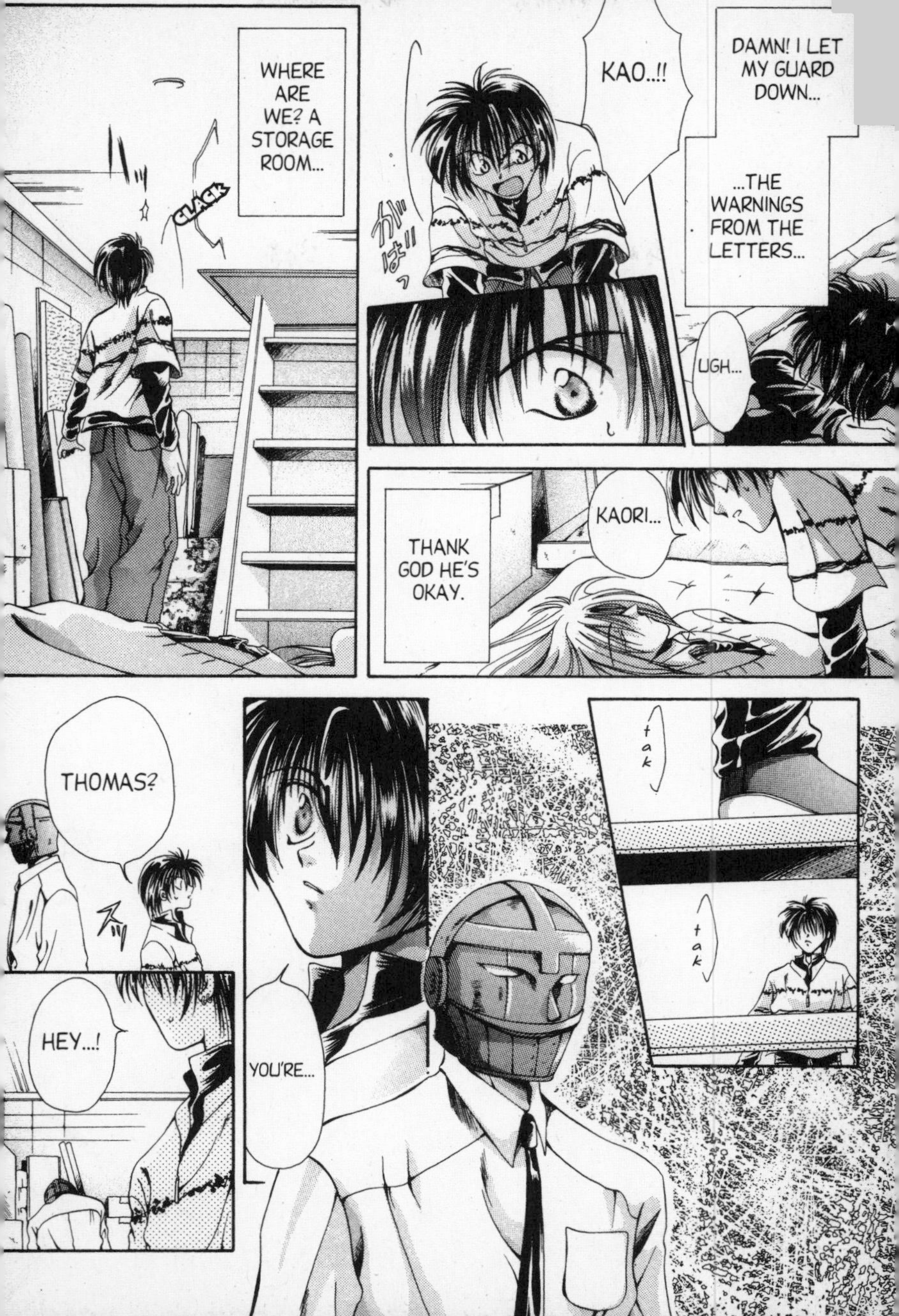

DAMN! I LET MY GUARD DOWN...
...THE WARNINGS FROM THE LETTERS...
UGH...
KAO..!!
がばっ
WHERE ARE WE? A STORAGE ROOM...
ハッ
CLACK
KAORI...
THANK GOD HE'S OKAY.
tak
tak
YOU'RE...
THOMAS?
スッ
HEY...!

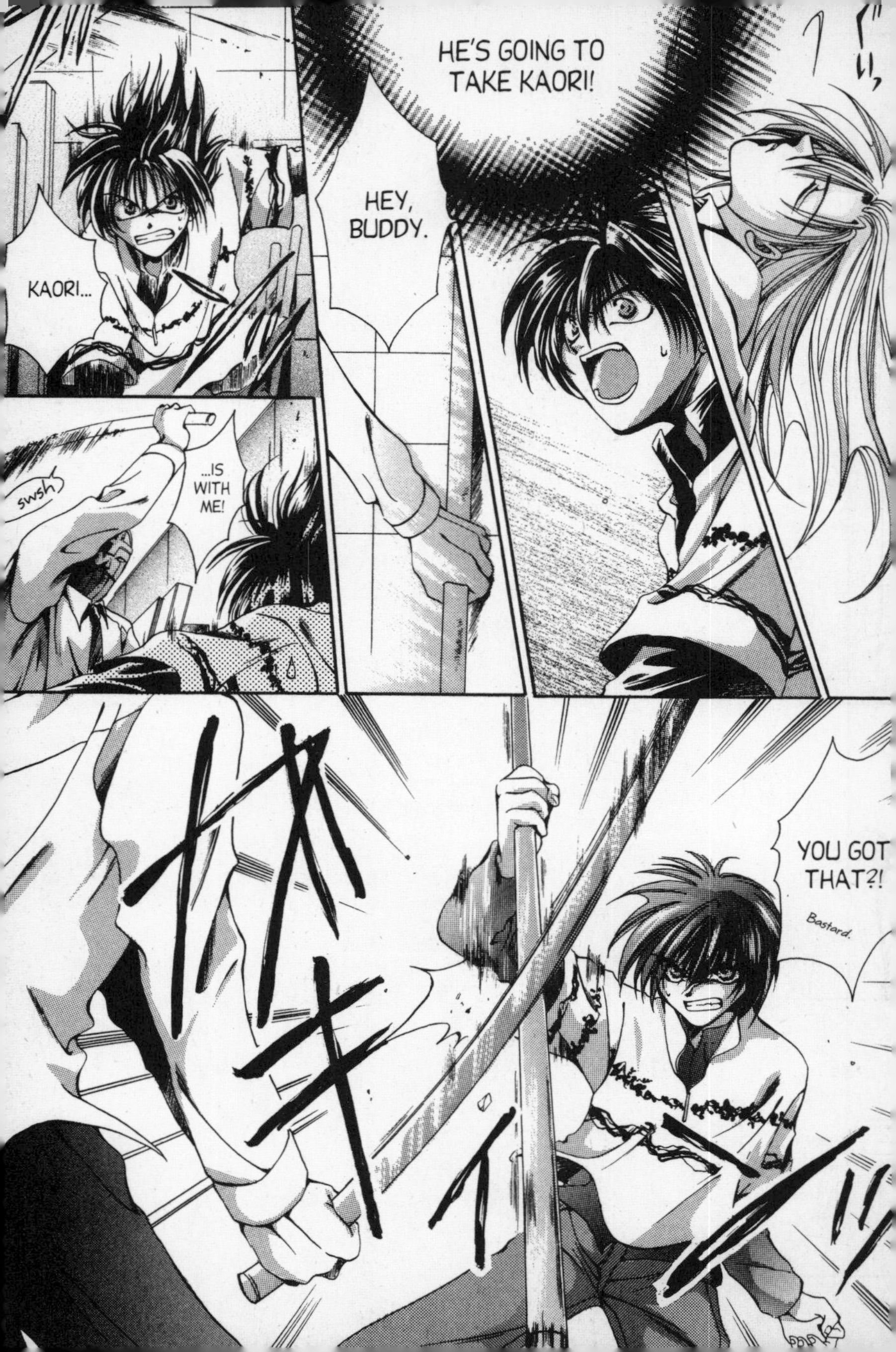
HE'S GOING TO TAKE KAORI!
HEY, BUDDY.
KAORI...
swsh
...IS WITH ME!
YOU GOT THAT?!
Bastard.

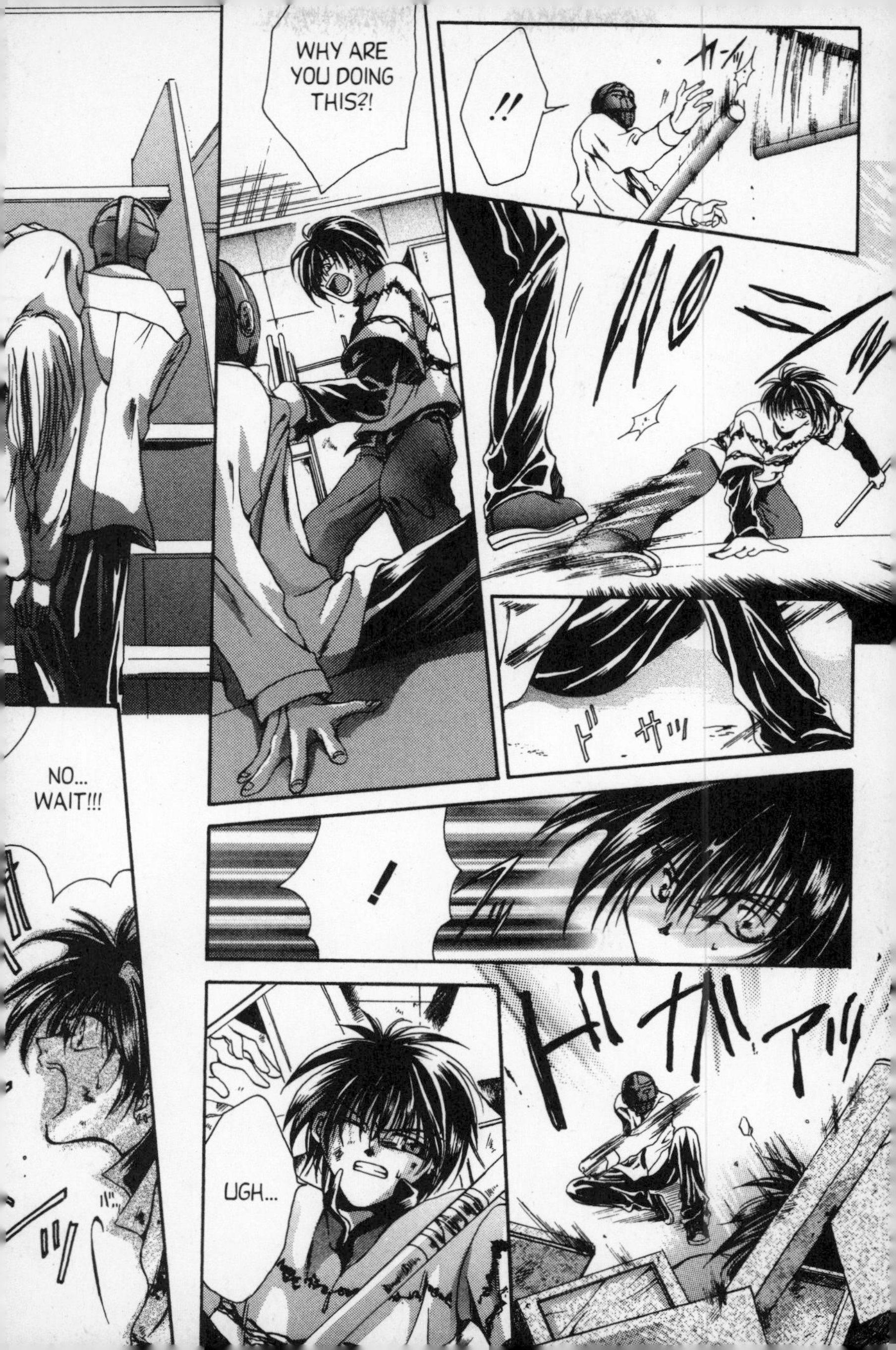
!!
WHY ARE YOU DOING THIS?!
!
UGH...
NO... WAIT!!!

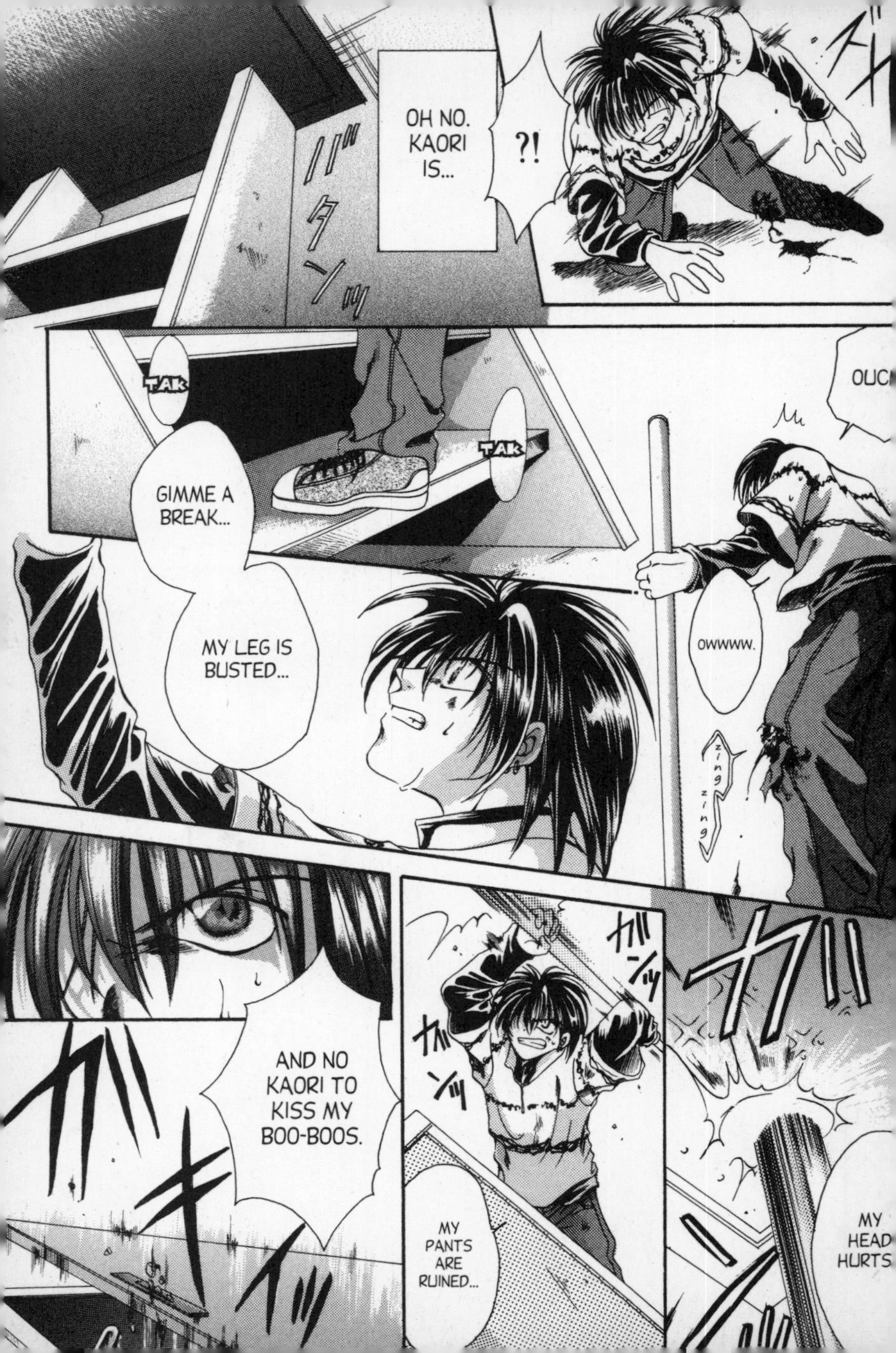
?!
OH NO. KAORI IS...
OUC
OWWWW.
zing zing
TAK
TAK
GIMME A BREAK...
MY LEG IS BUSTED...
MY HEAD HURTS
MY PANTS ARE RUINED...
AND NO KAORI TO KISS MY BOO-BOOS.

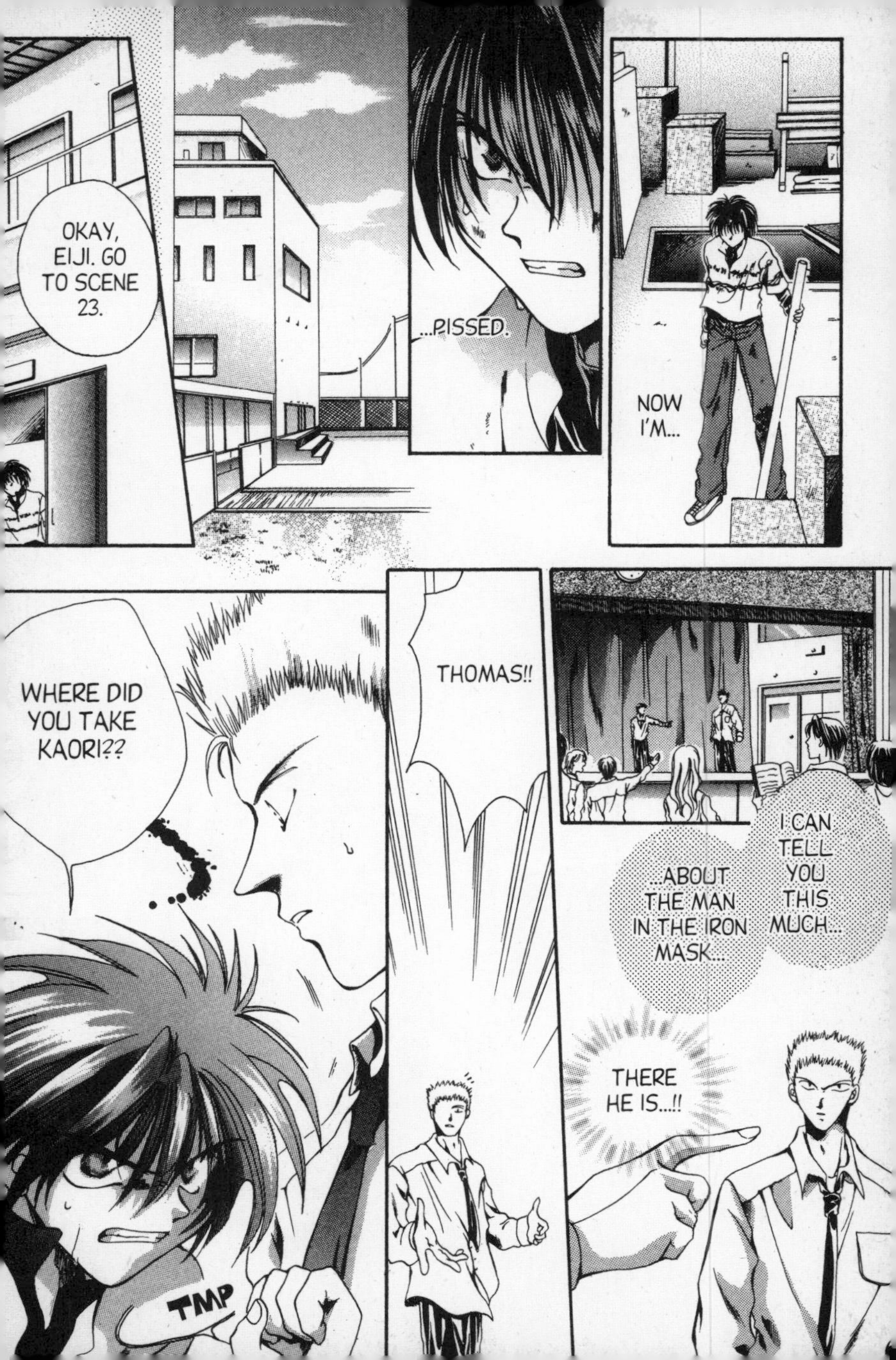
NOW I'M...
...PISSED.
OKAY, EIJI. GO TO SCENE 23.
I CAN TELL YOU THIS MUCH...
...ABOUT THE MAN IN THE IRON MASK...
THERE HE IS...!!
THOMAS!!
WHERE DID YOU TAKE KAORI??
TMP

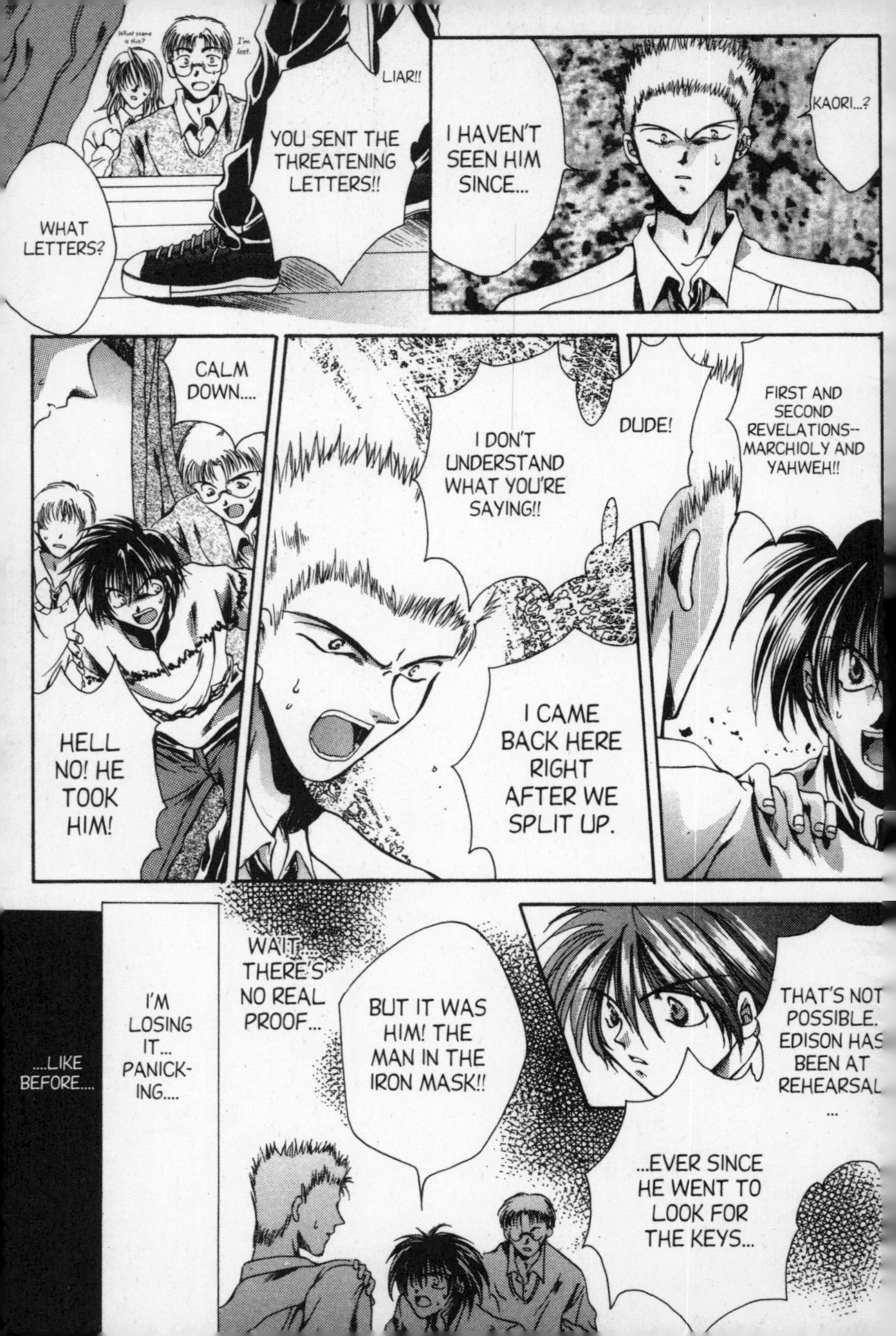
KAORI...?
I HAVEN'T SEEN HIM SINCE...
LIAR!!
YOU SENT THE THREATENING LETTERS!!
I'm lost.
What scene is this?
WHAT LETTERS?
FIRST AND SECOND REVELATIONS-- MARCHIOLY AND YAHWEH!!
DUDE!
I DON'T UNDERSTAND WHAT YOU'RE SAYING!!
I CAME BACK HERE RIGHT AFTER WE SPLIT UP.
CALM DOWN....
HELL NO! HE TOOK HIM!
THAT'S NOT POSSIBLE. EDISON HAS BEEN AT REHEARSAL...
...EVER SINCE HE WENT TO LOOK FOR THE KEYS...
BUT IT WAS HIM! THE MAN IN THE IRON MASK!!
WAIT... THERE'S NO REAL PROOF...
I'M LOSING IT... PANICK-ING....
...LIKE BEFORE....

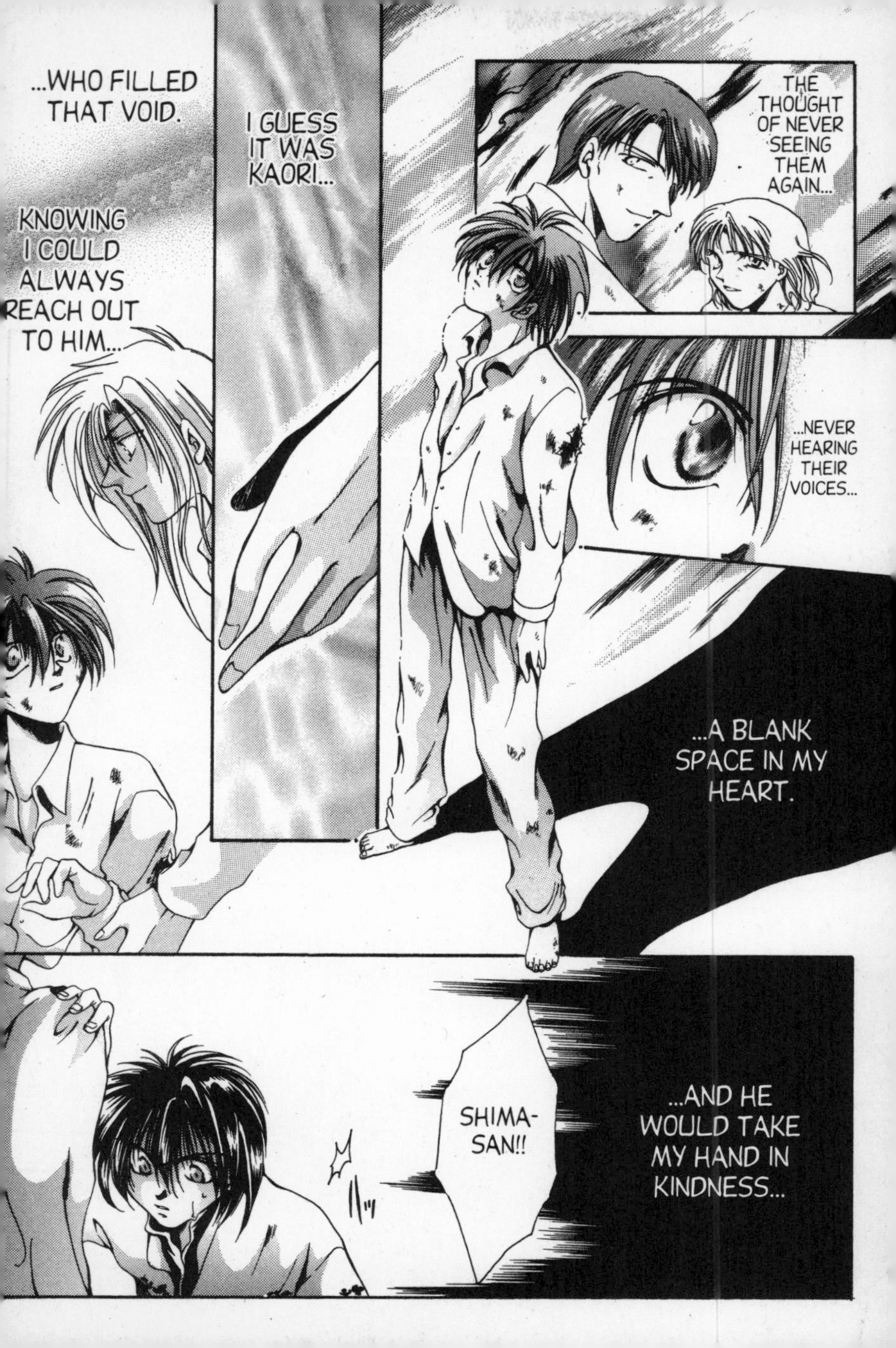
THE THOUGHT OF NEVER SEEING THEM AGAIN...
...NEVER HEARING THEIR VOICES...
...A BLANK SPACE IN MY HEART.
I GUESS IT WAS KAORI...
...WHO FILLED THAT VOID.
KNOWING I COULD ALWAYS REACH OUT TO HIM...
...AND HE WOULD TAKE MY HAND IN KINDNESS...
SHIMA-SAN!!

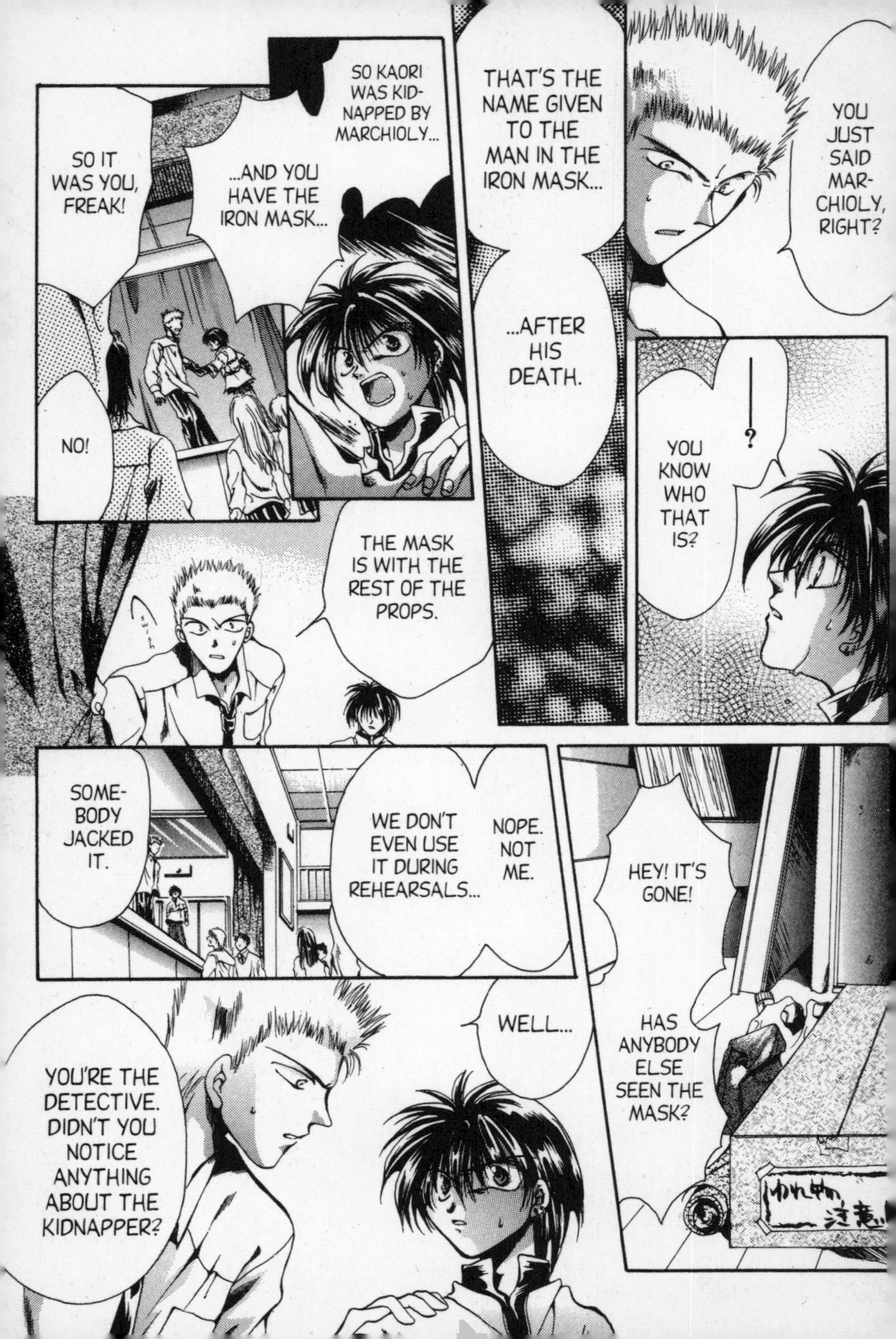
YOU JUST SAID MAR-CHIOLY, RIGHT?
—?
YOU KNOW WHO THAT IS?
THAT'S THE NAME GIVEN TO THE MAN IN THE IRON MASK...
...AFTER HIS DEATH.
SO KAORI WAS KID-NAPPED BY MARCHIOLY...
...AND YOU HAVE THE IRON MASK...
SO IT WAS YOU, FREAK!
NO!
THE MASK IS WITH THE REST OF THE PROPS.
HEY! IT'S GONE!
HAS ANYBODY ELSE SEEN THE MASK?
NOPE. NOT ME.
WE DON'T EVEN USE IT DURING REHEARSALS...
SOME-BODY JACKED IT.
WELL...
YOU'RE THE DETECTIVE. DIDN'T YOU NOTICE ANYTHING ABOUT THE KIDNAPPER?

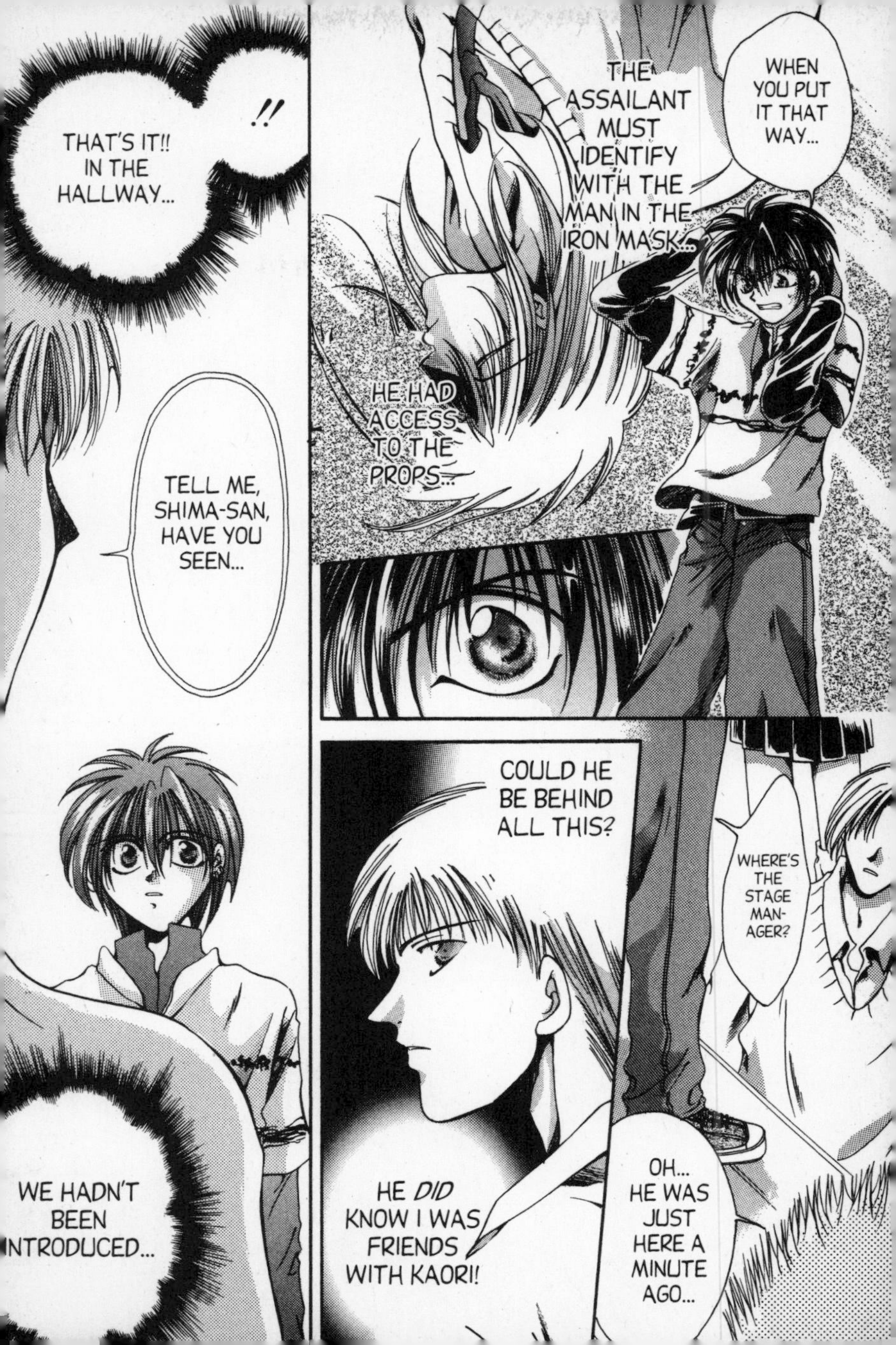
WHEN YOU PUT IT THAT WAY...
THE ASSAILANT MUST IDENTIFY WITH THE MAN IN THE IRON MASK...
HE HAD ACCESS TO THE PROPS...
!!
THAT'S IT!! IN THE HALLWAY...
TELL ME, SHIMA-SAN, HAVE YOU SEEN...
WHERE'S THE STAGE MAN-AGER?
OH... HE WAS JUST HERE A MINUTE AGO...
COULD HE BE BEHIND ALL THIS?
HE *DID* KNOW I WAS FRIENDS WITH KAORI!
WE HADN'T BEEN INTRODUCED...

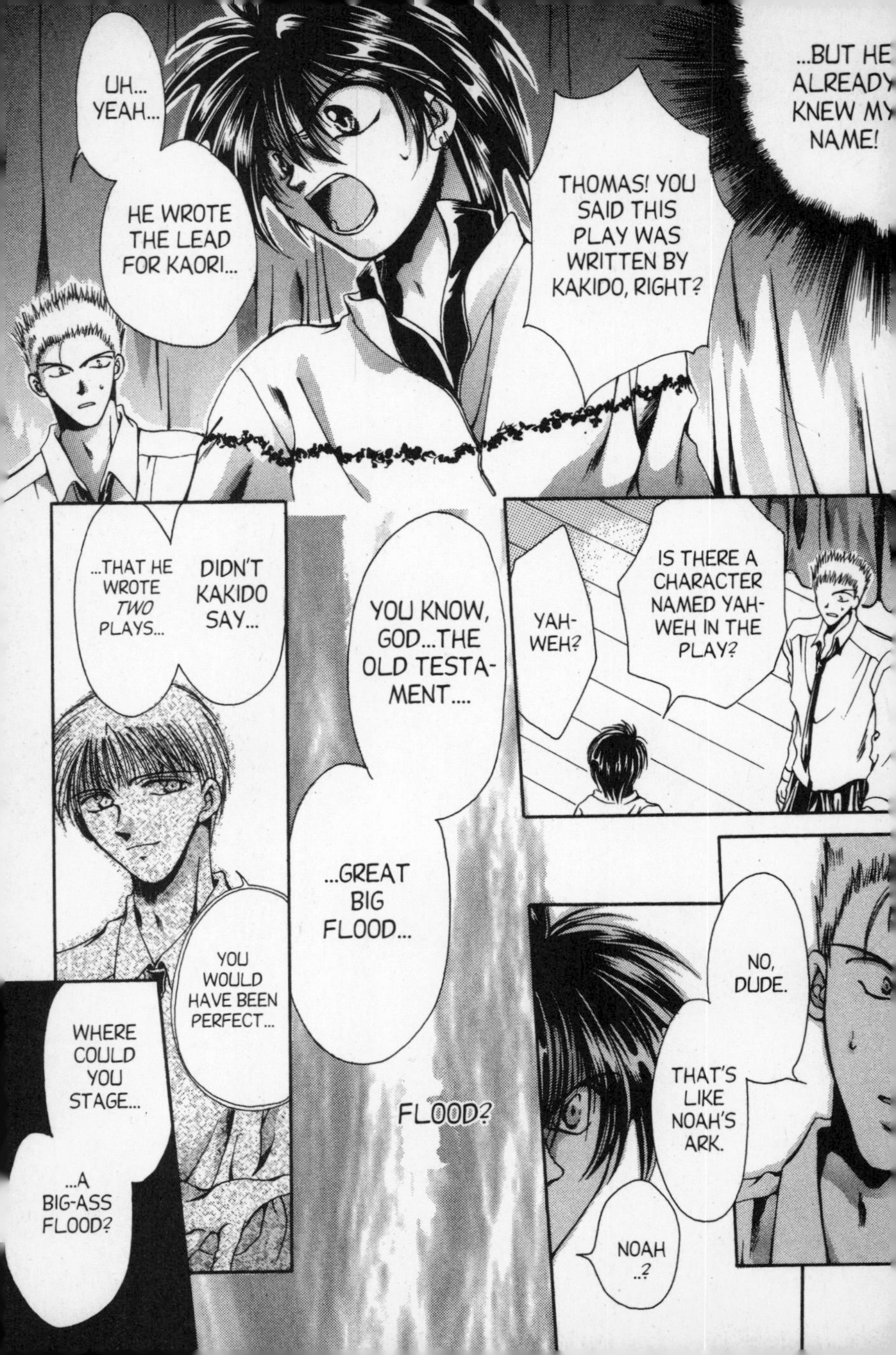
...BUT HE ALREADY KNEW MY NAME!
THOMAS! YOU SAID THIS PLAY WAS WRITTEN BY KAKIDO, RIGHT?
UH... YEAH...
HE WROTE THE LEAD FOR KAORI...
IS THERE A CHARACTER NAMED YAH-WEH IN THE PLAY?
YAH-WEH?
NO, DUDE.
THAT'S LIKE NOAH'S ARK.
NOAH ...?
YOU KNOW, GOD...THE OLD TESTA-MENT....
...GREAT BIG FLOOD...
FLOOD?
DIDN'T KAKIDO SAY...
...THAT HE WROTE *TWO* PLAYS...
YOU WOULD HAVE BEEN PERFECT...
WHERE COULD YOU STAGE...
...A BIG-ASS FLOOD?

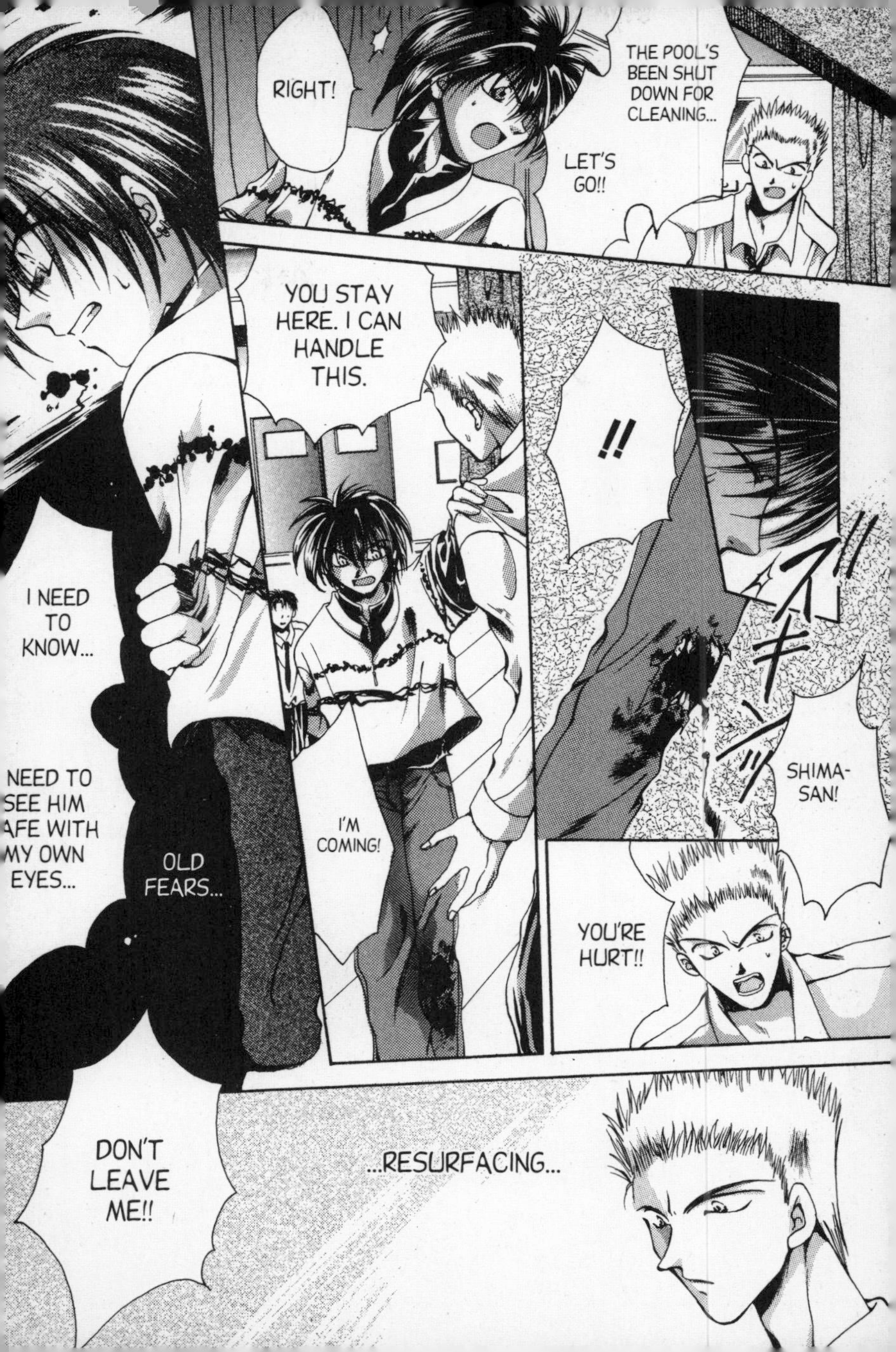
THE POOL'S BEEN SHUT DOWN FOR CLEANING...
LET'S GO!!
RIGHT!
!!
SHIMA-SAN!
YOU'RE HURT!!
YOU STAY HERE. I CAN HANDLE THIS.
I'M COMING!
I NEED TO KNOW...
NEED TO SEE HIM AFE WITH MY OWN EYES...
OLD FEARS...
...RESURFACING...
DON'T LEAVE ME!!

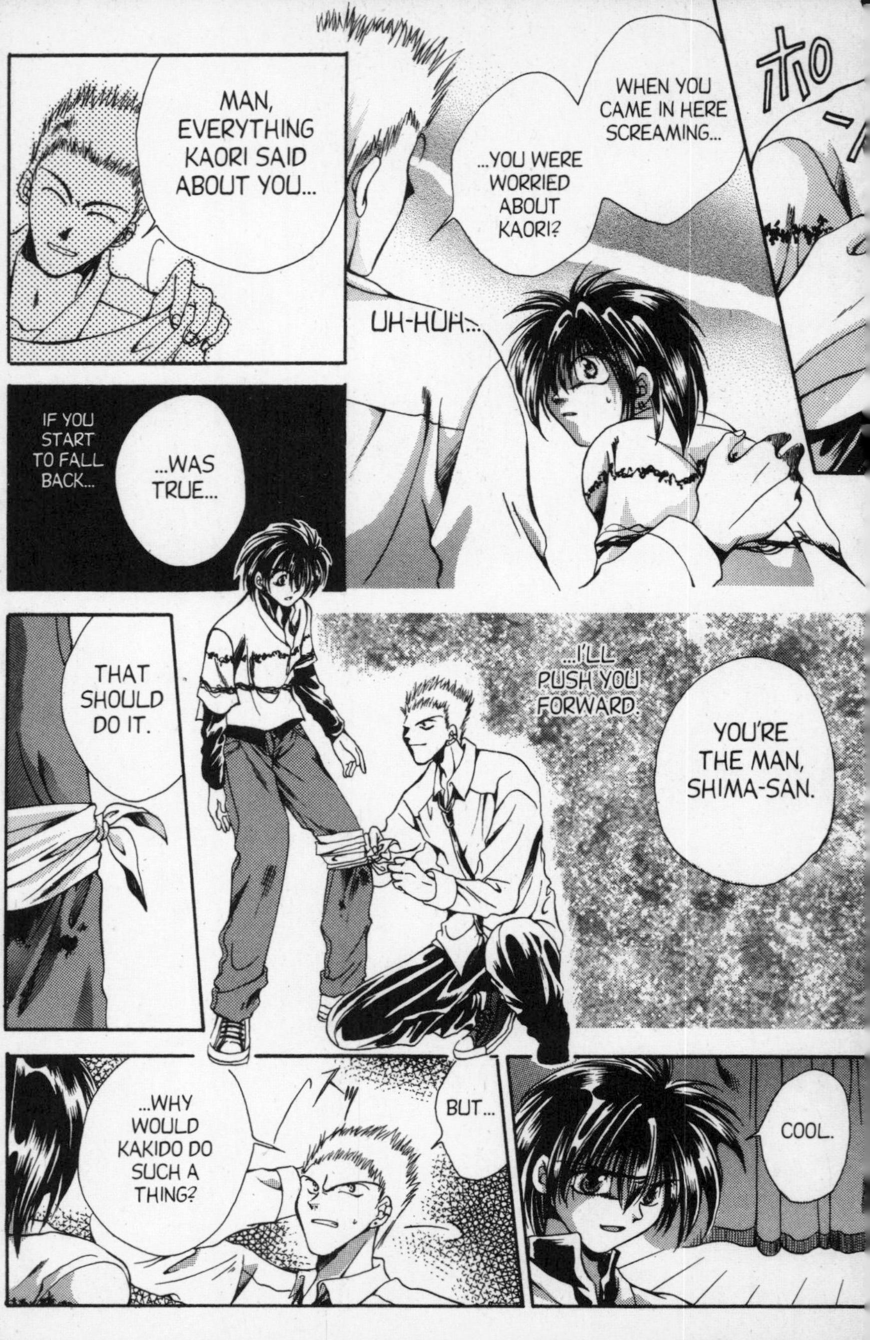
WHEN YOU CAME IN HERE SCREAMING...
...YOU WERE WORRIED ABOUT KAORI?
UH-HUH...
MAN, EVERYTHING KAORI SAID ABOUT YOU...
...WAS TRUE...
IF YOU START TO FALL BACK...
YOU'RE THE MAN, SHIMA-SAN.
...I'LL PUSH YOU FORWARD.
THAT SHOULD DO IT.
COOL.
BUT...
...WHY WOULD KAKIDO DO SUCH A THING?

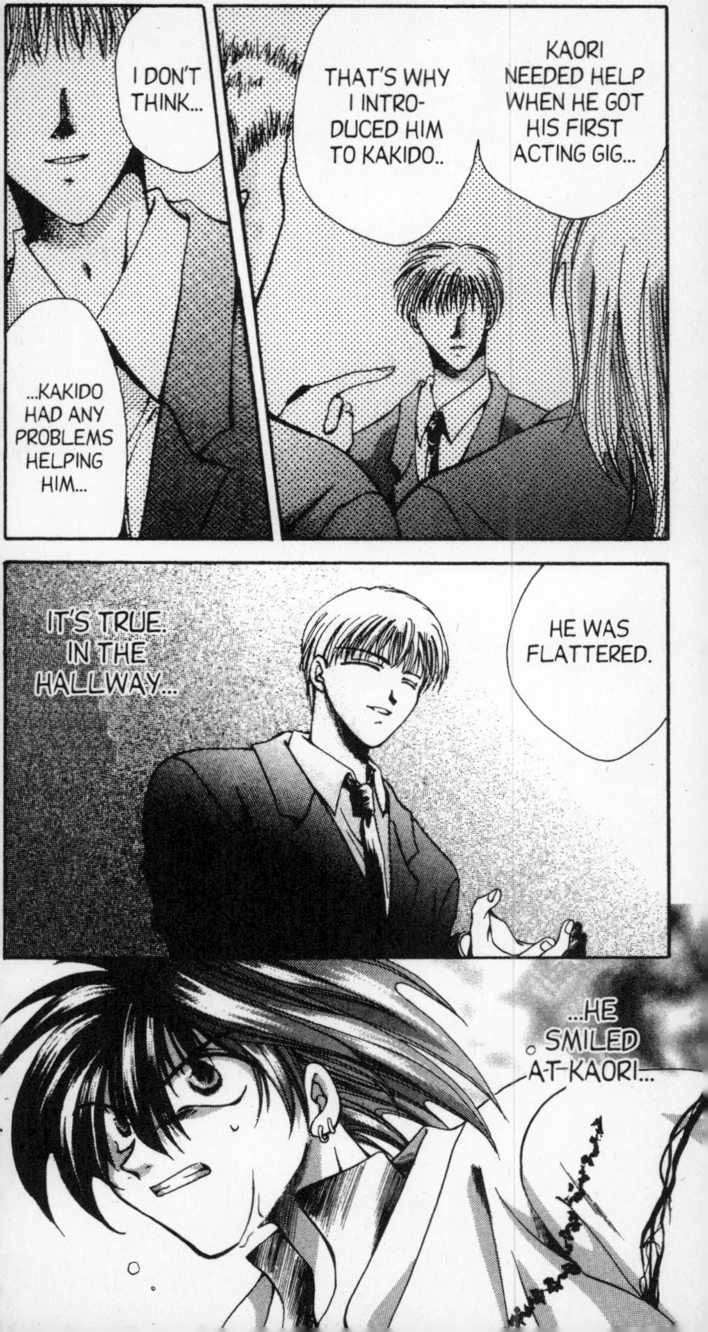
KAORI NEEDED HELP WHEN HE GOT HIS FIRST ACTING GIG...
THAT'S WHY I INTRODUCED HIM TO KAKIDO..
I DON'T THINK...
...KAKIDO HAD ANY PROBLEMS HELPING HIM...
HE WAS FLATTERED.
IT'S TRUE. IN THE HALLWAY...
...HE SMILED AT KAORI...

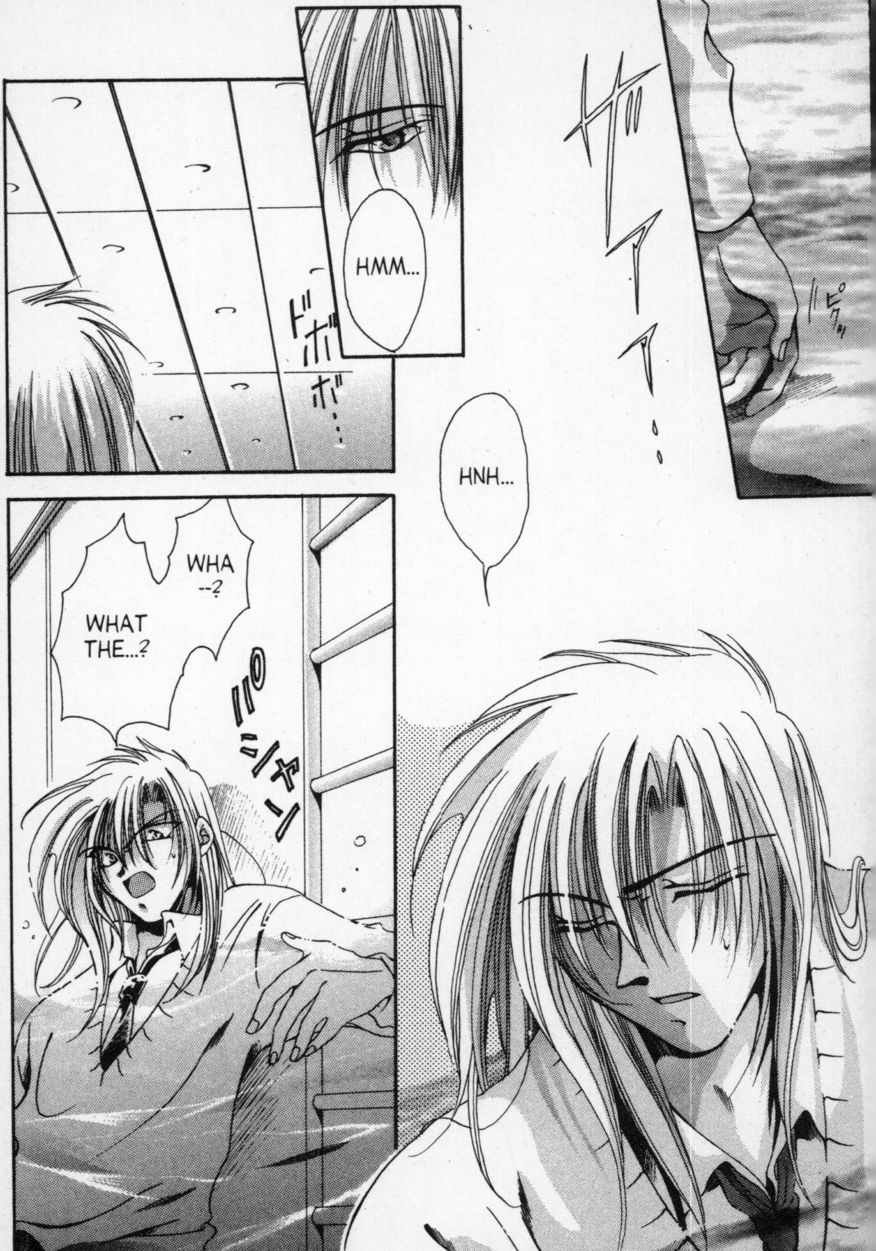
ザァァ。。
ピクッ
HMM...
ドボボボ…
HNH...
WHA --?
WHAT THE...?
パシャン

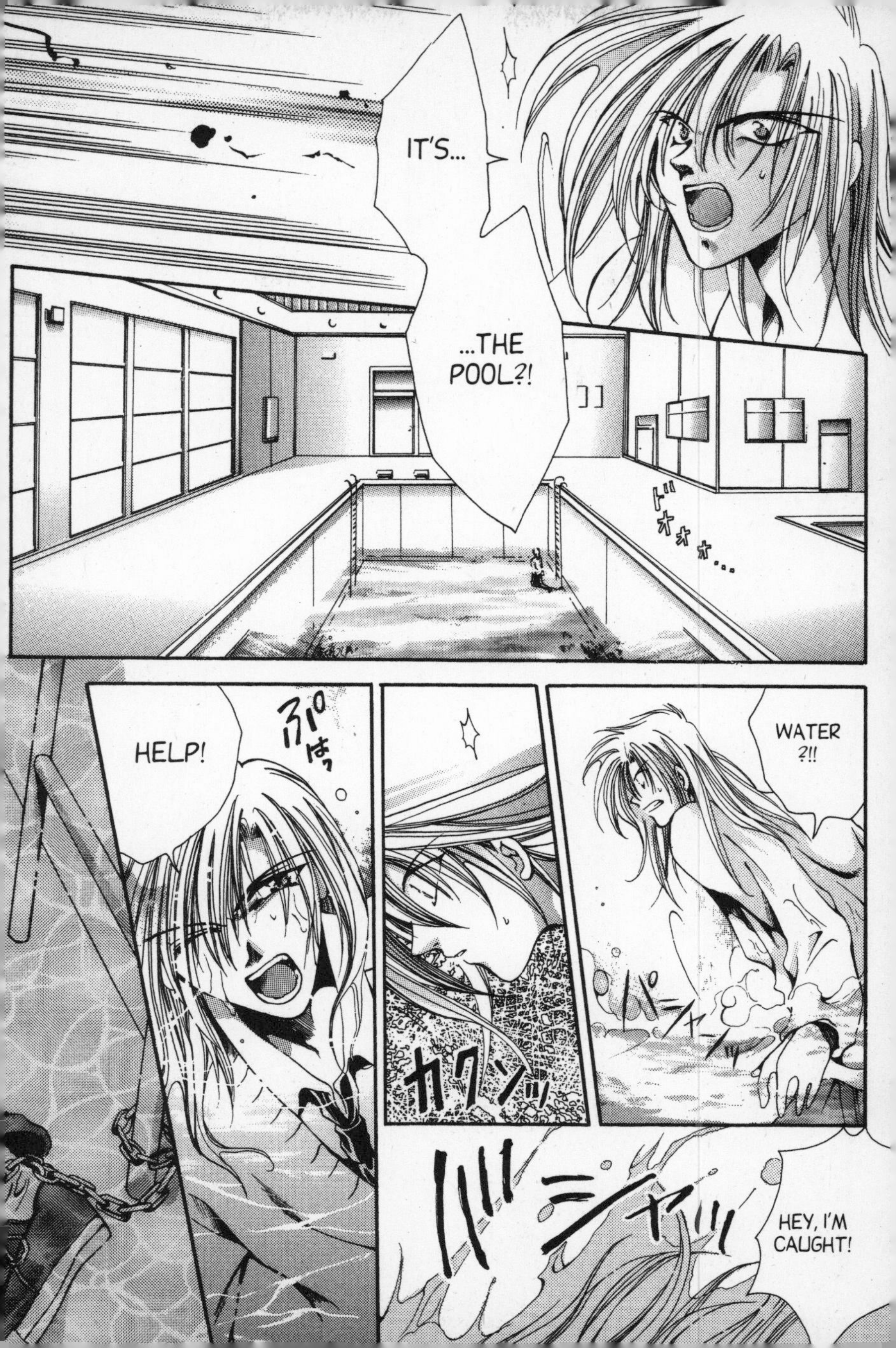

IT'S...
...THE POOL?!
ドオオオ...
WATER ?!!
パシャーッ
カクンッ
バシャッ
HEY, I'M CAUGHT!
HELP!
ぷはっ

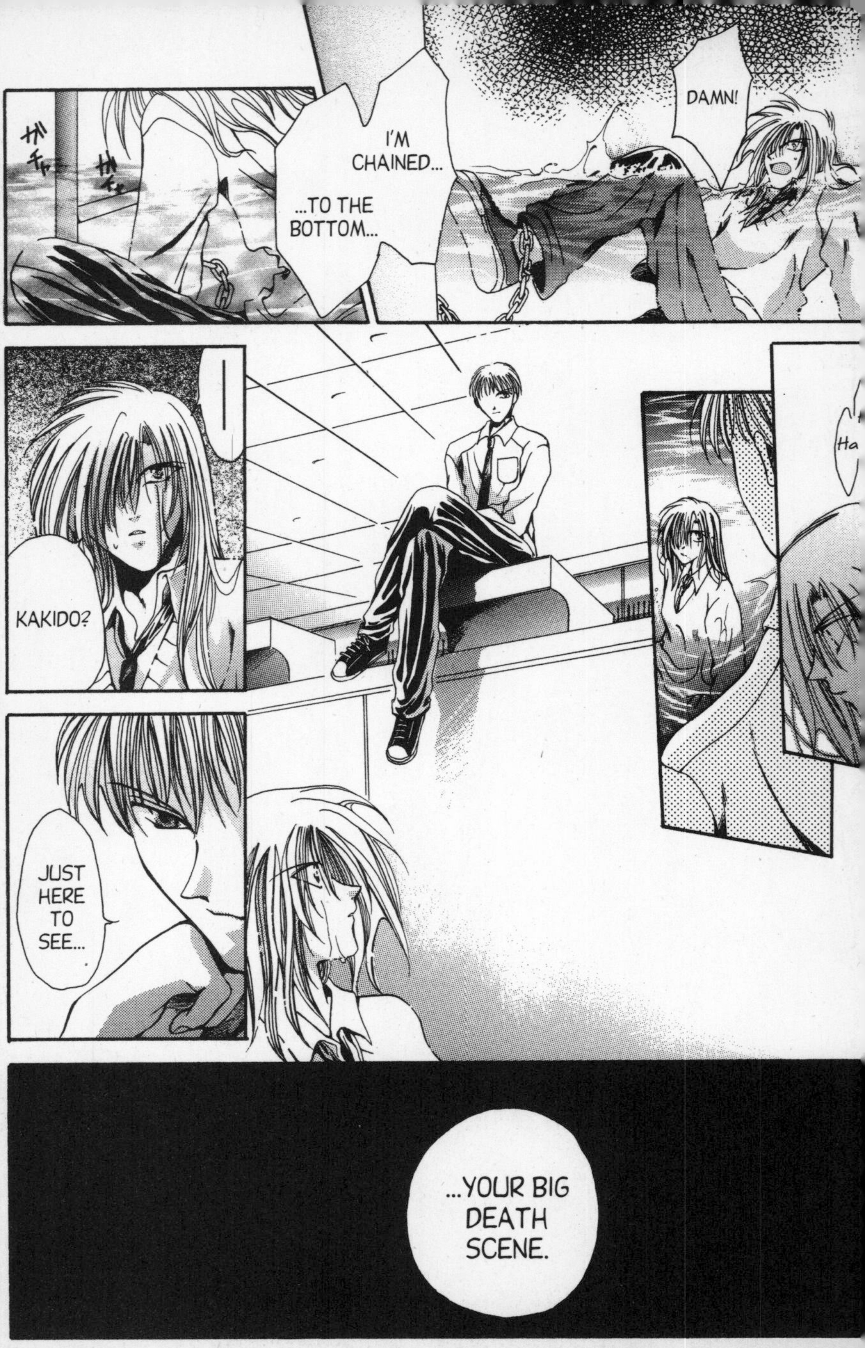
DAMN!
I'M CHAINED...
...TO THE BOTTOM...
ガチャ
ガチャ
Ha
|
KAKIDO?
JUST HERE TO SEE...
...YOUR BIG DEATH SCENE.

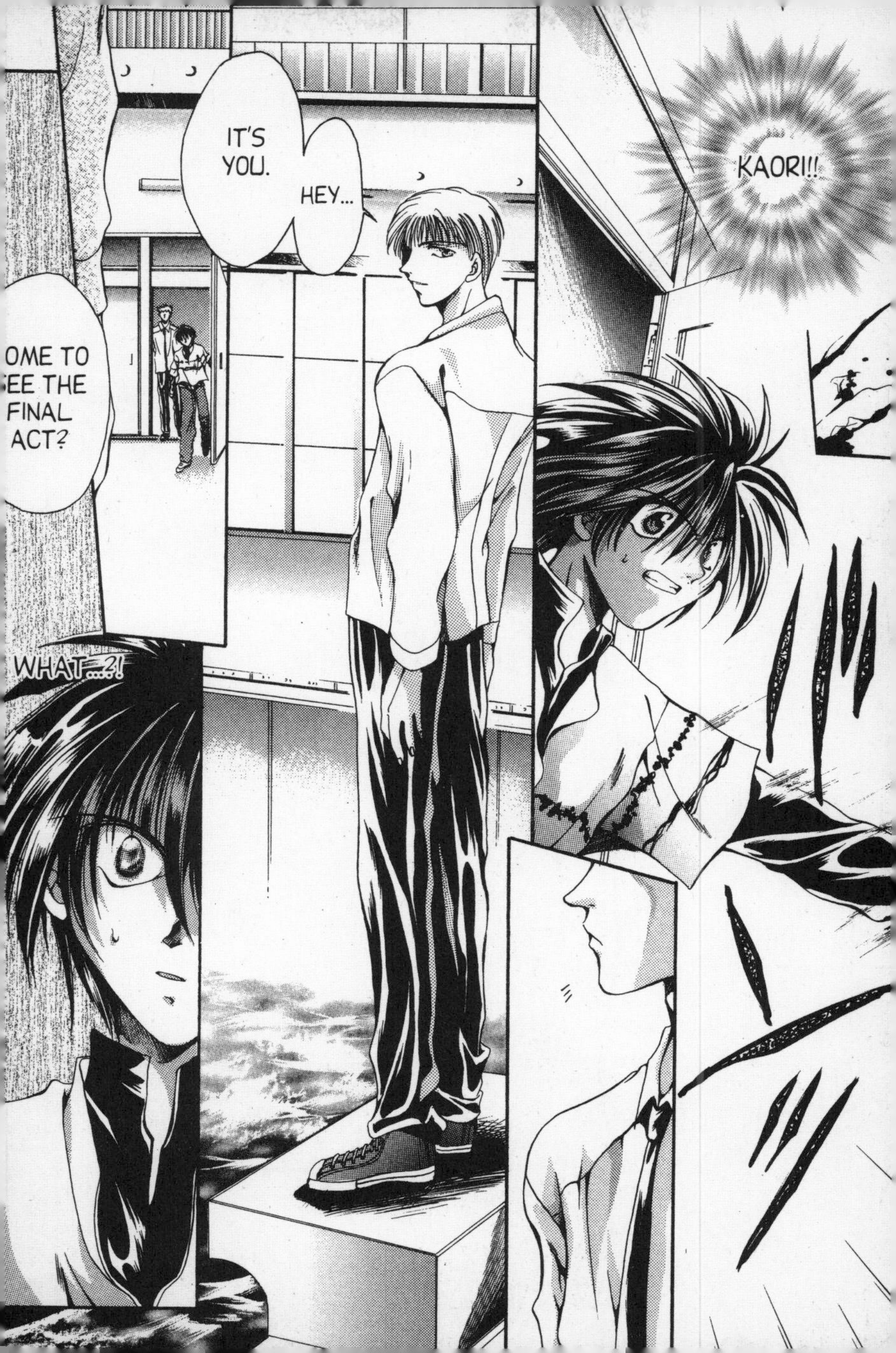
KAORI!!
HEY...
IT'S YOU.
OME TO EE THE FINAL ACT?
WHAT...?!

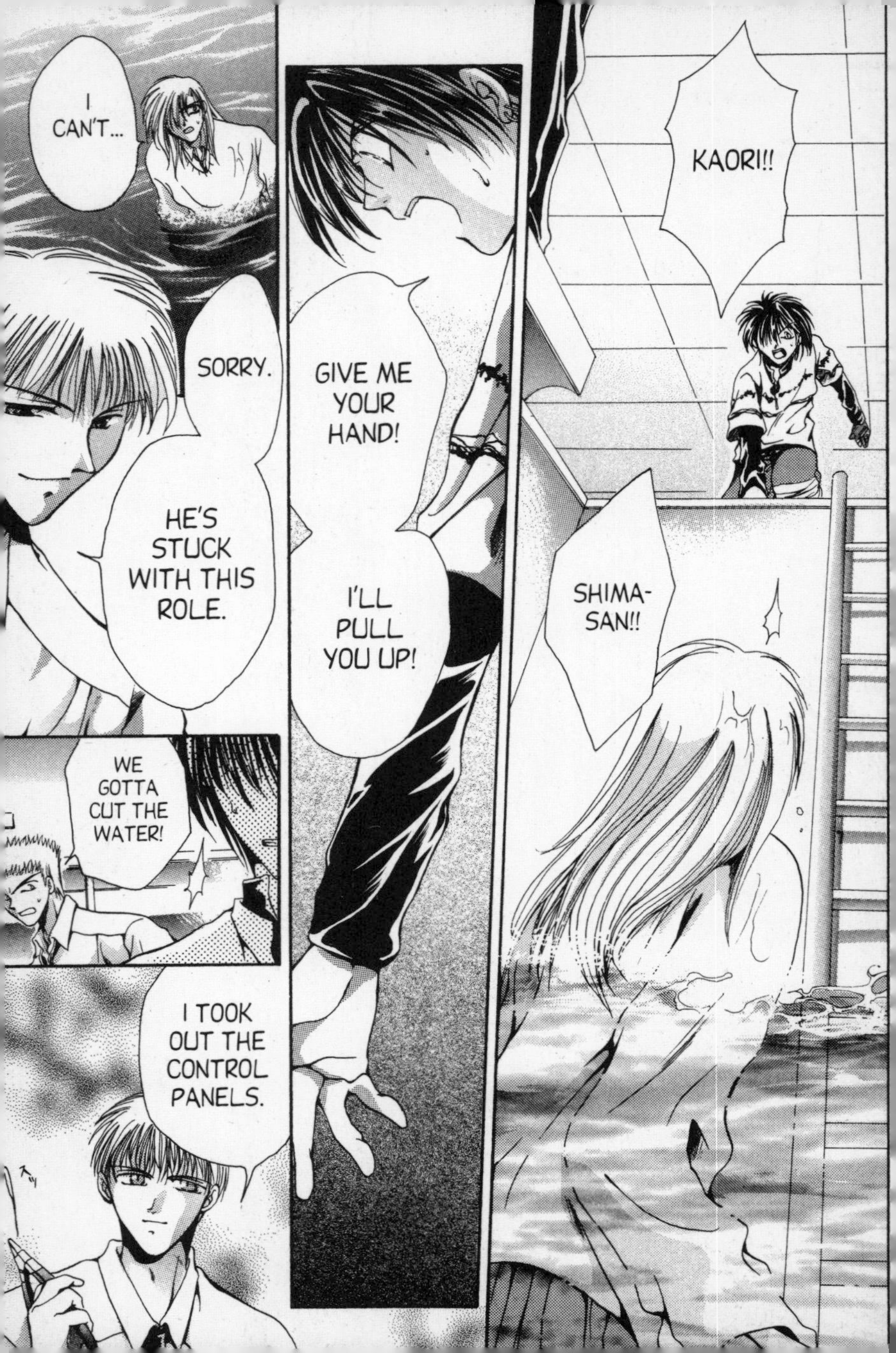
KAORI!!
SHIMA-SAN!!
GIVE ME YOUR HAND!
I'LL PULL YOU UP!
I CAN'T...
SORRY.
HE'S STUCK WITH THIS ROLE.
WE GOTTA CUT THE WATER!
I TOOK OUT THE CONTROL PANELS.

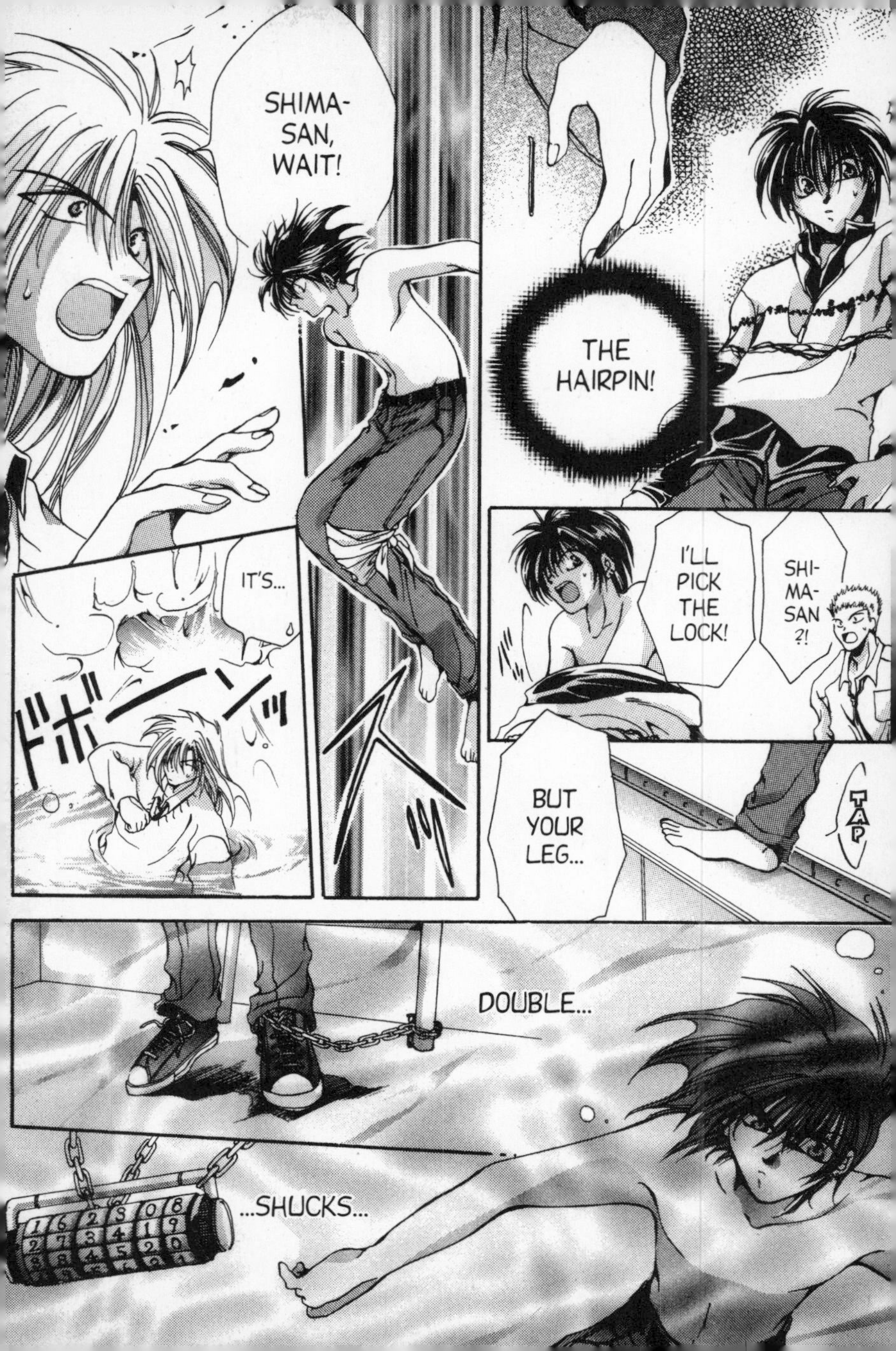
THE HAIRPIN!
SHI-MA-SAN?!
I'LL PICK THE LOCK!
TAP
BUT YOUR LEG...
SHIMA-SAN, WAIT!
ス
IT'S...
ドボーンッ
DOUBLE...
...SHUCKS...

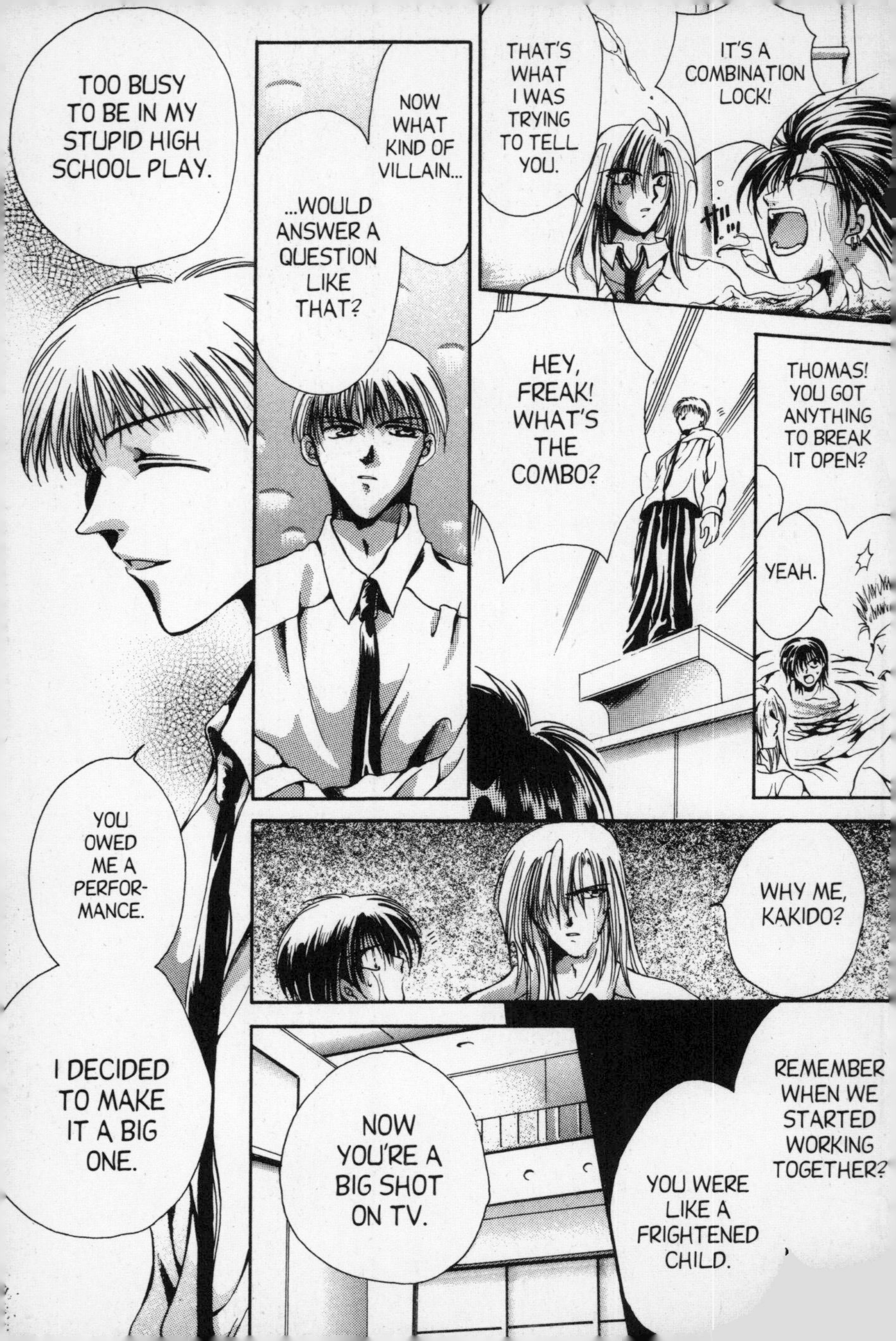
IT'S A COMBINATION LOCK!
THAT'S WHAT I WAS TRYING TO TELL YOU.
THOMAS! YOU GOT ANYTHING TO BREAK IT OPEN?
YEAH.
HEY, FREAK! WHAT'S THE COMBO?
NOW WHAT KIND OF VILLAIN...
...WOULD ANSWER A QUESTION LIKE THAT?
WHY ME, KAKIDO?
REMEMBER WHEN WE STARTED WORKING TOGETHER?
YOU WERE LIKE A FRIGHTENED CHILD.
NOW YOU'RE A BIG SHOT ON TV.
TOO BUSY TO BE IN MY STUPID HIGH SCHOOL PLAY.
YOU OWED ME A PERFORMANCE.
I DECIDED TO MAKE IT A BIG ONE.

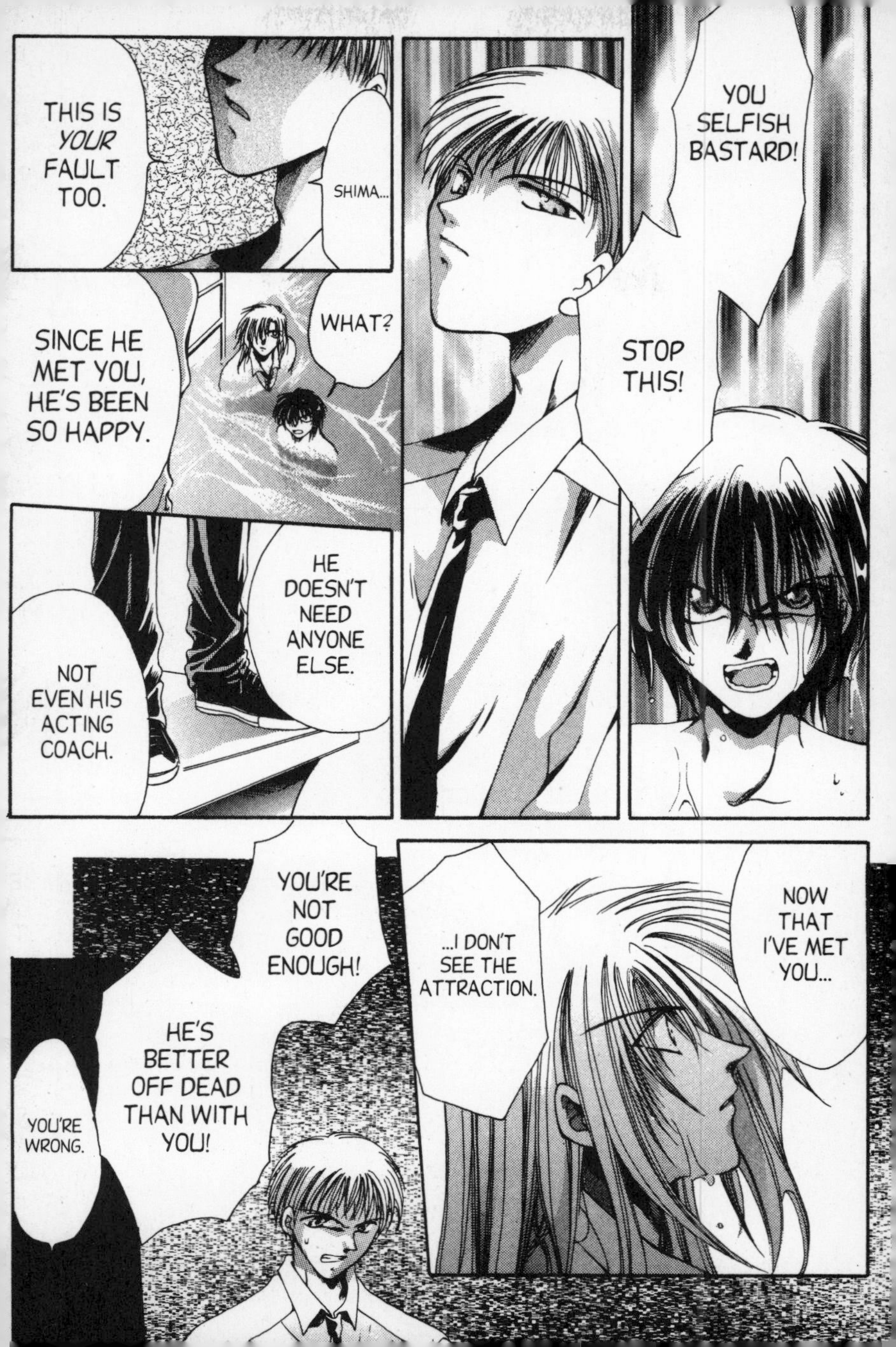
YOU SELFISH BASTARD!
STOP THIS!
THIS IS *YOUR* FAULT TOO.
SHIMA...
WHAT?
SINCE HE MET YOU, HE'S BEEN SO HAPPY.
HE DOESN'T NEED ANYONE ELSE.
NOT EVEN HIS ACTING COACH.
NOW THAT I'VE MET YOU...
...I DON'T SEE THE ATTRACTION.
YOU'RE NOT GOOD ENOUGH!
HE'S BETTER OFF DEAD THAN WITH YOU!
YOU'RE WRONG.

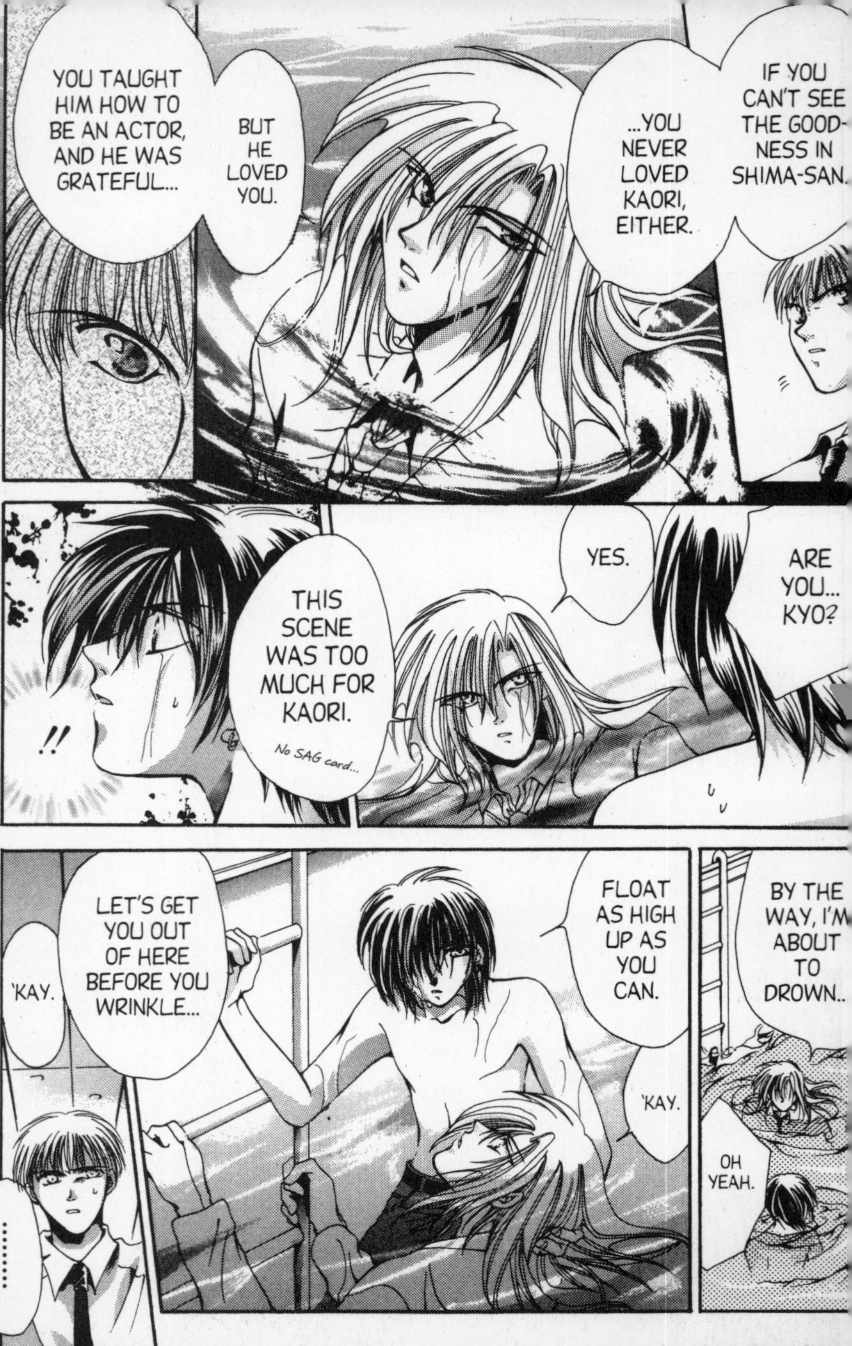
IF YOU CAN'T SEE THE GOODNESS IN SHIMA-SAN...
...YOU NEVER LOVED KAORI, EITHER.
YOU TAUGHT HIM HOW TO BE AN ACTOR, AND HE WAS GRATEFUL...
BUT HE LOVED YOU.
ARE YOU... KYO?
YES.
THIS SCENE WAS TOO MUCH FOR KAORI.
No SAG card...
!!
BY THE WAY, I'M ABOUT TO DROWN...
OH YEAH.
FLOAT AS HIGH UP AS YOU CAN.
'KAY.
LET'S GET YOU OUT OF HERE BEFORE YOU WRINKLE...
'KAY.
....

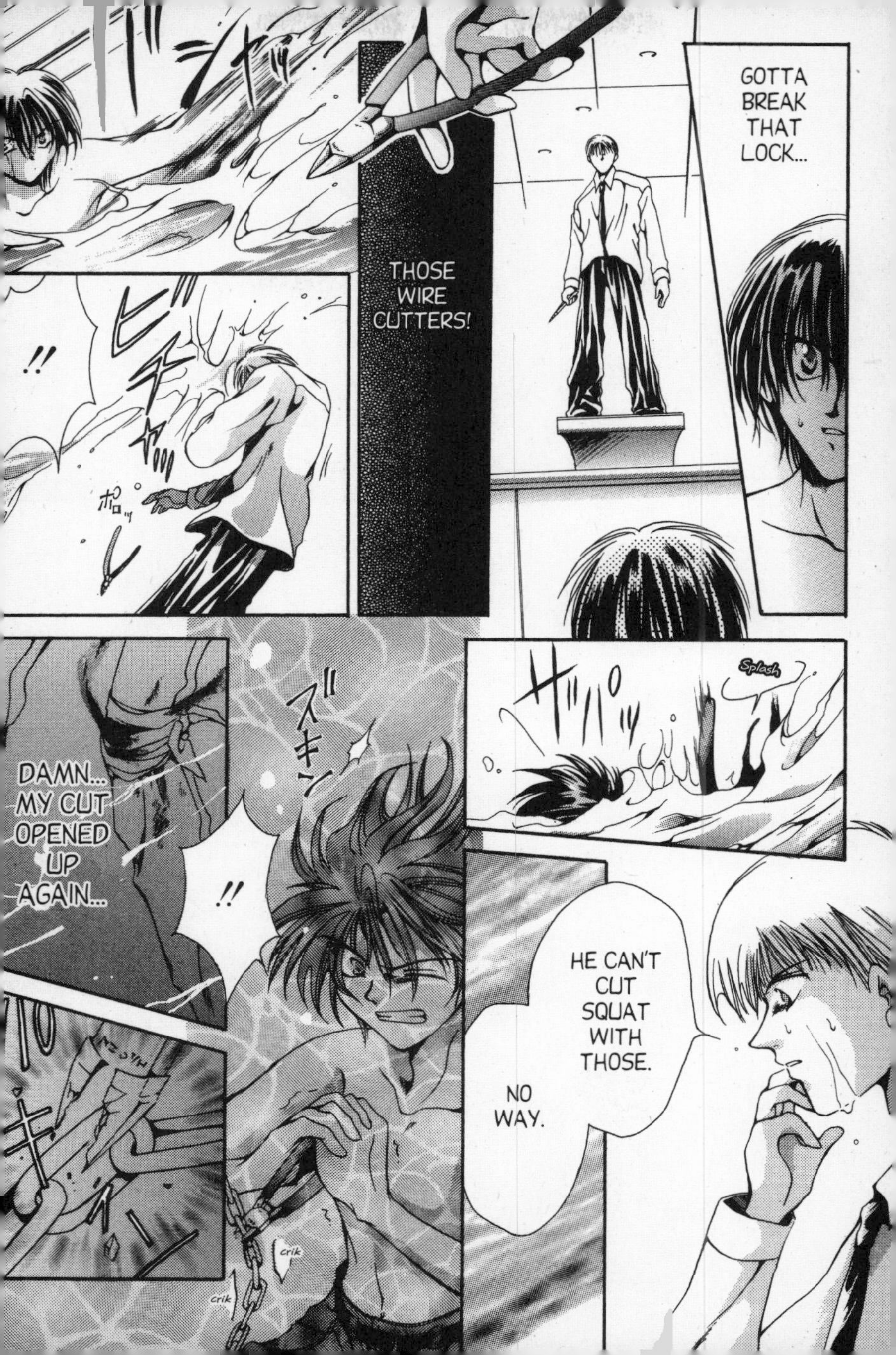
GOTTA BREAK THAT LOCK...
THOSE WIRE CUTTERS!
!!
Splash
HE CAN'T CUT SQUAT WITH THOSE.
NO WAY.
!!
DAMN... MY CUT OPENED UP AGAIN...
crik
crik

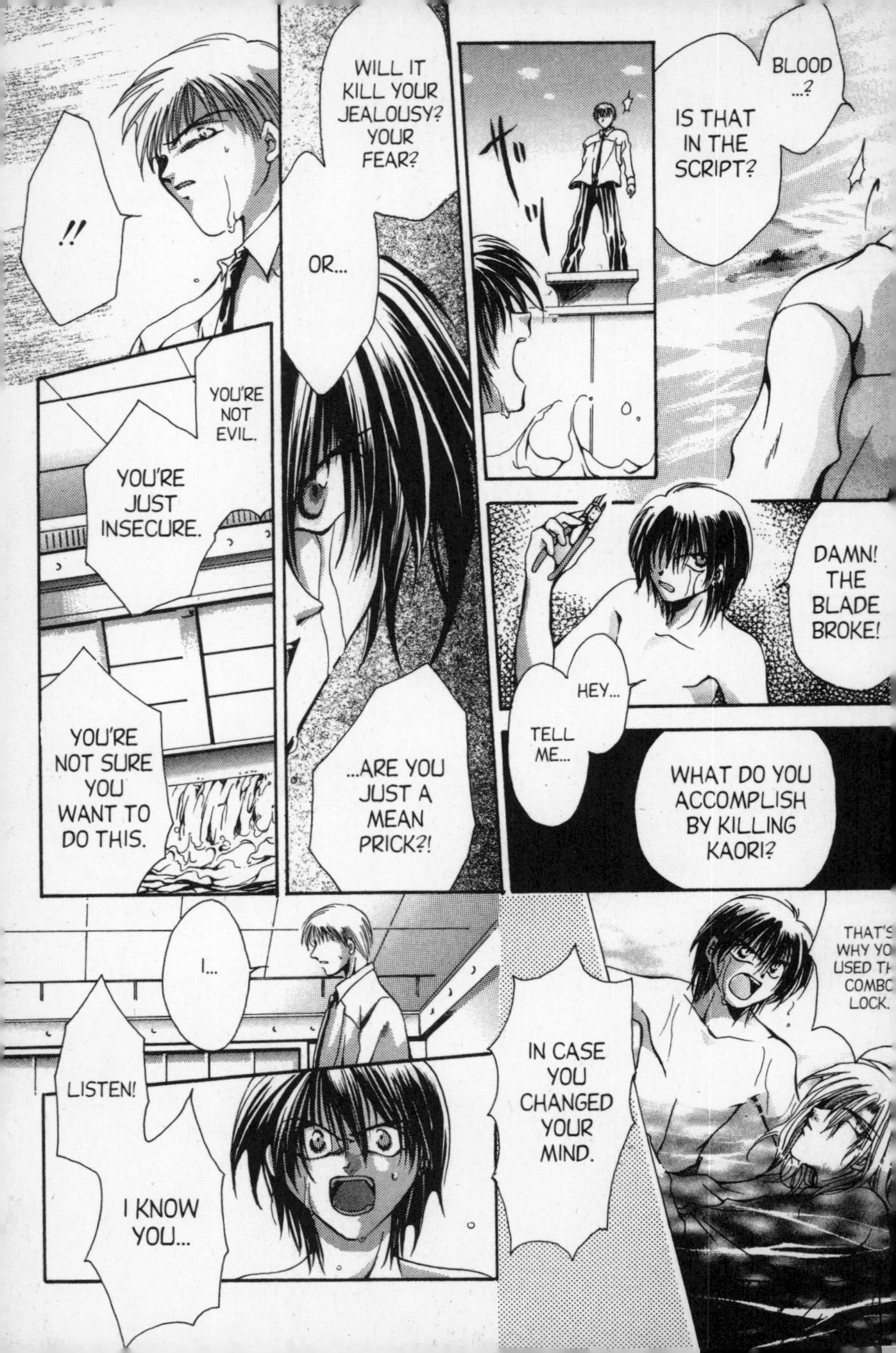
BLOOD ...?
IS THAT IN THE SCRIPT?
DAMN! THE BLADE BROKE!
HEY...
TELL ME...
WHAT DO YOU ACCOMPLISH BY KILLING KAORI?
WILL IT KILL YOUR JEALOUSY? YOUR FEAR?
OR...
...ARE YOU JUST A MEAN PRICK?!
!!
YOU'RE NOT EVIL.
YOU'RE JUST INSECURE.
YOU'RE NOT SURE YOU WANT TO DO THIS.
THAT'S WHY YO USED TH COMBO LOCK.
IN CASE YOU CHANGED YOUR MIND.
I...
LISTEN!
I KNOW YOU...

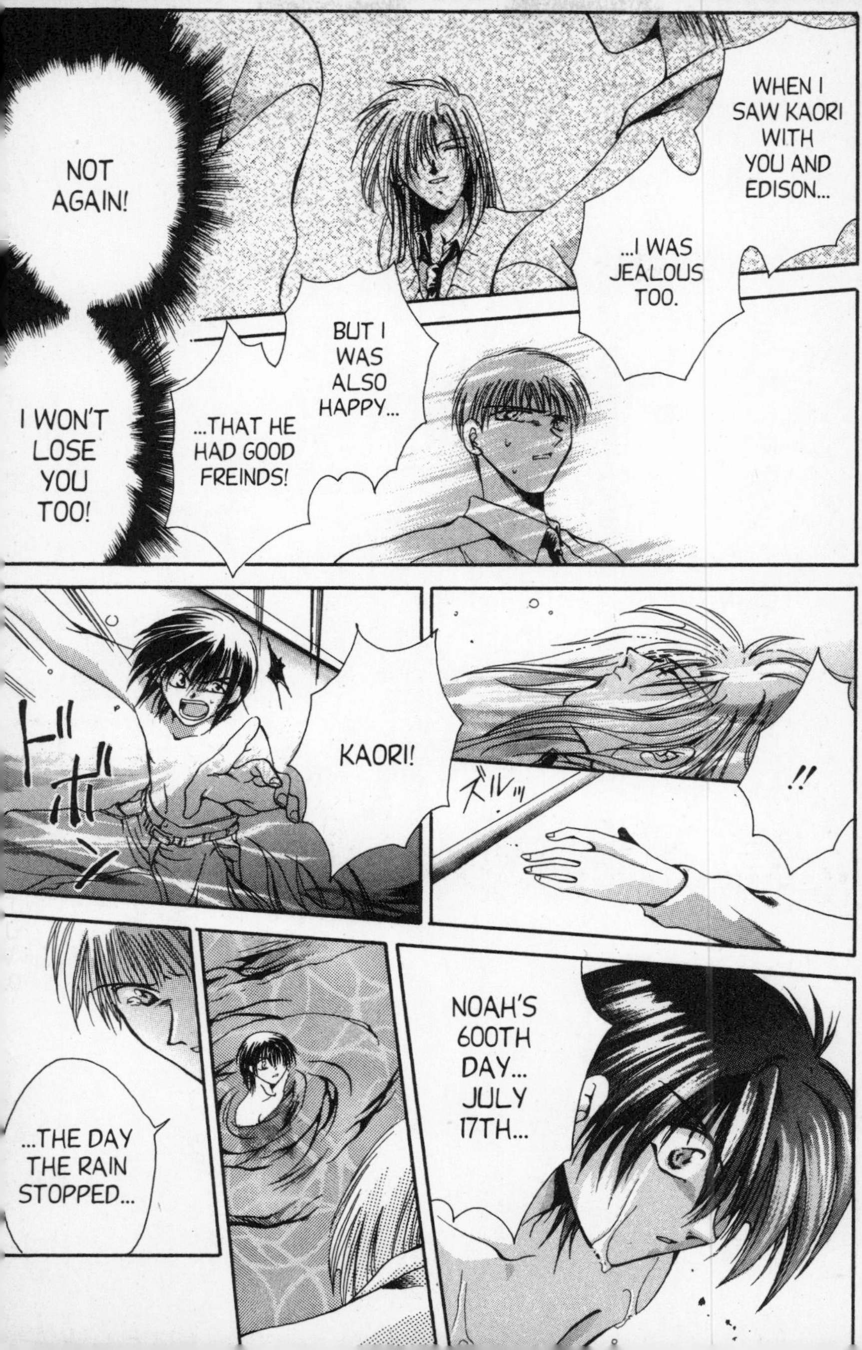
WHEN I SAW KAORI WITH YOU AND EDISON...
...I WAS JEALOUS TOO.
BUT I WAS ALSO HAPPY...
...THAT HE HAD GOOD FREINDS!
NOT AGAIN!
I WON'T LOSE YOU TOO!
!!
ズルッ
KAORI!
ドボン
NOAH'S 600TH DAY... JULY 17TH...
...THE DAY THE RAIN STOPPED...

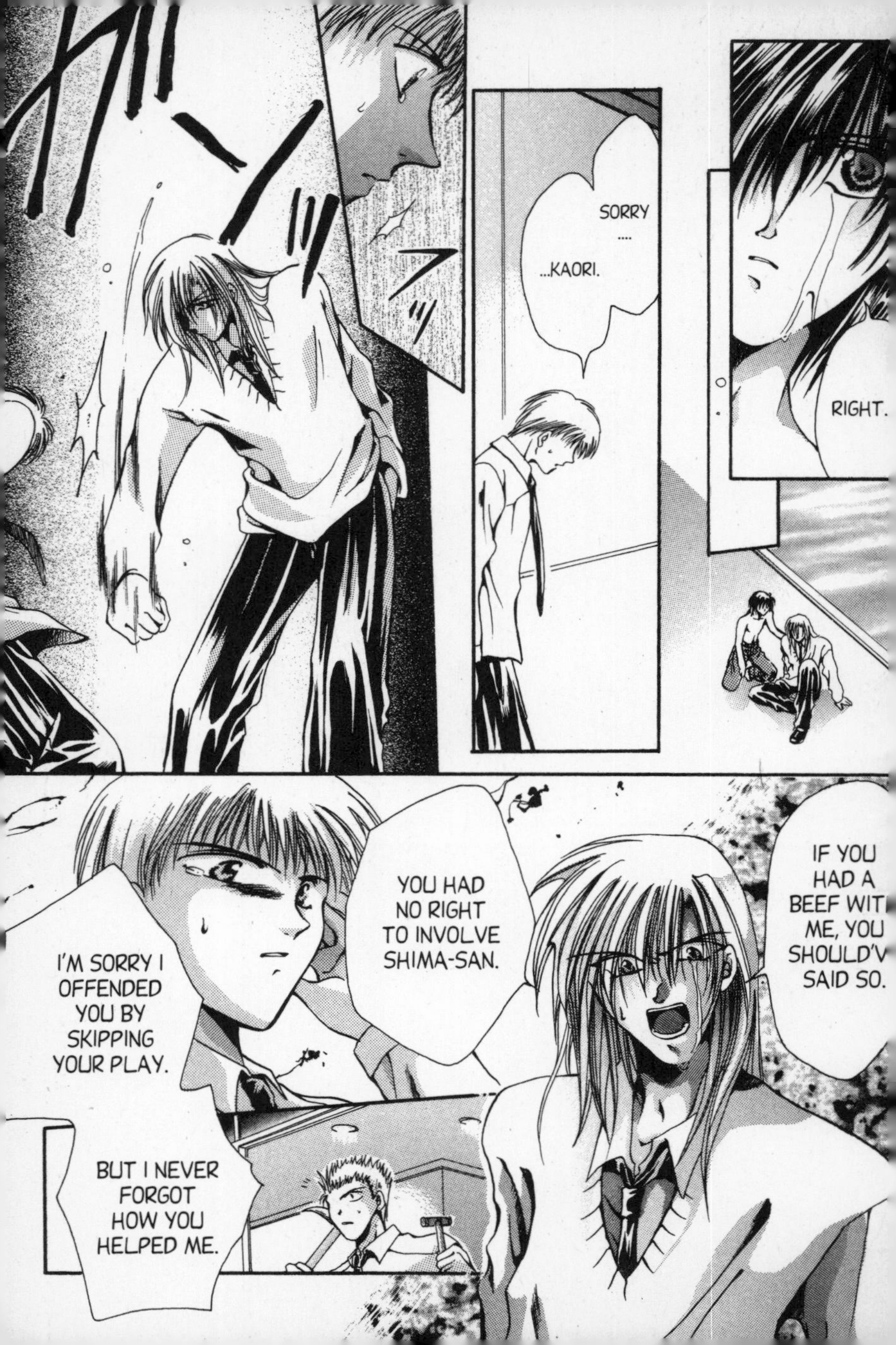
RIGHT.
SORRY ....KAORI.
IF YOU HAD A BEEF WIT ME, YOU SHOULD'V SAID SO.
YOU HAD NO RIGHT TO INVOLVE SHIMA-SAN.
I'M SORRY I OFFENDED YOU BY SKIPPING YOUR PLAY.
BUT I NEVER FORGOT HOW YOU HELPED ME.

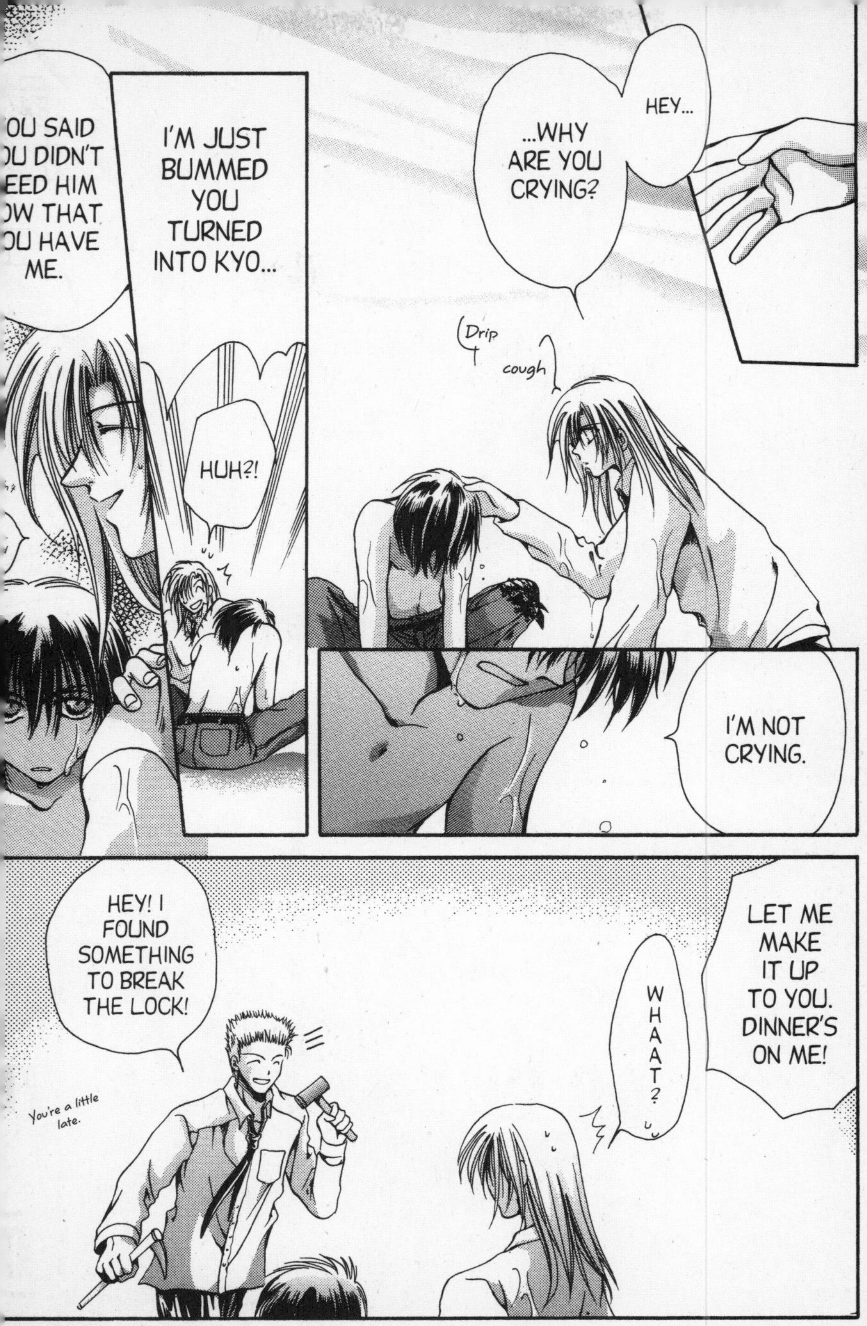
HEY...
...WHY ARE YOU CRYING?
Drip
cough
I'M NOT CRYING.
I'M JUST BUMMED YOU TURNED INTO KYO...
HUH?!
OU SAID OU DIDN'T EED HIM OW THAT OU HAVE ME.
LET ME MAKE IT UP TO YOU. DINNER'S ON ME!
WHAAT?
HEY! I FOUND SOMETHING TO BREAK THE LOCK!
You're a little late.

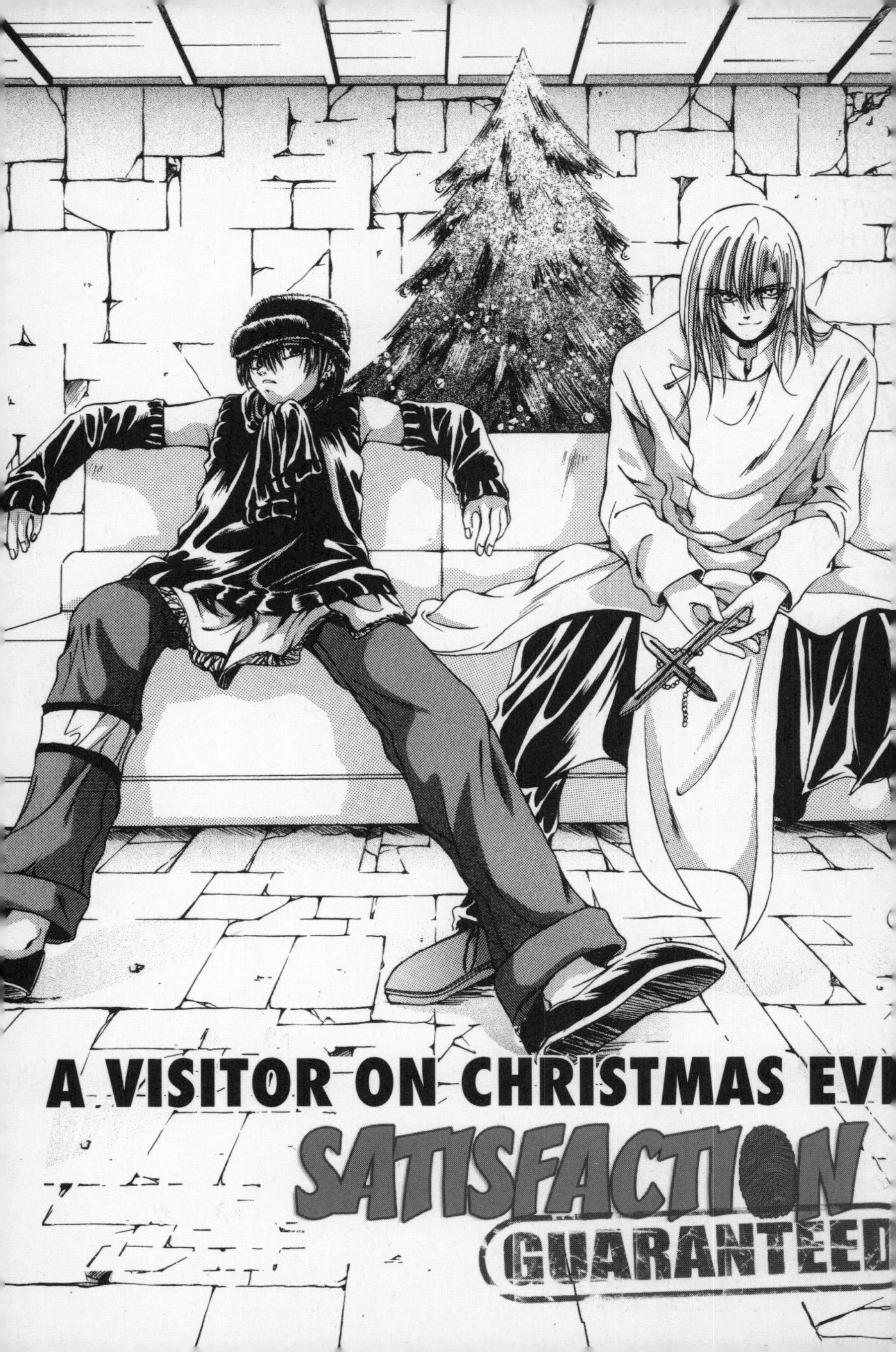
A VISITOR ON CHRISTMAS EV
SATISFACTION
GUARANTEED

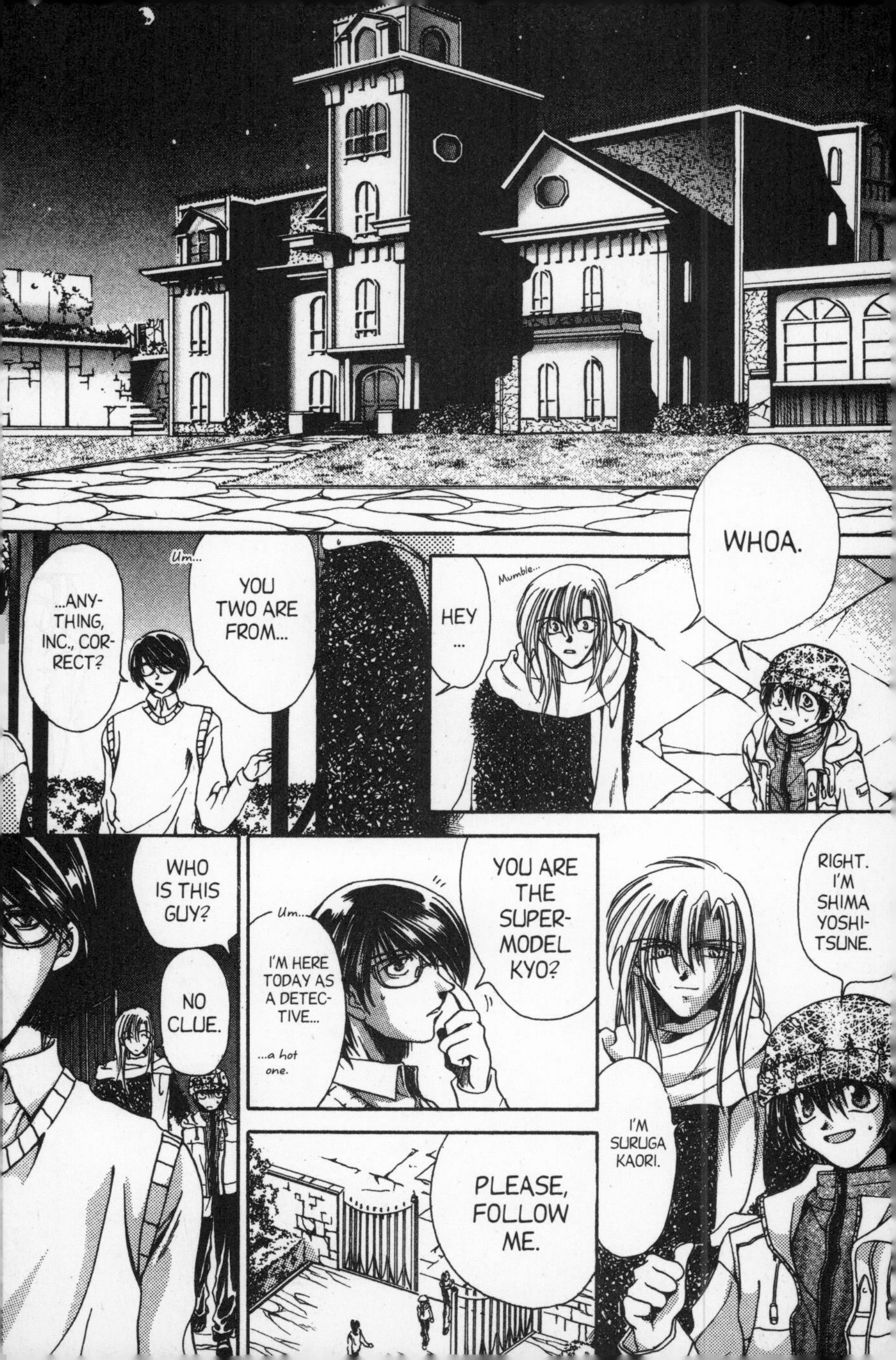
WHOA.
Mumble...
HEY ...
Um...
YOU TWO ARE FROM...
...ANY-THING, INC., COR-RECT?
RIGHT. I'M SHIMA YOSHI-TSUNE.
I'M SURUGA KAORI.
YOU ARE THE SUPER-MODEL KYO?
Um...
I'M HERE TODAY AS A DETEC-TIVE...
...a hot one.
PLEASE, FOLLOW ME.
WHO IS THIS GUY?
NO CLUE.

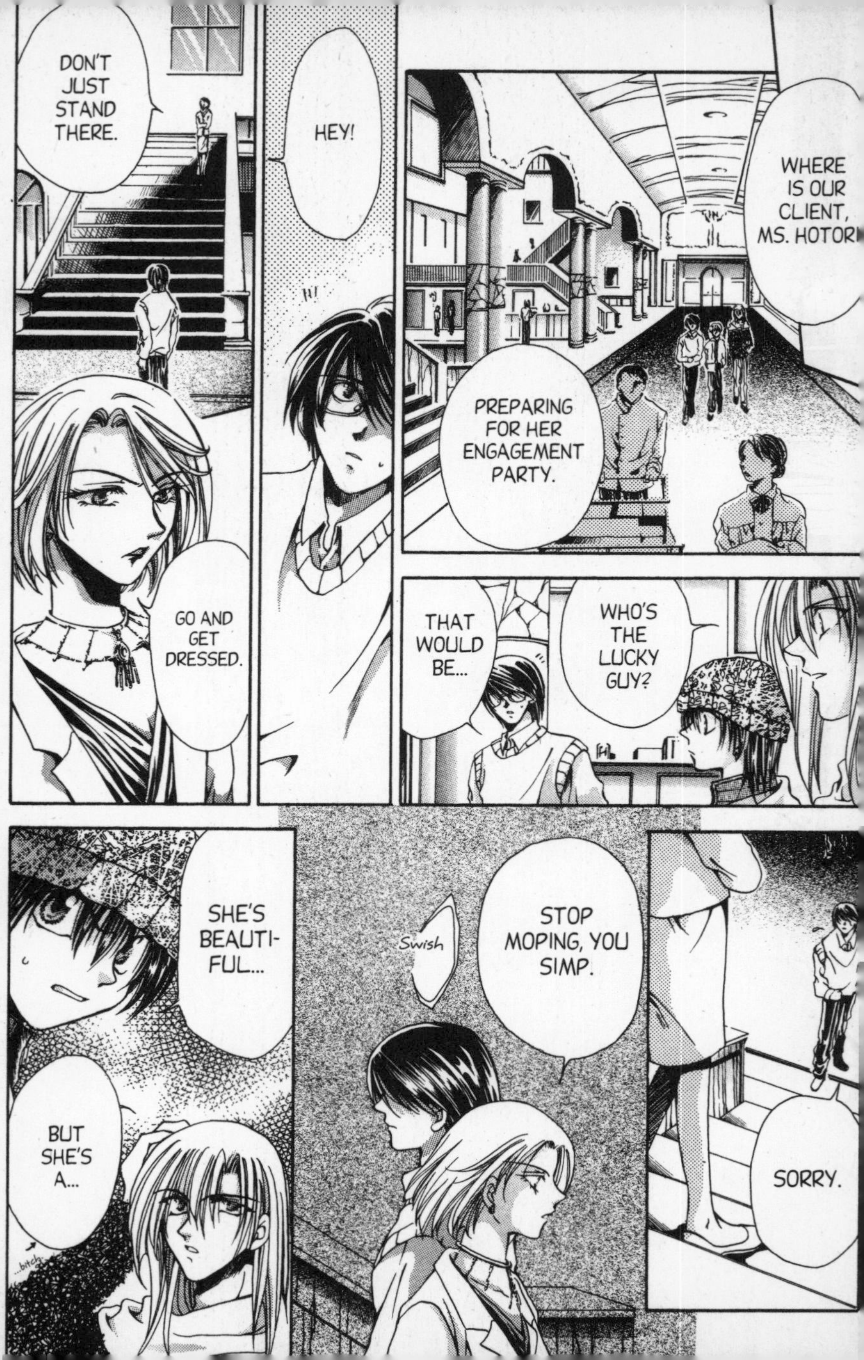
WHERE IS OUR CLIENT, MS. HOTORI
PREPARING FOR HER ENGAGEMENT PARTY.
WHO'S THE LUCKY GUY?
THAT WOULD BE...
HEY!
!!
DON'T JUST STAND THERE.
GO AND GET DRESSED.
SORRY.
STOP MOPING, YOU SIMP.
Swish
SHE'S BEAUTI-FUL...
BUT SHE'S A...
...bitch

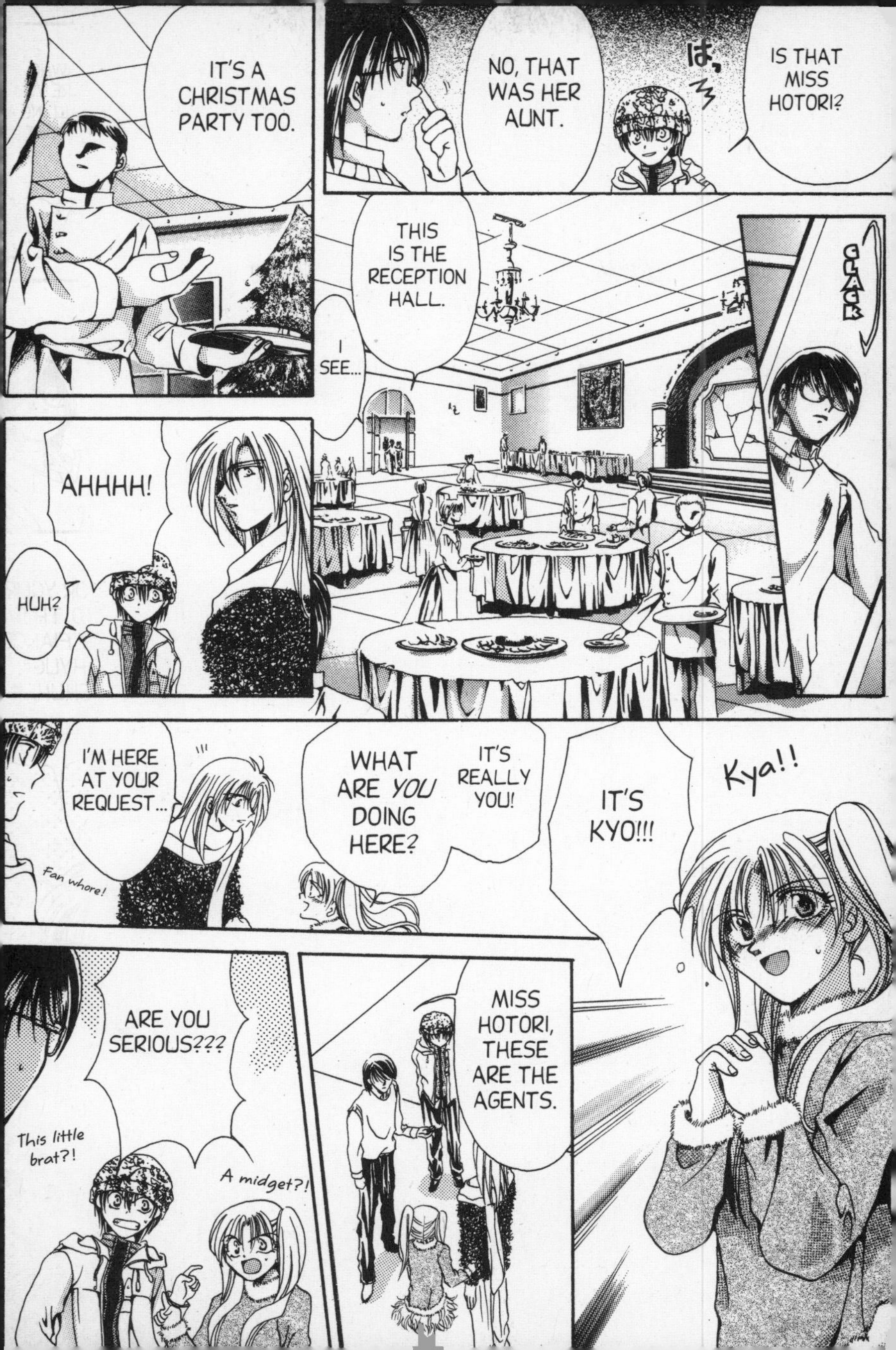

IS THAT MISS HOTORI⁈
は
NO, THAT WAS HER AUNT.
IT'S A CHRISTMAS PARTY TOO.
CLACK
THIS IS THE RECEPTION HALL.
I SEE...
AHHHH!
HUH?
Kya!!
IT'S KYO!!!
IT'S REALLY YOU!
WHAT ARE *YOU* DOING HERE?
I'M HERE AT YOUR REQUEST...
Fan whore!
MISS HOTORI, THESE ARE THE AGENTS.
ARE YOU SERIOUS???
This little brat?!
A midget?!

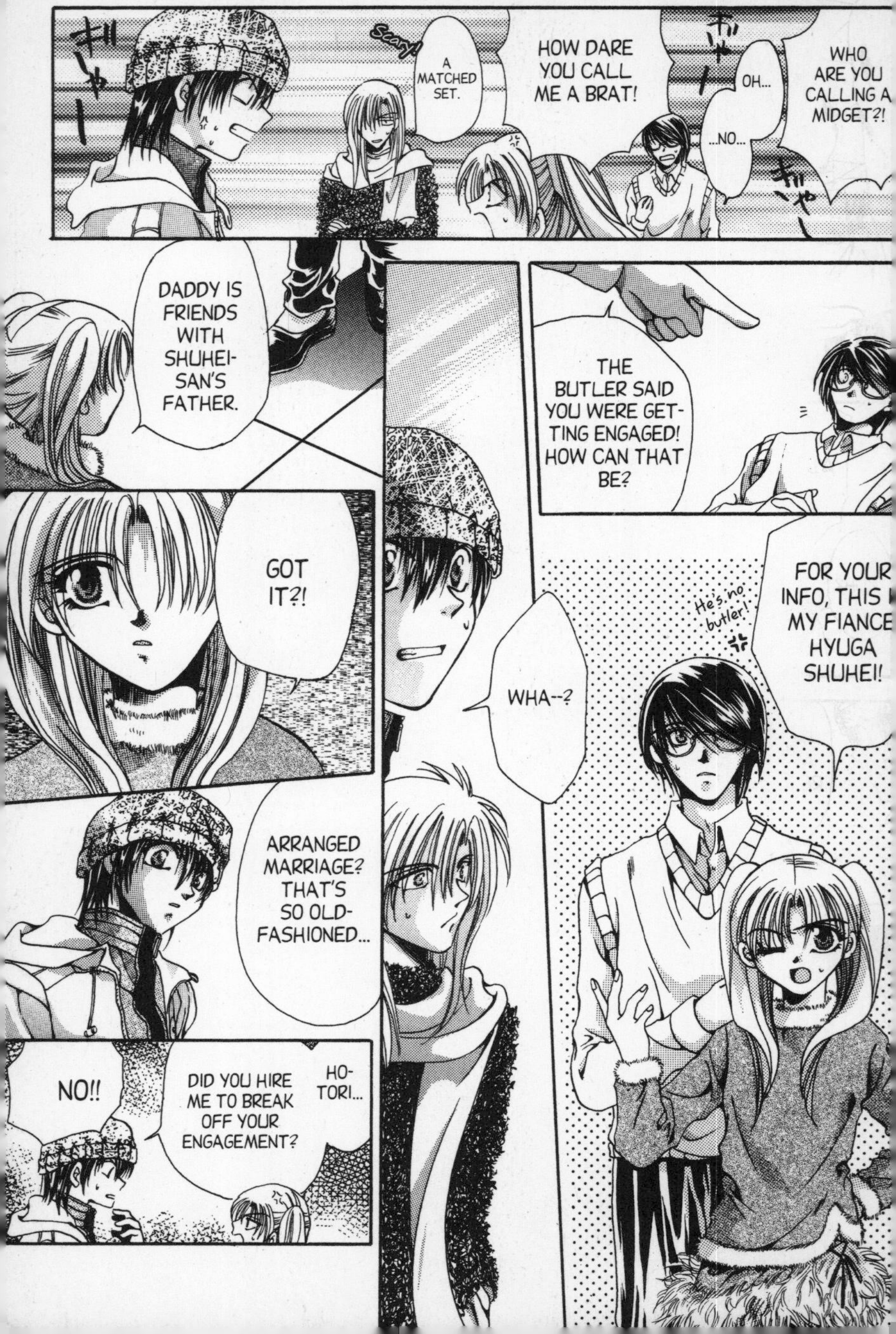
WHO ARE YOU CALLING A MIDGET?!
OH...
...NO...
HOW DARE YOU CALL ME A BRAT!
A MATCHED SET.
Scary!
THE BUTLER SAID YOU WERE GETTING ENGAGED! HOW CAN THAT BE?
FOR YOUR INFO, THIS I MY FIANCE HYUGA SHUHEI!
He's no butler!
WHA--?
DADDY IS FRIENDS WITH SHUHEI-SAN'S FATHER.
GOT IT?!
ARRANGED MARRIAGE? THAT'S SO OLD-FASHIONED...
HO-TORI...
DID YOU HIRE ME TO BREAK OFF YOUR ENGAGEMENT?
NO!!

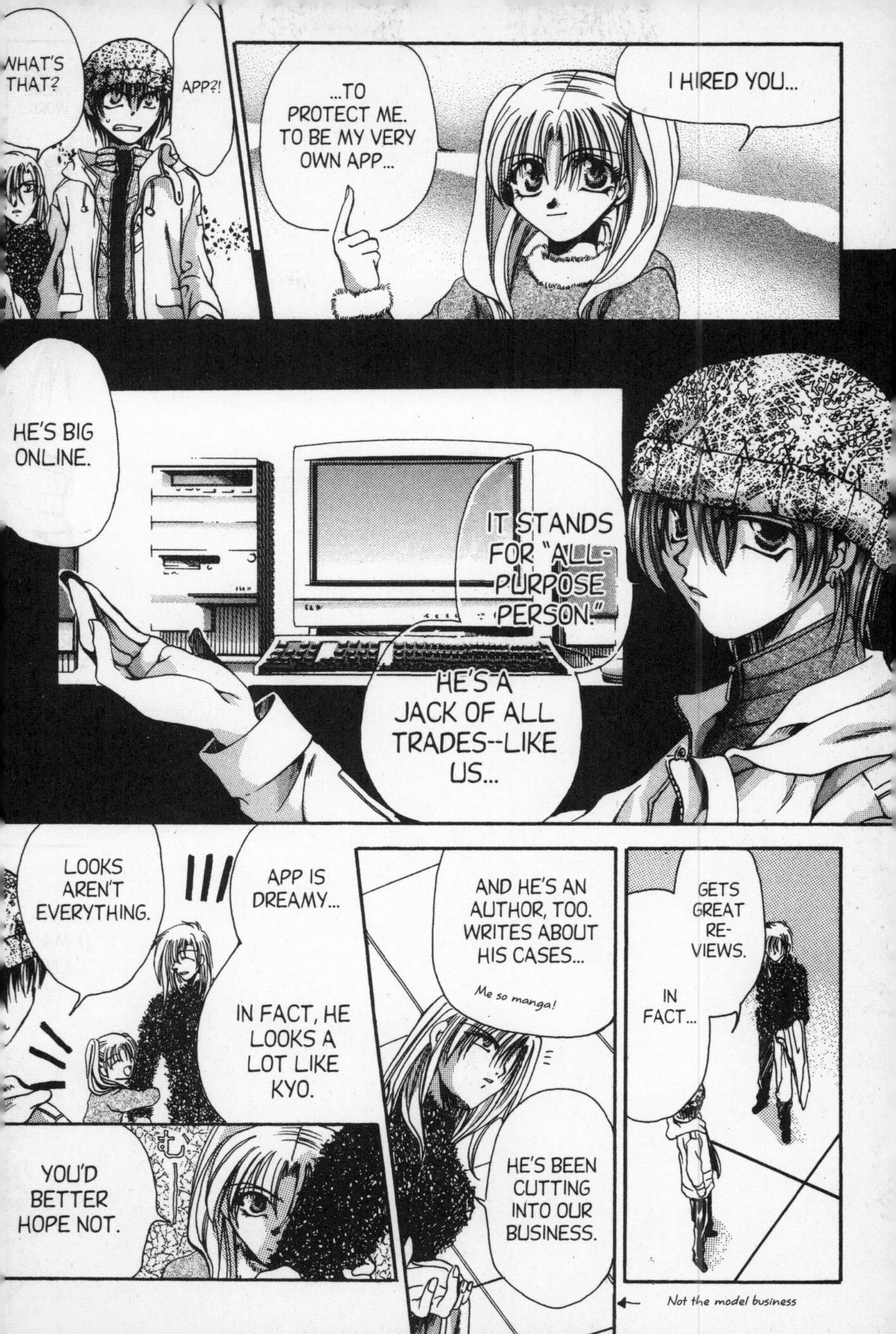
I HIRED YOU...
...TO PROTECT ME. TO BE MY VERY OWN APP...
APP?!
WHAT'S THAT?
IT STANDS FOR "ALL-PURPOSE PERSON."
HE'S A JACK OF ALL TRADES--LIKE US...
HE'S BIG ONLINE.
GETS GREAT RE-VIEWS.
IN FACT...
AND HE'S AN AUTHOR, TOO. WRITES ABOUT HIS CASES...
Me so manga!
HE'S BEEN CUTTING INTO OUR BUSINESS.
APP IS DREAMY...
LOOKS AREN'T EVERYTHING.
IN FACT, HE LOOKS A LOT LIKE KYO.
YOU'D BETTER HOPE NOT.

Not the model business

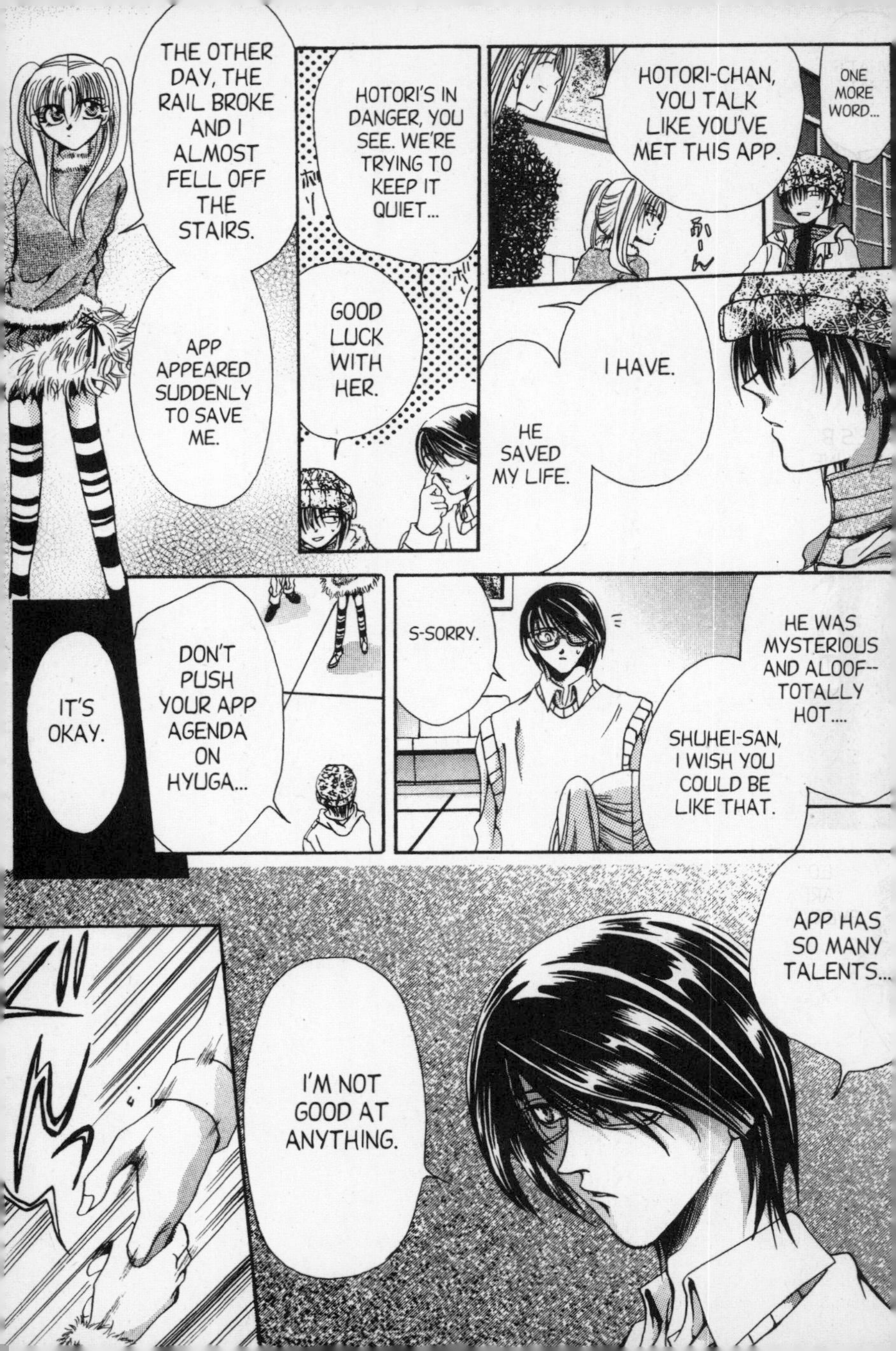
ONE MORE WORD...
HOTORI-CHAN, YOU TALK LIKE YOU'VE MET THIS APP.
I HAVE.
HE SAVED MY LIFE.
HOTORI'S IN DANGER, YOU SEE. WE'RE TRYING TO KEEP IT QUIET...
GOOD LUCK WITH HER.
THE OTHER DAY, THE RAIL BROKE AND I ALMOST FELL OFF THE STAIRS.
APP APPEARED SUDDENLY TO SAVE ME.
HE WAS MYSTERIOUS AND ALOOF-- TOTALLY HOT....
SHUHEI-SAN, I WISH YOU COULD BE LIKE THAT.
S-SORRY.
DON'T PUSH YOUR APP AGENDA ON HYUGA...
IT'S OKAY.
APP HAS SO MANY TALENTS...
I'M NOT GOOD AT ANYTHING.

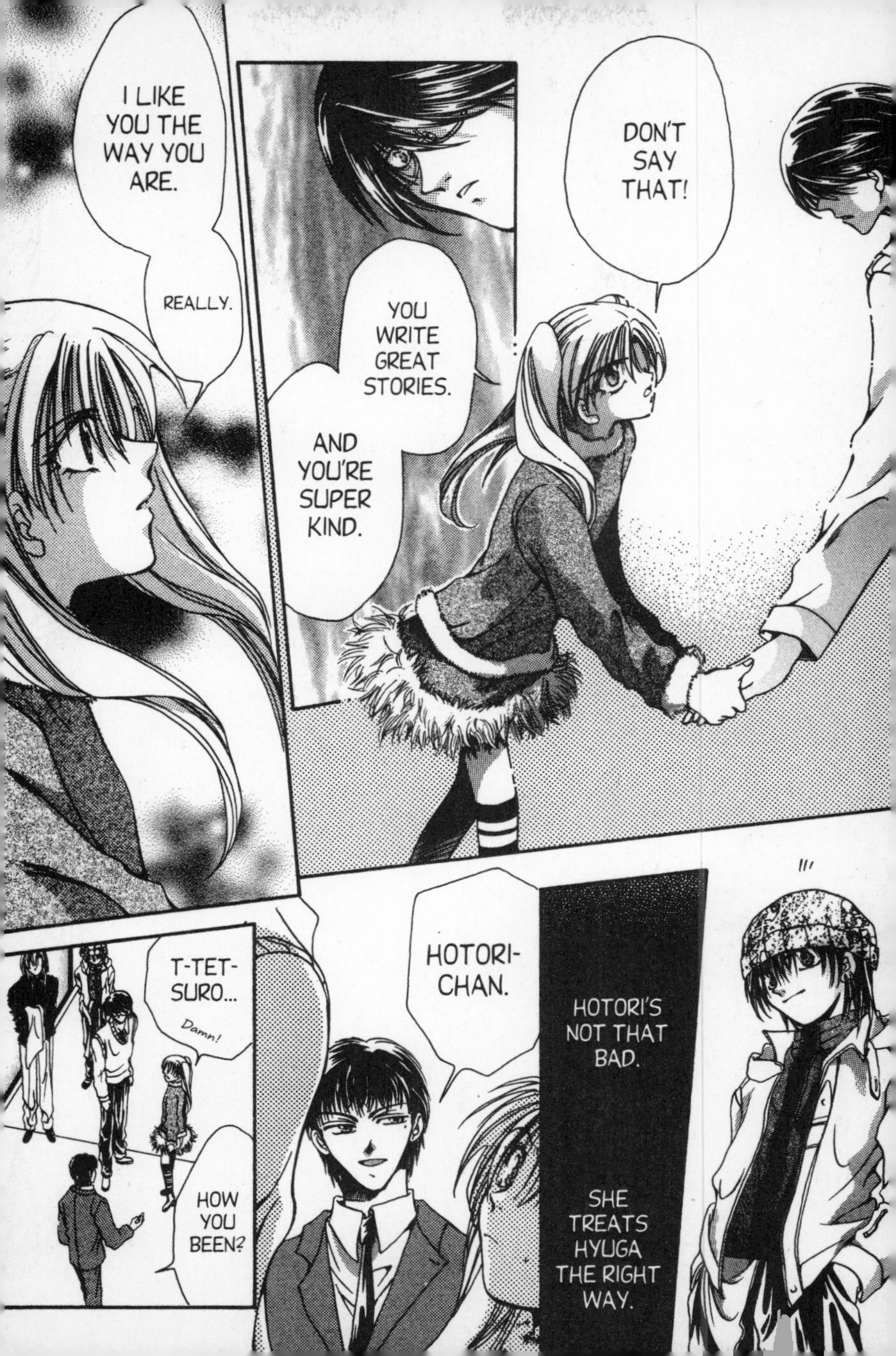
DON'T SAY THAT!
YOU WRITE GREAT STORIES.
AND YOU'RE SUPER KIND.
I LIKE YOU THE WAY YOU ARE.
REALLY.
HOTORI'S NOT THAT BAD.
SHE TREATS HYUGA THE RIGHT WAY.
HOTORI-CHAN.
T-TET-SURO...
Damn!
HOW YOU BEEN?

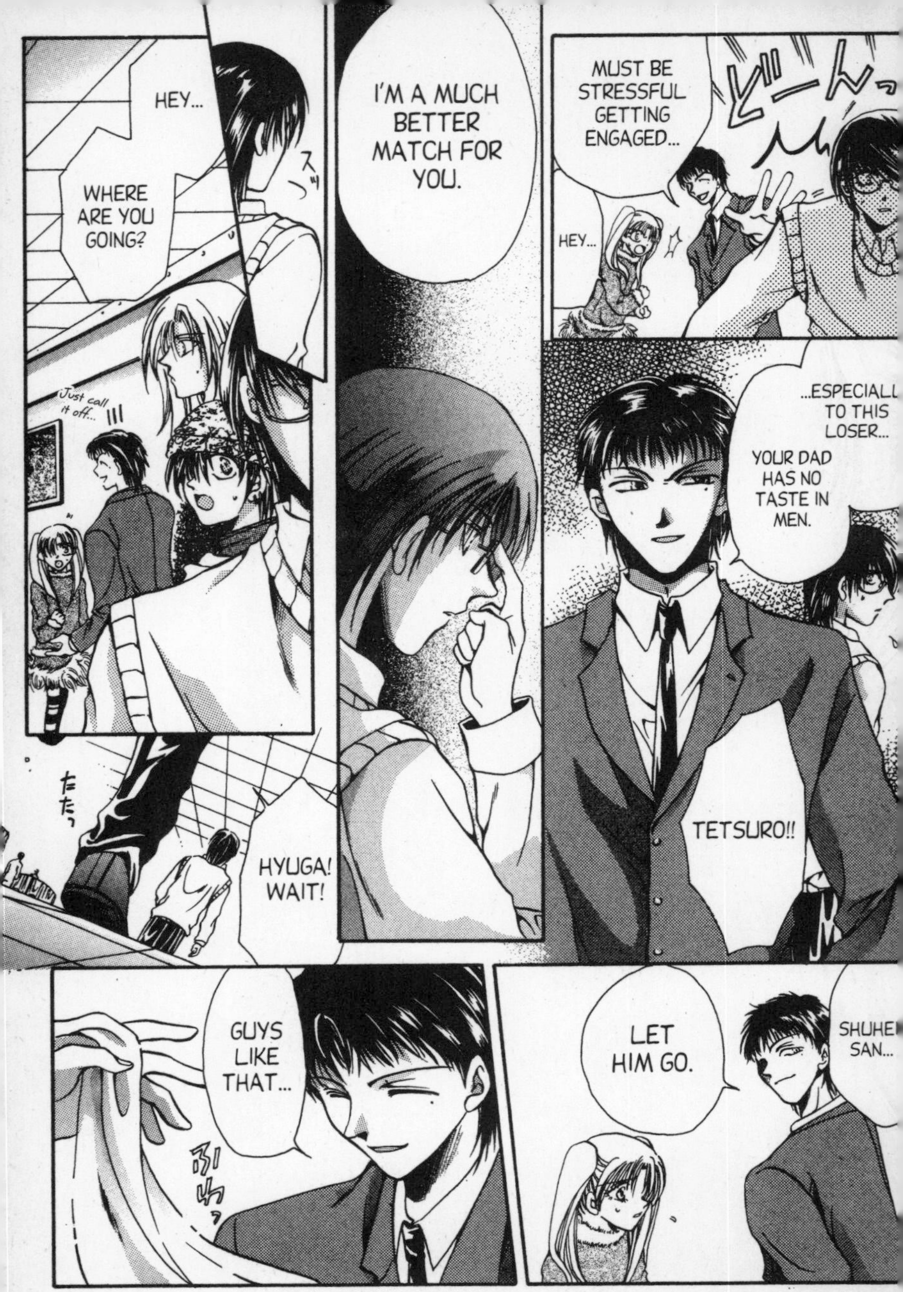

どーんっ
MUST BE STRESSFUL GETTING ENGAGED...
HEY...
...ESPECIALL TO THIS LOSER...
YOUR DAD HAS NO TASTE IN MEN.
TETSURO!!
I'M A MUCH BETTER MATCH FOR YOU.
HEY...
WHERE ARE YOU GOING?
Just call it off...
HYUGA! WAIT!
SHUHE SAN...
LET HIM GO.
GUYS LIKE THAT...

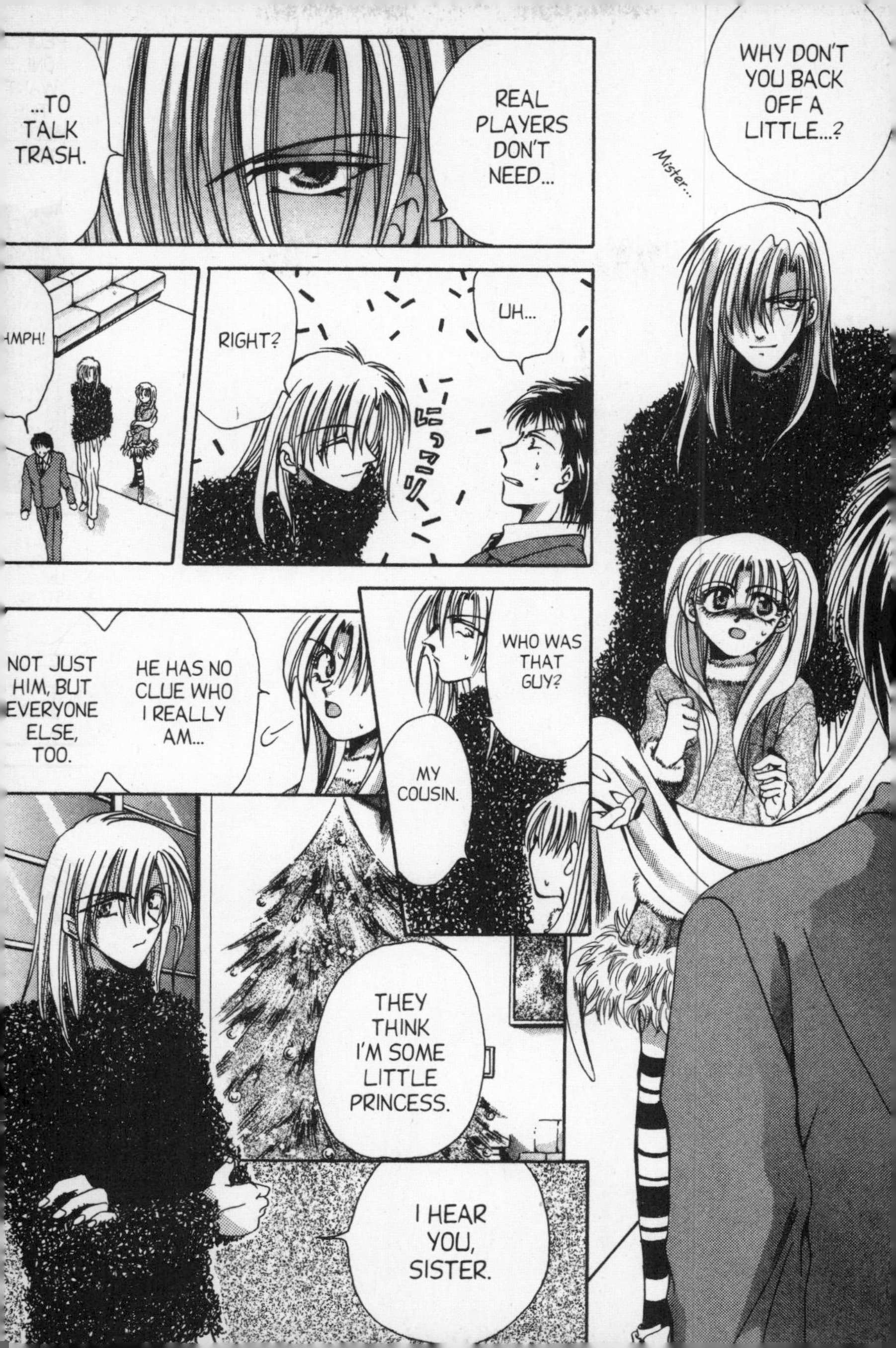
WHY DON'T YOU BACK OFF A LITTLE...?
Mister...
REAL PLAYERS DON'T NEED...
...TO TALK TRASH.
UH...
RIGHT?
HMPH!
WHO WAS THAT GUY?
MY COUSIN.
HE HAS NO CLUE WHO I REALLY AM...
NOT JUST HIM, BUT EVERYONE ELSE, TOO.
THEY THINK I'M SOME LITTLE PRINCESS.
I HEAR YOU, SISTER.

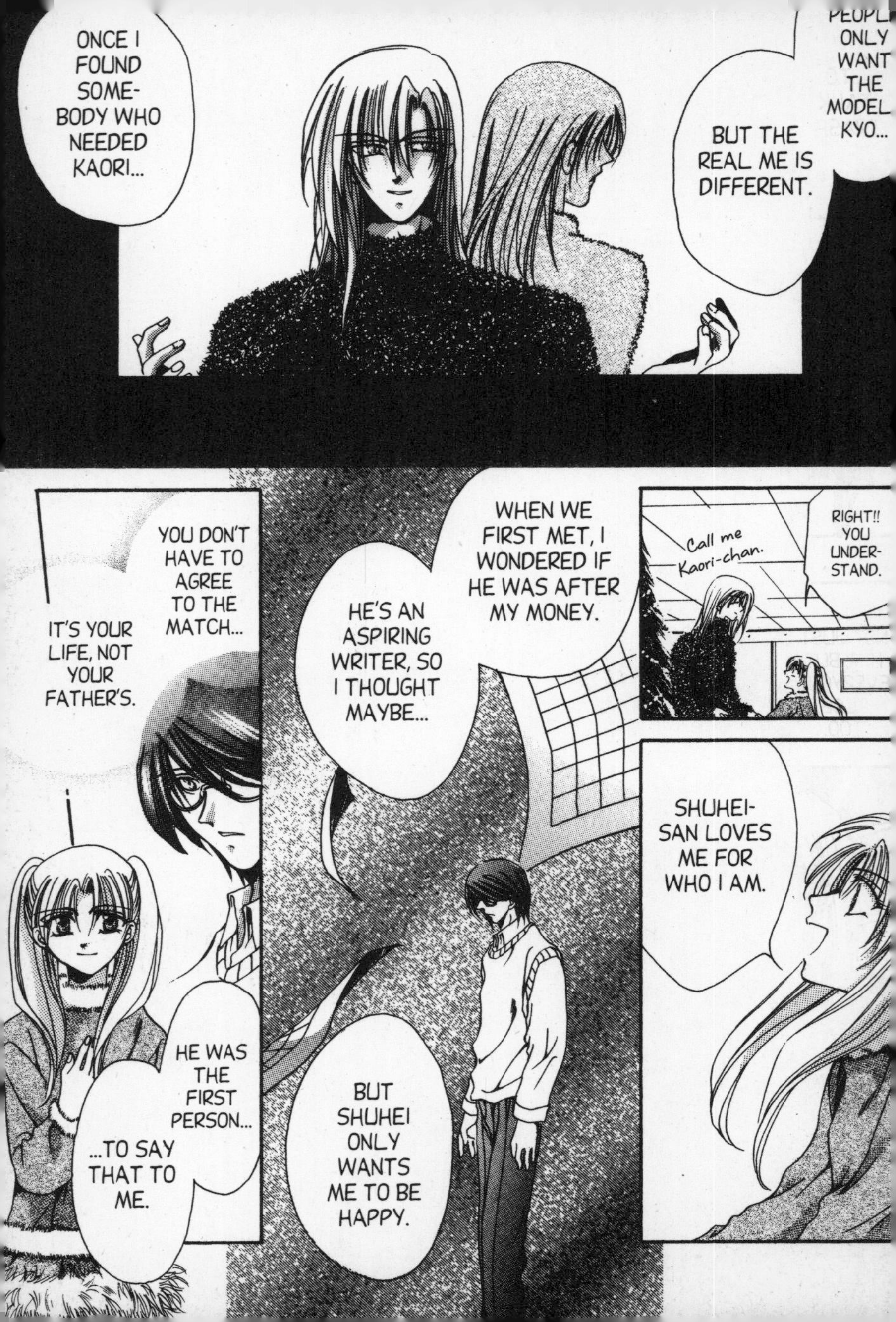
PEOPL ONLY WANT THE MODEL KYO...
BUT THE REAL ME IS DIFFERENT.
ONCE I FOUND SOME-BODY WHO NEEDED KAORI...
RIGHT!! YOU UNDER-STAND.
Call me Kaori-chan.
WHEN WE FIRST MET, I WONDERED IF HE WAS AFTER MY MONEY.
HE'S AN ASPIRING WRITER, SO I THOUGHT MAYBE...
SHUHEI-SAN LOVES ME FOR WHO I AM.
BUT SHUHEI ONLY WANTS ME TO BE HAPPY.
YOU DON'T HAVE TO AGREE TO THE MATCH...
IT'S YOUR LIFE, NOT YOUR FATHER'S.
HE WAS THE FIRST PERSON...
...TO SAY THAT TO ME.

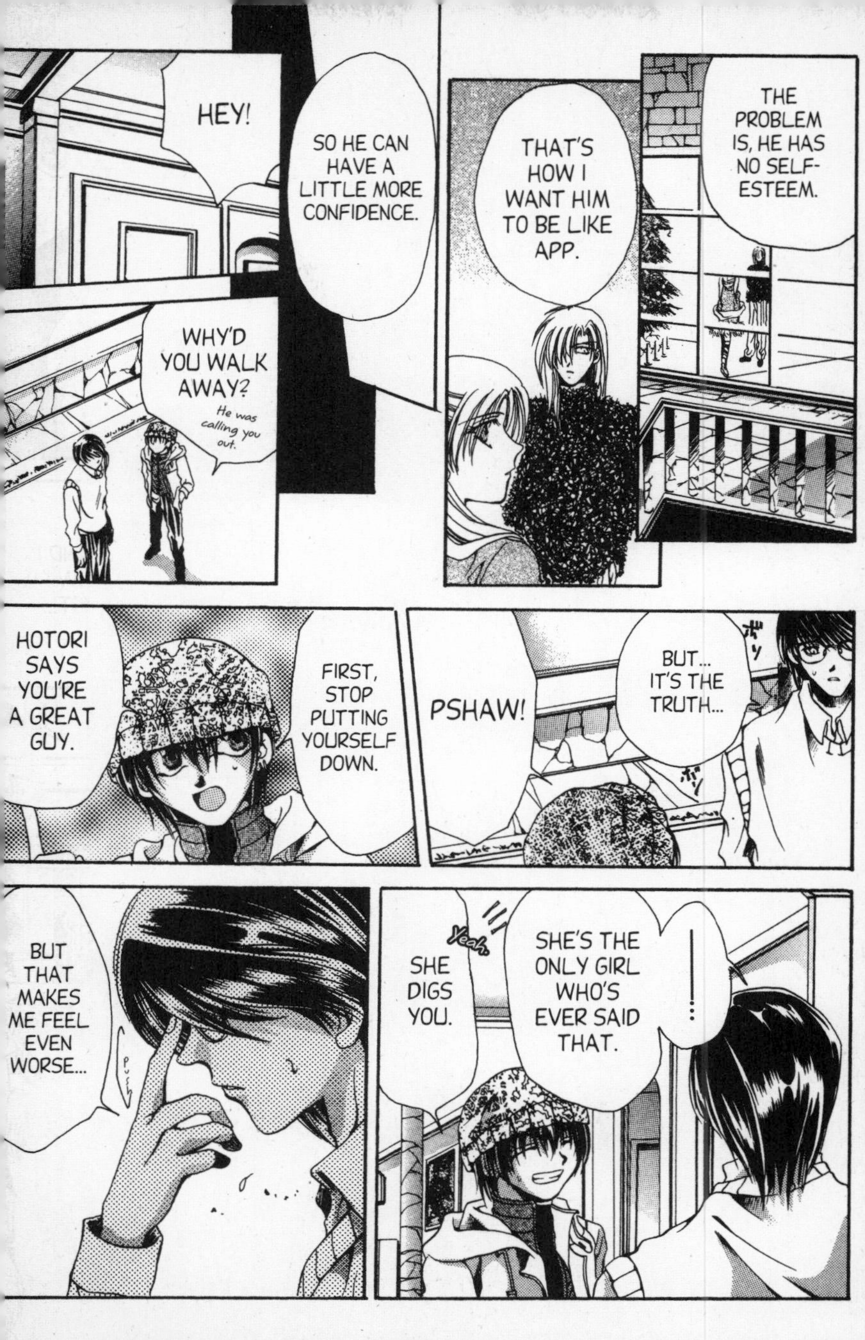
THE PROBLEM IS, HE HAS NO SELF-ESTEEM.
THAT'S HOW I WANT HIM TO BE LIKE APP.
SO HE CAN HAVE A LITTLE MORE CONFIDENCE.
HEY!
WHY'D YOU WALK AWAY?
He was calling you out.
BUT... IT'S THE TRUTH...
PSHAW!
FIRST, STOP PUTTING YOURSELF DOWN.
HOTORI SAYS YOU'RE A GREAT GUY.
......
SHE'S THE ONLY GIRL WHO'S EVER SAID THAT.
Yeah.
SHE DIGS YOU.
BUT THAT MAKES ME FEEL EVEN WORSE...

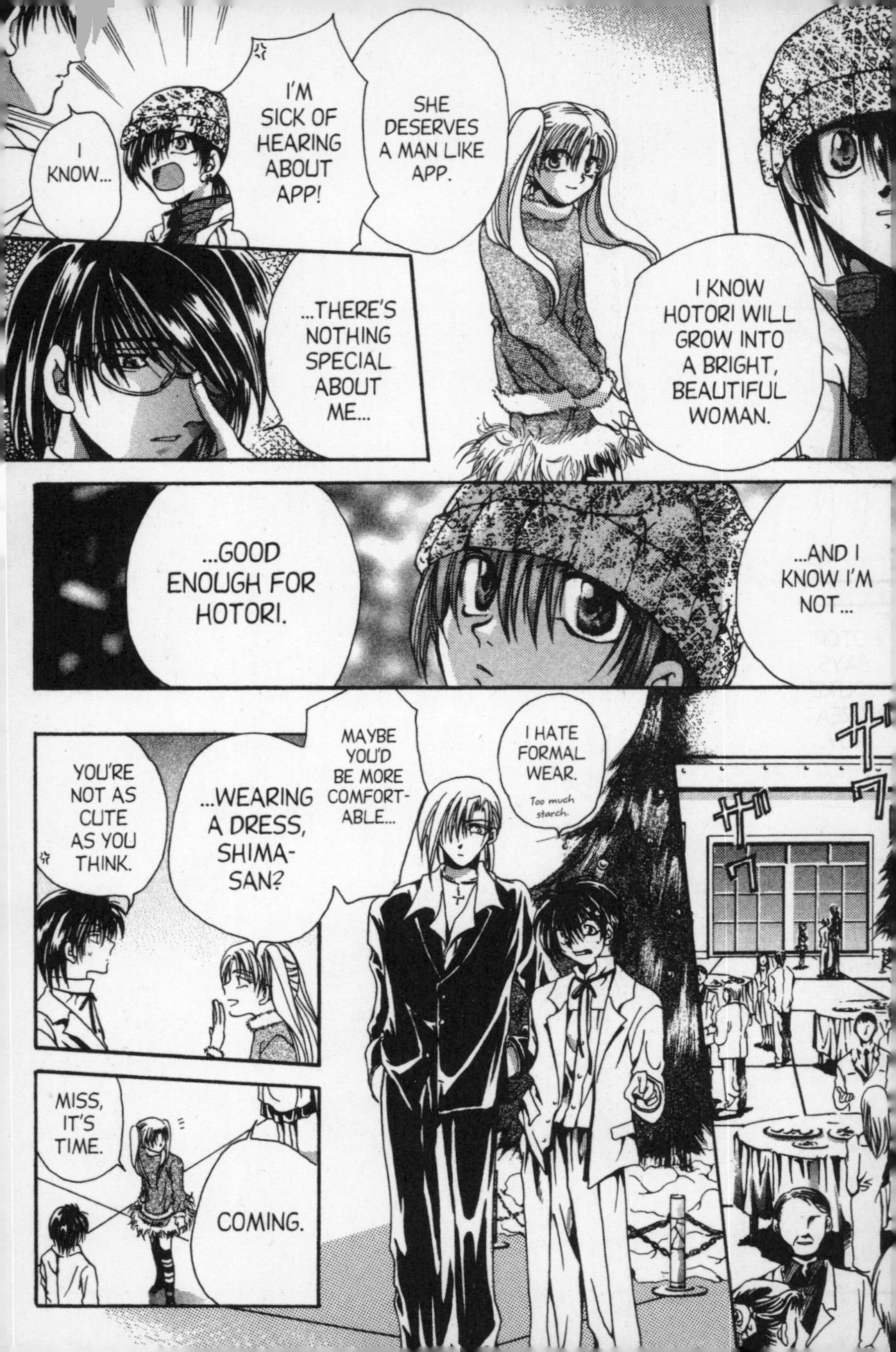
I KNOW HOTORI WILL GROW INTO A BRIGHT, BEAUTIFUL WOMAN.
SHE DESERVES A MAN LIKE APP.
I'M SICK OF HEARING ABOUT APP!
I KNOW...
...THERE'S NOTHING SPECIAL ABOUT ME...
...AND I KNOW I'M NOT...
...GOOD ENOUGH FOR HOTORI.
I HATE FORMAL WEAR.
Too much starch.
MAYBE YOU'D BE MORE COMFORT-ABLE...
...WEARING A DRESS, SHIMA-SAN?
YOU'RE NOT AS CUTE AS YOU THINK.
MISS, IT'S TIME.
COMING.

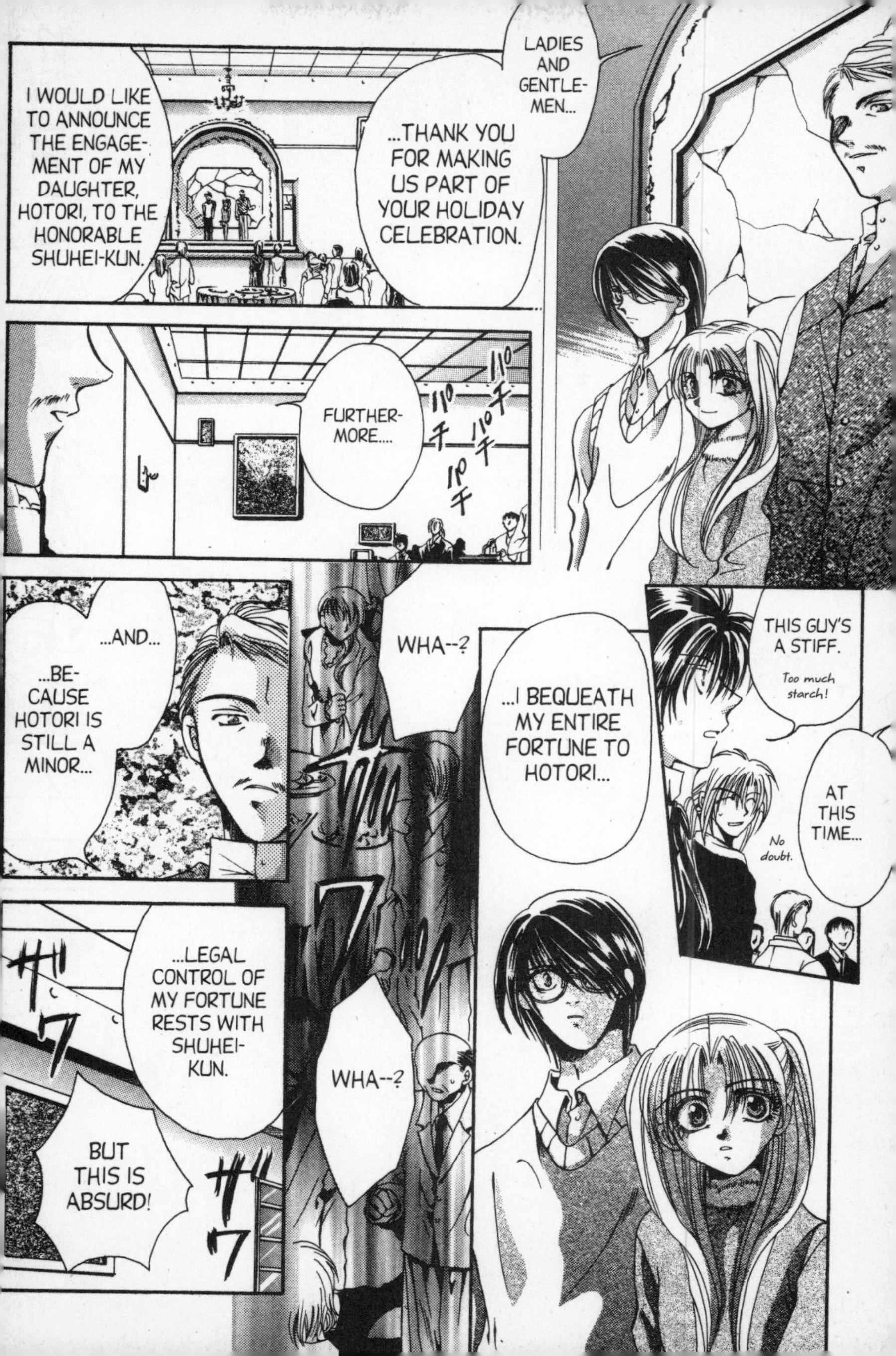

LADIES AND GENTLEMEN...
...THANK YOU FOR MAKING US PART OF YOUR HOLIDAY CELEBRATION.
I WOULD LIKE TO ANNOUNCE THE ENGAGEMENT OF MY DAUGHTER, HOTORI, TO THE HONORABLE SHUHEI-KUN.
パチ
パチ
パチ
パチ
FURTHERMORE....
THIS GUY'S A STIFF.
Too much starch!
AT THIS TIME...
No doubt.
...I BEQUEATH MY ENTIRE FORTUNE TO HOTORI...
WHA--?
...AND...
...BECAUSE HOTORI IS STILL A MINOR...
WHA--?
...LEGAL CONTROL OF MY FORTUNE RESTS WITH SHUHEI-KUN.
ザワ
ザワ
BUT THIS IS ABSURD!

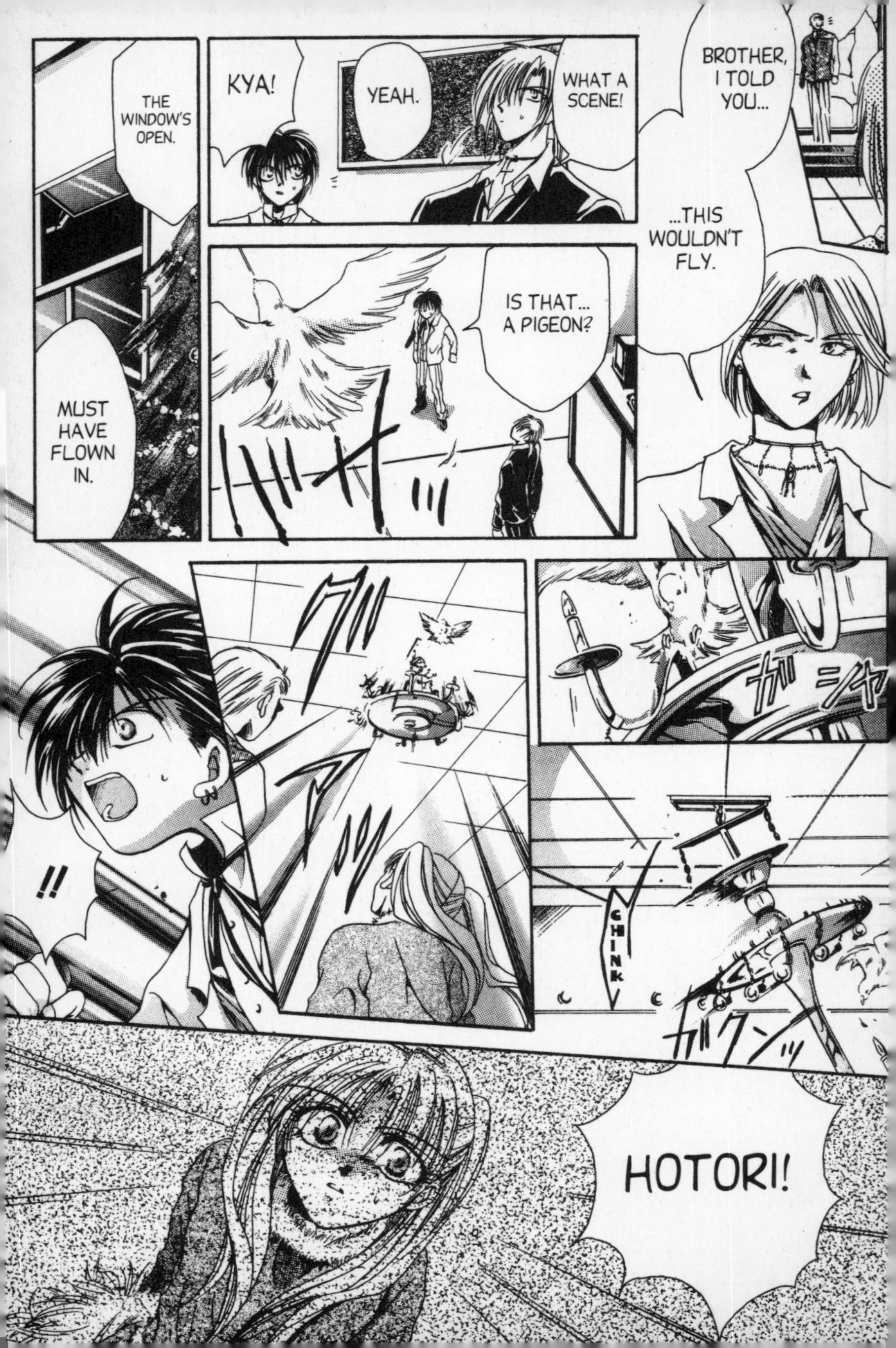
BROTHER, I TOLD YOU...
...THIS WOULDN'T FLY.
WHAT A SCENE!
YEAH.
KYA!
IS THAT... A PIGEON?
THE WINDOW'S OPEN.
MUST HAVE FLOWN IN.
CHINK
!!
HOTORI!

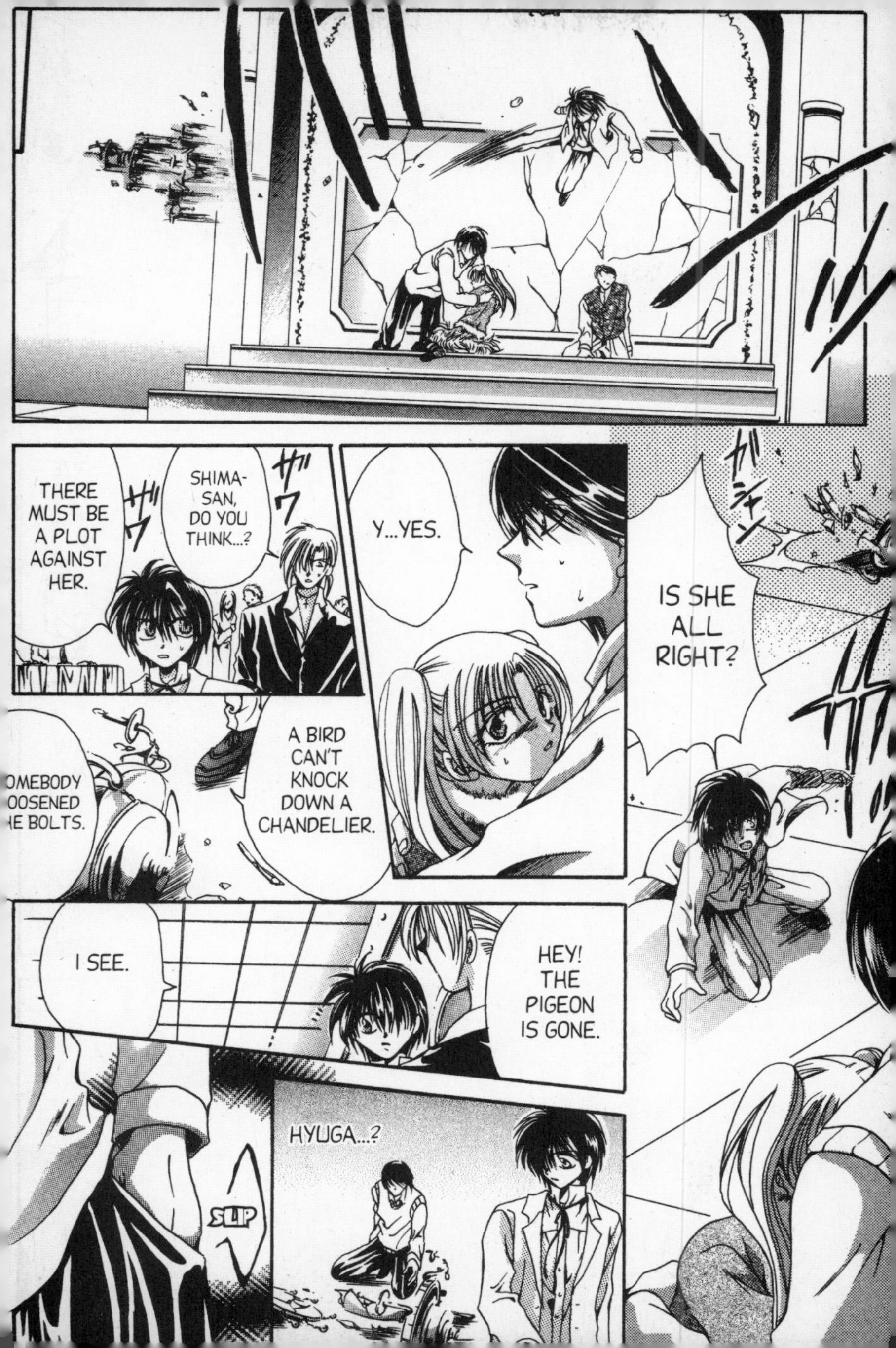

ガシャン
IS SHE ALL RIGHT?
Y...YES.
ザワ
SHIMA-SAN, DO YOU THINK...?
ザワ
THERE MUST BE A PLOT AGAINST HER.
A BIRD CAN'T KNOCK DOWN A CHANDELIER.
OMEBODY OOSENED HE BOLTS.
HEY! THE PIGEON IS GONE.
I SEE.
HYUGA...?
SLIP

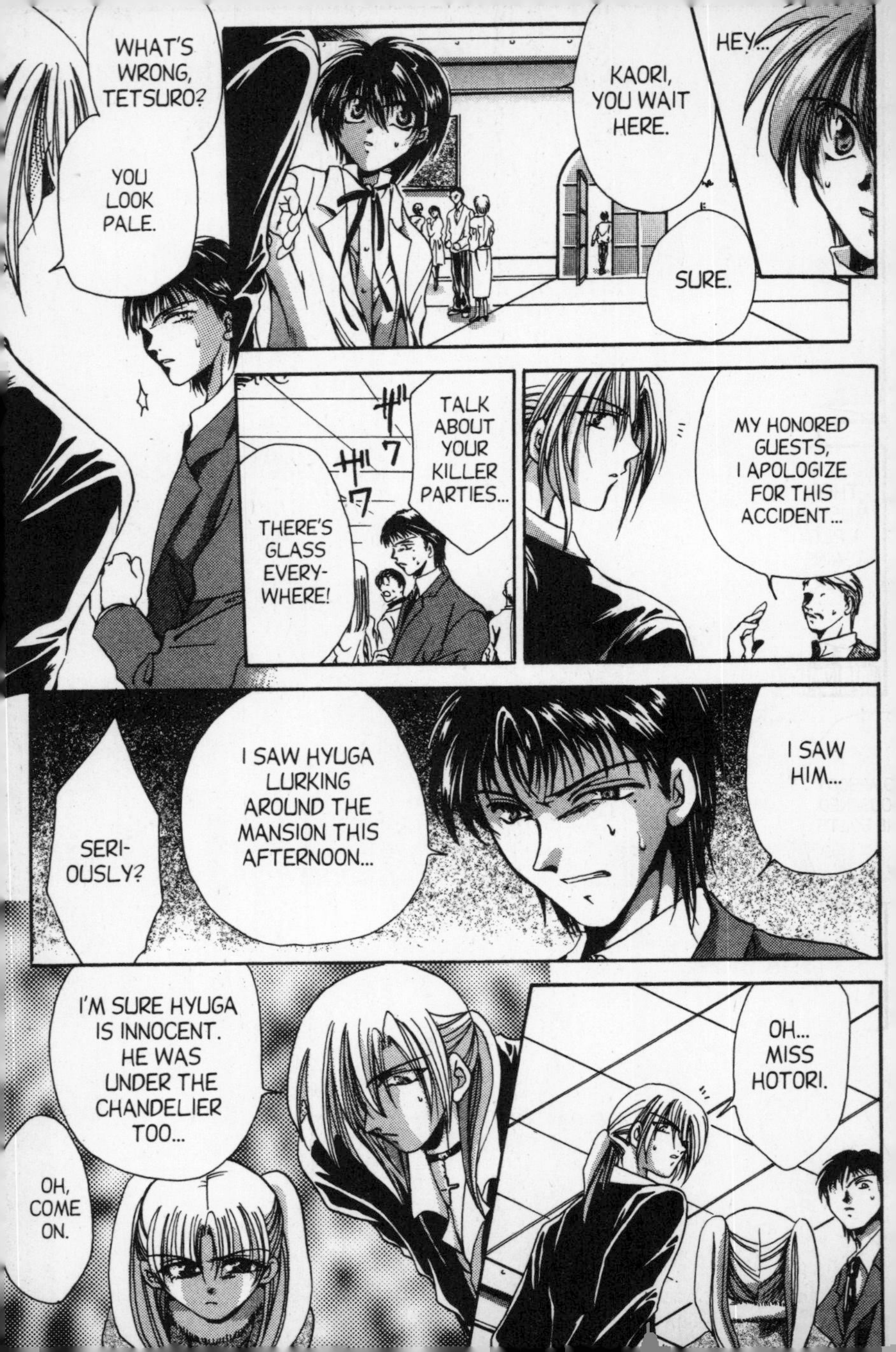
HEY...
KAORI, YOU WAIT HERE.
SURE.
WHAT'S WRONG, TETSURO?
YOU LOOK PALE.
MY HONORED GUESTS, I APOLOGIZE FOR THIS ACCIDENT...
TALK ABOUT YOUR KILLER PARTIES...
ザワ
ザワ
THERE'S GLASS EVERY-WHERE!
I SAW HIM...
I SAW HYUGA LURKING AROUND THE MANSION THIS AFTERNOON...
SERI-OUSLY?
OH... MISS HOTORI.
I'M SURE HYUGA IS INNOCENT. HE WAS UNDER THE CHANDELIER TOO...
OH, COME ON.

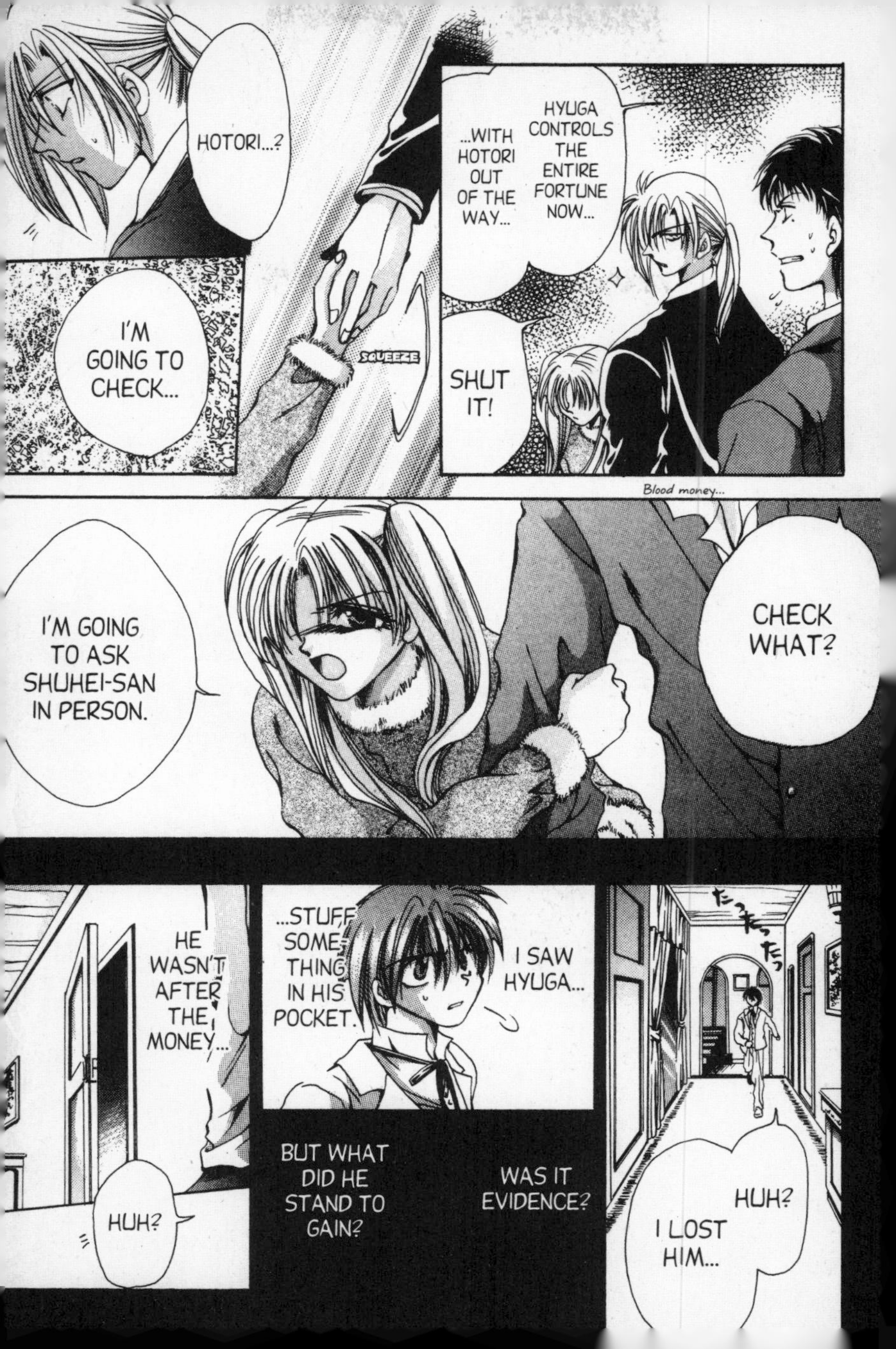

...WITH HOTORI OUT OF THE WAY... HYUGA CONTROLS THE ENTIRE FORTUNE NOW...
SHUT IT!
Blood money...
HOTORI...?
I'M GOING TO CHECK...
SQUEEZE
CHECK WHAT?
I'M GOING TO ASK SHUHEI-SAN IN PERSON.
HUH?
I LOST HIM...
I SAW HYUGA...
...STUFF SOMETHING IN HIS POCKET.
WAS IT EVIDENCE?
BUT WHAT DID HE STAND TO GAIN?
HE WASN'T AFTER THE MONEY...
HUH?

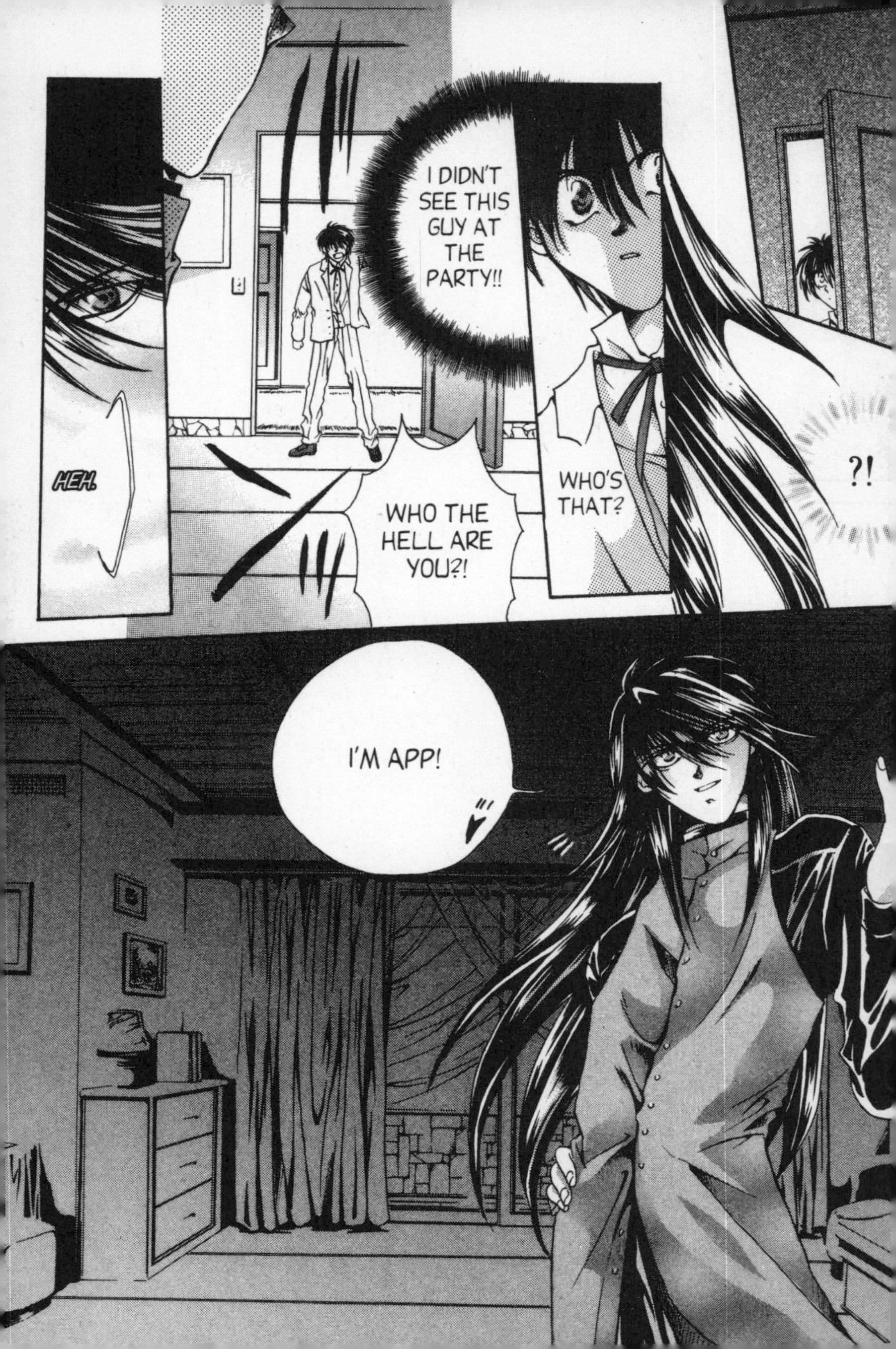
?!
WHO'S THAT?
I DIDN'T SEE THIS GUY AT THE PARTY!!
WHO THE HELL ARE YOU?!
HEH.
I'M APP!

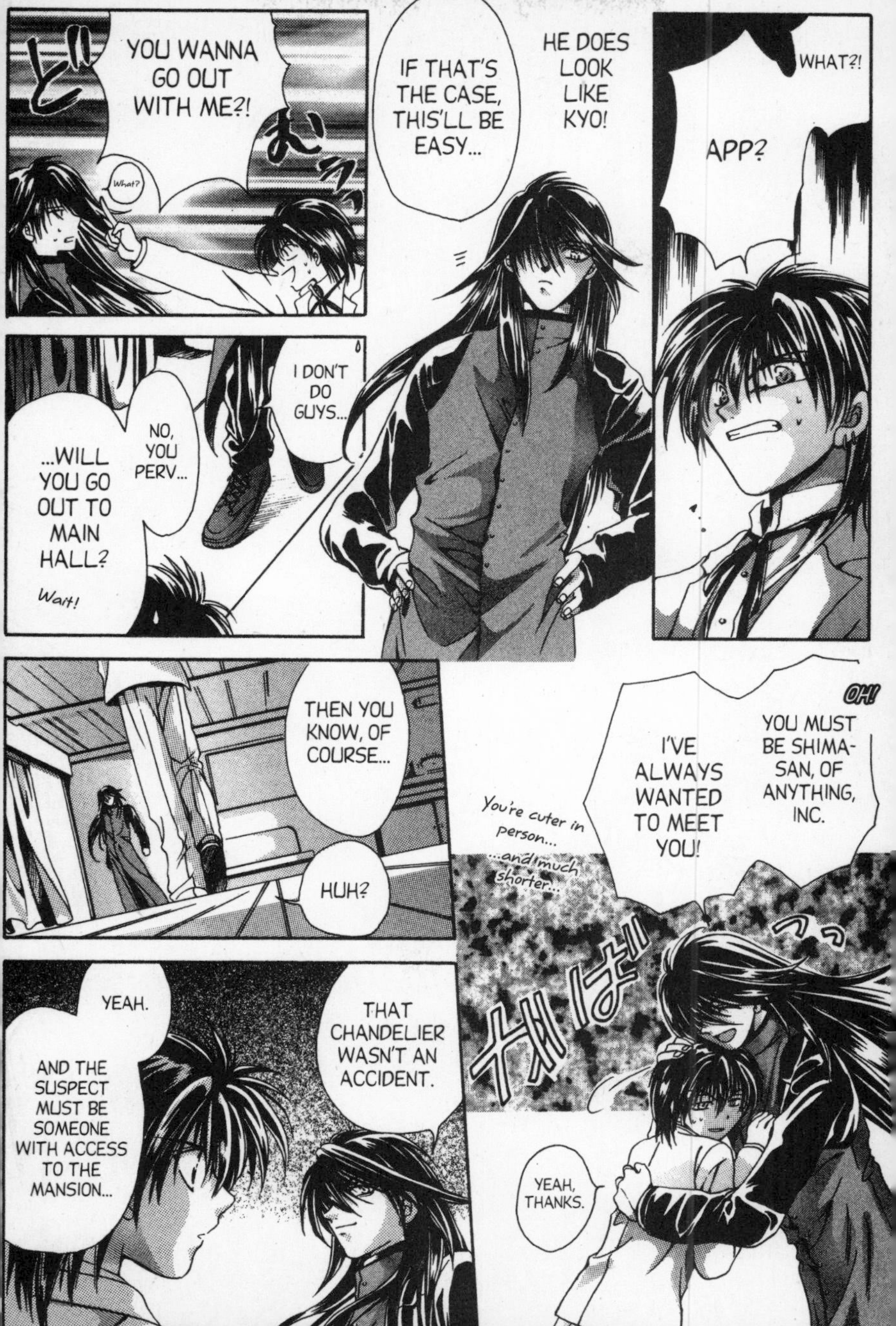
WHAT?!
APP?
HE DOES LOOK LIKE KYO!
IF THAT'S THE CASE, THIS'LL BE EASY...
YOU WANNA GO OUT WITH ME?!
What?
I DON'T DO GUYS...
NO, YOU PERV...
...WILL YOU GO OUT TO MAIN HALL?
Wait!
OH!
YOU MUST BE SHIMA-SAN, OF ANYTHING, INC.
I'VE ALWAYS WANTED TO MEET YOU!
You're cuter in person...
...and much shorter...
YEAH, THANKS.
THEN YOU KNOW, OF COURSE...
HUH?
THAT CHANDELIER WASN'T AN ACCIDENT.
YEAH.
AND THE SUSPECT MUST BE SOMEONE WITH ACCESS TO THE MANSION...

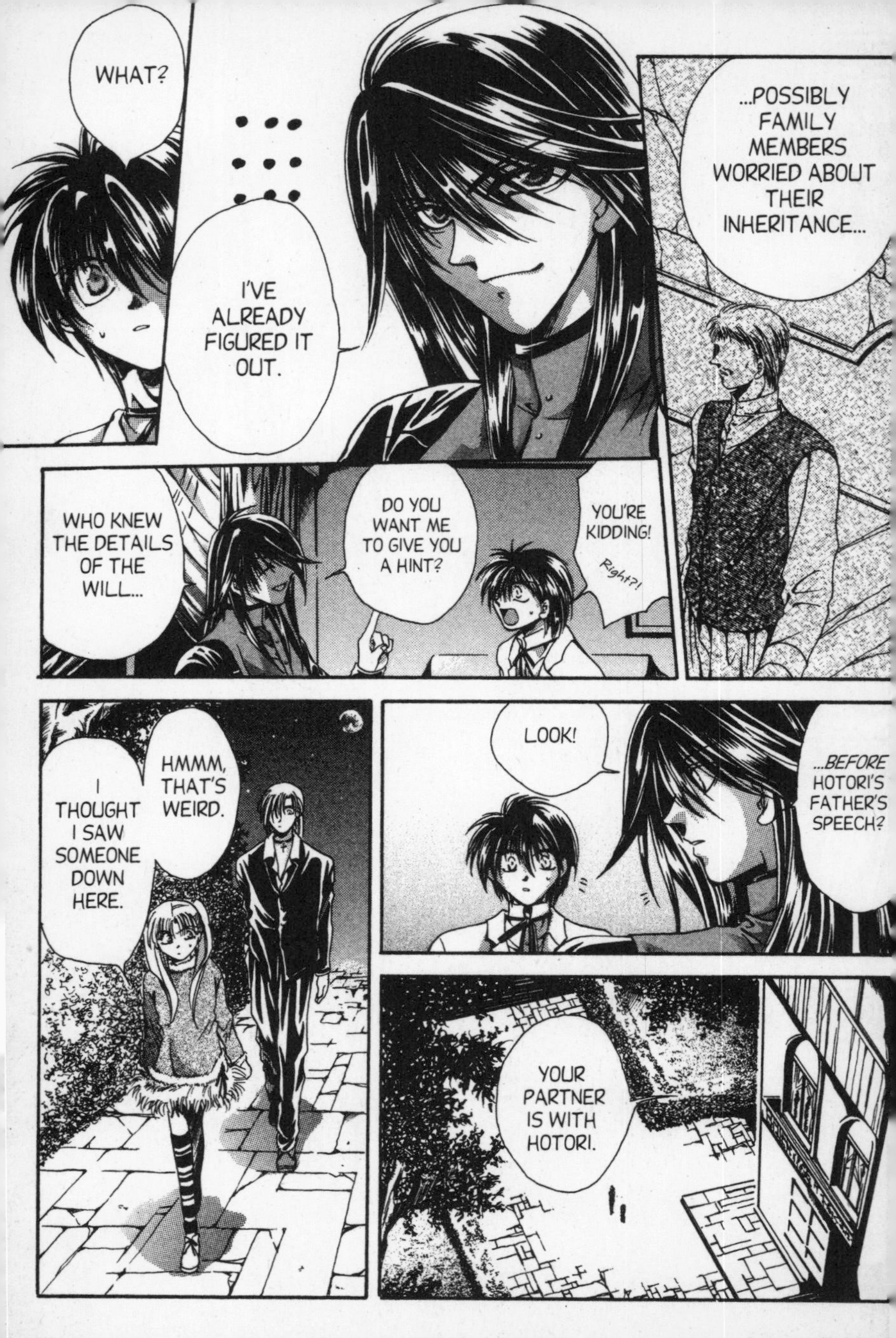
...POSSIBLY FAMILY MEMBERS WORRIED ABOUT THEIR INHERITANCE...
...
I'VE ALREADY FIGURED IT OUT.
WHAT?
YOU'RE KIDDING! Right?!
DO YOU WANT ME TO GIVE YOU A HINT?
WHO KNEW THE DETAILS OF THE WILL...
...*BEFORE* HOTORI'S FATHER'S SPEECH?
LOOK!
YOUR PARTNER IS WITH HOTORI.
HMMM, THAT'S WEIRD.
I THOUGHT I SAW SOMEONE DOWN HERE.

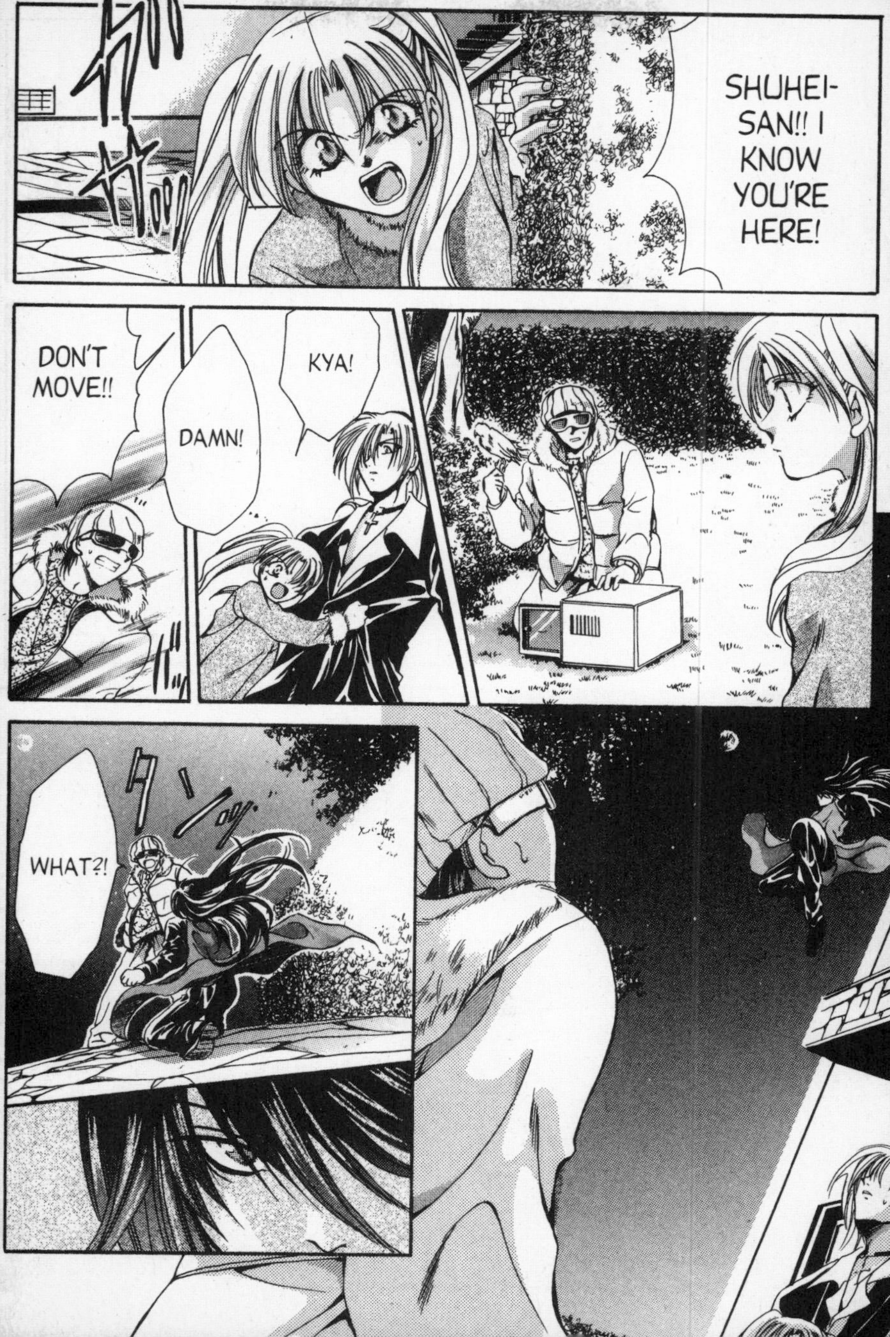
SHUHEI-SAN!! I KNOW YOU'RE HERE!
KYA!
DAMN!
DON'T MOVE!!
WHAT?!

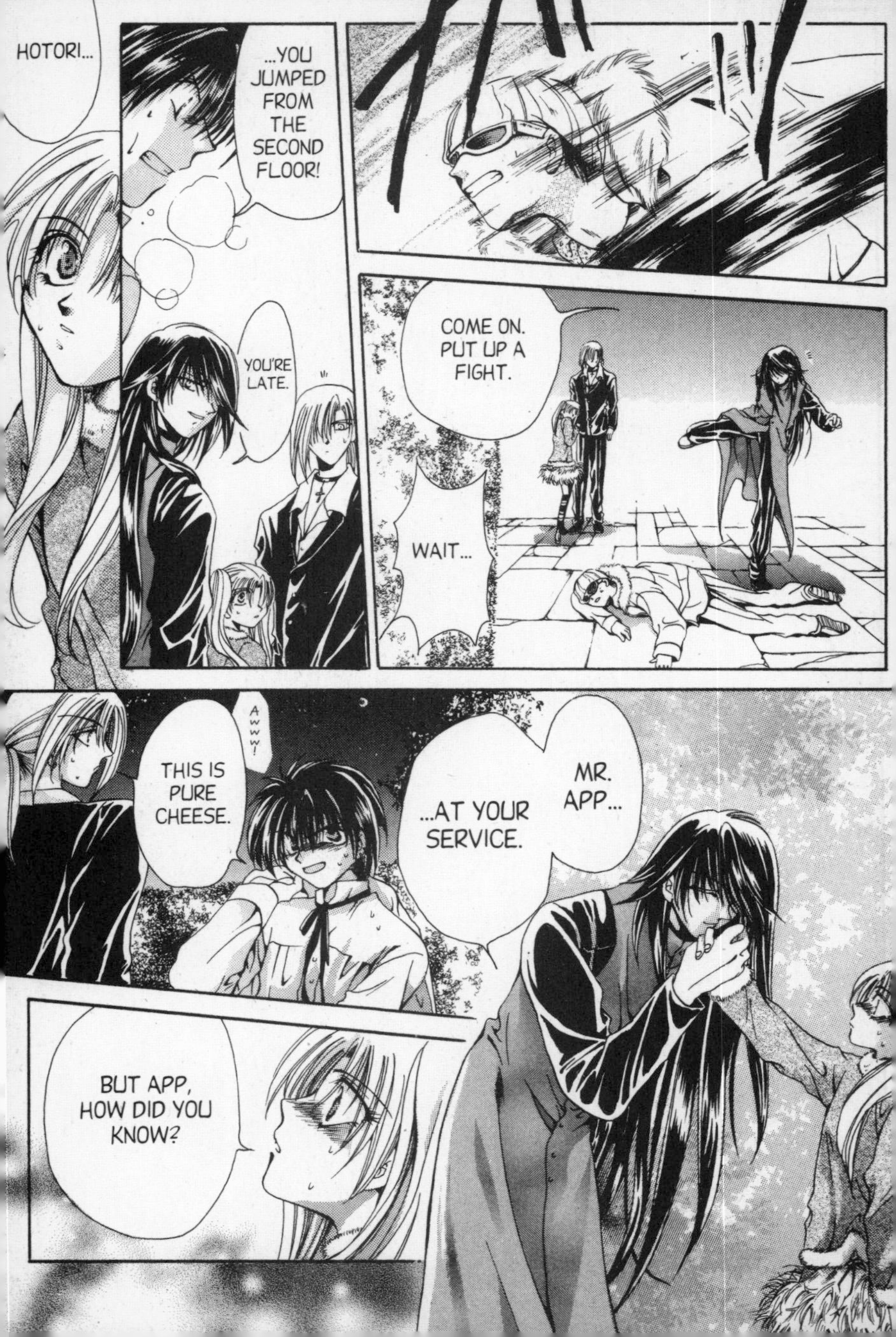
COME ON. PUT UP A FIGHT.
WAIT...
...YOU JUMPED FROM THE SECOND FLOOR!
HOTORI...
YOU'RE LATE.
MR. APP...
...AT YOUR SERVICE.
AWWW!
THIS IS PURE CHEESE.
BUT APP, HOW DID YOU KNOW?

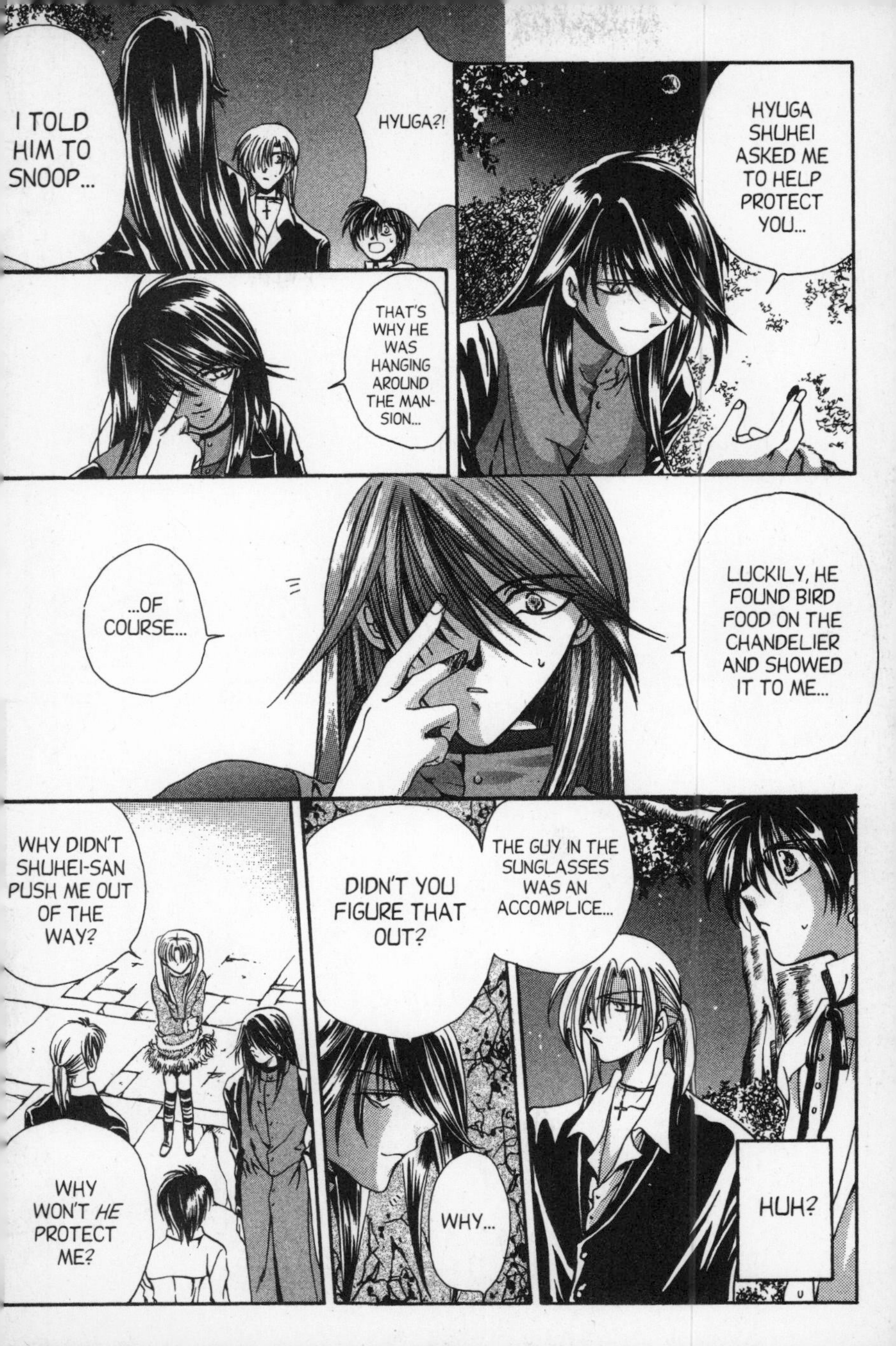
HYUGA SHUHEI ASKED ME TO HELP PROTECT YOU...
HYUGA?!
I TOLD HIM TO SNOOP...
THAT'S WHY HE WAS HANGING AROUND THE MANSION...
LUCKILY, HE FOUND BIRD FOOD ON THE CHANDELIER AND SHOWED IT TO ME...
...OF COURSE...
THE GUY IN THE SUNGLASSES WAS AN ACCOMPLICE...
DIDN'T YOU FIGURE THAT OUT?
HUH?
WHY...
WHY DIDN'T SHUHEI-SAN PUSH ME OUT OF THE WAY?
WHY WON'T *HE* PROTECT ME?

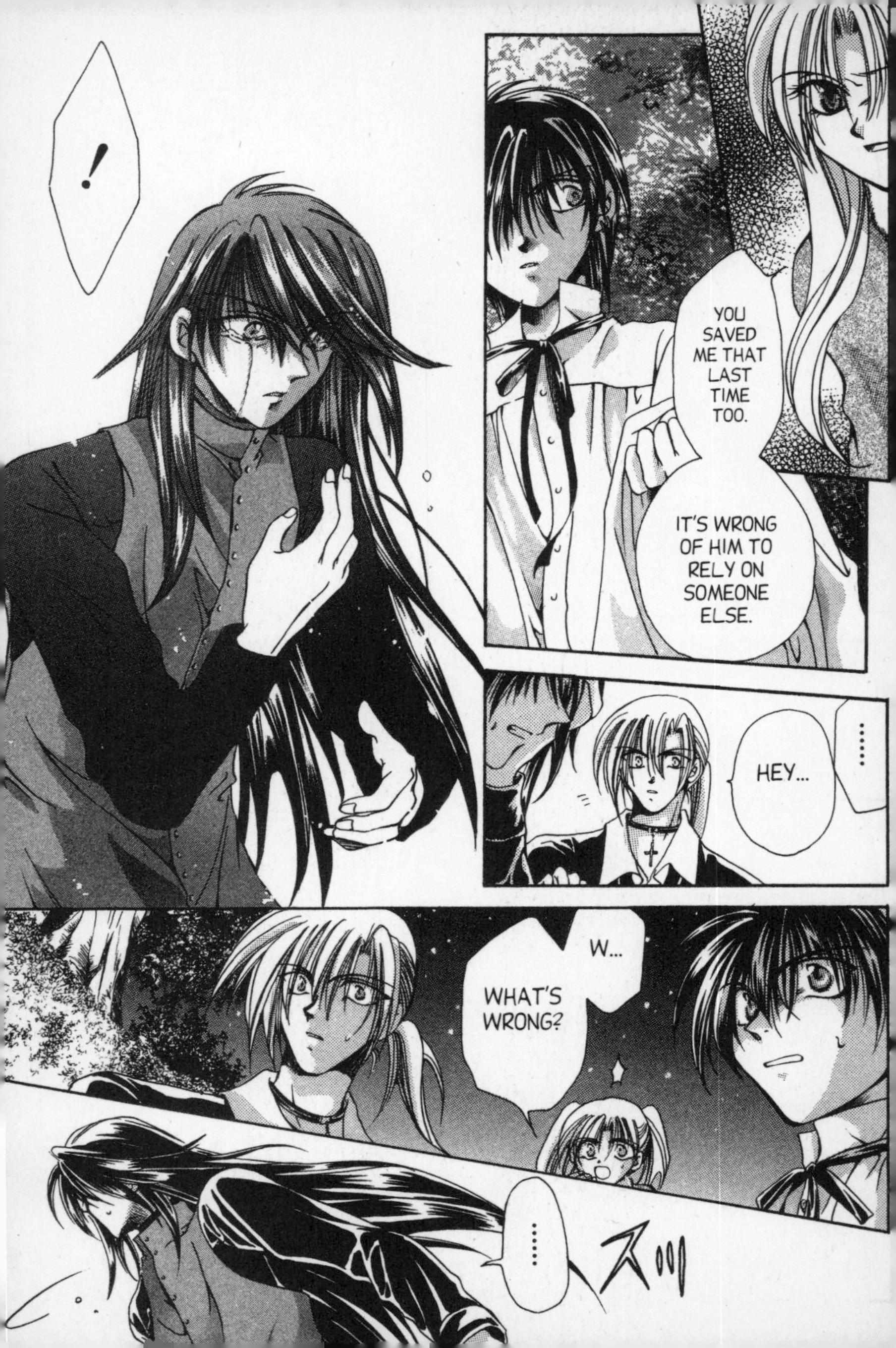
YOU SAVED ME THAT LAST TIME TOO.
IT'S WRONG OF HIM TO RELY ON SOMEONE ELSE.
......
HEY...
!
W...
WHAT'S WRONG?
......
ス

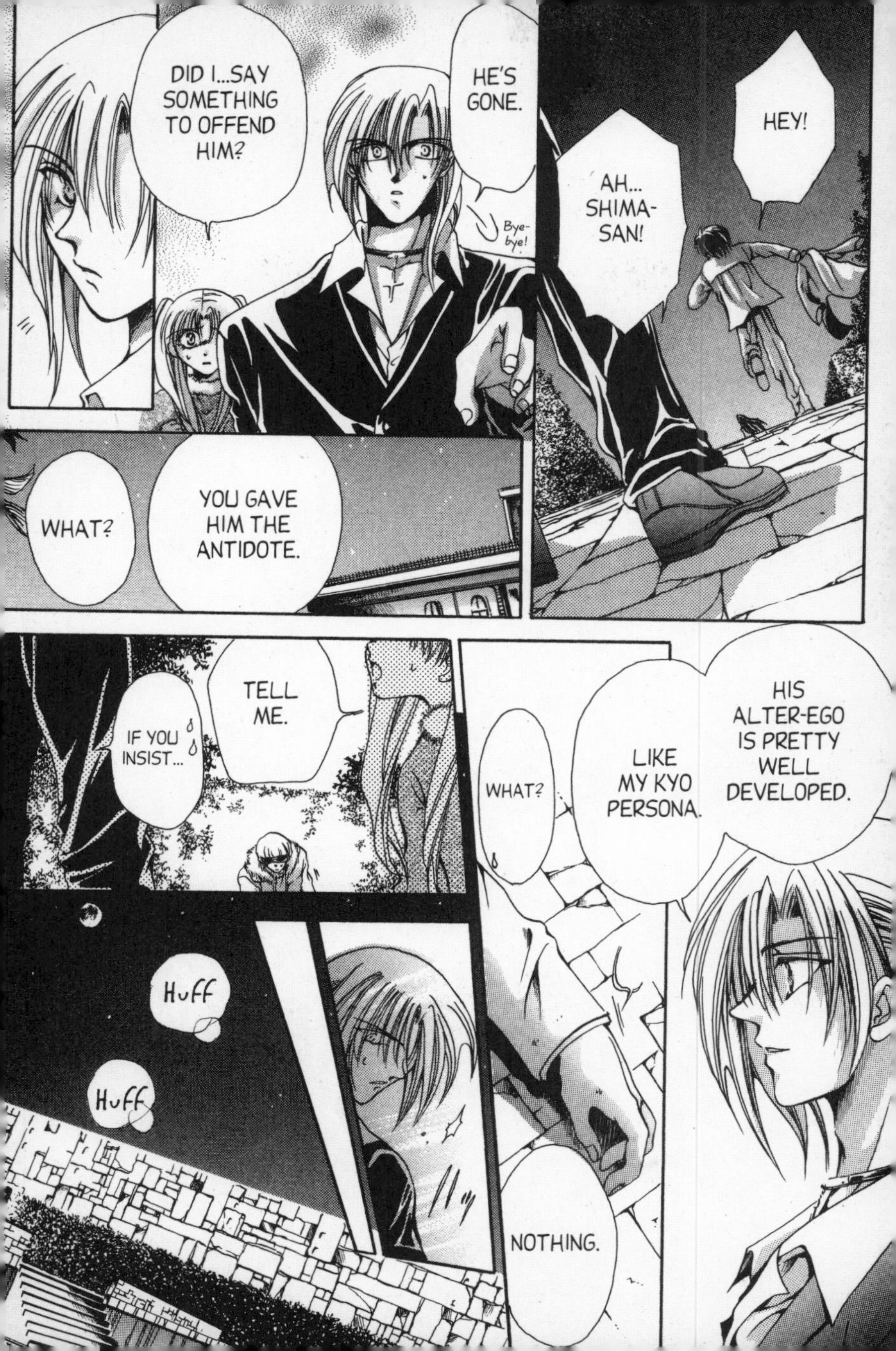
HEY!
AH... SHIMA-SAN!
HE'S GONE.
Bye-bye!
DID I...SAY SOMETHING TO OFFEND HIM?
YOU GAVE HIM THE ANTIDOTE.
WHAT?
HIS ALTER-EGO IS PRETTY WELL DEVELOPED.
LIKE MY KYO PERSONA.
WHAT?
NOTHING.
TELL ME.
IF YOU INSIST...
Huff
Huff

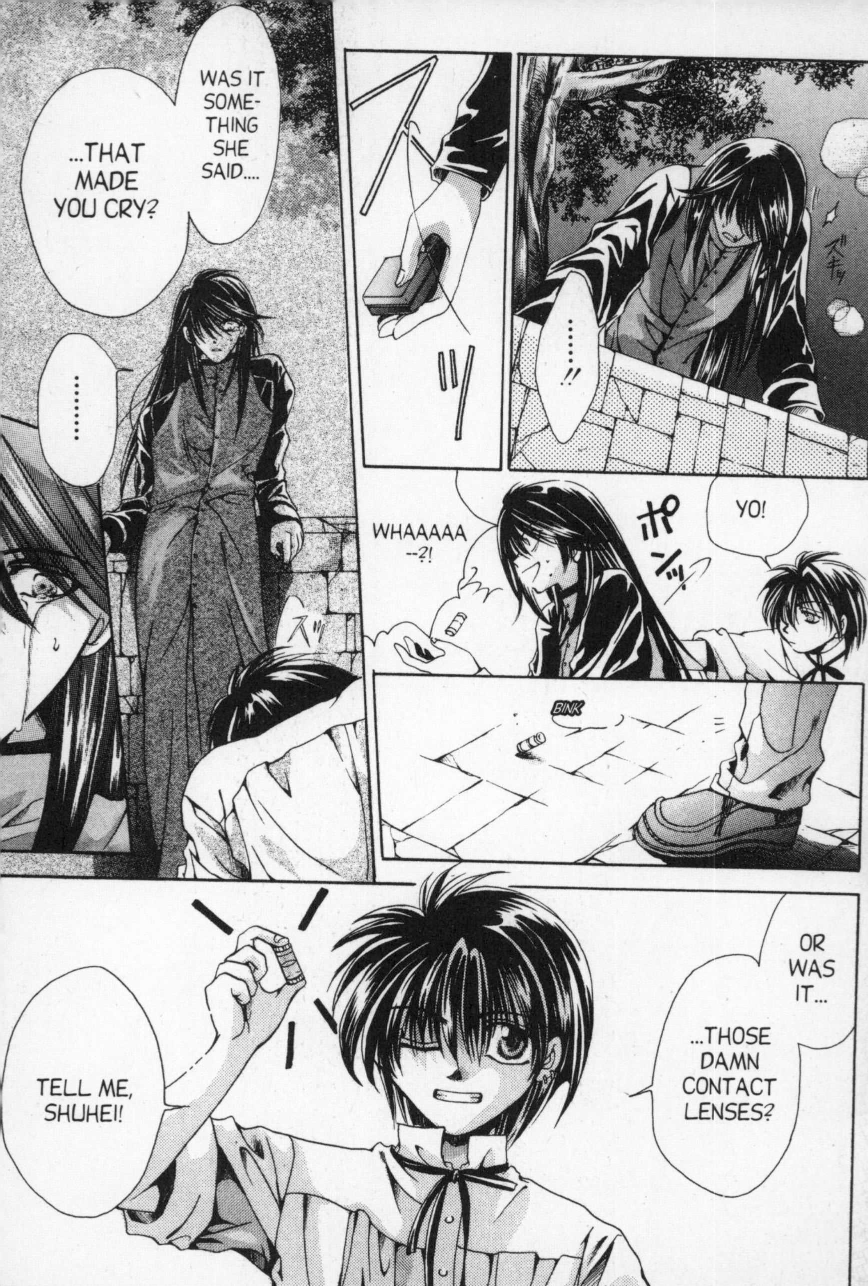
......!!
ズキッ
YO!
ポンッ
WHAAAAA --?!
BINK
WAS IT SOMETHING SHE SAID....
...THAT MADE YOU CRY?
......
スッ
OR WAS IT...
...THOSE DAMN CONTACT LENSES?
TELL ME, SHUHEI!

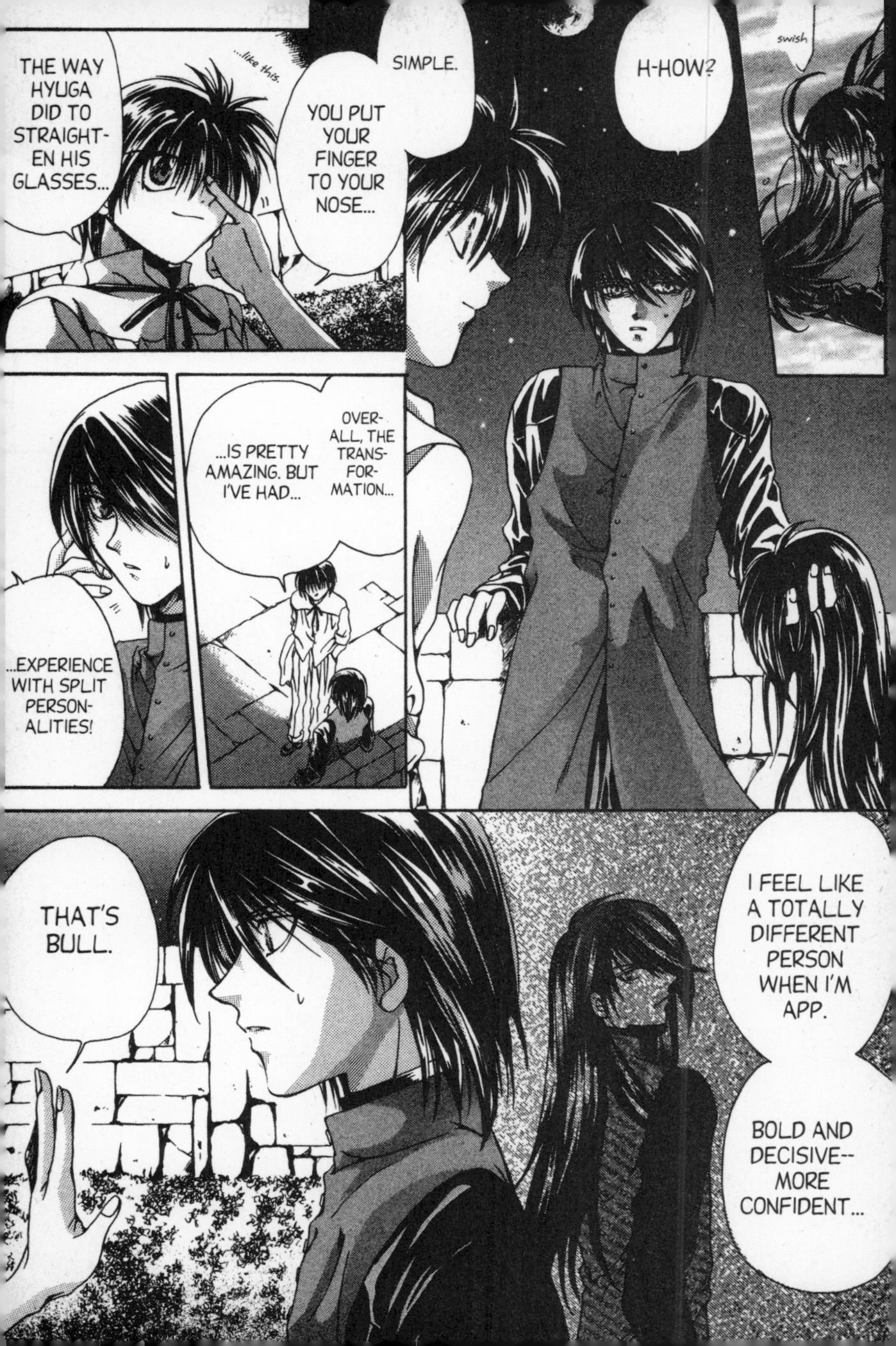
swish
H-HOW?
SIMPLE.
YOU PUT YOUR FINGER TO YOUR NOSE...
...like this.
THE WAY HYUGA DID TO STRAIGHT-EN HIS GLASSES...
OVER-ALL, THE TRANS-FOR-MATION...
...IS PRETTY AMAZING. BUT I'VE HAD...
...EXPERIENCE WITH SPLIT PERSON-ALITIES!
I FEEL LIKE A TOTALLY DIFFERENT PERSON WHEN I'M APP.
BOLD AND DECISIVE-- MORE CONFIDENT...
THAT'S BULL.

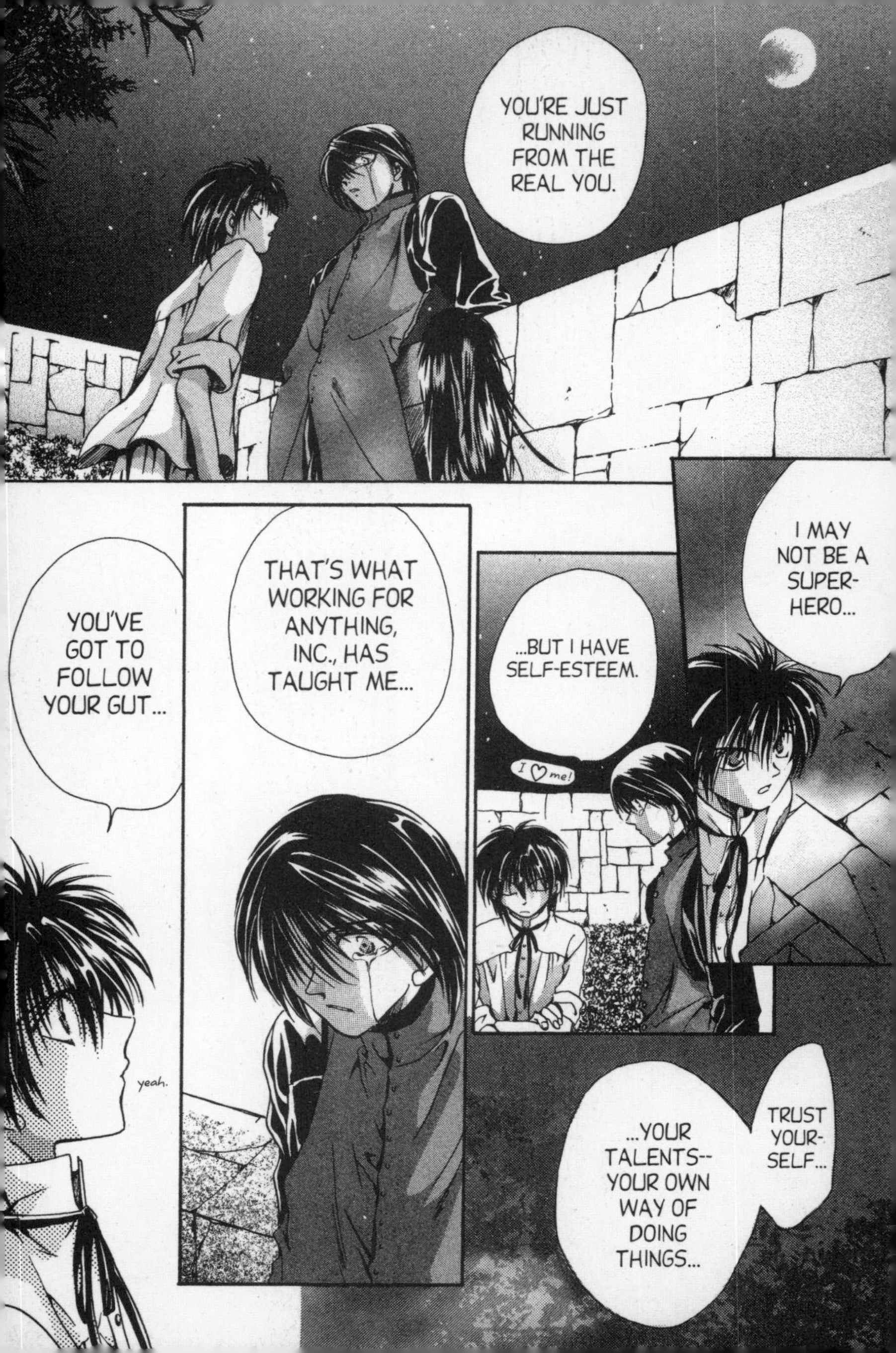
YOU'RE JUST RUNNING FROM THE REAL YOU.
I MAY NOT BE A SUPER-HERO...
...BUT I HAVE SELF-ESTEEM.
I ♡ me!
THAT'S WHAT WORKING FOR ANYTHING, INC., HAS TAUGHT ME...
YOU'VE GOT TO FOLLOW YOUR GUT...
yeah.
TRUST YOURSELF...
...YOUR TALENTS-- YOUR OWN WAY OF DOING THINGS...

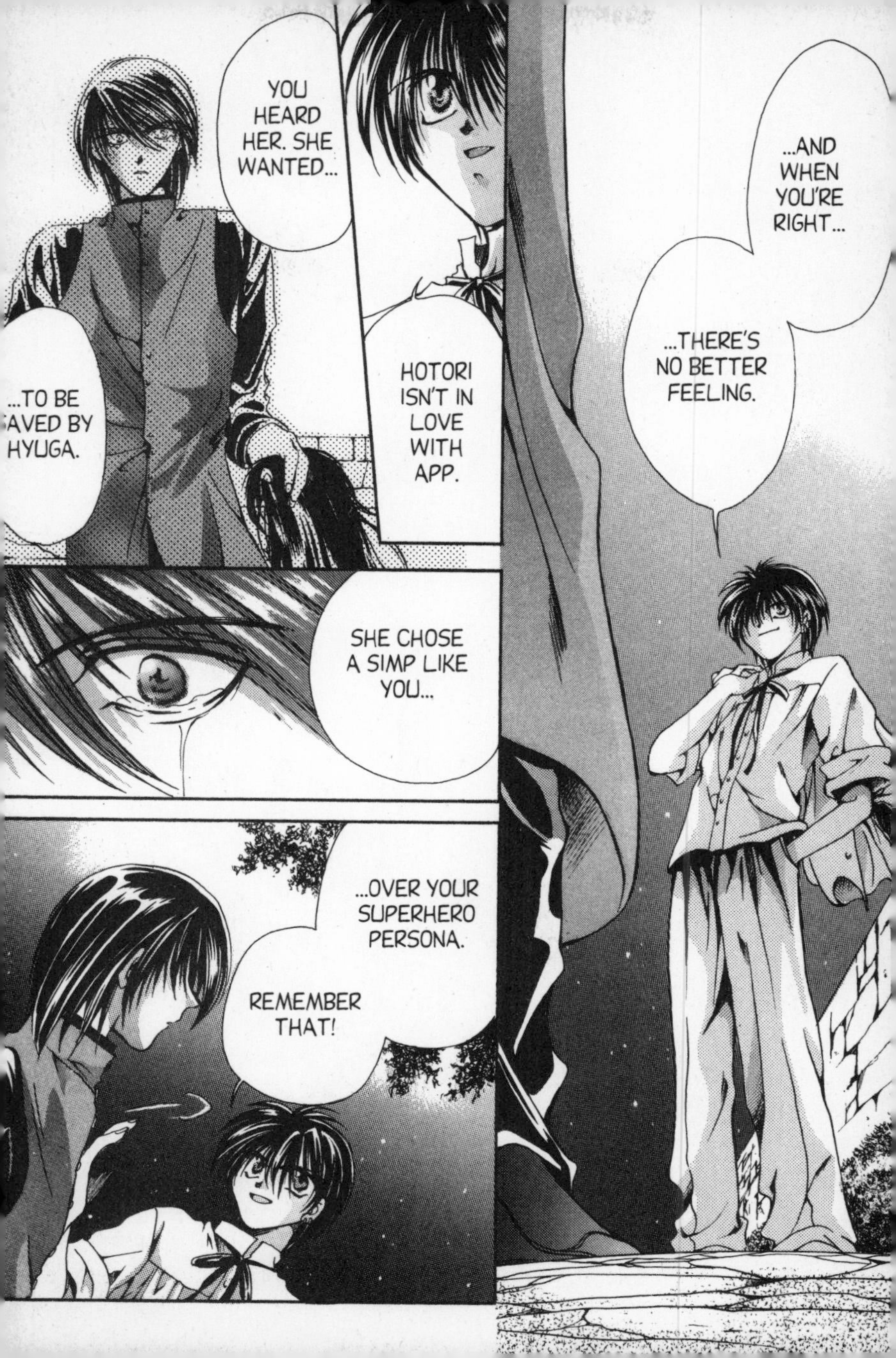
...AND WHEN YOU'RE RIGHT...
...THERE'S NO BETTER FEELING.
HOTORI ISN'T IN LOVE WITH APP.
YOU HEARD HER. SHE WANTED...
...TO BE AVED BY HYUGA.
SHE CHOSE A SIMP LIKE YOU...
...OVER YOUR SUPERHERO PERSONA.
REMEMBER THAT!

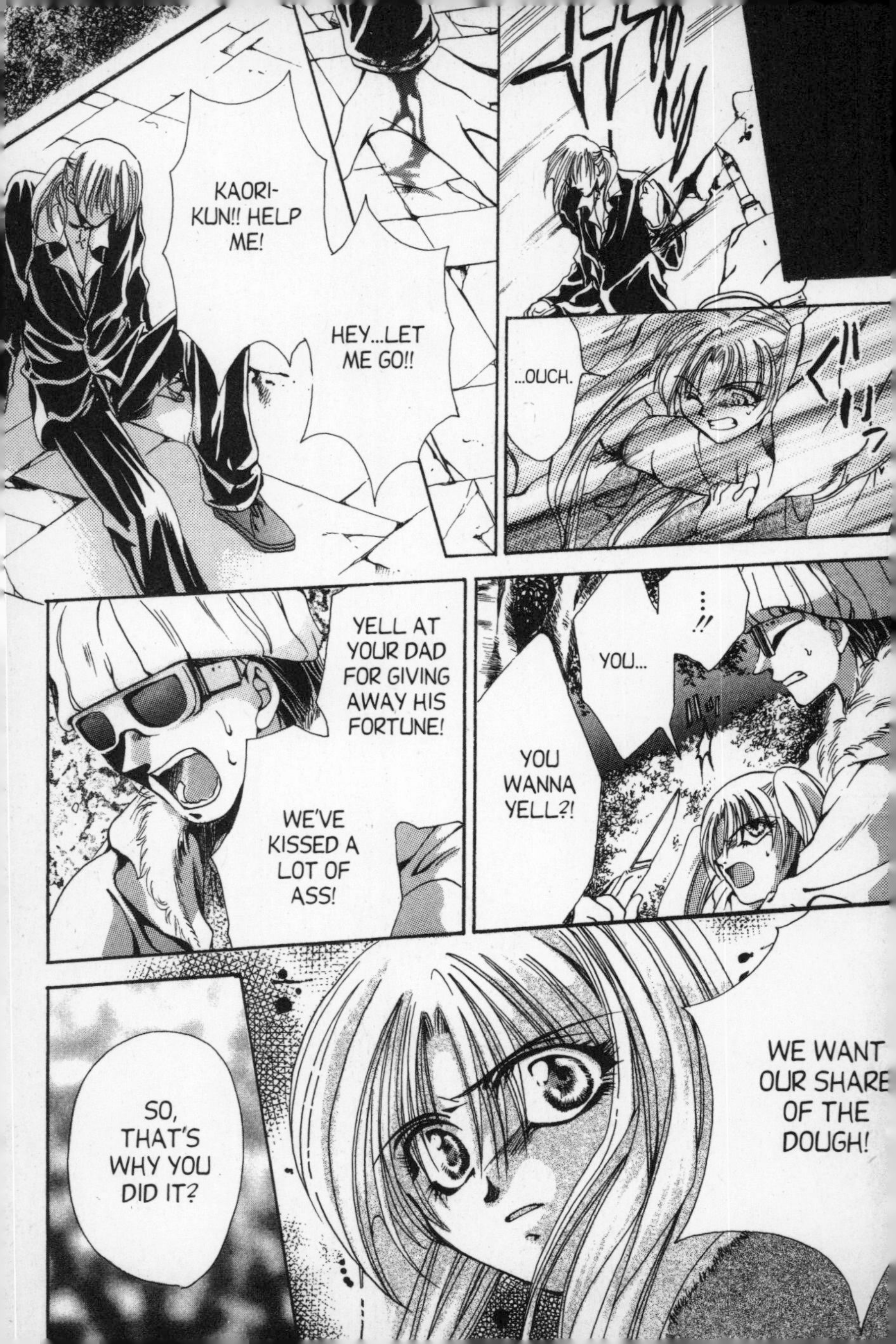
...OUCH.
HEY...LET ME GO!!
KAORI-KUN!! HELP ME!
...!!
YOU...
YOU WANNA YELL?!
YELL AT YOUR DAD FOR GIVING AWAY HIS FORTUNE!
WE'VE KISSED A LOT OF ASS!
WE WANT OUR SHARE OF THE DOUGH!
SO, THAT'S WHY YOU DID IT?

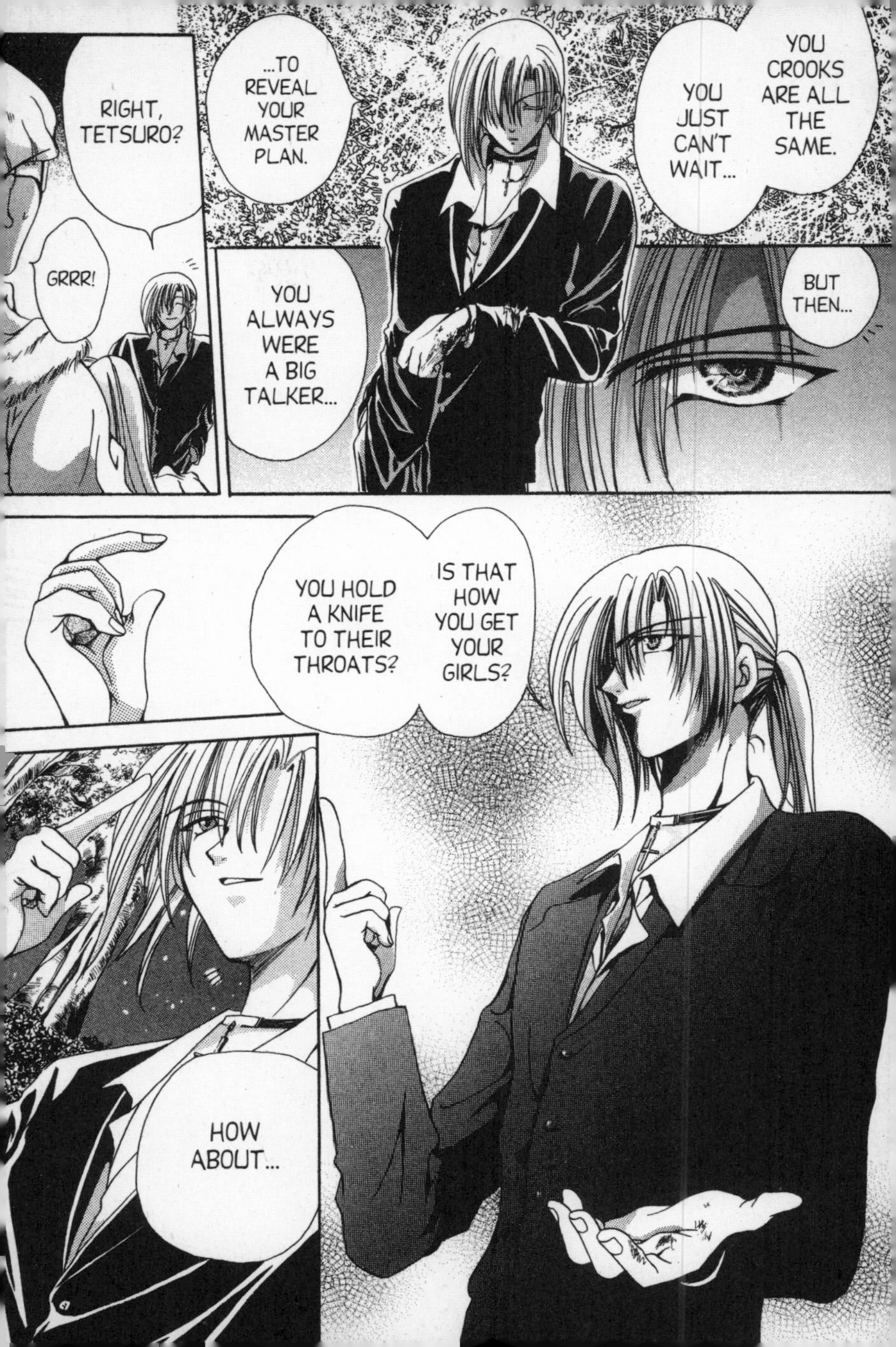
YOU CROOKS ARE ALL THE SAME.
YOU JUST CAN'T WAIT...
...TO REVEAL YOUR MASTER PLAN.
BUT THEN...
YOU ALWAYS WERE A BIG TALKER...
RIGHT, TETSURO?
GRRR!
IS THAT HOW YOU GET YOUR GIRLS?
YOU HOLD A KNIFE TO THEIR THROATS?
HOW ABOUT...

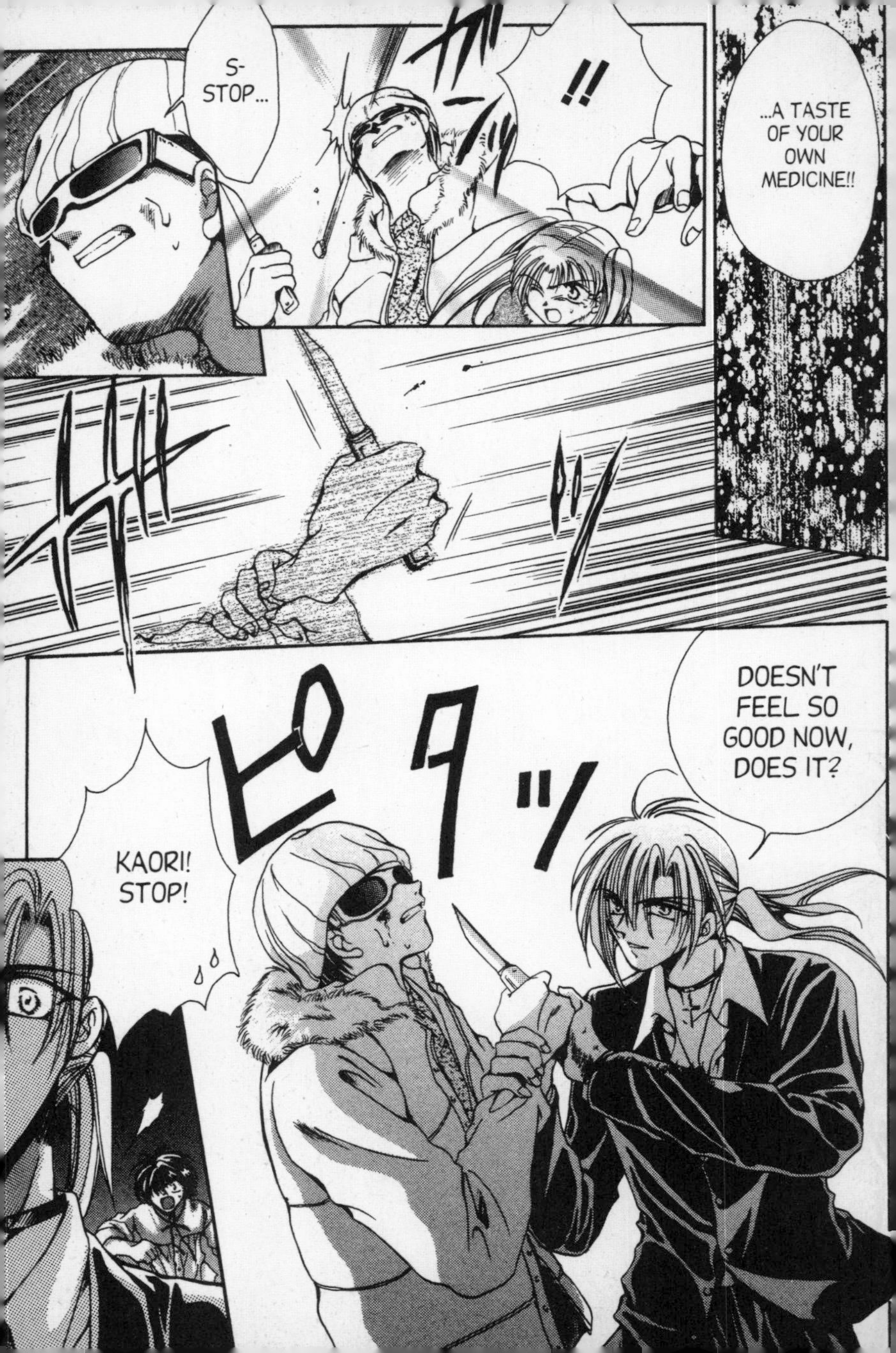
...A TASTE OF YOUR OWN MEDICINE!!
!!
S- STOP...
DOESN'T FEEL SO GOOD NOW, DOES IT?
ピタッ
KAORI! STOP!

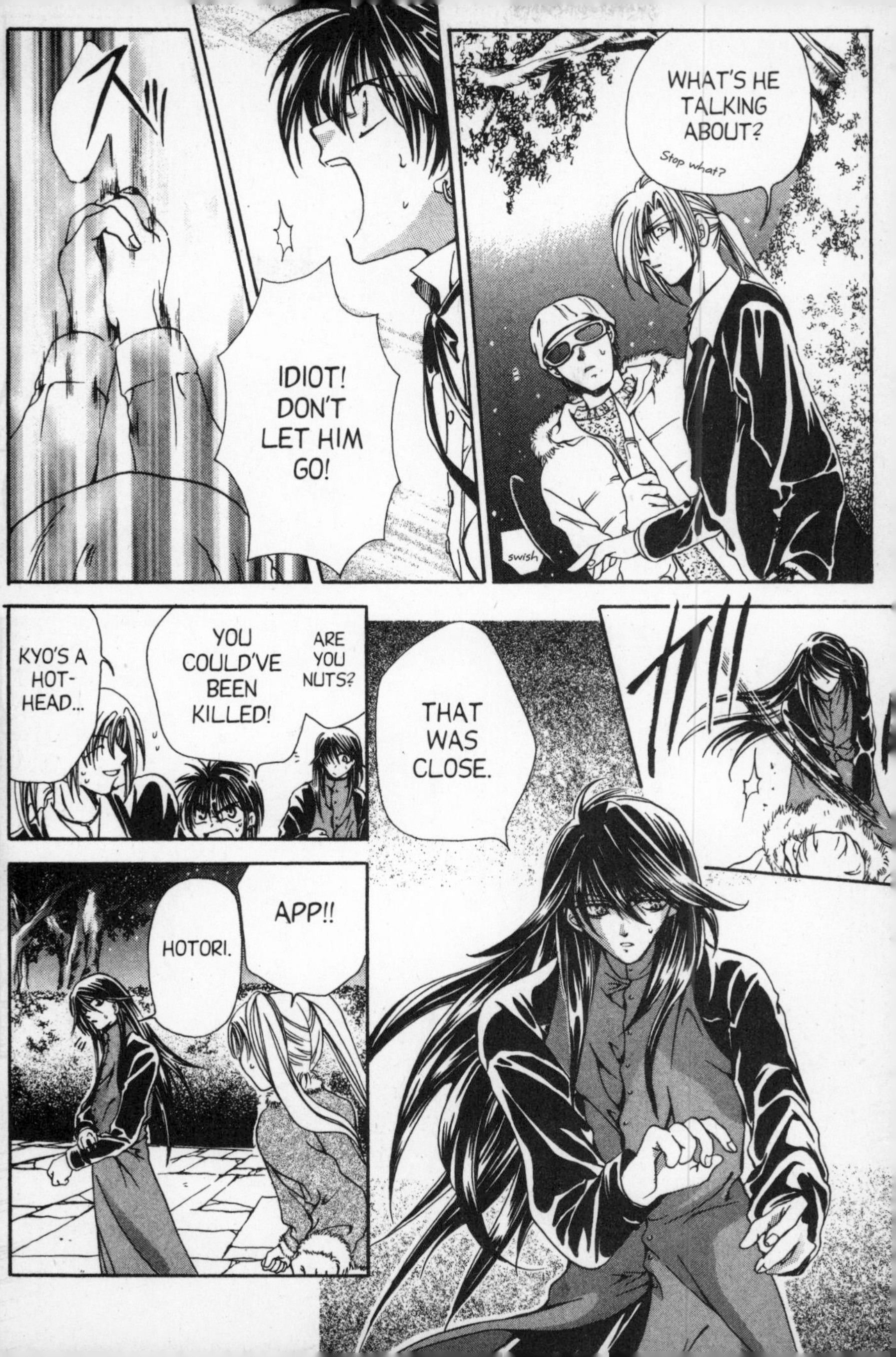
WHAT'S HE TALKING ABOUT?
Stop what?
swish
IDIOT! DON'T LET HIM GO!
THAT WAS CLOSE.
ARE YOU NUTS?
YOU COULD'VE BEEN KILLED!
KYO'S A HOT-HEAD...
APP!!
HOTORI.

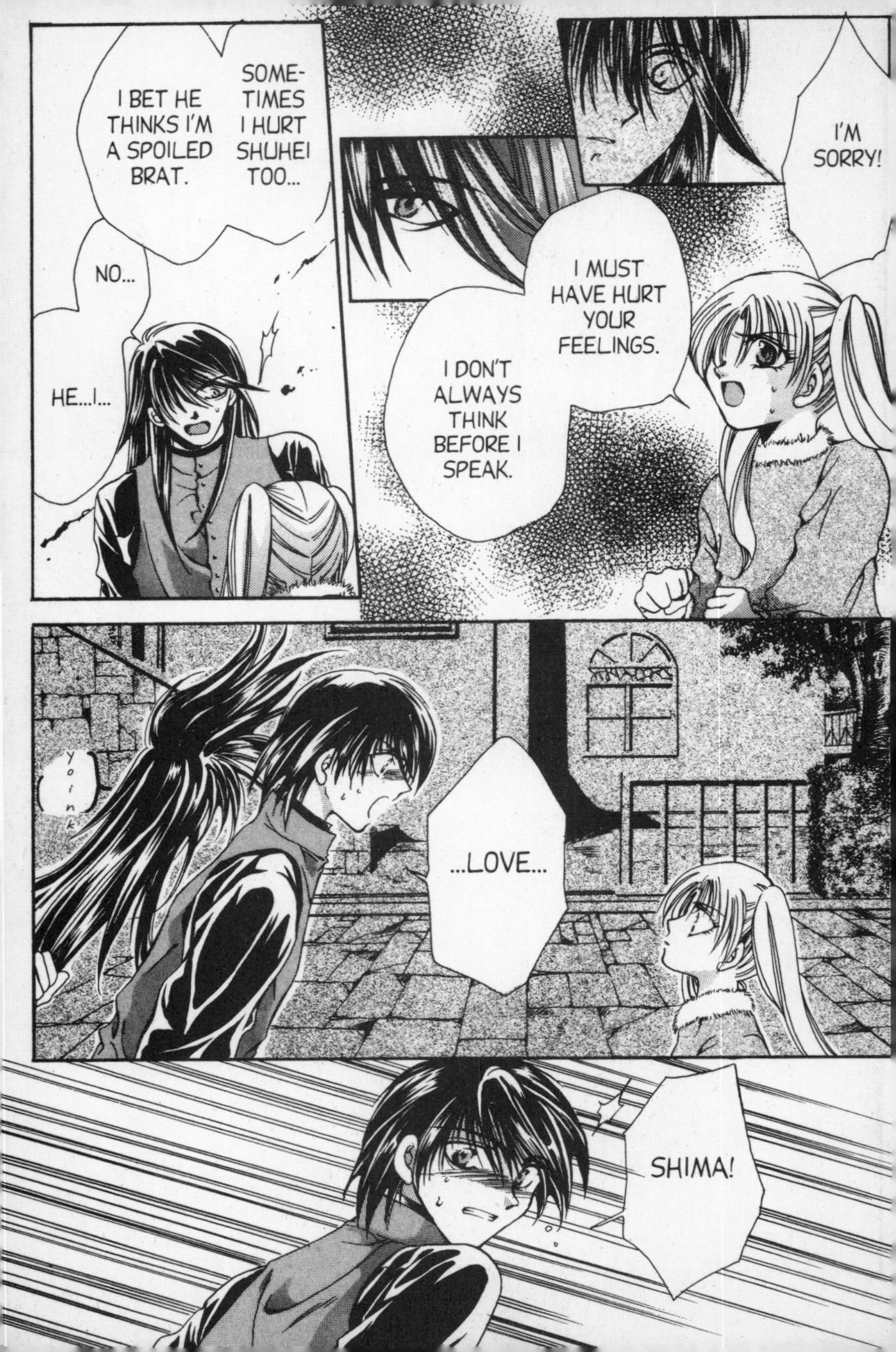

I'M SORRY!
I MUST HAVE HURT YOUR FEELINGS.
I DON'T ALWAYS THINK BEFORE I SPEAK.
SOMETIMES I HURT SHUHEI TOO...
I BET HE THINKS I'M A SPOILED BRAT.
NO...
HE...I...
...LOVE...
yoink
SHIMA!

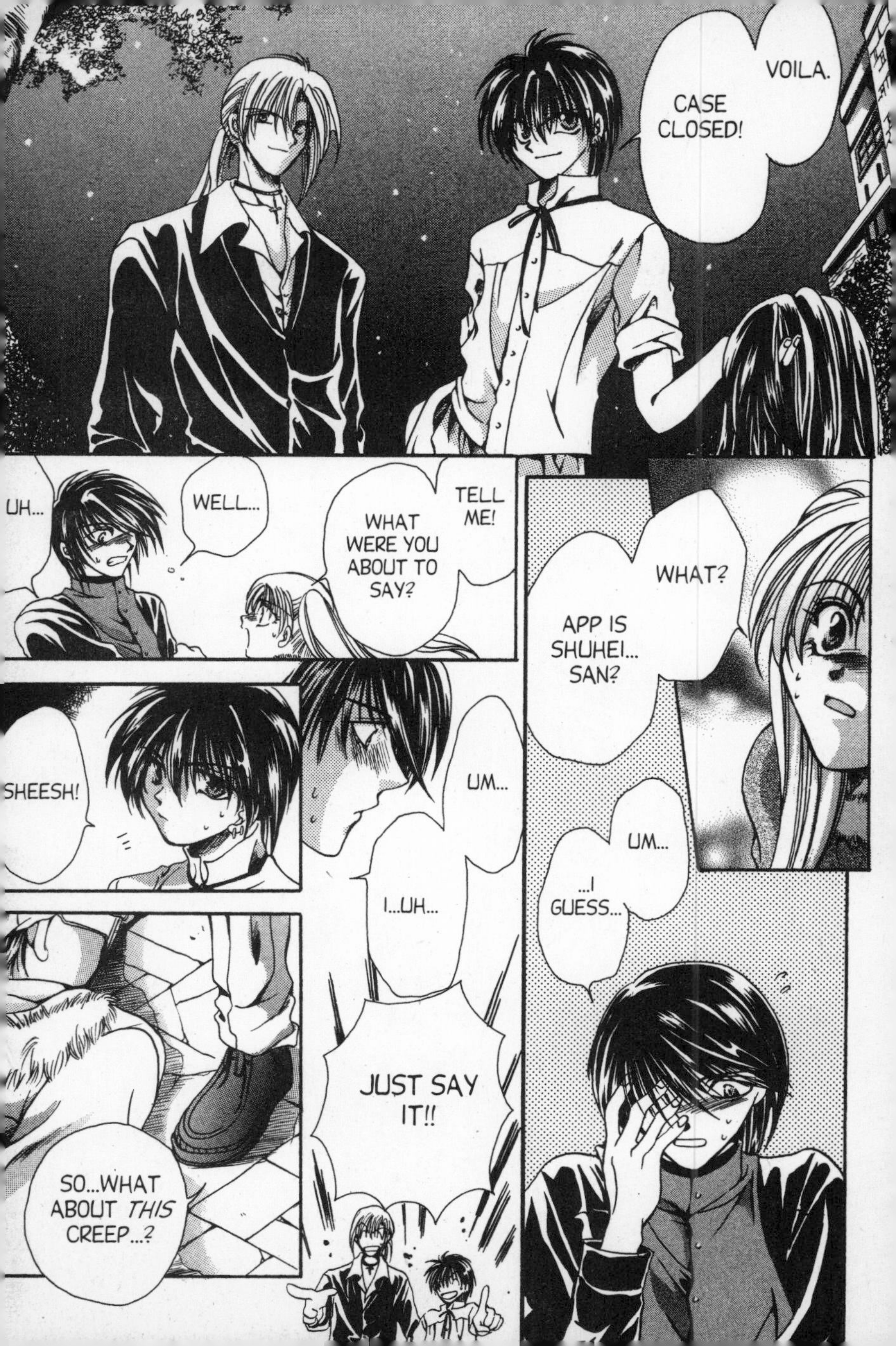

VOILA.
CASE CLOSED!
WHAT?
APP IS SHUHEI... SAN?
UM...
...I GUESS...
TELL ME!
WHAT WERE YOU ABOUT TO SAY?
WELL...
UH...
UM...
I...UH...
JUST SAY IT!!
SHEESH!
SO...WHAT ABOUT *THIS* CREEP...?

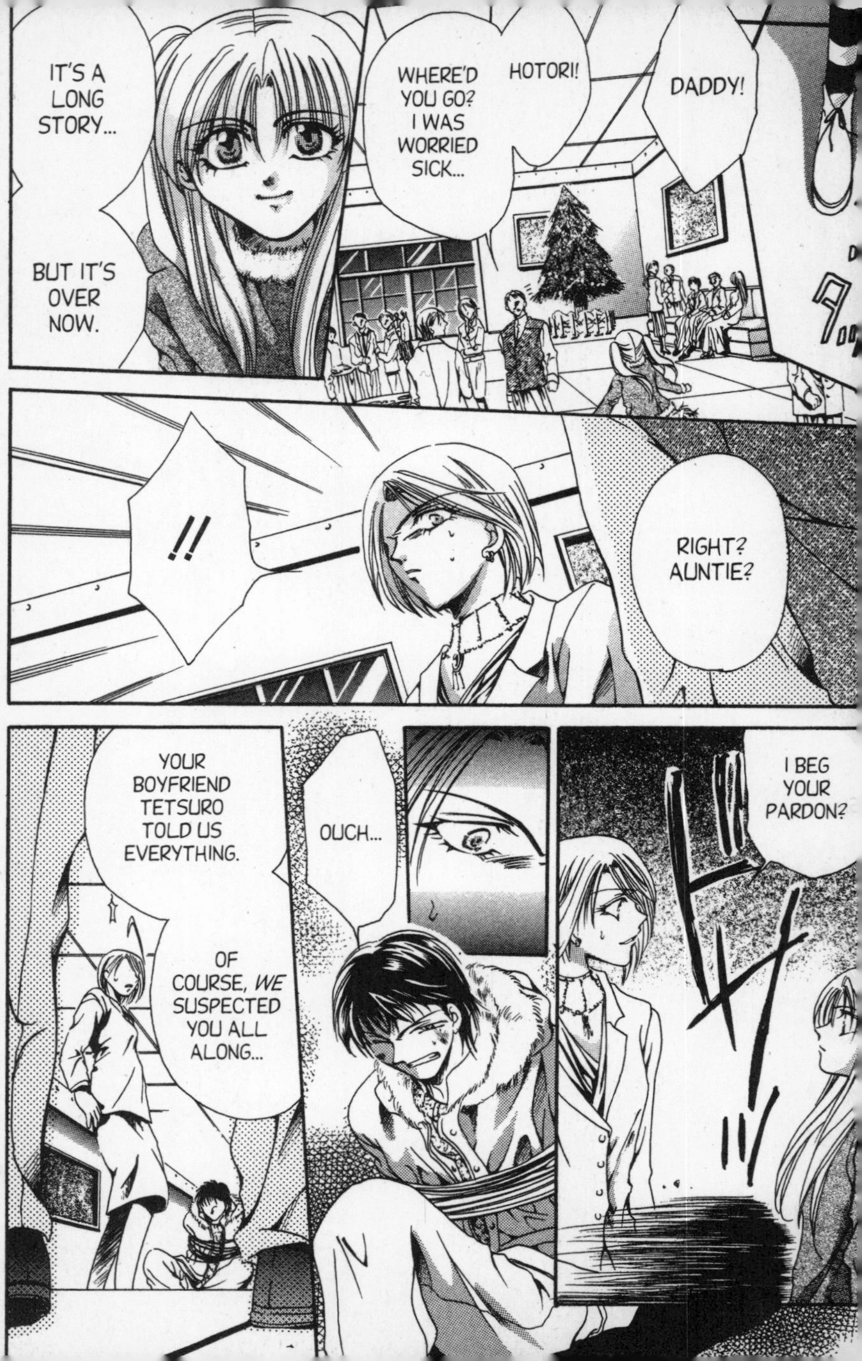
DADDY!
HOTORI!
WHERE'D YOU GO? I WAS WORRIED SICK...
IT'S A LONG STORY...
BUT IT'S OVER NOW.
RIGHT? AUNTIE?
!!
I BEG YOUR PARDON?
OUCH...
YOUR BOYFRIEND TETSURO TOLD US EVERYTHING.
OF COURSE, *WE* SUSPECTED YOU ALL ALONG...

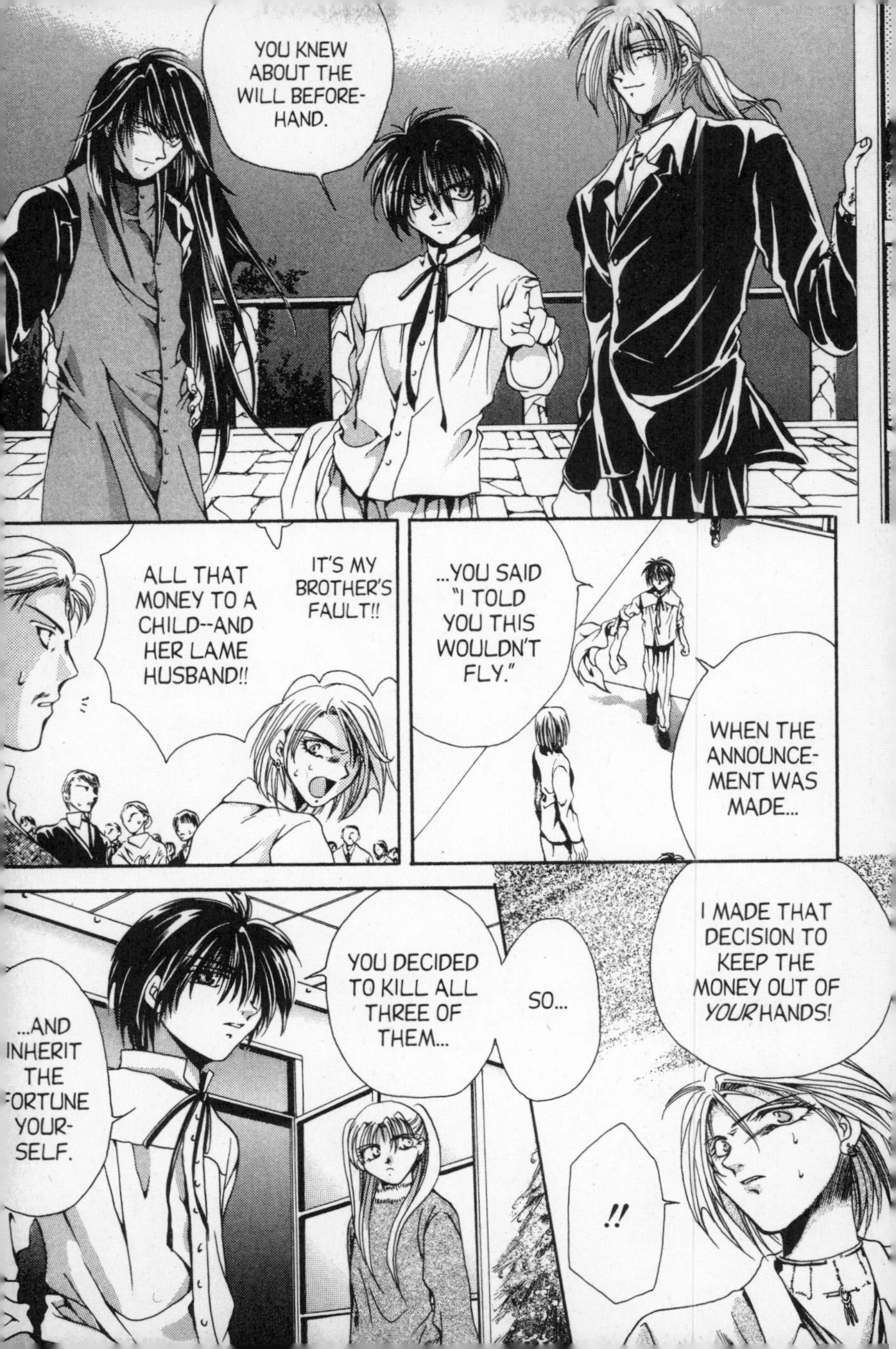
YOU KNEW ABOUT THE WILL BEFORE-HAND.
WHEN THE ANNOUNCE-MENT WAS MADE...
...YOU SAID "I TOLD YOU THIS WOULDN'T FLY."
IT'S MY BROTHER'S FAULT!!
ALL THAT MONEY TO A CHILD--AND HER LAME HUSBAND!!
I MADE THAT DECISION TO KEEP THE MONEY OUT OF *YOUR* HANDS!
!!
SO...
YOU DECIDED TO KILL ALL THREE OF THEM...
...AND INHERIT THE FORTUNE YOUR-SELF.

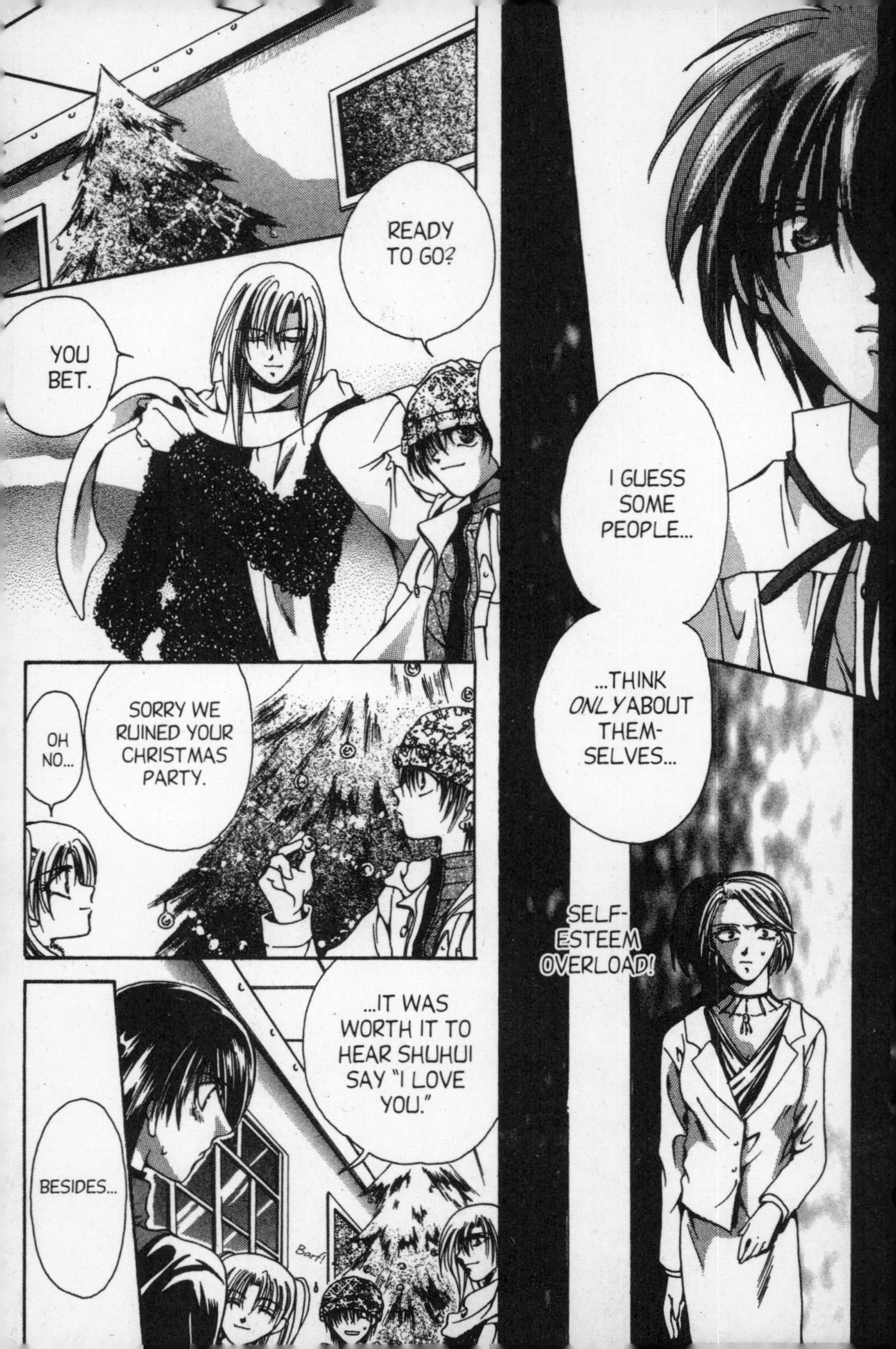
I GUESS SOME PEOPLE...
...THINK *ONLY* ABOUT THEM-SELVES...
SELF-ESTEEM OVERLOAD!
READY TO GO?
YOU BET.
SORRY WE RUINED YOUR CHRISTMAS PARTY.
OH NO...
...IT WAS WORTH IT TO HEAR SHUHUI SAY "I LOVE YOU."
BESIDES...
Barf!

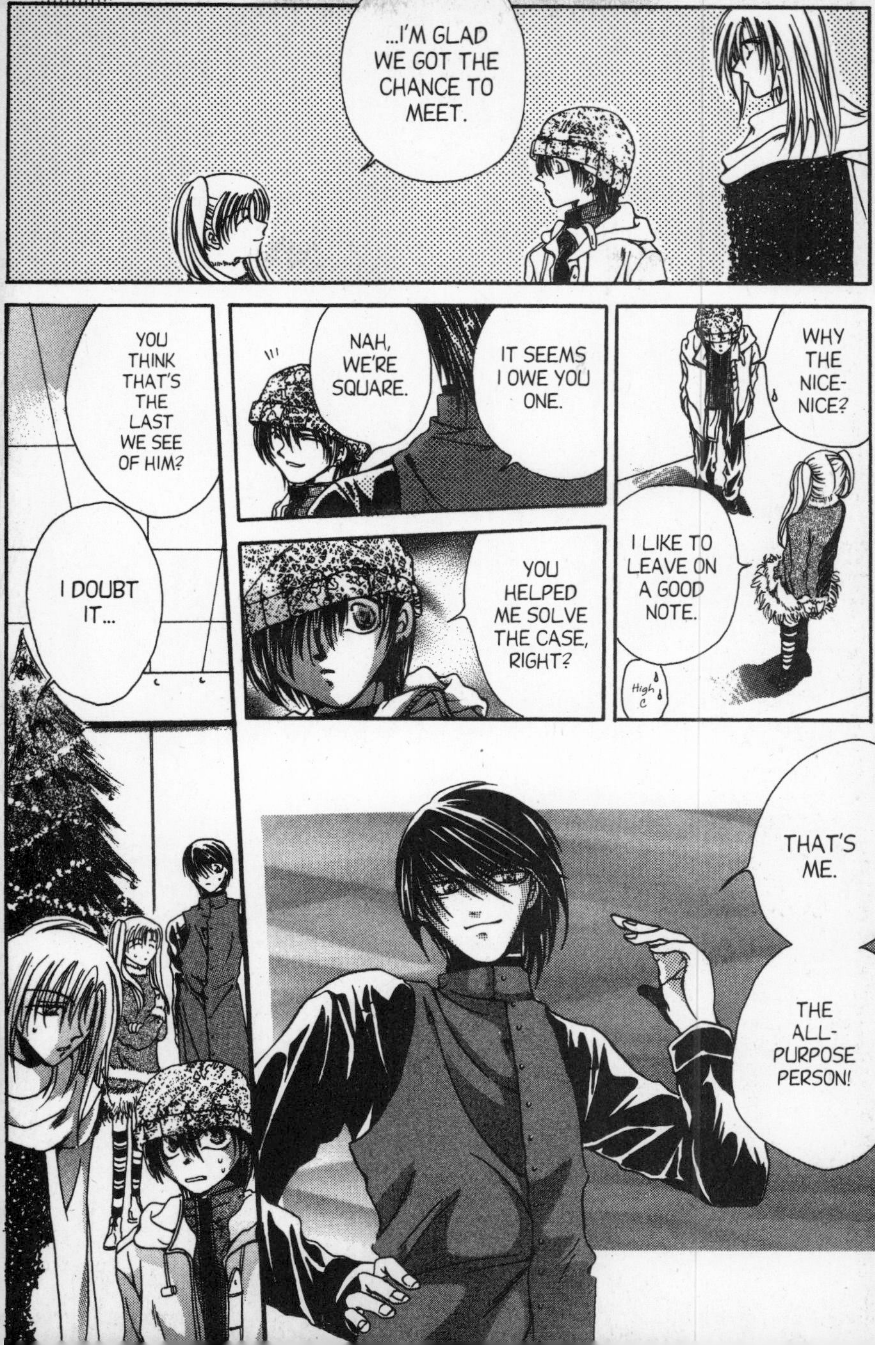
...I'M GLAD WE GOT THE CHANCE TO MEET.
WHY THE NICE-NICE?
I LIKE TO LEAVE ON A GOOD NOTE.
High C
IT SEEMS I OWE YOU ONE.
NAH, WE'RE SQUARE.
YOU HELPED ME SOLVE THE CASE, RIGHT?
THAT'S ME.
THE ALL-PURPOSE PERSON!
YOU THINK THAT'S THE LAST WE SEE OF HIM?
I DOUBT IT...

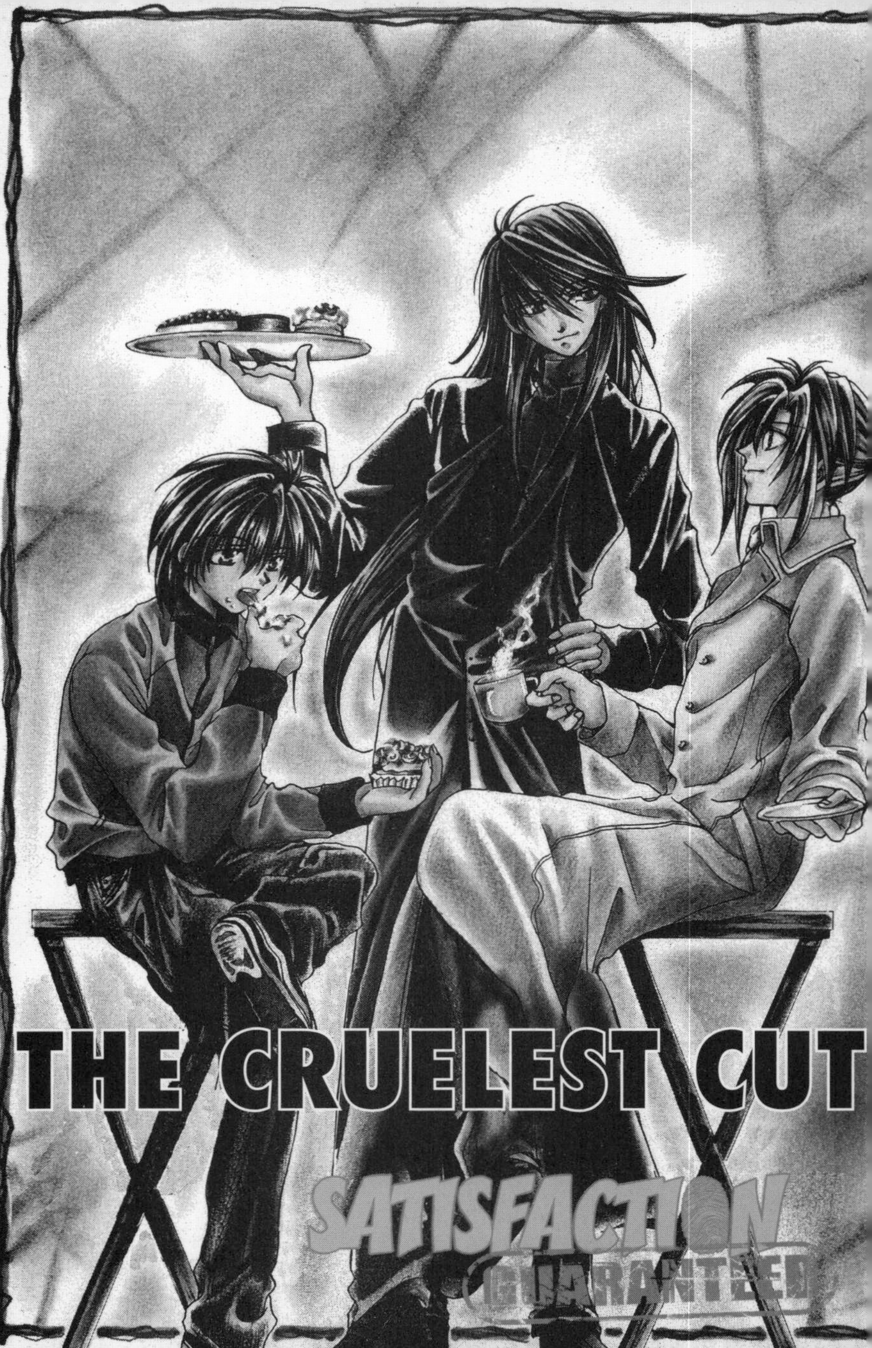
THE CRUELEST CUT
SATISFACTION
GUARANTEED

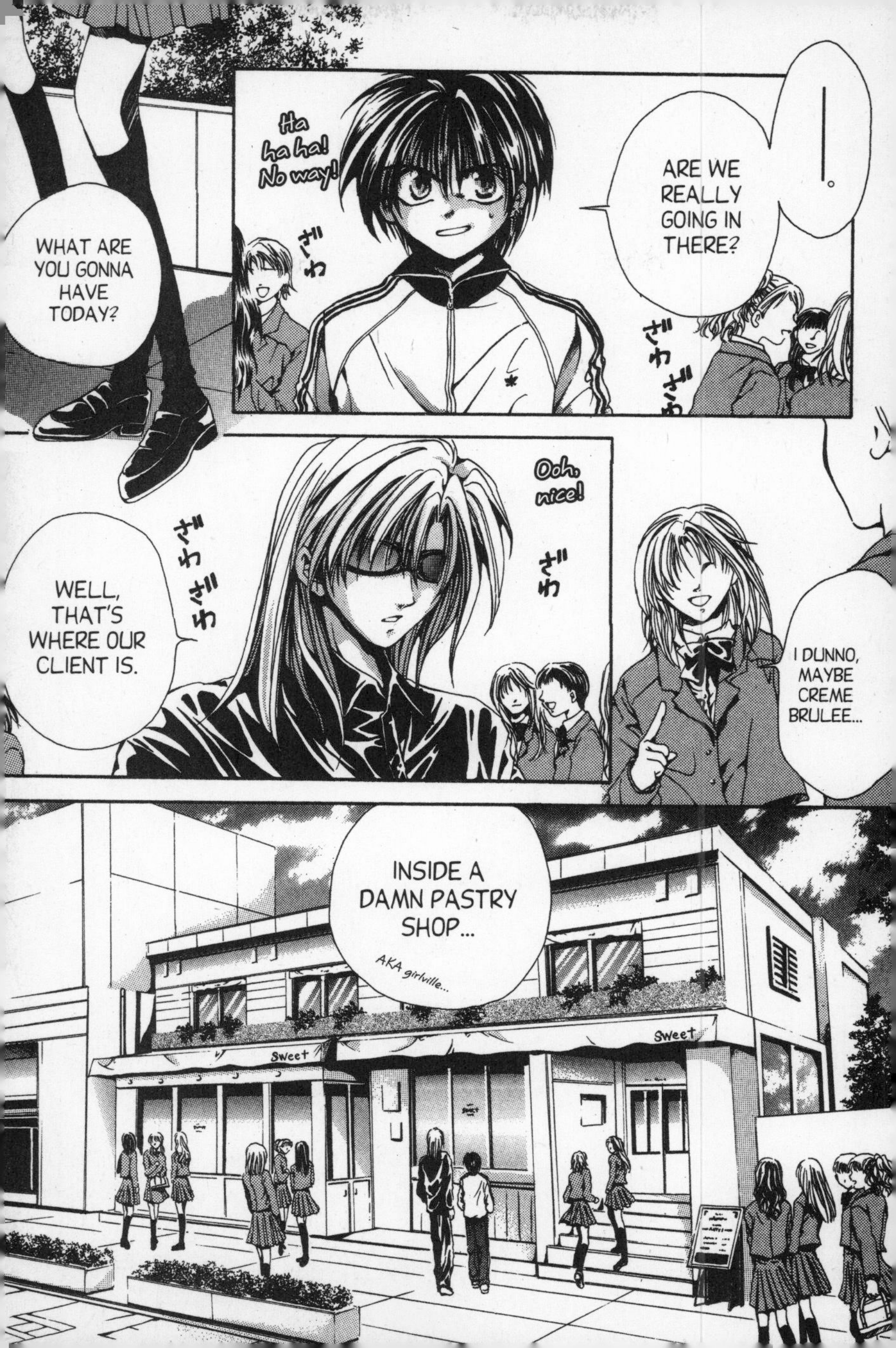
!
ARE WE REALLY GOING IN THERE?
ざわ ざわ
Ha ha ha! No way!
ざわ
WHAT ARE YOU GONNA HAVE TODAY?
I DUNNO, MAYBE CREME BRULEE...
Ooh, nice!
ざわ
ざわ ざわ
WELL, THAT'S WHERE OUR CLIENT IS.
INSIDE A DAMN PASTRY SHOP...
AKA girlville...
Sweet
Sweet

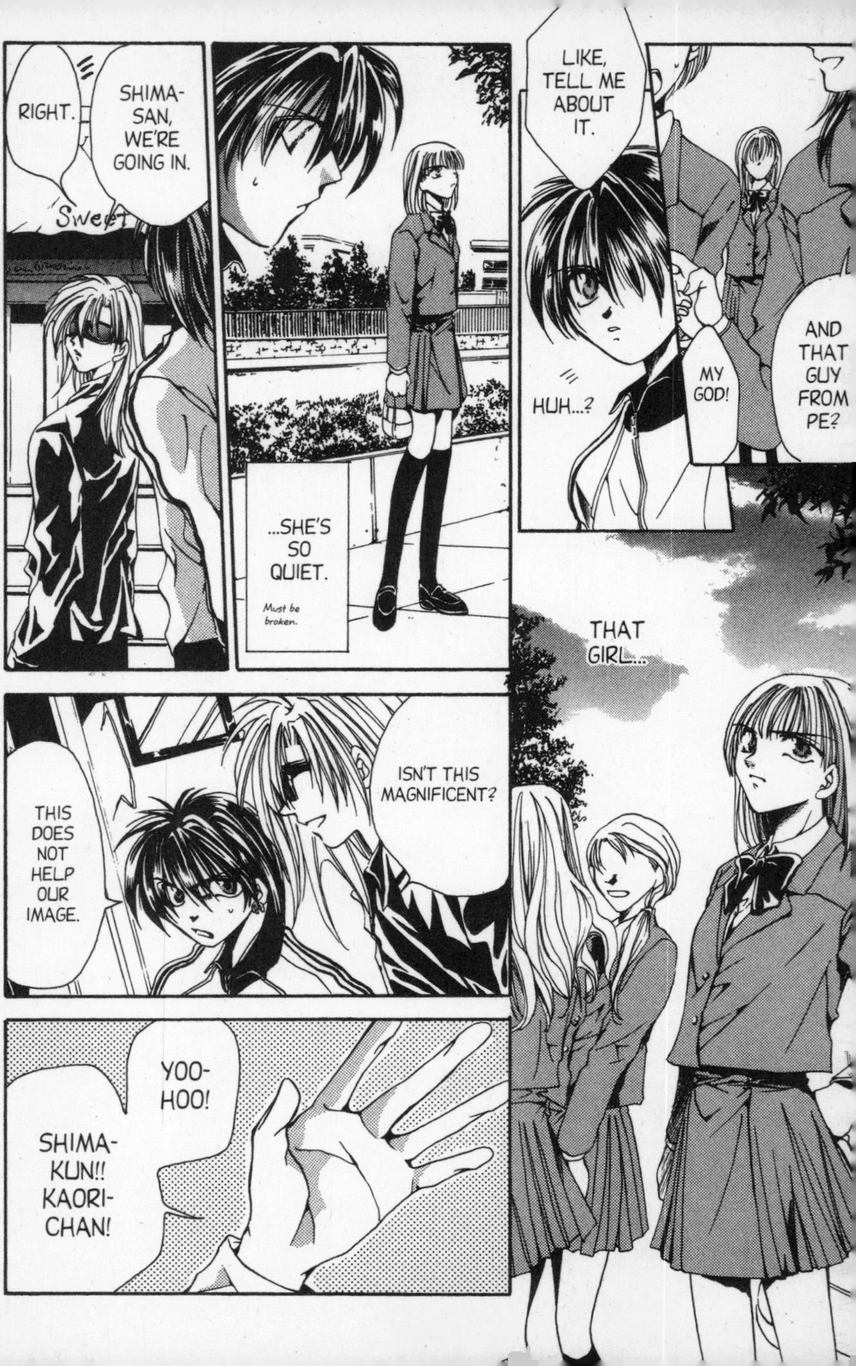
AND THAT GUY FROM PE?
MY GOD!
LIKE, TELL ME ABOUT IT.
HUH...?
...SHE'S SO QUIET.
Must be broken.
SHIMA-SAN, WE'RE GOING IN.
RIGHT.
Sweet
THAT GIRL...
ISN'T THIS MAGNIFICENT?
THIS DOES NOT HELP OUR IMAGE.
YOO-HOO!
SHIMA-KUN!! KAORI-CHAN!

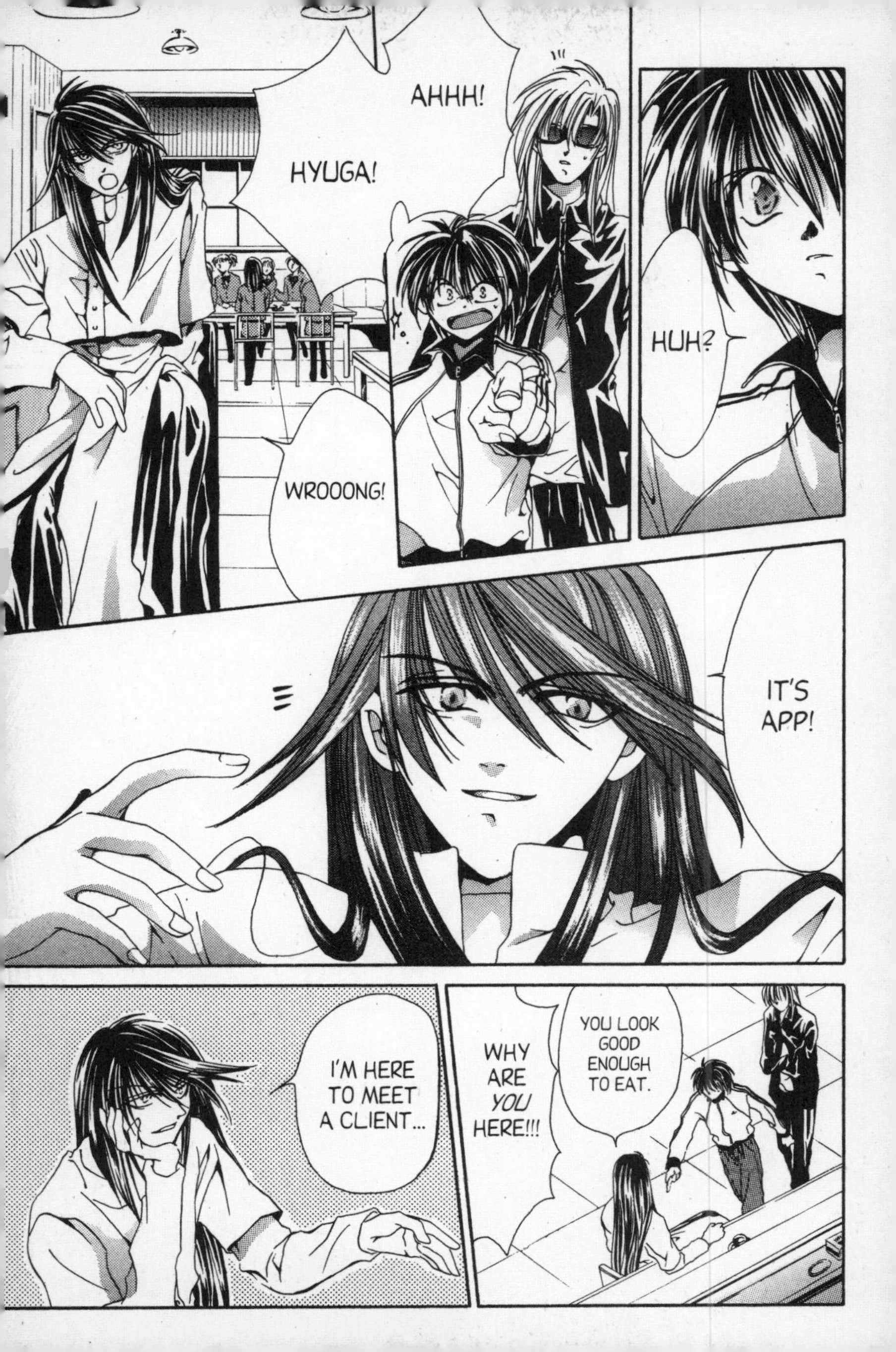

HUH?
AHHH!
HYUGA!
WROOONG!
IT'S APP!
YOU LOOK GOOD ENOUGH TO EAT.
WHY ARE *YOU* HERE!!!
I'M HERE TO MEET A CLIENT...

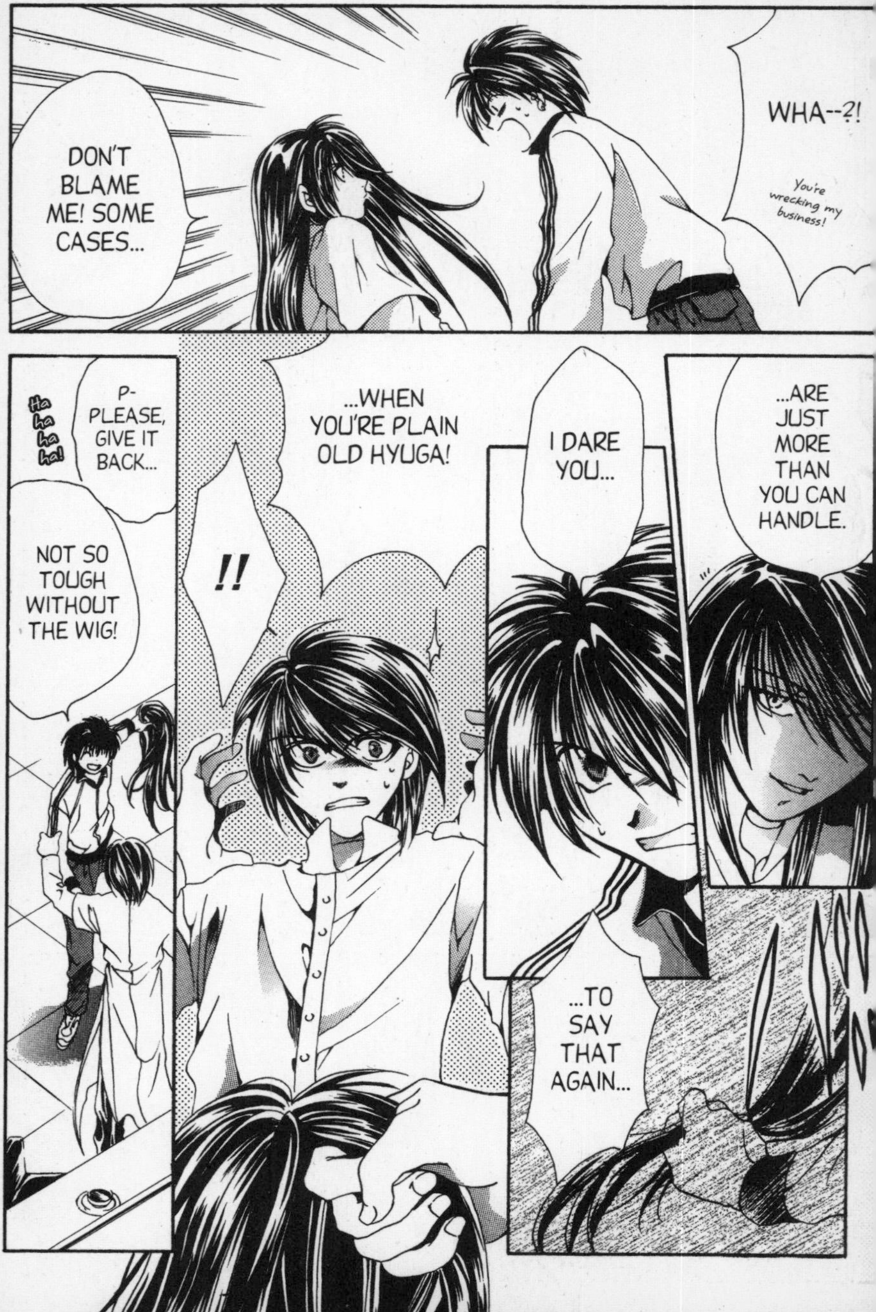
WHA--?!
You're wrecking my business!
DON'T BLAME ME! SOME CASES...
...ARE JUST MORE THAN YOU CAN HANDLE.
I DARE YOU...
...TO SAY THAT AGAIN...
...WHEN YOU'RE PLAIN OLD HYUGA!
!!
P-PLEASE, GIVE IT BACK...
Ha ha ha ha!
NOT SO TOUGH WITHOUT THE WIG!

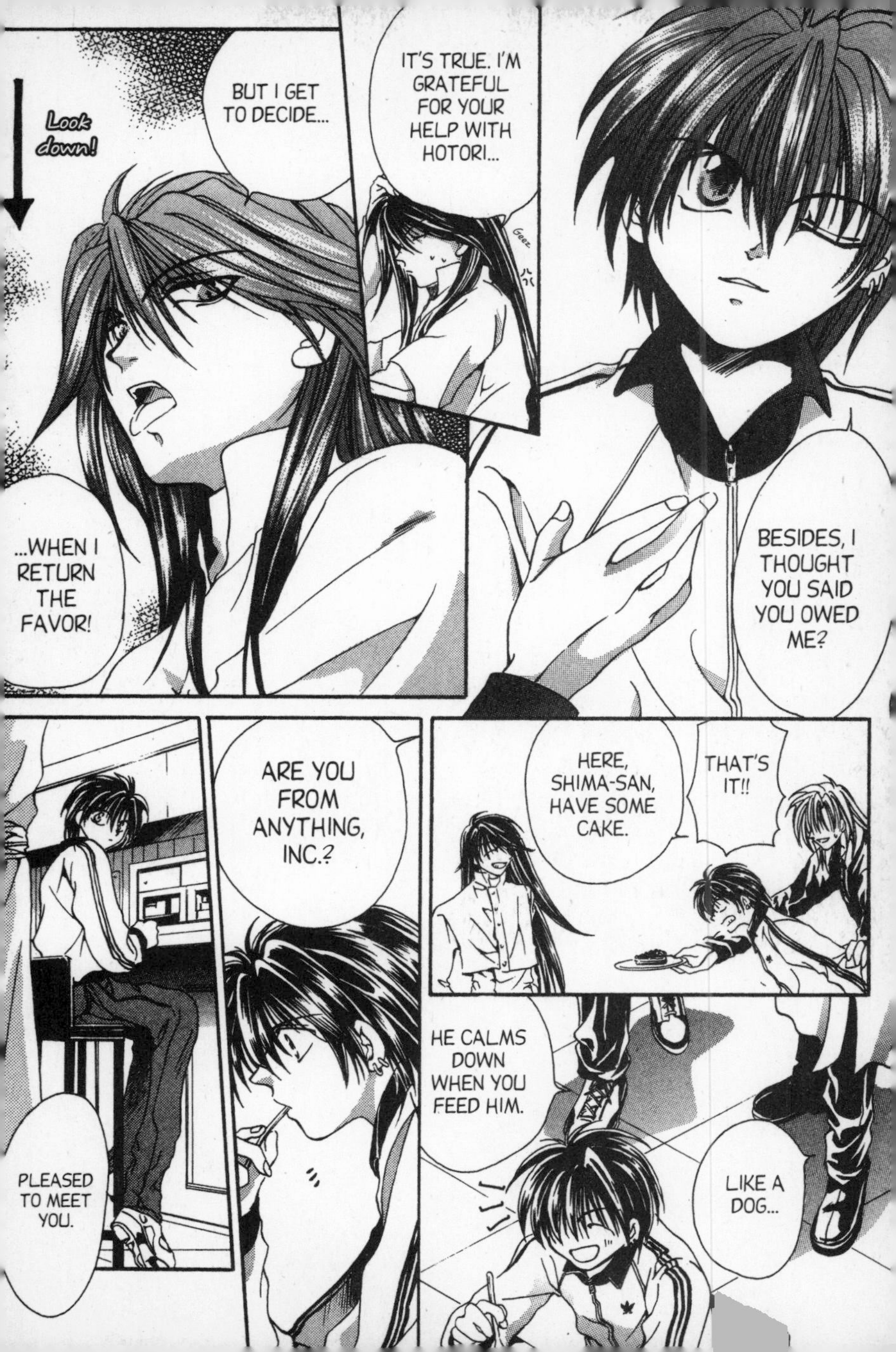
BESIDES, I THOUGHT YOU SAID YOU OWED ME?
IT'S TRUE. I'M GRATEFUL FOR YOUR HELP WITH HOTORI...
Geez
BUT I GET TO DECIDE...
Look down!
...WHEN I RETURN THE FAVOR!
THAT'S IT!!
HERE, SHIMA-SAN, HAVE SOME CAKE.
HE CALMS DOWN WHEN YOU FEED HIM.
LIKE A DOG...
ARE YOU FROM ANYTHING, INC.?
PLEASED TO MEET YOU.

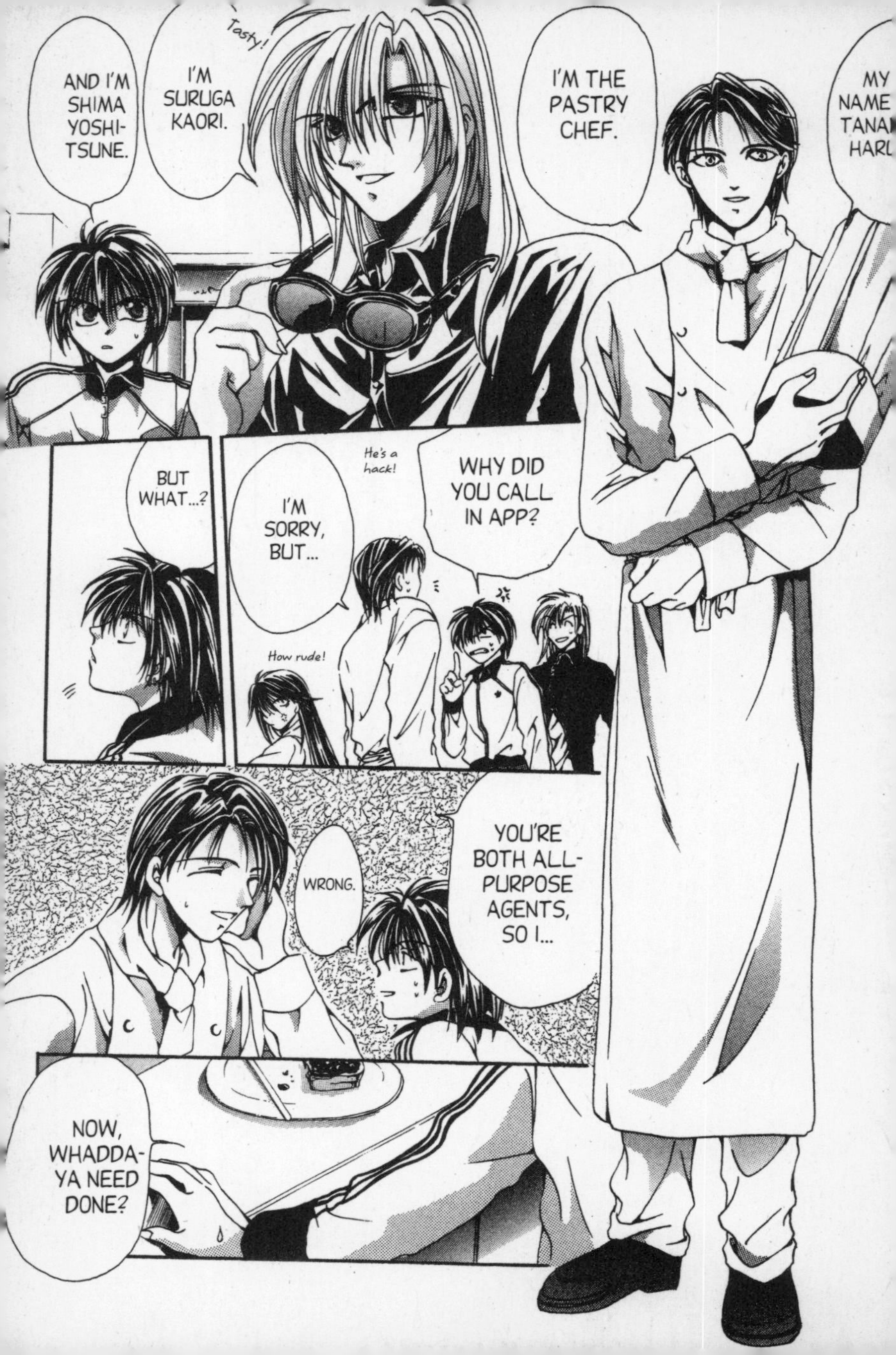
MY NAME TANA HAR
I'M THE PASTRY CHEF.
I'M SURUGA KAORI.
Tasty!
AND I'M SHIMA YOSHI-TSUNE.
WHY DID YOU CALL IN APP?
He's a hack!
I'M SORRY, BUT...
How rude!
BUT WHAT...?
YOU'RE BOTH ALL-PURPOSE AGENTS, SO I...
WRONG.
NOW, WHADDA-YA NEED DONE?

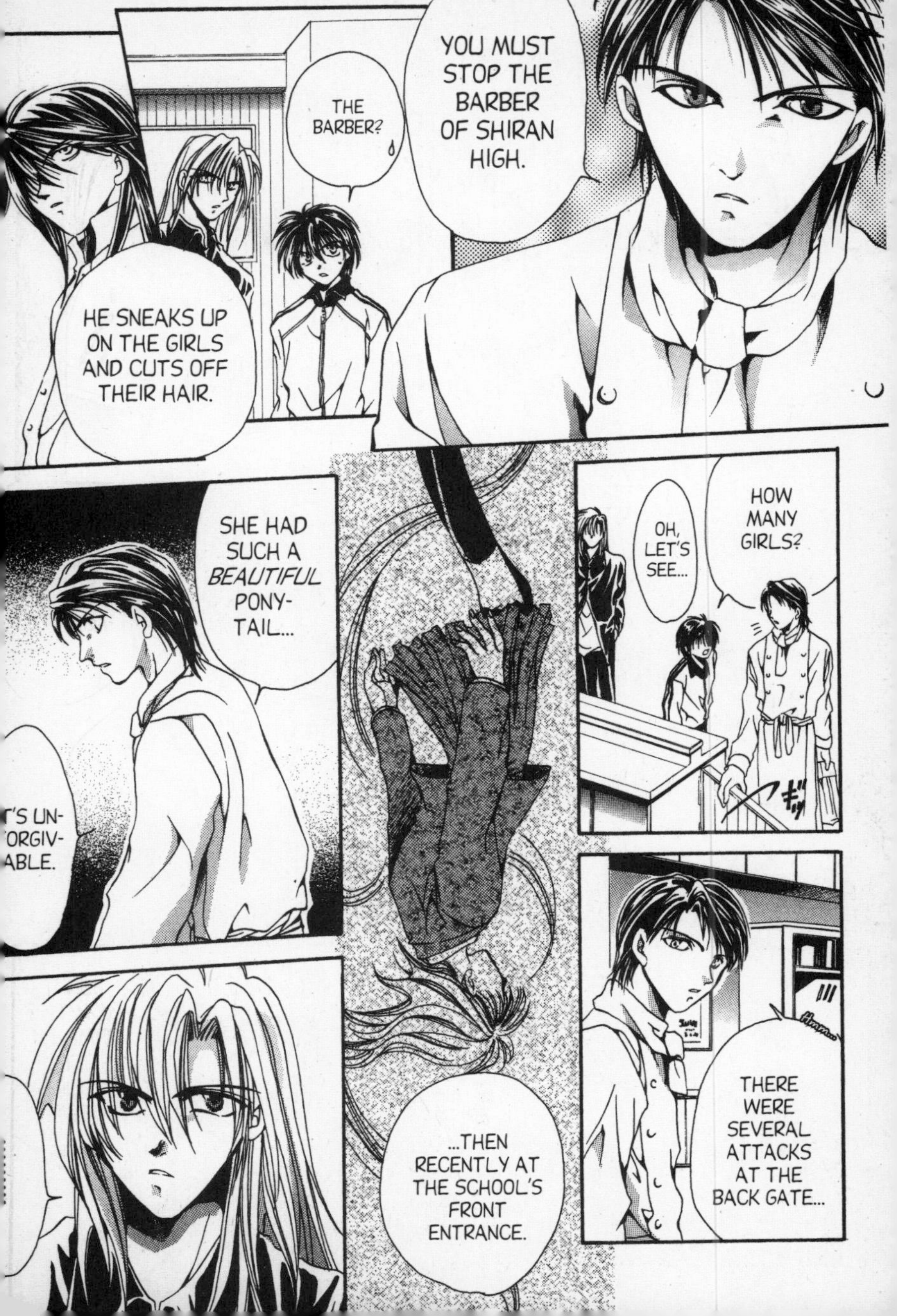
YOU MUST STOP THE BARBER OF SHIRAN HIGH.
THE BARBER?
HE SNEAKS UP ON THE GIRLS AND CUTS OFF THEIR HAIR.
HOW MANY GIRLS?
OH, LET'S SEE...
ギッ
THERE WERE SEVERAL ATTACKS AT THE BACK GATE...
...THEN RECENTLY AT THE SCHOOL'S FRONT ENTRANCE.
SHE HAD SUCH A *BEAUTIFUL* PONY-TAIL...
'S UN-ORGIV-ABLE.

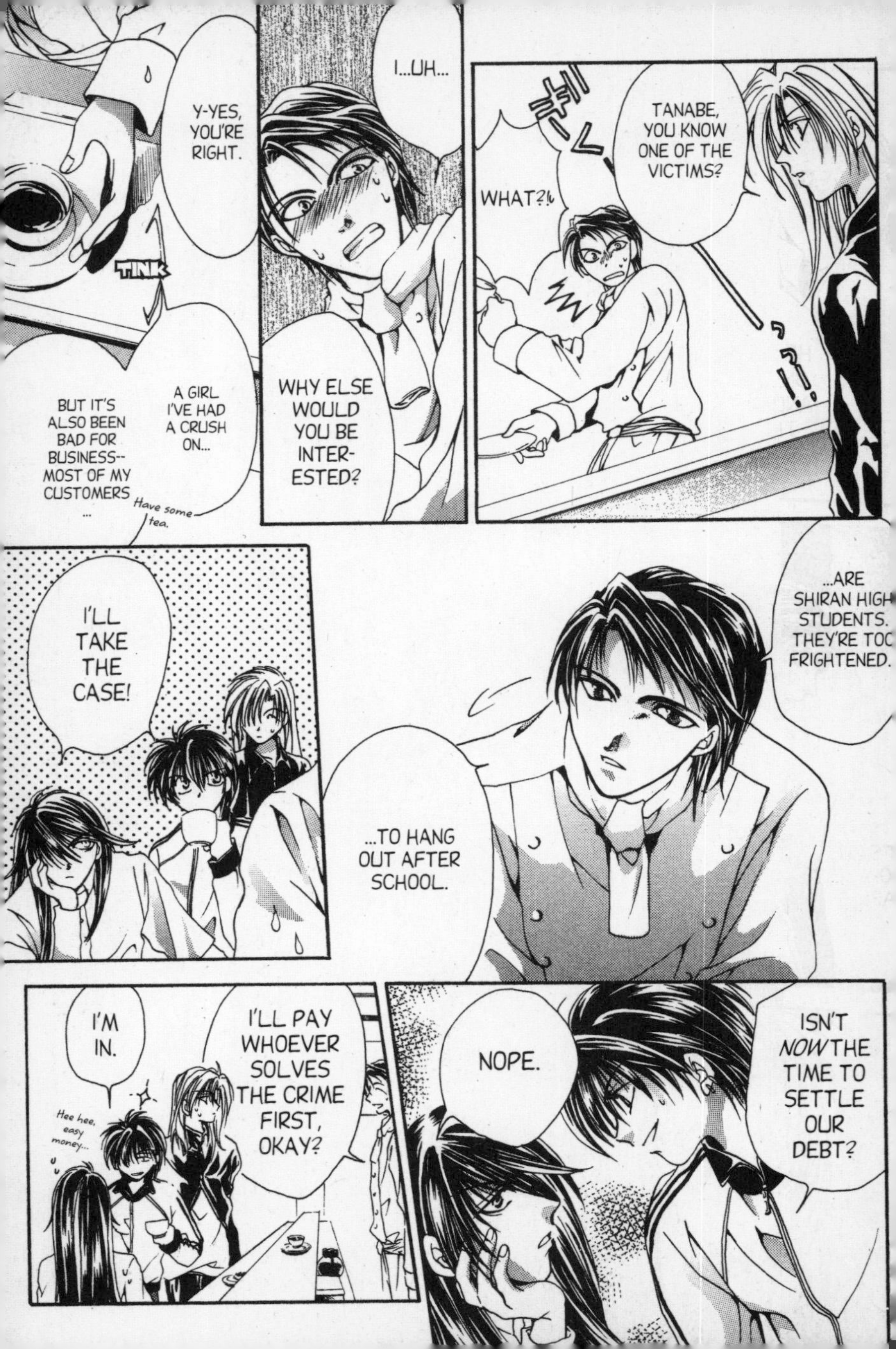
TANABE, YOU KNOW ONE OF THE VICTIMS?
WHAT?!
?!!
I...UH...
WHY ELSE WOULD YOU BE INTERESTED?
Y-YES, YOU'RE RIGHT.
TINK
A GIRL I'VE HAD A CRUSH ON...
BUT IT'S ALSO BEEN BAD FOR BUSINESS--MOST OF MY CUSTOMERS ...
Have some tea.
...ARE SHIRAN HIGH STUDENTS. THEY'RE TOO FRIGHTENED.
...TO HANG OUT AFTER SCHOOL.
I'LL TAKE THE CASE!
ISN'T *NOW* THE TIME TO SETTLE OUR DEBT?
NOPE.
I'LL PAY WHOEVER SOLVES THE CRIME FIRST, OKAY?
I'M IN.
Hee hee, easy money...

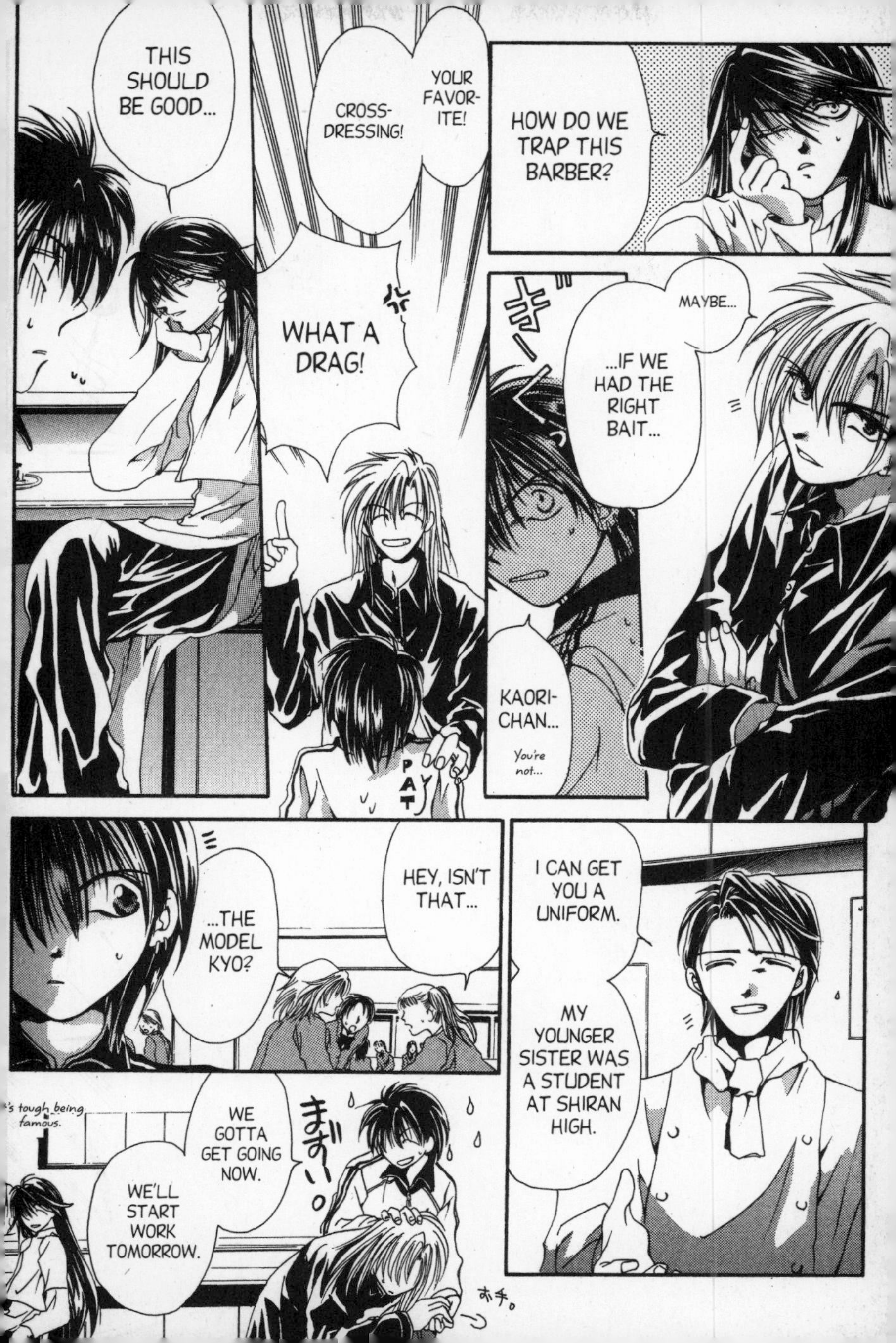
HOW DO WE TRAP THIS BARBER?
MAYBE...
...IF WE HAD THE RIGHT BAIT...
KAORI-CHAN...
You're not...
YOUR FAVOR-ITE!
CROSS-DRESSING!
WHAT A DRAG!
PAT PAT
THIS SHOULD BE GOOD...
I CAN GET YOU A UNIFORM.
MY YOUNGER SISTER WAS A STUDENT AT SHIRAN HIGH.
HEY, ISN'T THAT...
...THE MODEL KYO?
's tough being famous.
WE GOTTA GET GOING NOW.
WE'LL START WORK TOMORROW.
まずい。
お手。

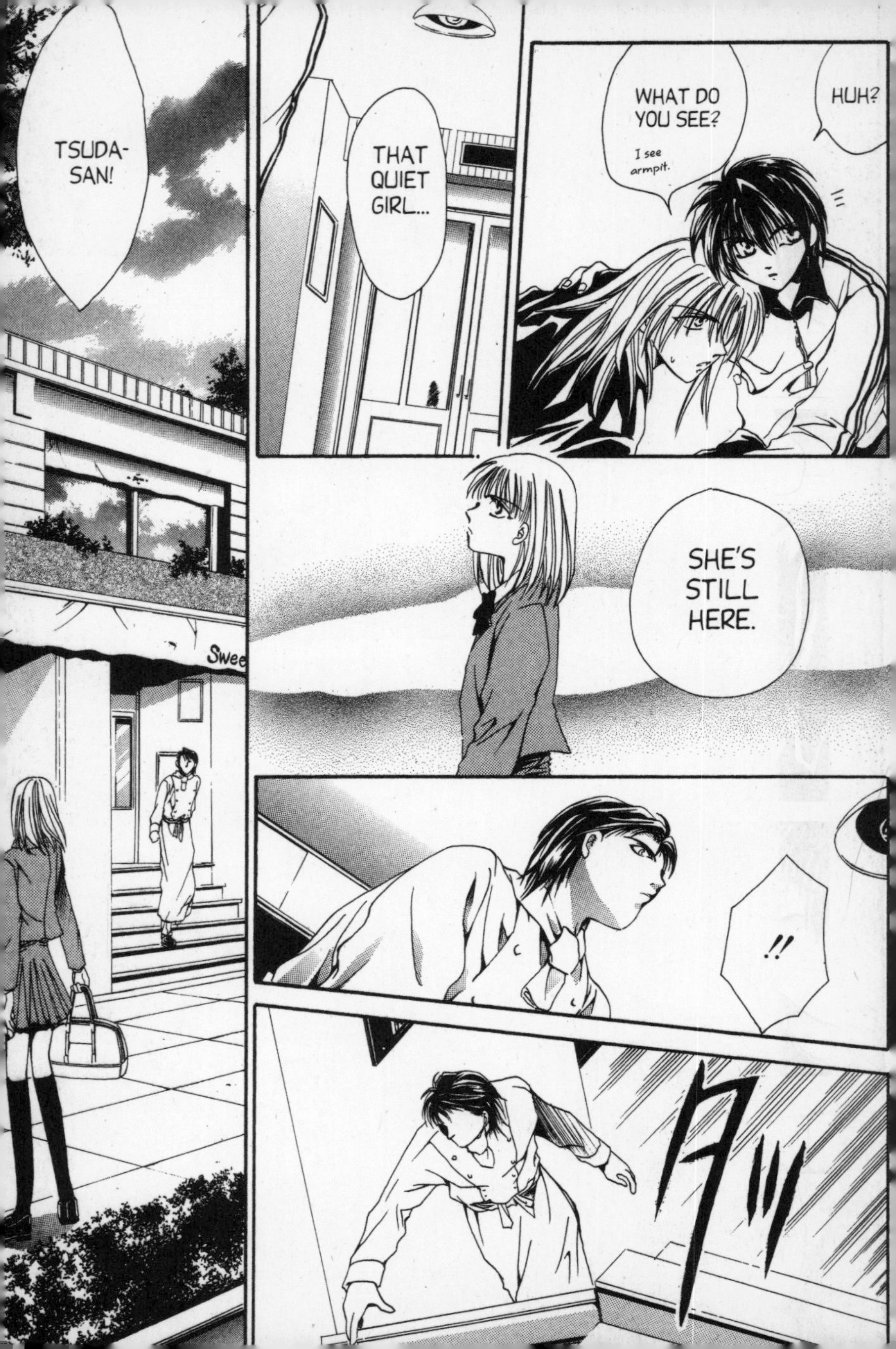

HUH?
WHAT DO YOU SEE?
I see armpit.
THAT QUIET GIRL...
SHE'S STILL HERE.
!!
ダッ
TSUDA-SAN!
Swee

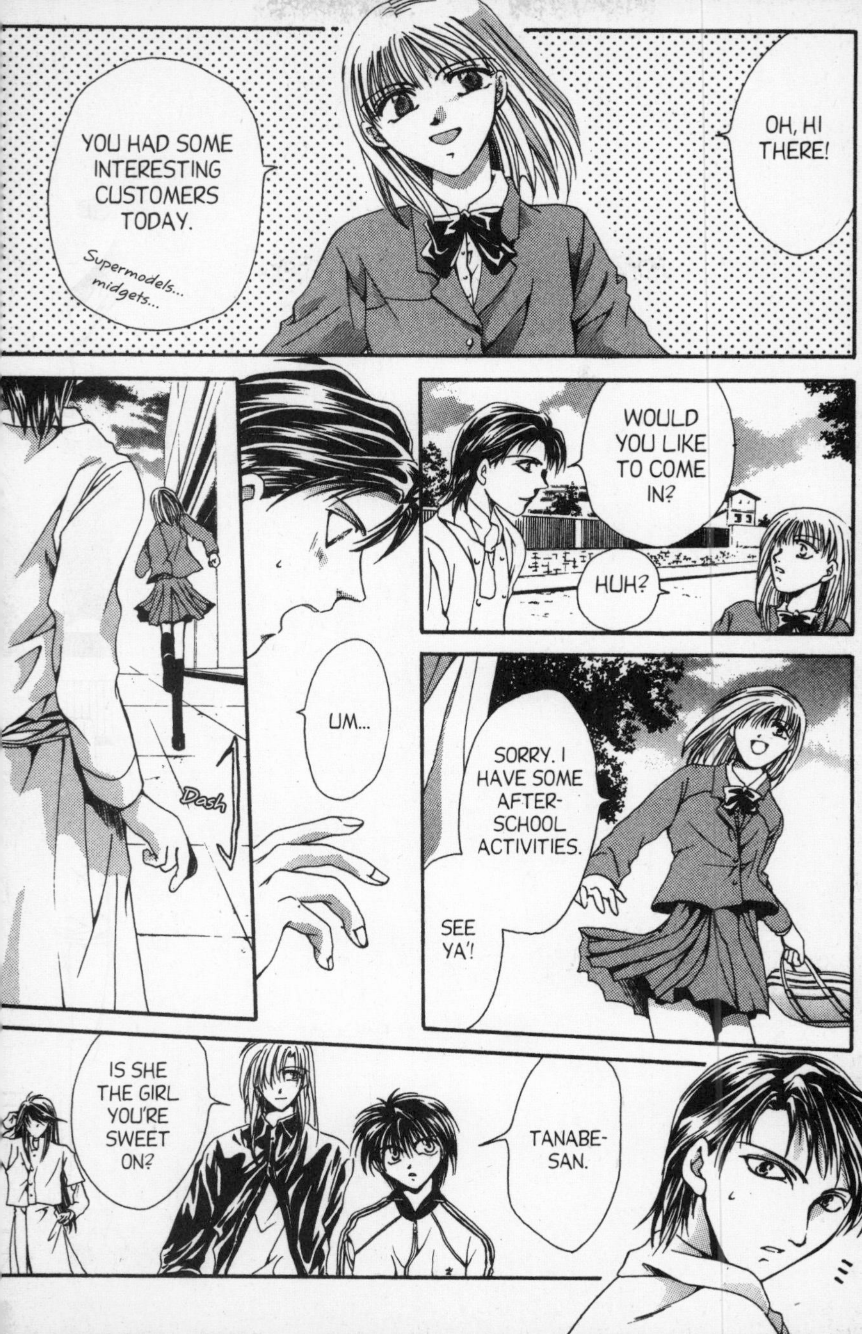
OH, HI THERE!
YOU HAD SOME INTERESTING CUSTOMERS TODAY.
Supermodels... midgets...
WOULD YOU LIKE TO COME IN?
HUH?
SORRY. I HAVE SOME AFTER-SCHOOL ACTIVITIES.
SEE YA'!
UM...
Dash
TANABE-SAN.
IS SHE THE GIRL YOU'RE SWEET ON?

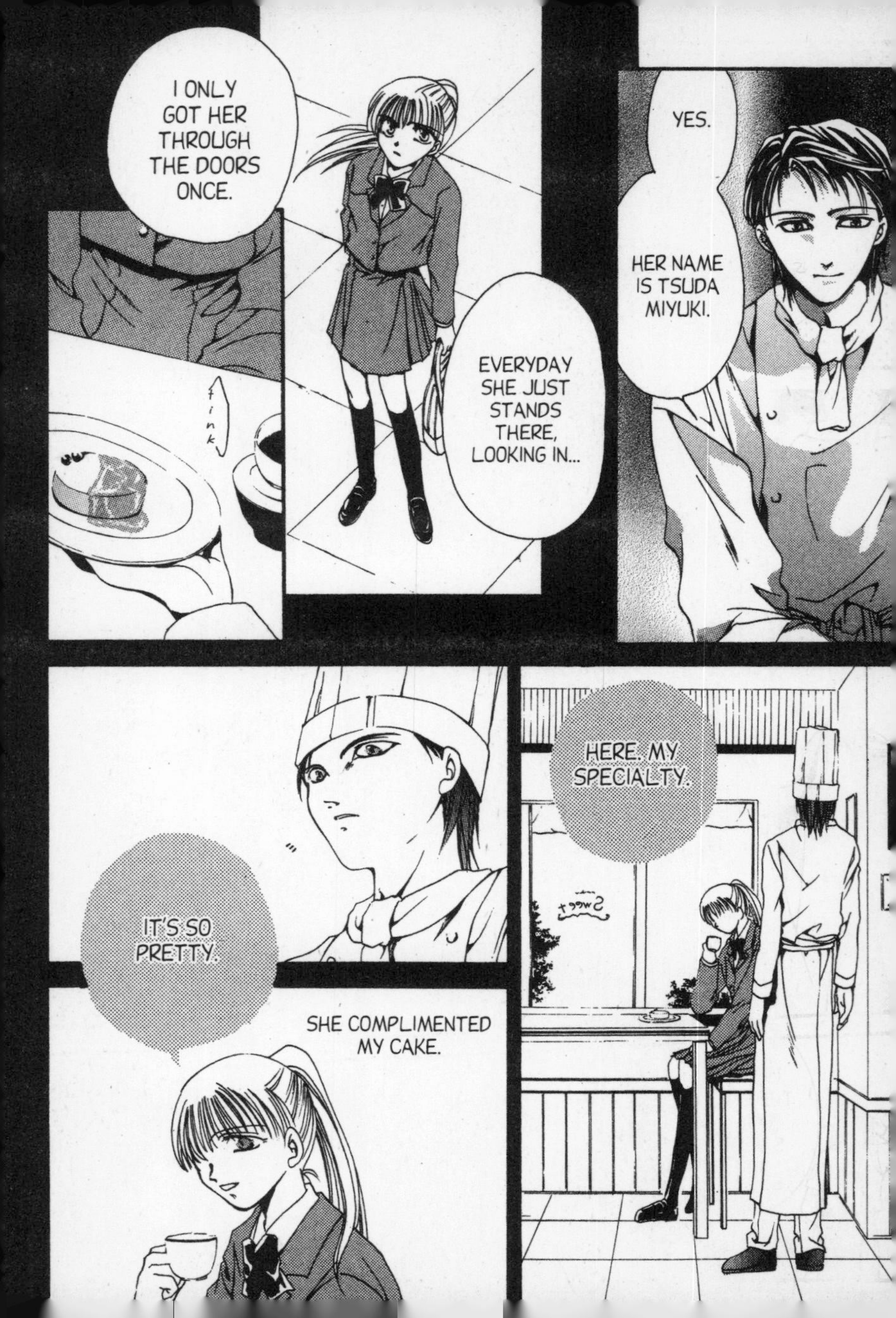
YES.
HER NAME IS TSUDA MIYUKI.
EVERYDAY SHE JUST STANDS THERE, LOOKING IN...
I ONLY GOT HER THROUGH THE DOORS ONCE.
tink
HERE. MY SPECIALTY.
IT'S SO PRETTY.
SHE COMPLIMENTED MY CAKE.

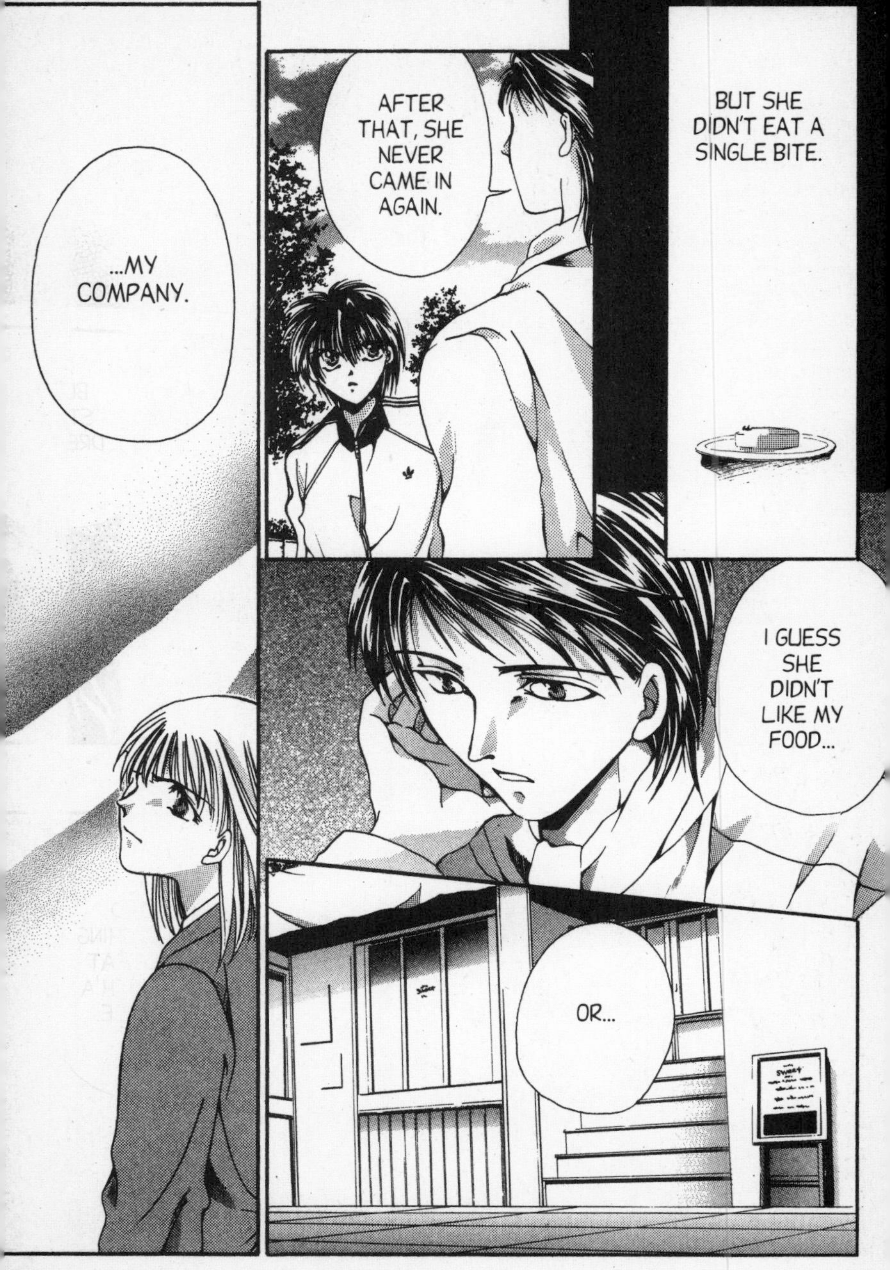
BUT SHE DIDN'T EAT A SINGLE BITE.
AFTER THAT, SHE NEVER CAME IN AGAIN.
I GUESS SHE DIDN'T LIKE MY FOOD...
OR...
...MY COMPANY.

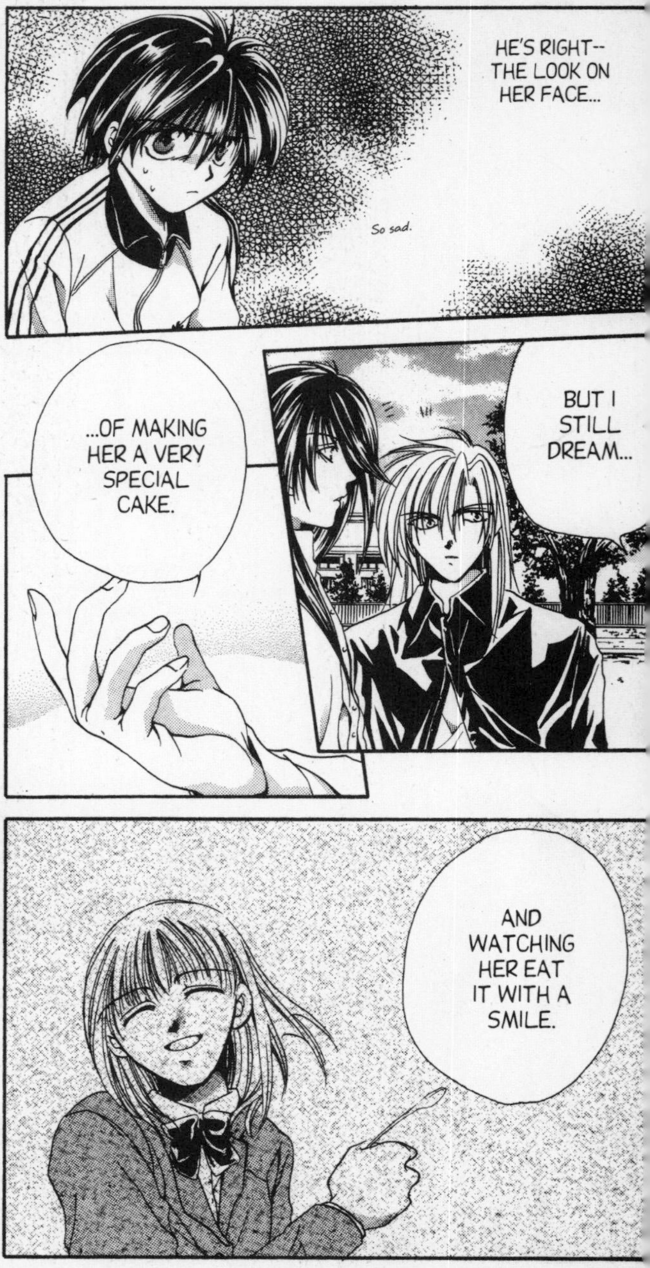
HE'S RIGHT-- THE LOOK ON HER FACE...
So sad.
BUT I STILL DREAM...
...OF MAKING HER A VERY SPECIAL CAKE.
AND WATCHING HER EAT IT WITH A SMILE.

Greetings! I'm Saenagi Ryo.

Born November 28th Sagittarius, type O blood. 163 cm tall
Turn-ons: Coffee, tea, cheese, Norman Rockwell
Turn-offs: Dried fruits, grapes, pushy people
Favorite bands: Scudelia Electro, Mr. Children, Brilliant Green, L'arc, and many more.
Favorite celebrity: I've always loved the comedy duo and variety show hosts, Downtown!
That's me in a nutshell!

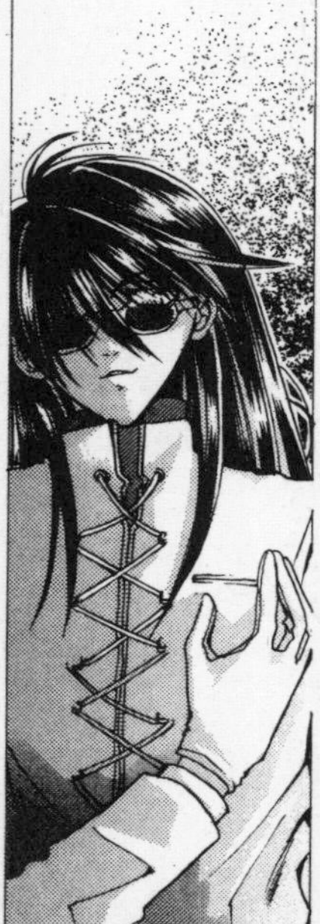

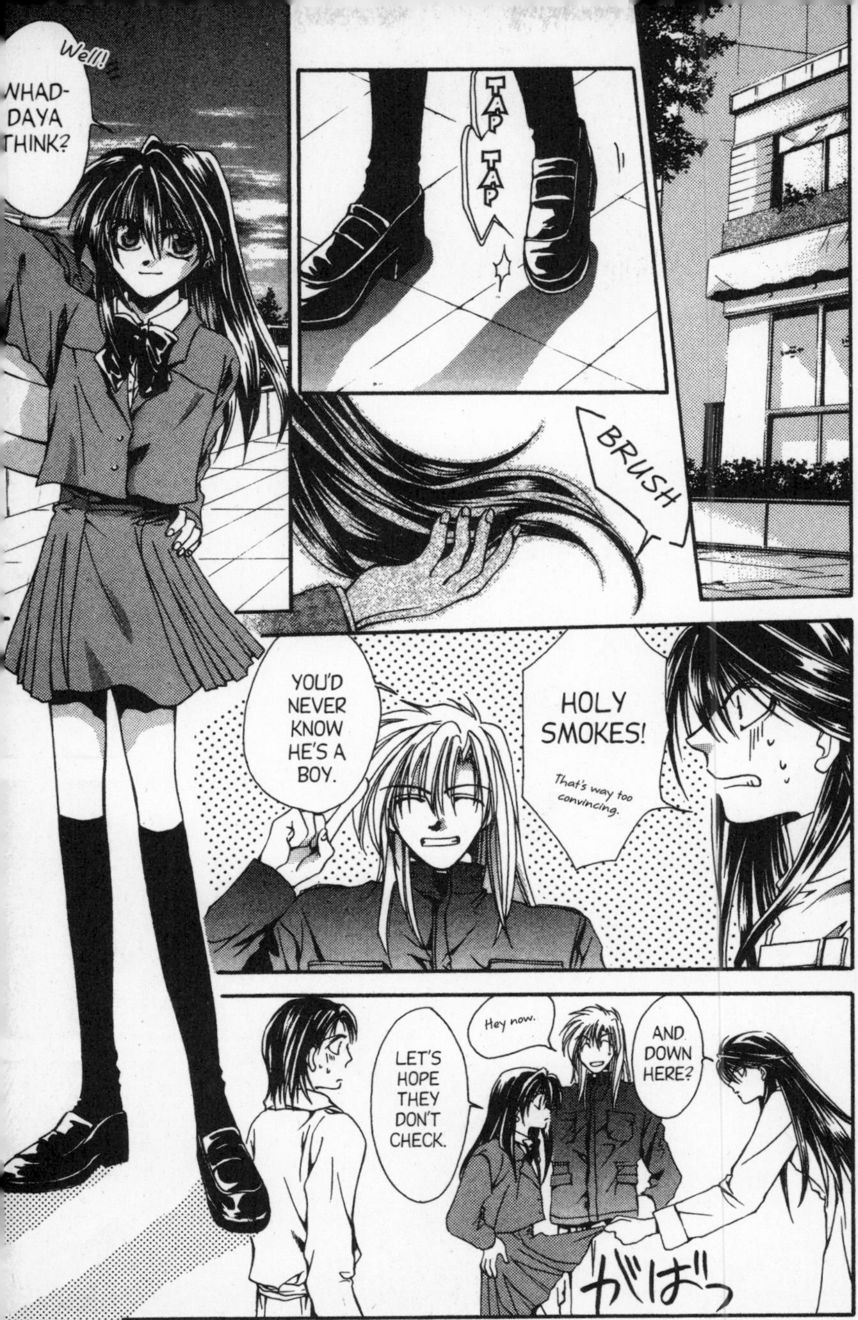
TAP TAP
BRUSH
HOLY SMOKES!
That's way too convincing.
YOU'D NEVER KNOW HE'S A BOY.
AND DOWN HERE?
Hey now.
LET'S HOPE THEY DON'T CHECK.
がばっ
Well!
WHAD-DAYA THINK?

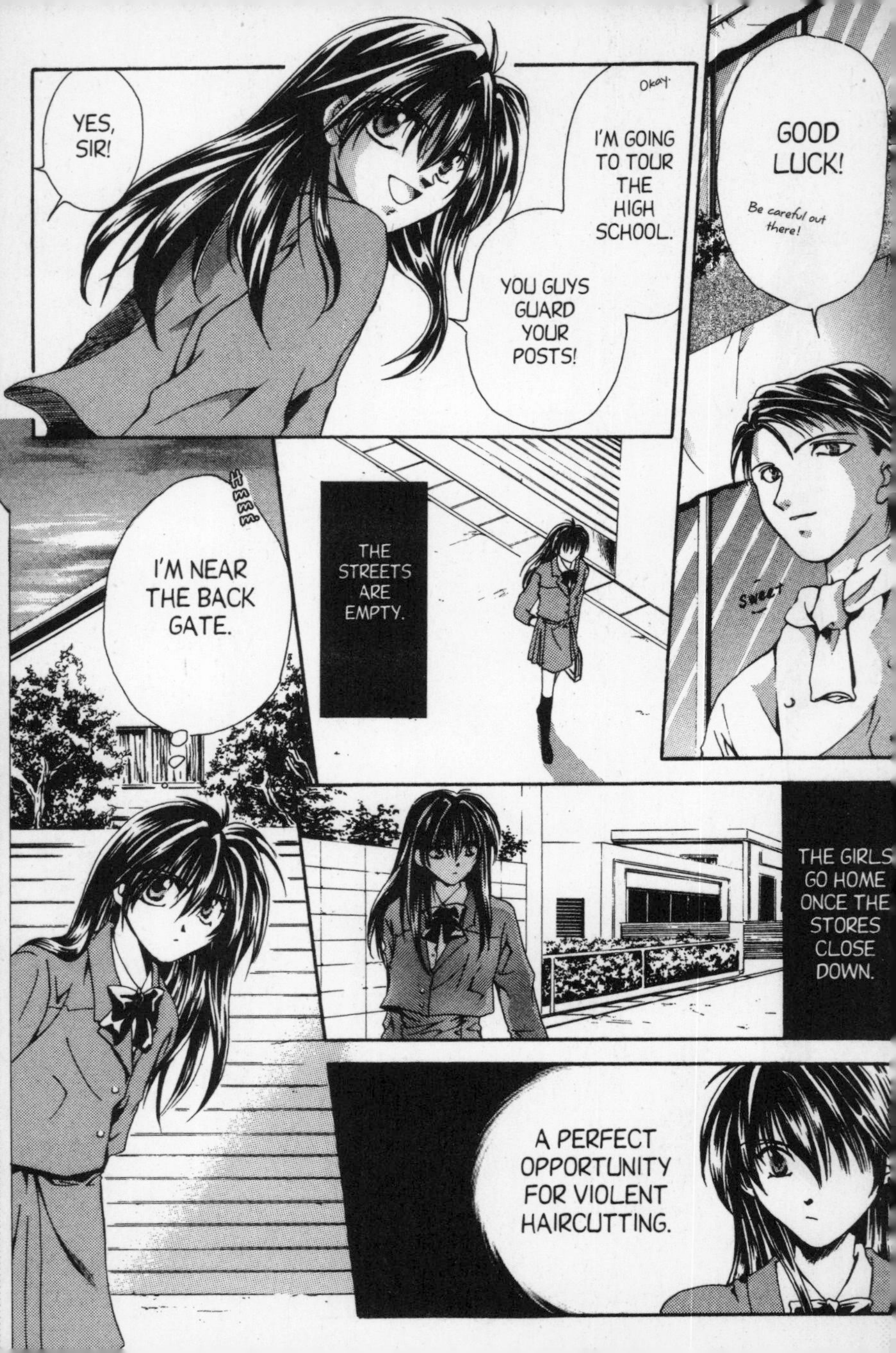
GOOD LUCK!
Be careful out there!
Okay.
I'M GOING TO TOUR THE HIGH SCHOOL.
YOU GUYS GUARD YOUR POSTS!
YES, SIR!
Sweat
THE STREETS ARE EMPTY.
Hmmm
I'M NEAR THE BACK GATE.
THE GIRLS GO HOME ONCE THE STORES CLOSE DOWN.
A PERFECT OPPORTUNITY FOR VIOLENT HAIRCUTTING.

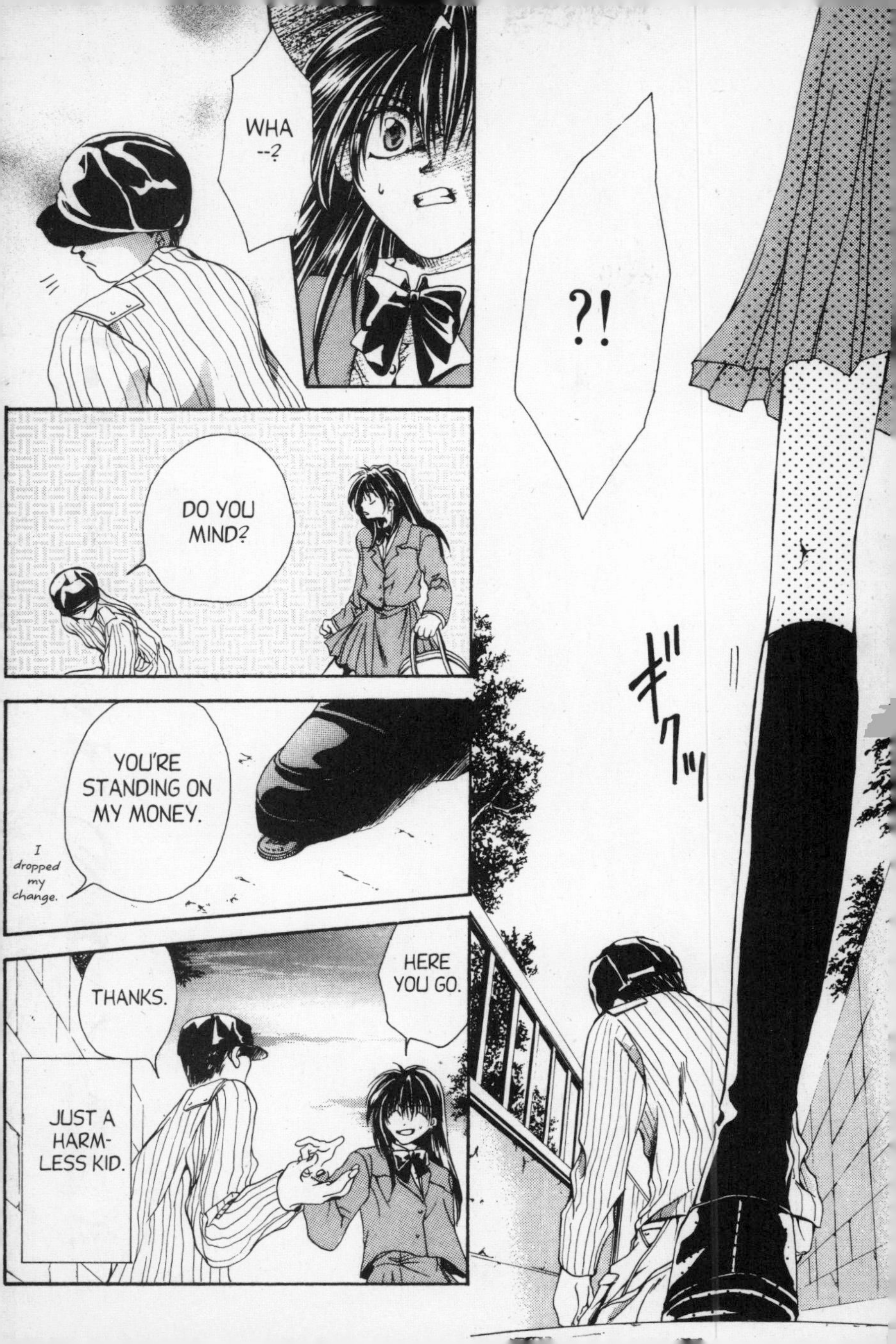
?!
ギクッ
WHA --?
DO YOU MIND?
YOU'RE STANDING ON MY MONEY.
I dropped my change.
HERE YOU GO.
THANKS.
JUST A HARM-LESS KID.

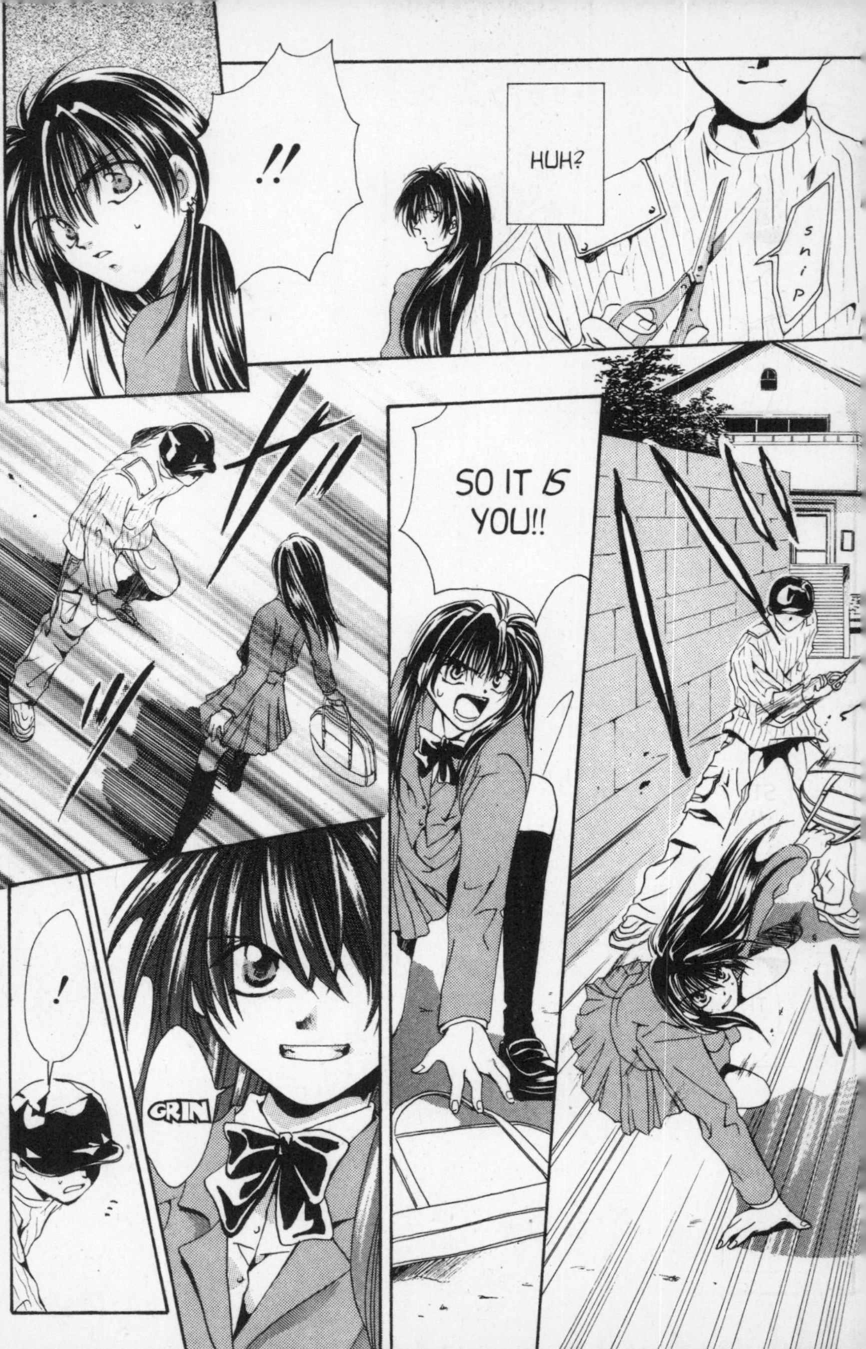
HUH?
snip
!!
SO IT IS YOU!!
GRIN
!

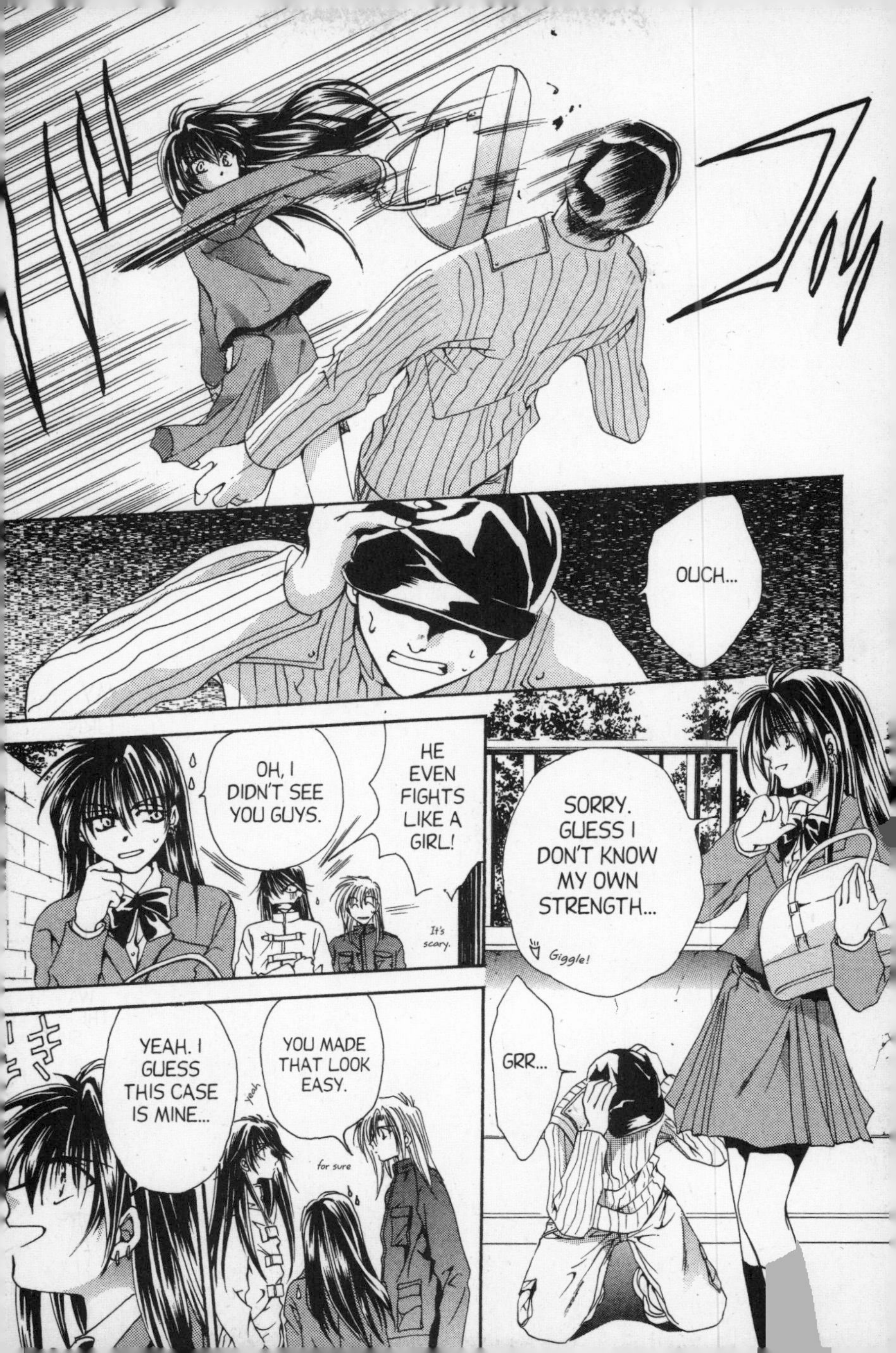
OUCH...
SORRY. GUESS I DON'T KNOW MY OWN STRENGTH...
Giggle!
GRR...
HE EVEN FIGHTS LIKE A GIRL!
OH, I DIDN'T SEE YOU GUYS.
It's scary.
YOU MADE THAT LOOK EASY.
YEAH. I GUESS THIS CASE IS MINE...
yeah
for sure

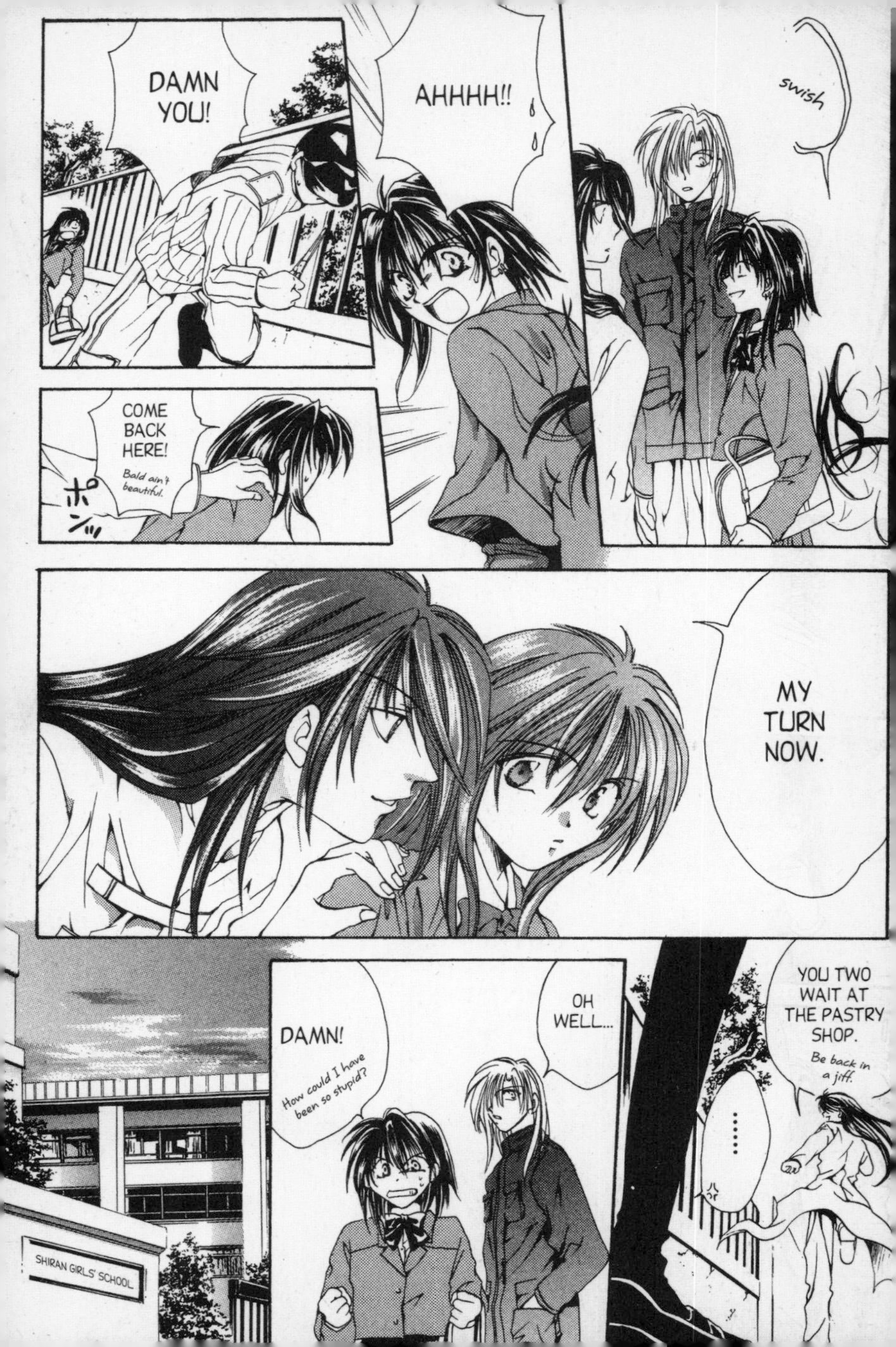
swish
AHHHH!!
DAMN YOU!
COME BACK HERE!
Bald ain't beautiful.
ポンッ
MY TURN NOW.
YOU TWO WAIT AT THE PASTRY SHOP.
Be back in a jiff.
……
OH WELL...
DAMN!
How could I have been so stupid?
SHIRAN GIRLS' SCHOOL

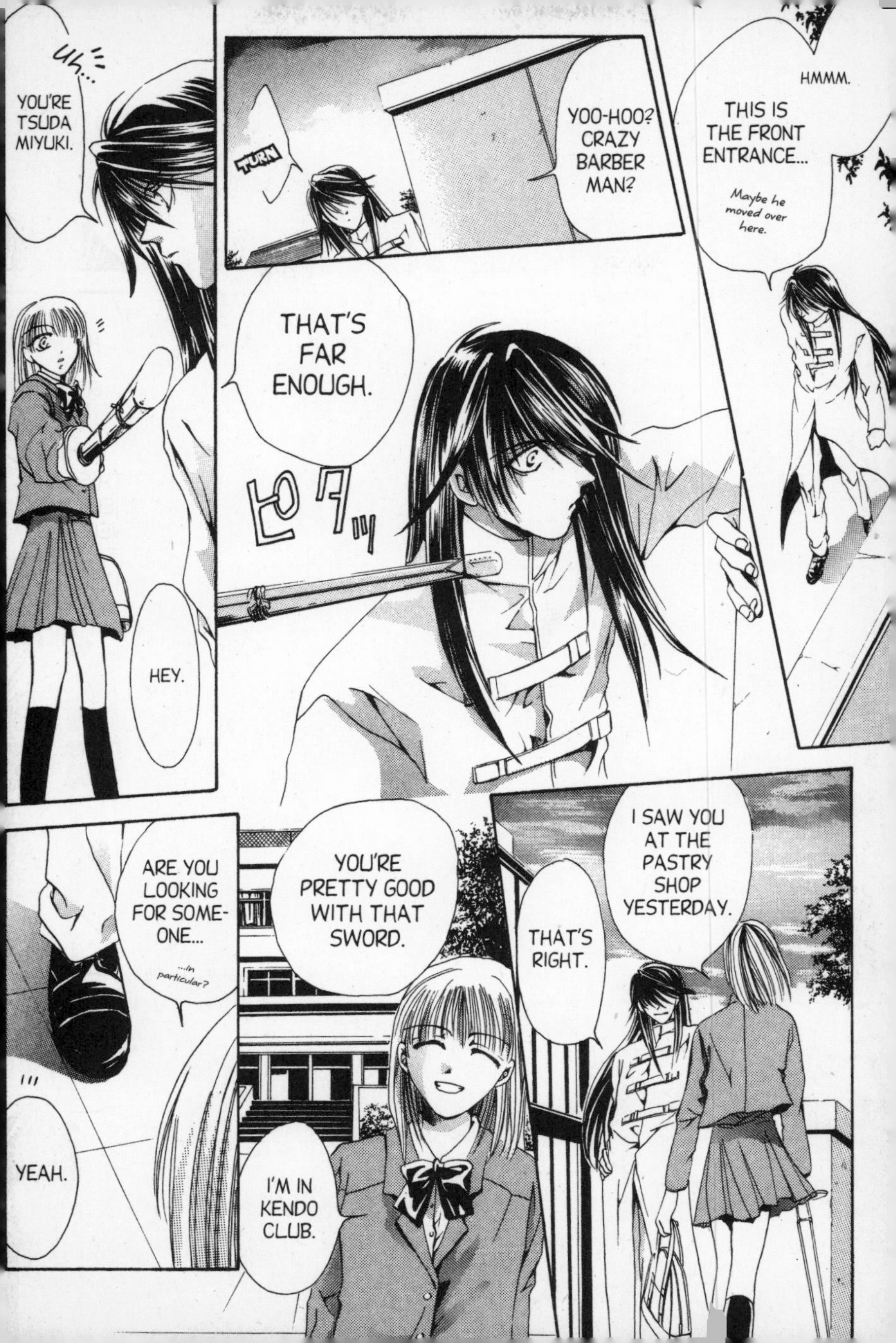
HMMM.
THIS IS THE FRONT ENTRANCE...
Maybe he moved over here.
YOO-HOO? CRAZY BARBER MAN?
TURN
THAT'S FAR ENOUGH.
Uh...
YOU'RE TSUDA MIYUKI.
HEY.
I SAW YOU AT THE PASTRY SHOP YESTERDAY.
THAT'S RIGHT.
YOU'RE PRETTY GOOD WITH THAT SWORD.
I'M IN KENDO CLUB.
ARE YOU LOOKING FOR SOME-ONE...
...in particular?
YEAH.

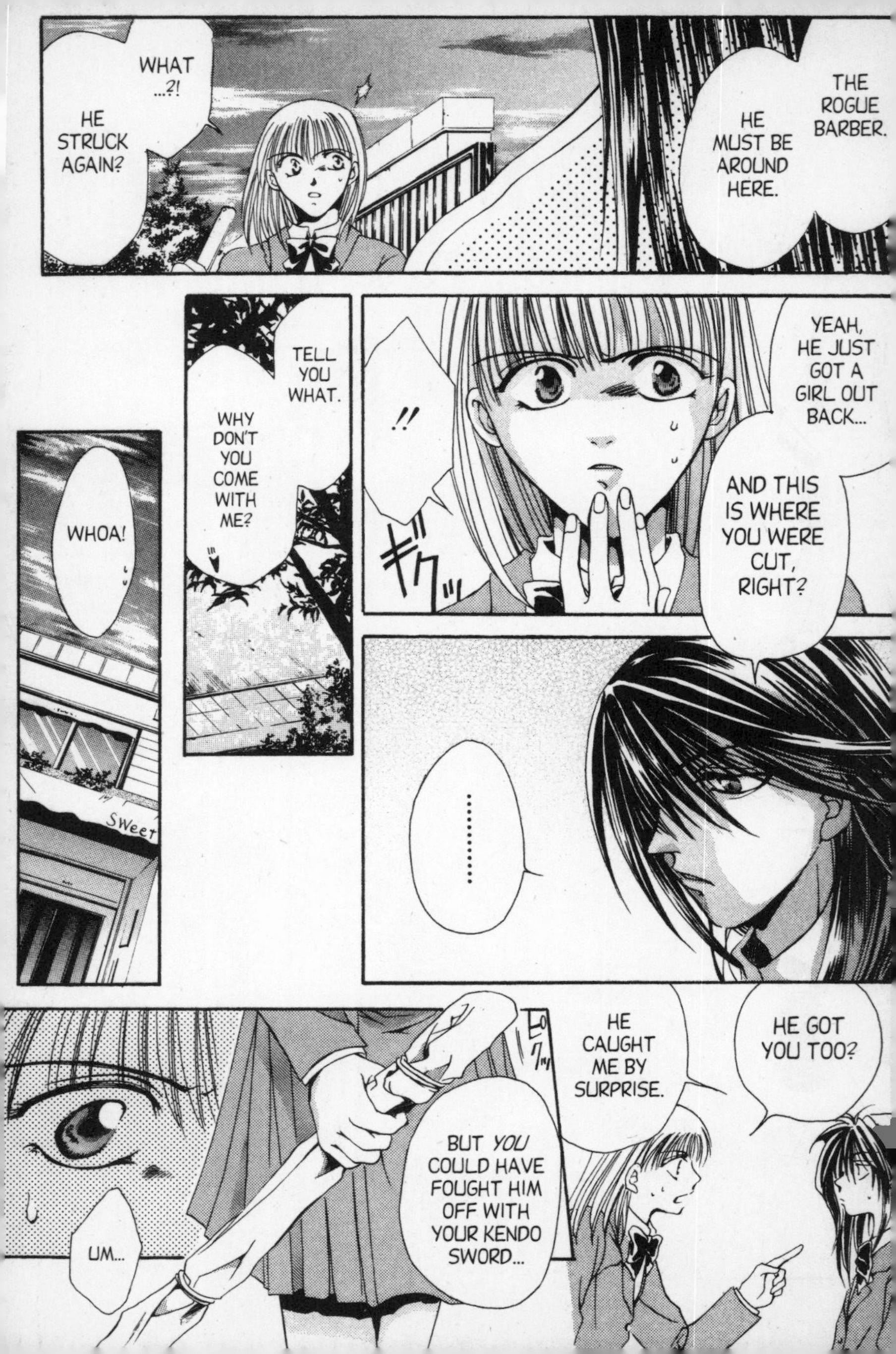
THE ROGUE BARBER.
HE MUST BE AROUND HERE.
WHAT ...?!
HE STRUCK AGAIN?
YEAH, HE JUST GOT A GIRL OUT BACK...
AND THIS IS WHERE YOU WERE CUT, RIGHT?
!!
ギクッ
TELL YOU WHAT.
WHY DON'T YOU COME WITH ME?
......
WHOA!
Sweet
HE GOT YOU TOO?
HE CAUGHT ME BY SURPRISE.
BUT YOU COULD HAVE FOUGHT HIM OFF WITH YOUR KENDO SWORD...
UM...

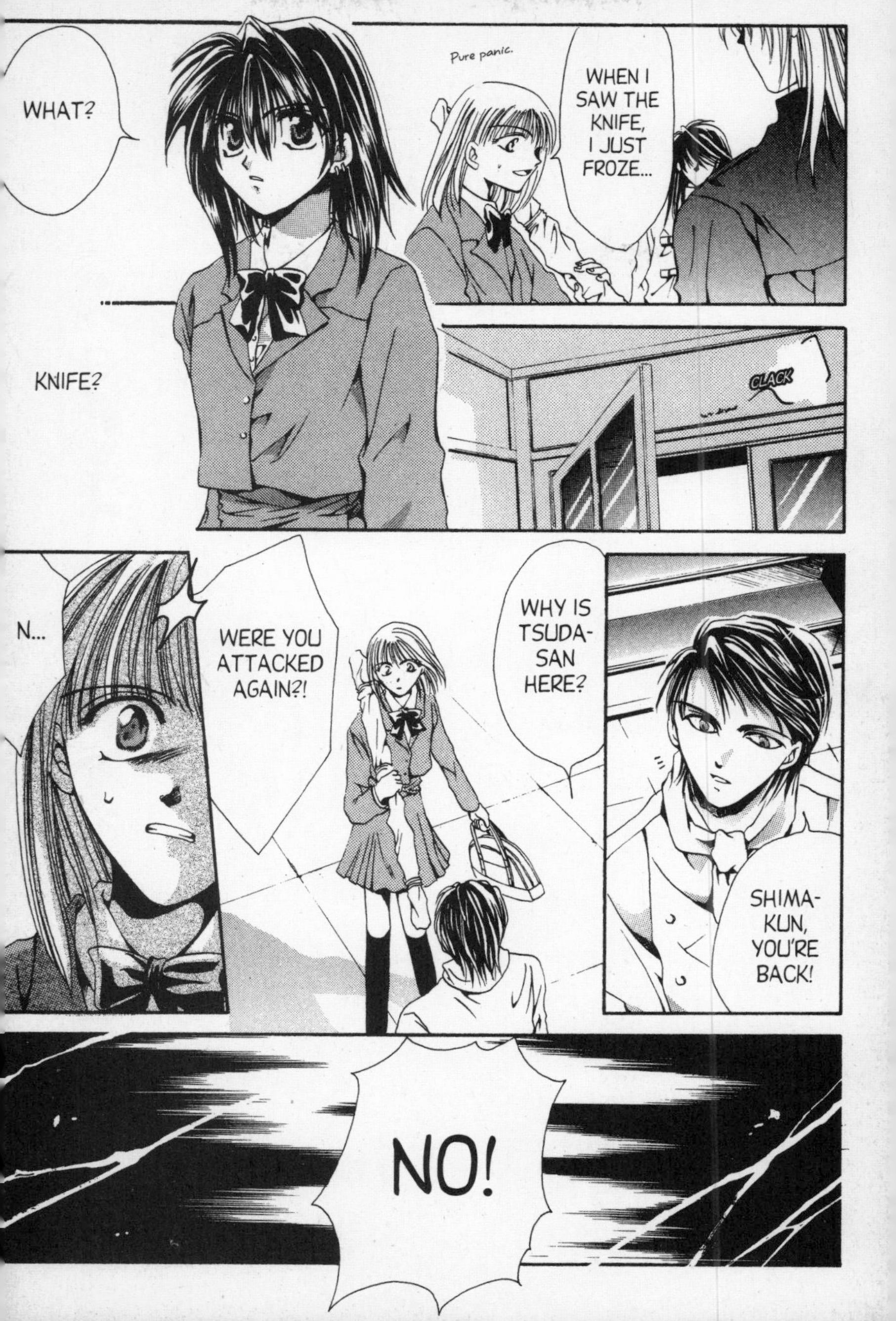
Pure panic.
WHEN I SAW THE KNIFE, I JUST FROZE...
WHAT?
CLACK
KNIFE?
SHIMA-KUN, YOU'RE BACK!
WHY IS TSUDA-SAN HERE?
WERE YOU ATTACKED AGAIN?!
N...
NO!

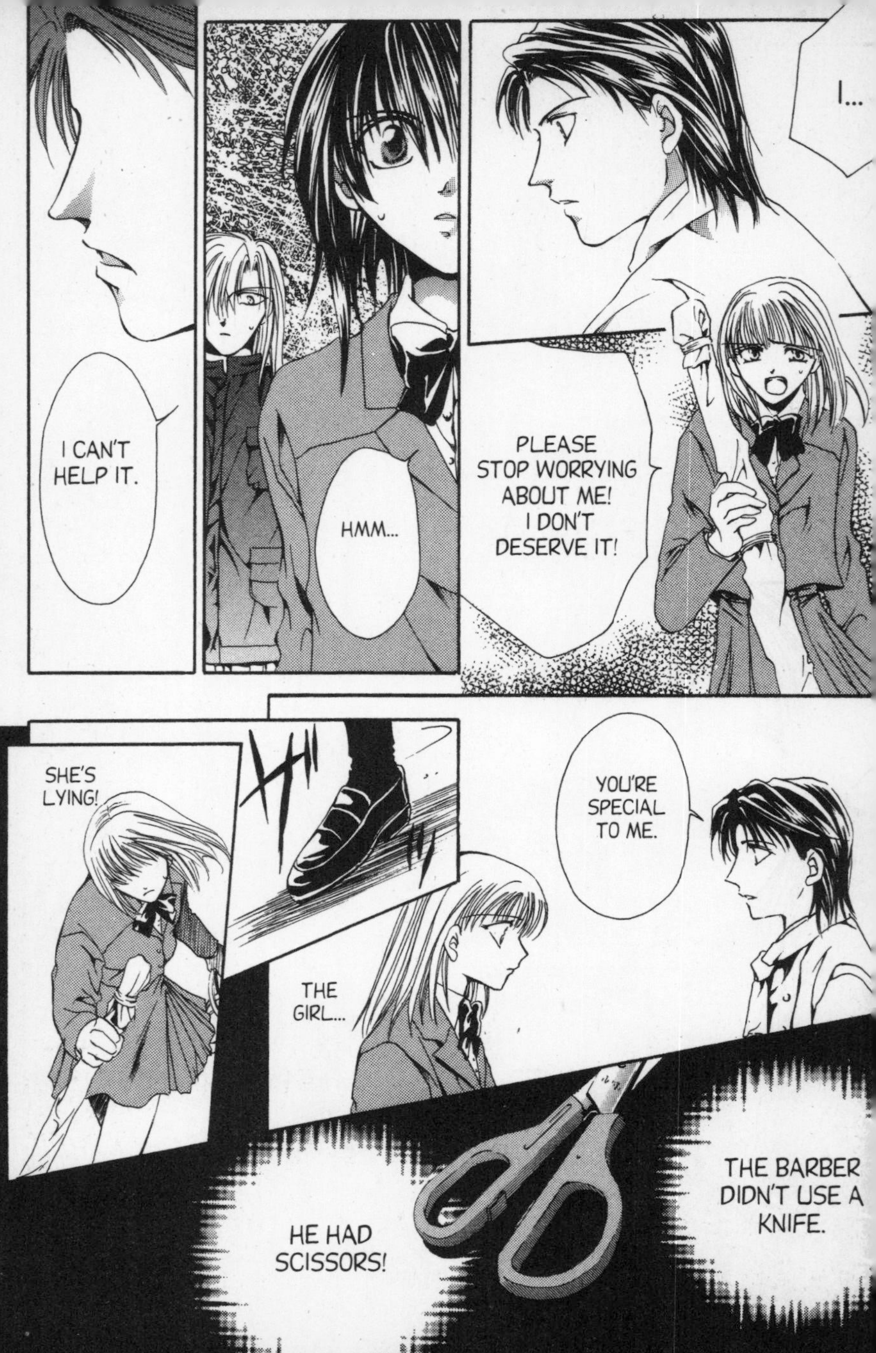
I...
PLEASE STOP WORRYING ABOUT ME! I DON'T DESERVE IT!
HMM...
I CAN'T HELP IT.
YOU'RE SPECIAL TO ME.
THE GIRL...
SHE'S LYING!
THE BARBER DIDN'T USE A KNIFE.
HE HAD SCISSORS!

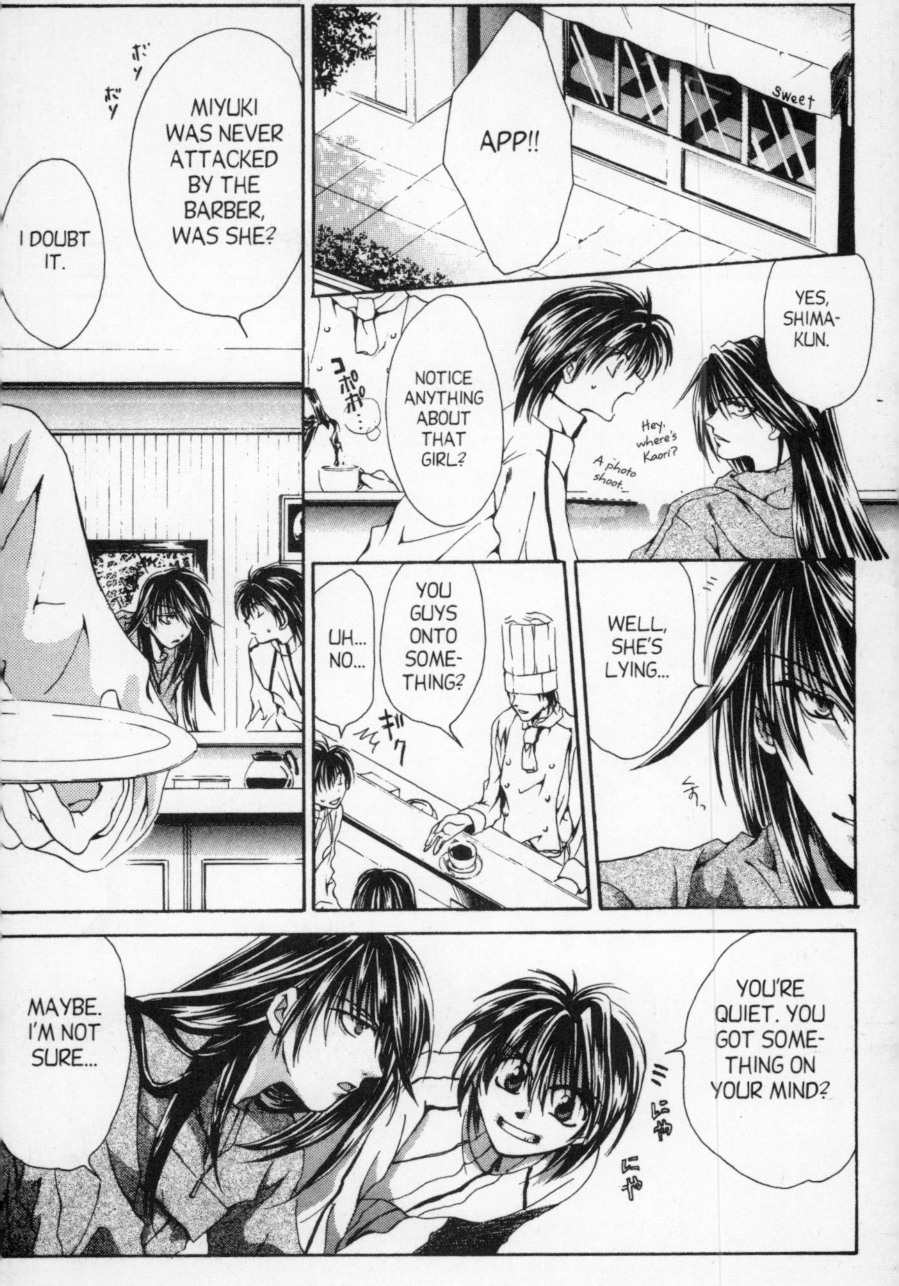
Sweet
APP!!
MIYUKI WAS NEVER ATTACKED BY THE BARBER, WAS SHE?
ボソ ボソ
I DOUBT IT.
YES, SHIMA-KUN.
NOTICE ANYTHING ABOUT THAT GIRL?
Hey, where's Kaori?
A photo shoot.
コポポ…
WELL, SHE'S LYING...
YOU GUYS ONTO SOMETHING?
UH... NO...
ギクッ
YOU'RE QUIET. YOU GOT SOMETHING ON YOUR MIND?
にや にや
MAYBE. I'M NOT SURE...

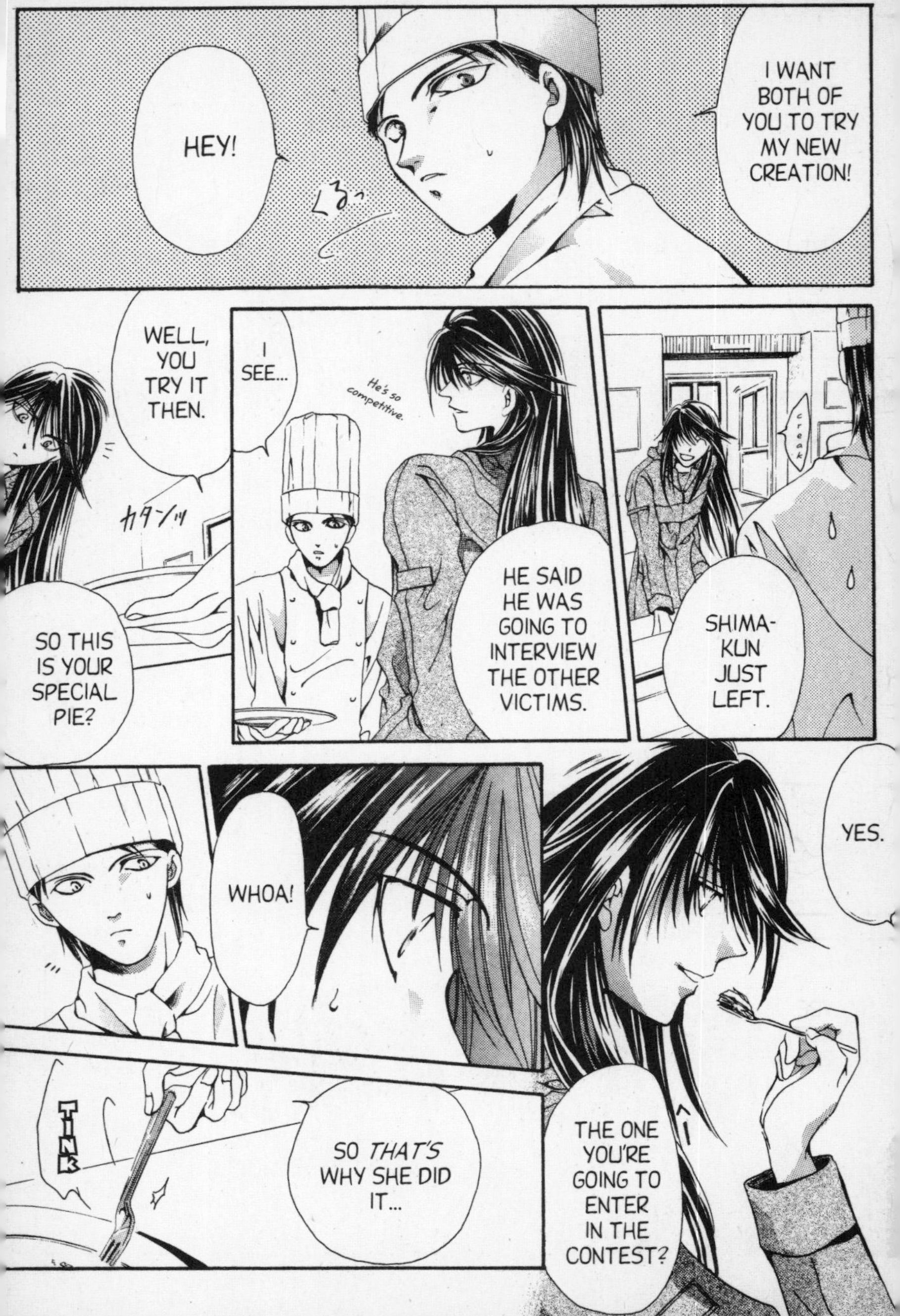
I WANT BOTH OF YOU TO TRY MY NEW CREATION!
HEY!
くるっ
SHIMA-KUN JUST LEFT.
creak
HE SAID HE WAS GOING TO INTERVIEW THE OTHER VICTIMS.
I SEE...
He's so competitive.
WELL, YOU TRY IT THEN.
カタンッ
SO THIS IS YOUR SPECIAL PIE?
YES.
THE ONE YOU'RE GOING TO ENTER IN THE CONTEST?
WHOA!
SO *THAT'S* WHY SHE DID IT...
TINK

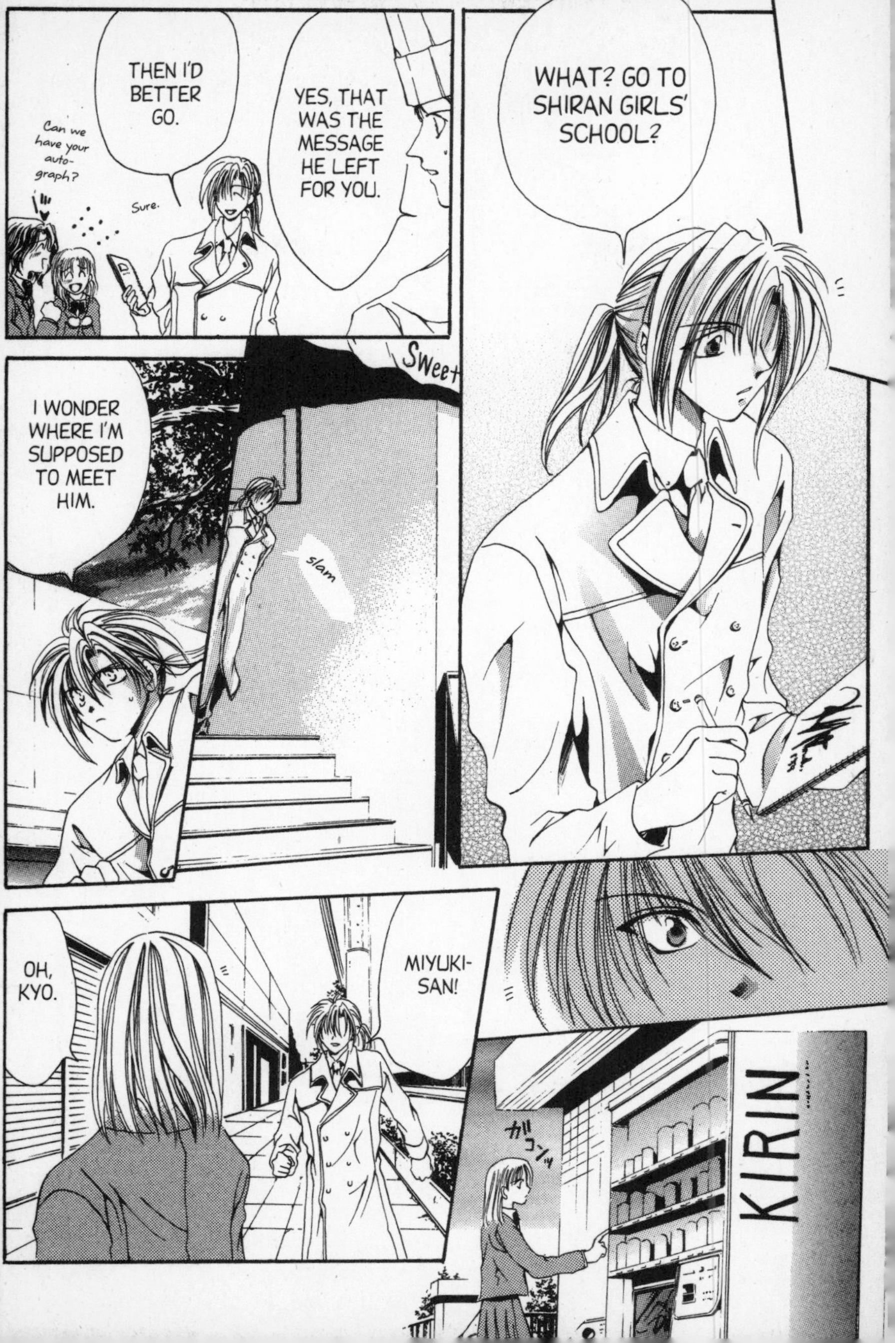
WHAT? GO TO SHIRAN GIRLS' SCHOOL?
YES, THAT WAS THE MESSAGE HE LEFT FOR YOU.
THEN I'D BETTER GO.
Can we have your autograph?
Sure.
Sweet
I WONDER WHERE I'M SUPPOSED TO MEET HIM.
slam
KIRIN
ガコンッ
MIYUKI-SAN!
OH, KYO.

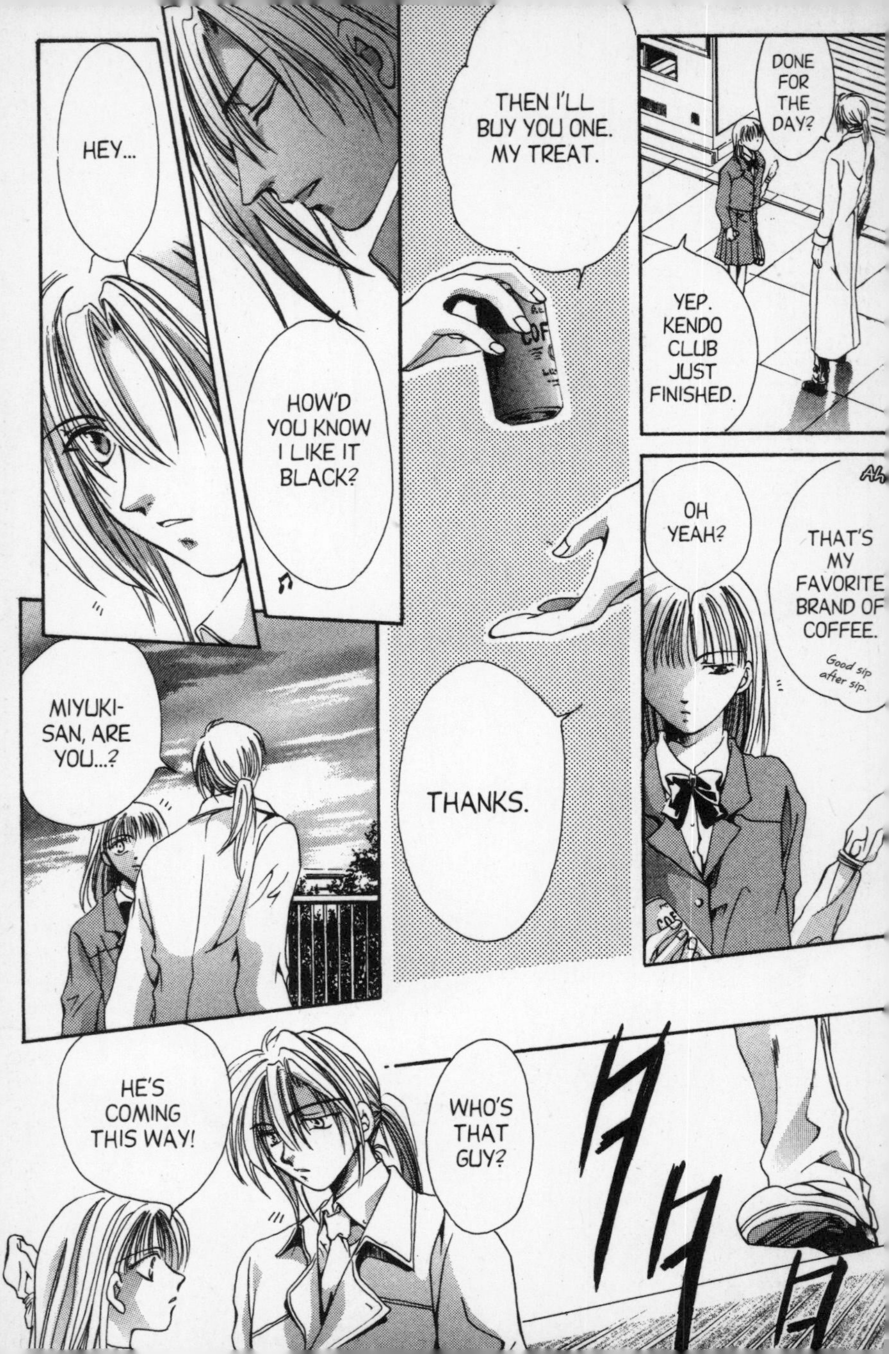
DONE FOR THE DAY?
YEP. KENDO CLUB JUST FINISHED.
Ah
THAT'S MY FAVORITE BRAND OF COFFEE.
Good sip after sip.
OH YEAH?
THEN I'LL BUY YOU ONE. MY TREAT.
THANKS.
HEY...
HOW'D YOU KNOW I LIKE IT BLACK?
MIYUKI-SAN, ARE YOU...?
WHO'S THAT GUY?
HE'S COMING THIS WAY!

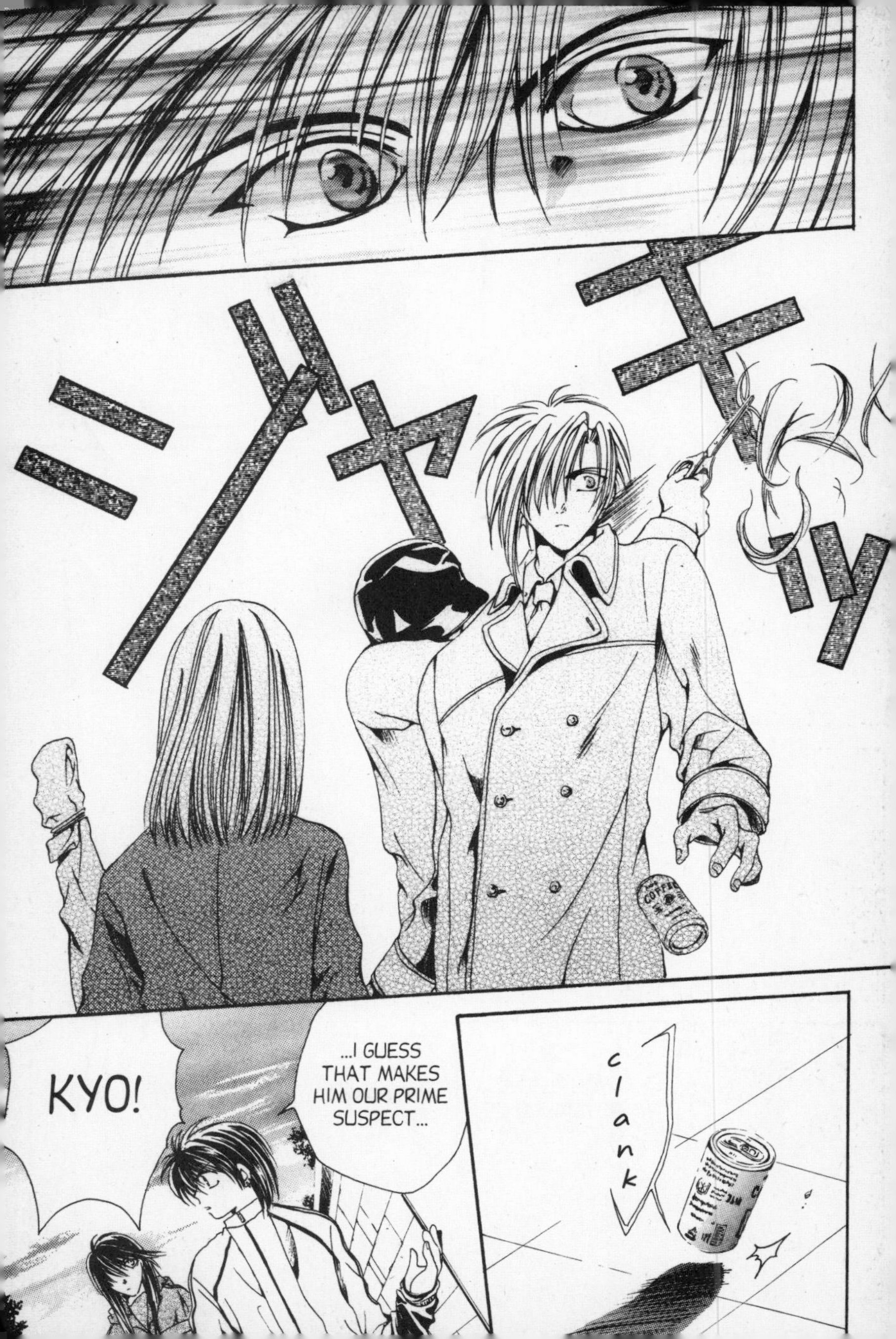
ジャキッ
clank
...I GUESS THAT MAKES HIM OUR PRIME SUSPECT...
KYO!

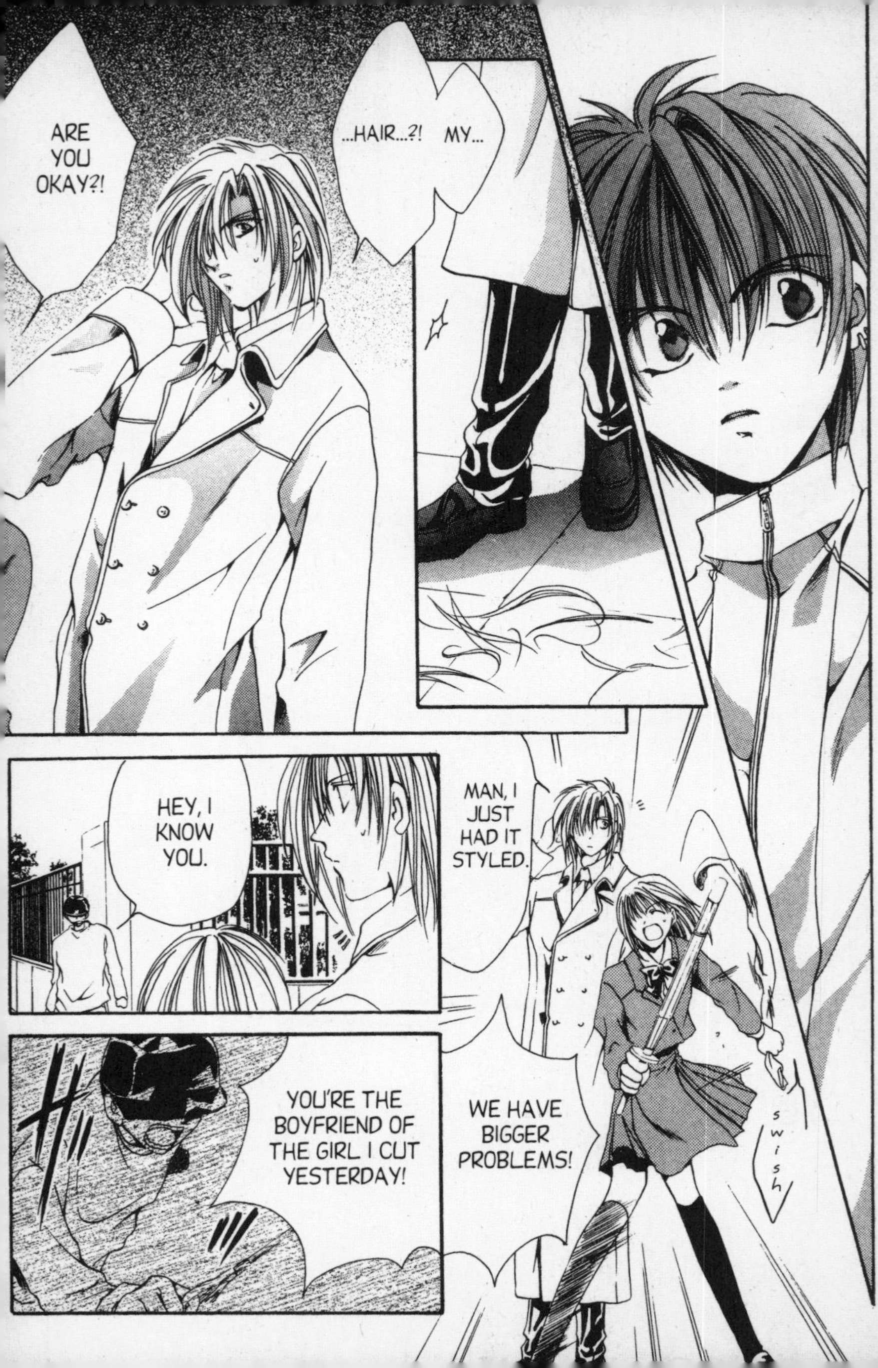
MY...
...HAIR...?!
ARE YOU OKAY?!
MAN, I JUST HAD IT STYLED.
WE HAVE BIGGER PROBLEMS!
swish
HEY, I KNOW YOU.
YOU'RE THE BOYFRIEND OF THE GIRL I CUT YESTERDAY!

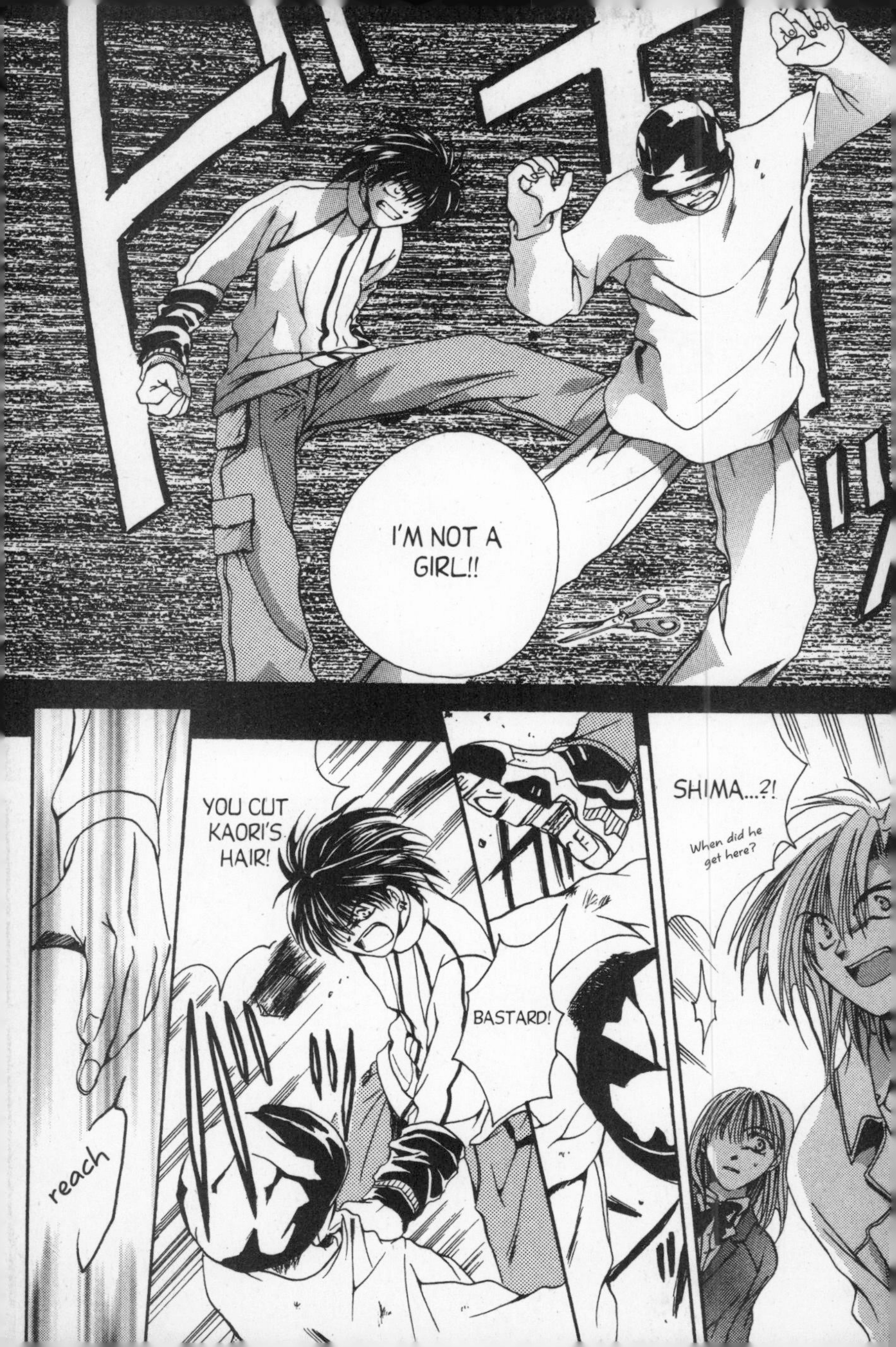
I'M NOT A GIRL!!
SHIMA...?!
When did he get here?
YOU CUT KAORI'S HAIR!
BASTARD!
reach

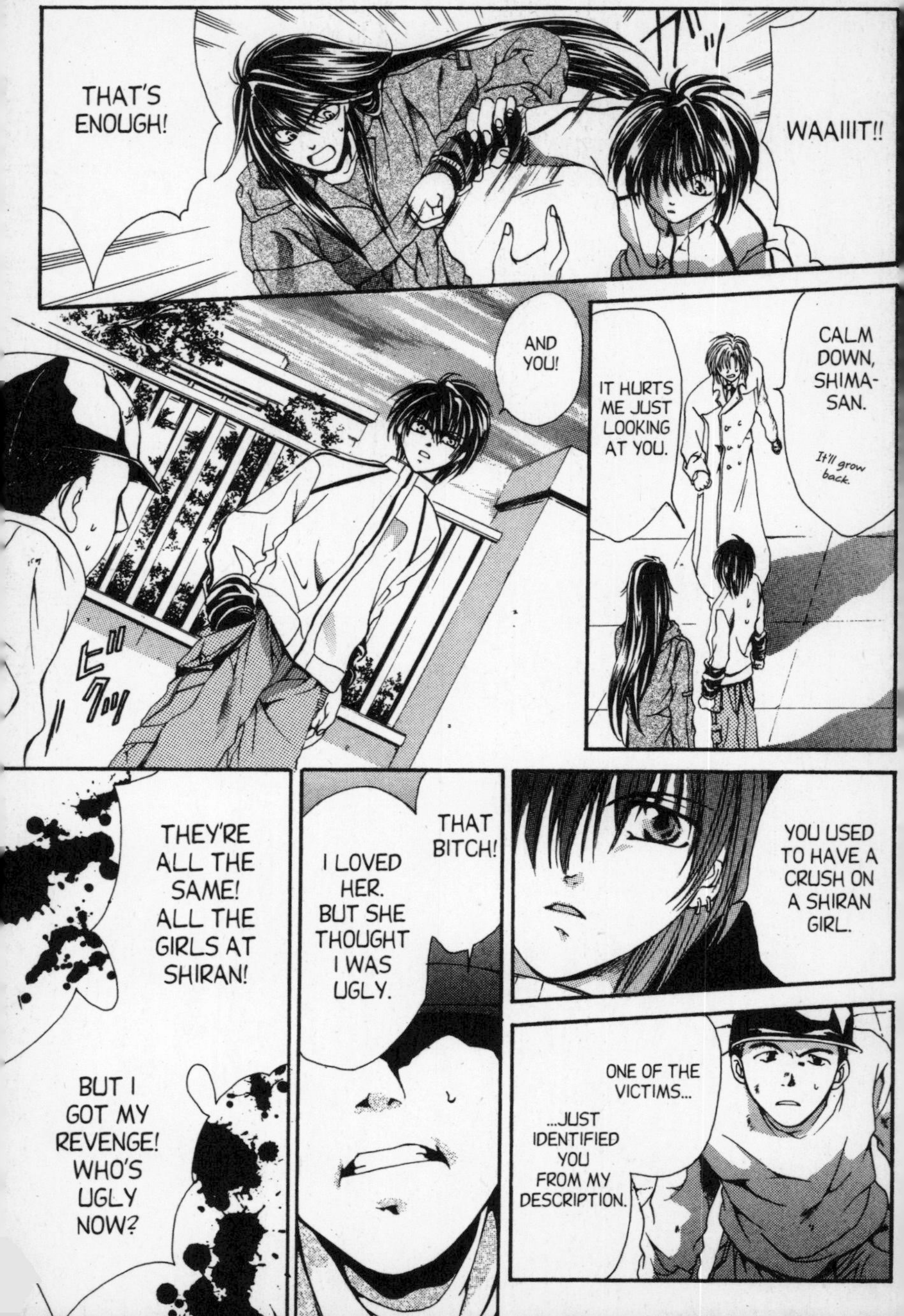
WAAIIIT!!
THAT'S ENOUGH!
CALM DOWN, SHIMA-SAN.
It'll grow back.
IT HURTS ME JUST LOOKING AT YOU.
AND YOU!
YOU USED TO HAVE A CRUSH ON A SHIRAN GIRL.
ONE OF THE VICTIMS...
...JUST IDENTIFIED YOU FROM MY DESCRIPTION.
THAT BITCH!
I LOVED HER. BUT SHE THOUGHT I WAS UGLY.
THEY'RE ALL THE SAME! ALL THE GIRLS AT SHIRAN!
BUT I GOT MY REVENGE! WHO'S UGLY NOW?

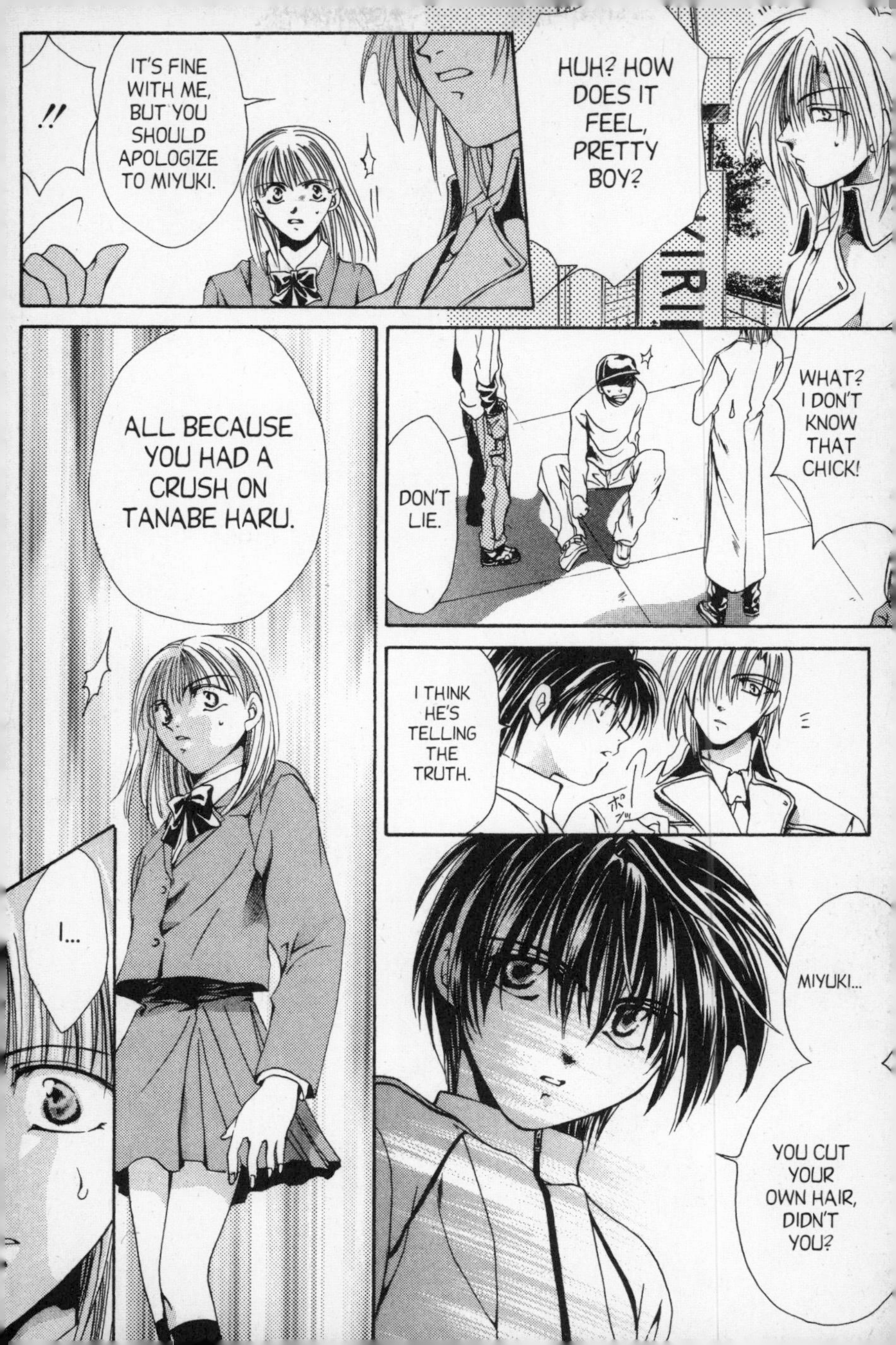
HUH? HOW DOES IT FEEL, PRETTY BOY?
IT'S FINE WITH ME, BUT YOU SHOULD APOLOGIZE TO MIYUKI.
!!
WHAT? I DON'T KNOW THAT CHICK!
DON'T LIE.
I THINK HE'S TELLING THE TRUTH.
MIYUKI...
YOU CUT YOUR OWN HAIR, DIDN'T YOU?
ALL BECAUSE YOU HAD A CRUSH ON TANABE HARU.
I...

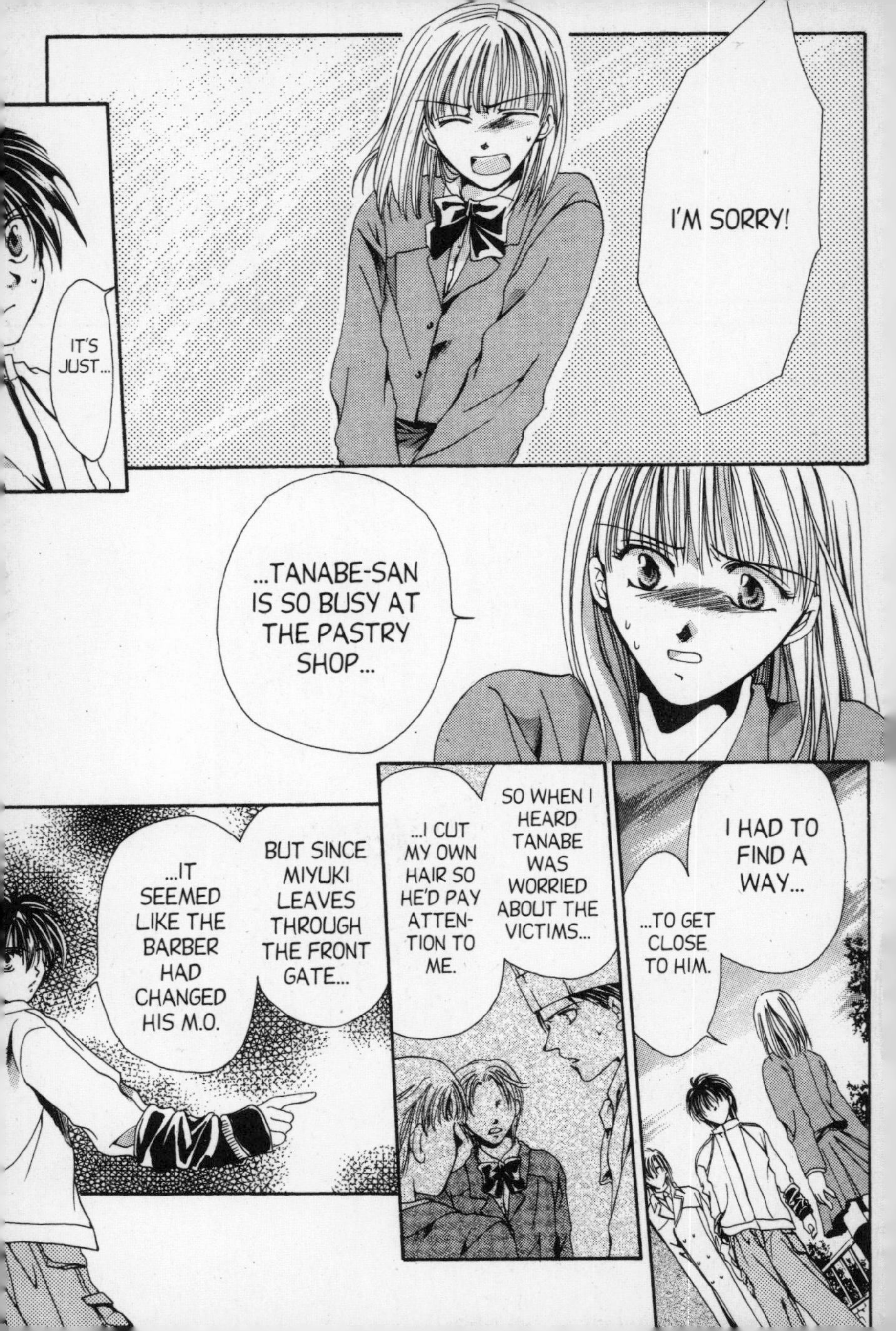
I'M SORRY!
IT'S JUST...
...TANABE-SAN IS SO BUSY AT THE PASTRY SHOP...
I HAD TO FIND A WAY...
...TO GET CLOSE TO HIM.
SO WHEN I HEARD TANABE WAS WORRIED ABOUT THE VICTIMS...
...I CUT MY OWN HAIR SO HE'D PAY ATTEN-TION TO ME.
BUT SINCE MIYUKI LEAVES THROUGH THE FRONT GATE...
...IT SEEMED LIKE THE BARBER HAD CHANGED HIS M.O.

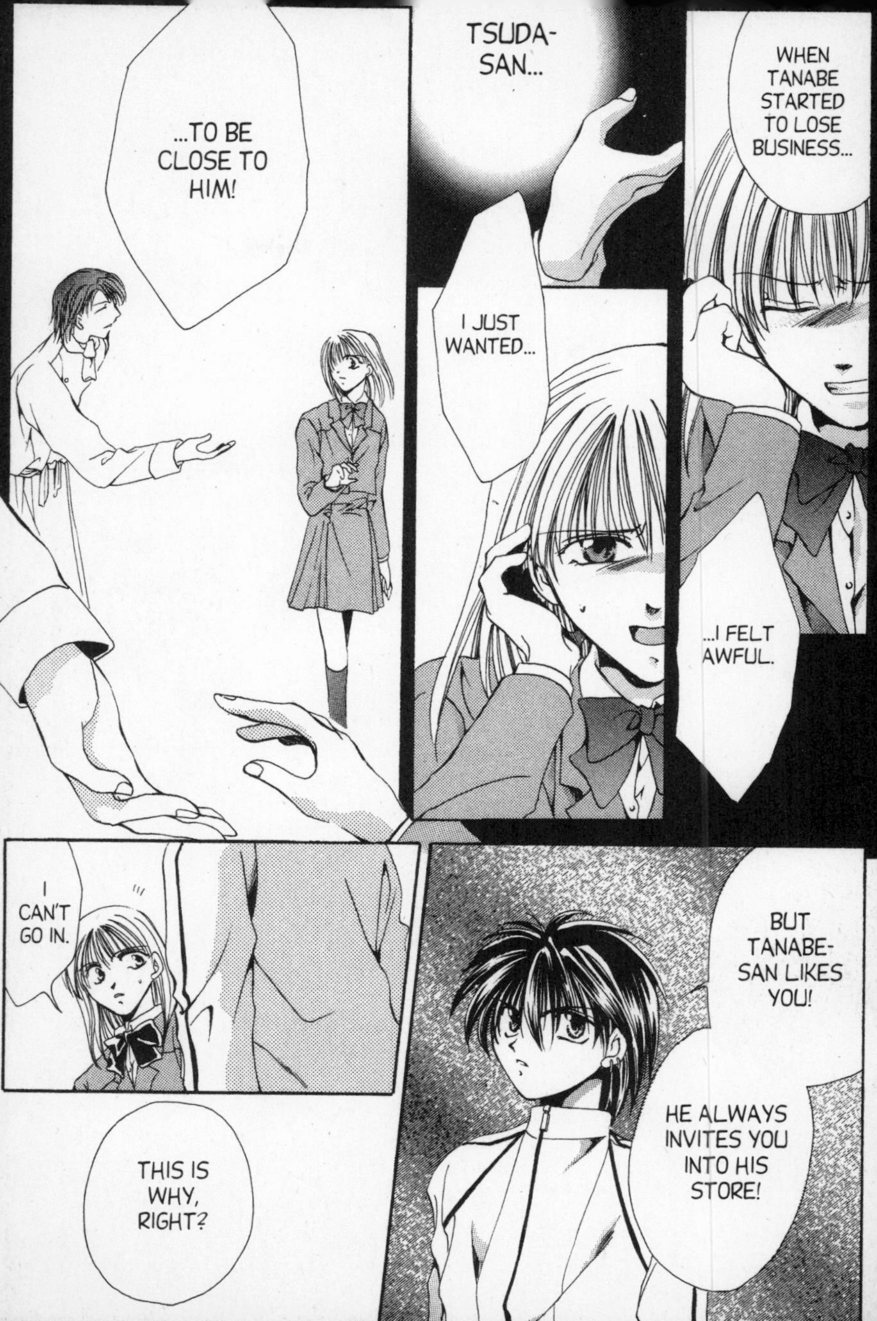
WHEN TANABE STARTED TO LOSE BUSINESS...
...I FELT AWFUL.
TSUDA-SAN...
I JUST WANTED...
...TO BE CLOSE TO HIM!
BUT TANABE-SAN LIKES YOU!
HE ALWAYS INVITES YOU INTO HIS STORE!
I CAN'T GO IN.
THIS IS WHY, RIGHT?

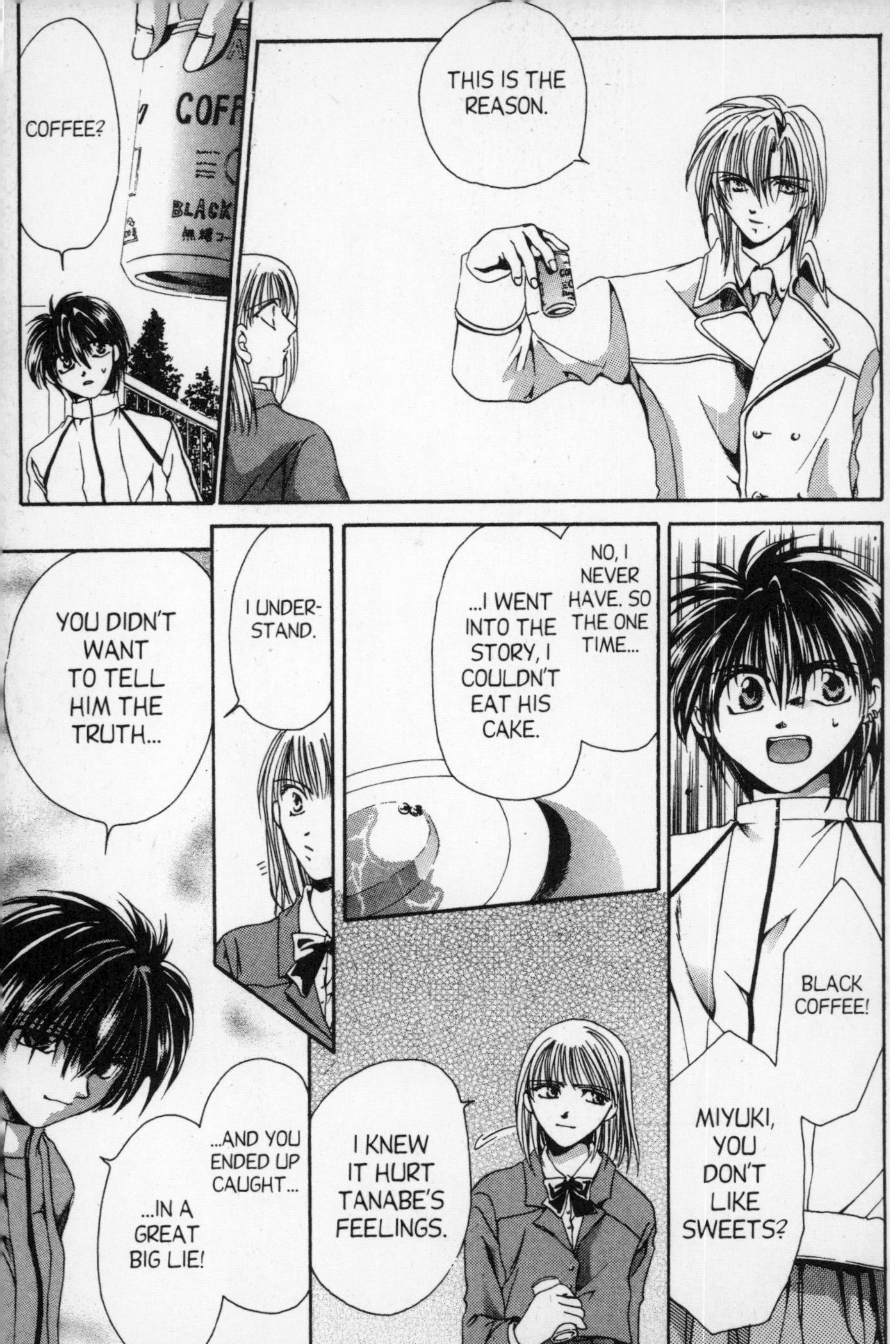
THIS IS THE REASON.
COFFEE?
BLACK COFFEE!
MIYUKI, YOU DON'T LIKE SWEETS?
NO, I NEVER HAVE. SO THE ONE TIME...
...I WENT INTO THE STORY, I COULDN'T EAT HIS CAKE.
I UNDER-STAND.
YOU DIDN'T WANT TO TELL HIM THE TRUTH...
I KNEW IT HURT TANABE'S FEELINGS.
...AND YOU ENDED UP CAUGHT...
...IN A GREAT BIG LIE!

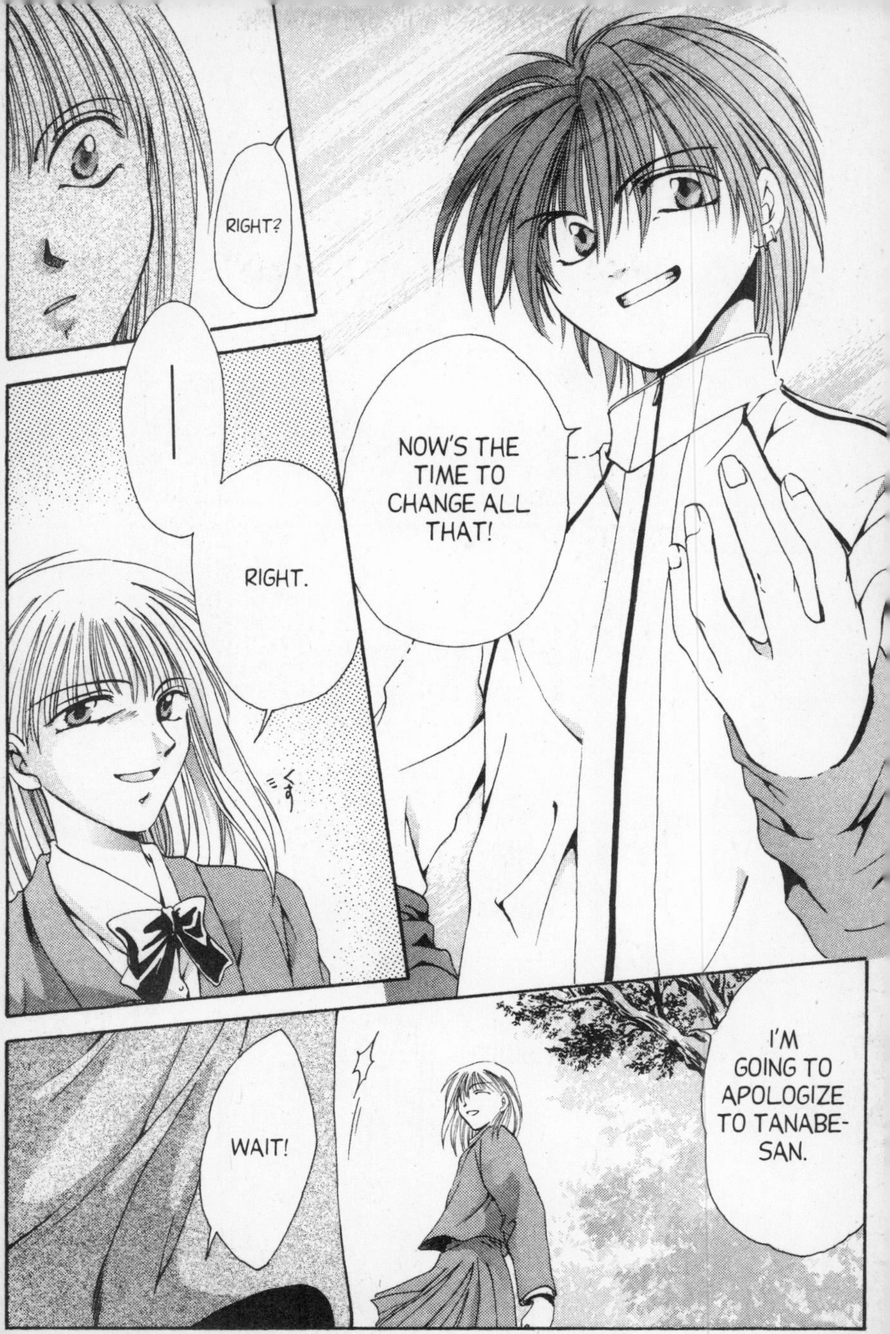
NOW'S THE TIME TO CHANGE ALL THAT!
RIGHT?
—
RIGHT.
くす
I'M GOING TO APOLOGIZE TO TANABE-SAN.
WAIT!

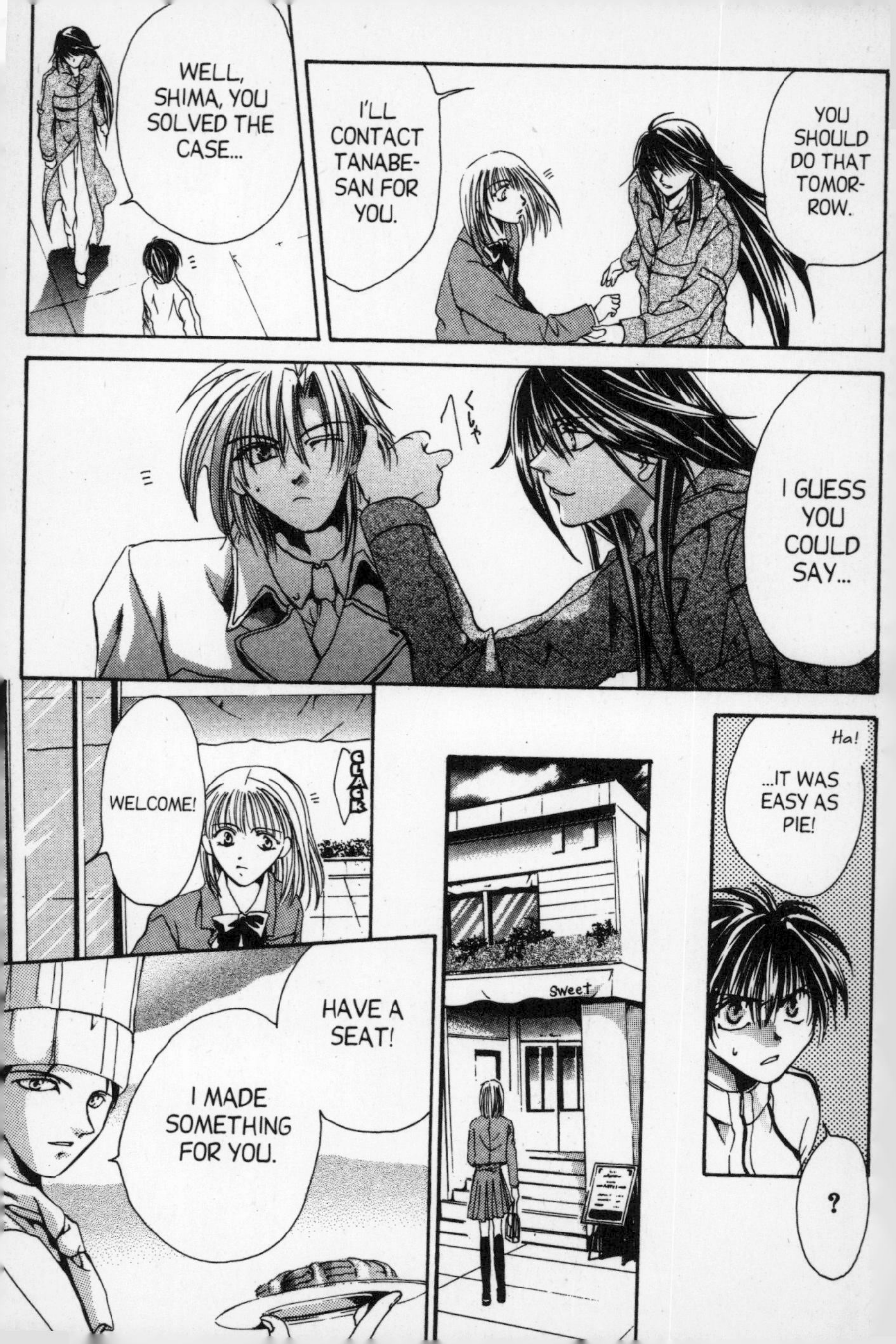
YOU SHOULD DO THAT TOMORROW.
I'LL CONTACT TANABE-SAN FOR YOU.
WELL, SHIMA, YOU SOLVED THE CASE...
くしゃ
I GUESS YOU COULD SAY...
Ha!
...IT WAS EASY AS PIE!
?
Sweet
CLACK
WELCOME!
HAVE A SEAT!
I MADE SOMETHING FOR YOU.

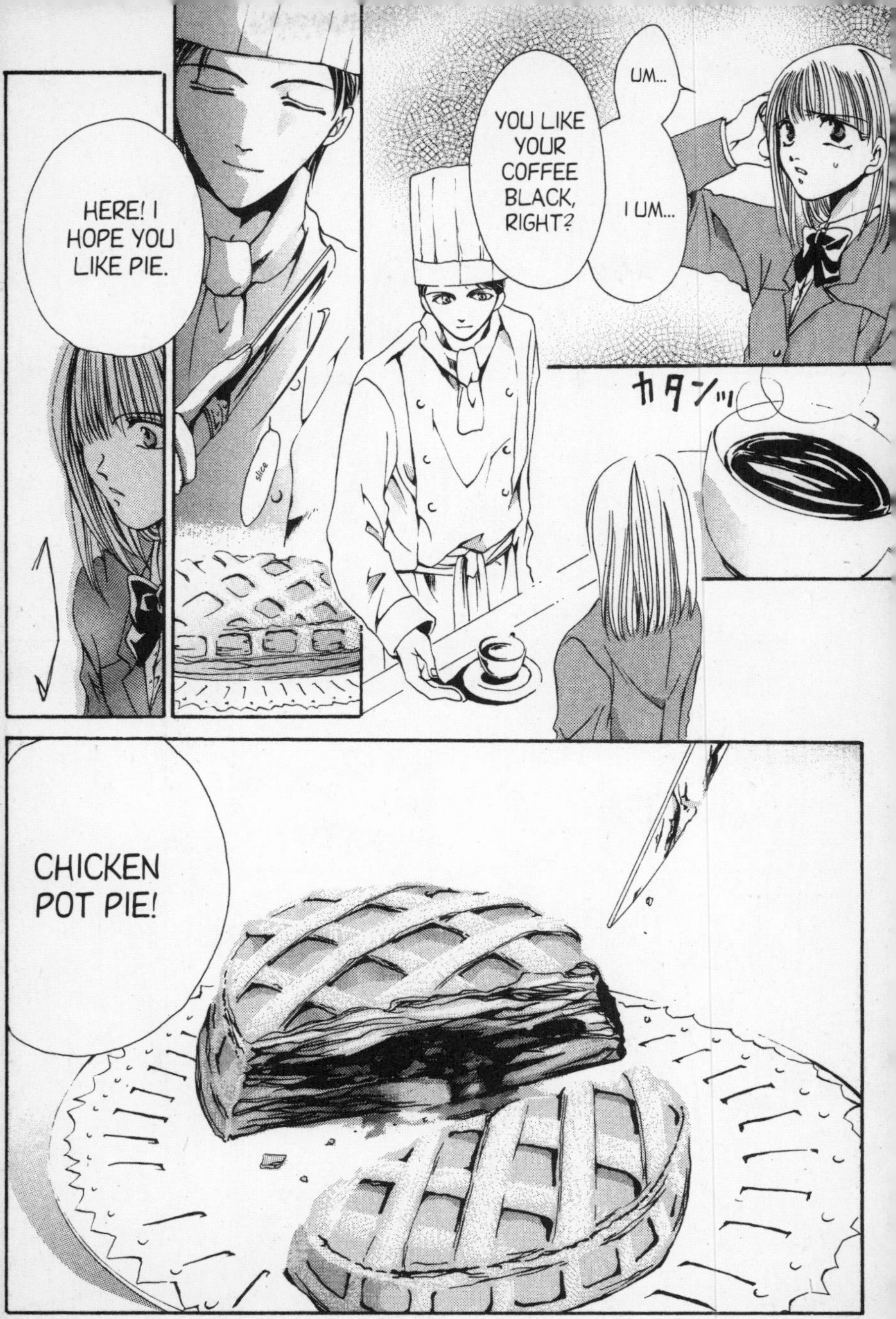
UM...
YOU LIKE YOUR COFFEE BLACK, RIGHT?
I UM...
カタンッ
slice
HERE! I HOPE YOU LIKE PIE.
CHICKEN POT PIE!

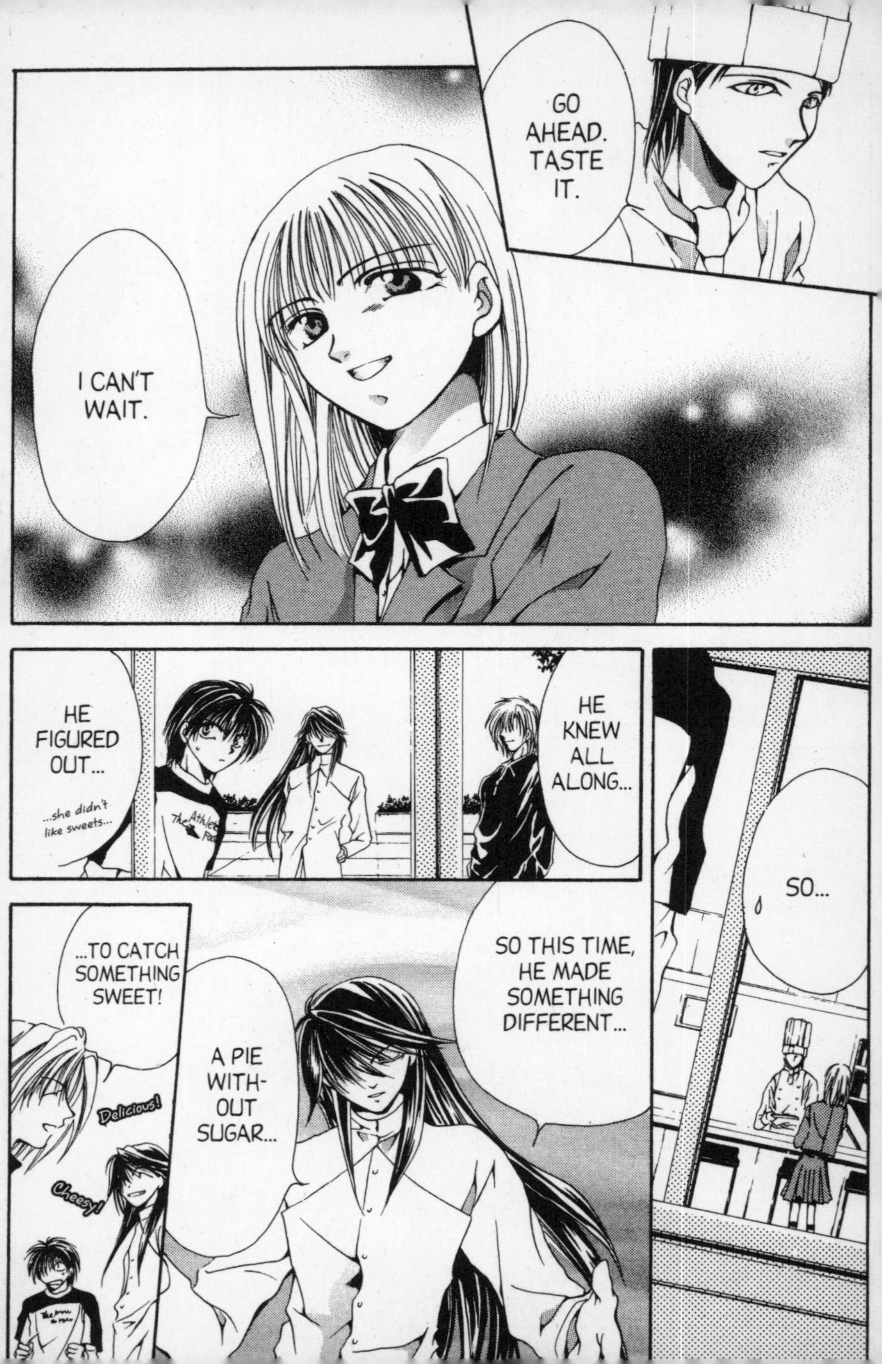
GO AHEAD. TASTE IT.
I CAN'T WAIT.
SO...
HE KNEW ALL ALONG...
HE FIGURED OUT...
...she didn't like sweets...
SO THIS TIME, HE MADE SOMETHING DIFFERENT...
A PIE WITH-OUT SUGAR...
...TO CATCH SOMETHING SWEET!
Delicious!
Cheesy!

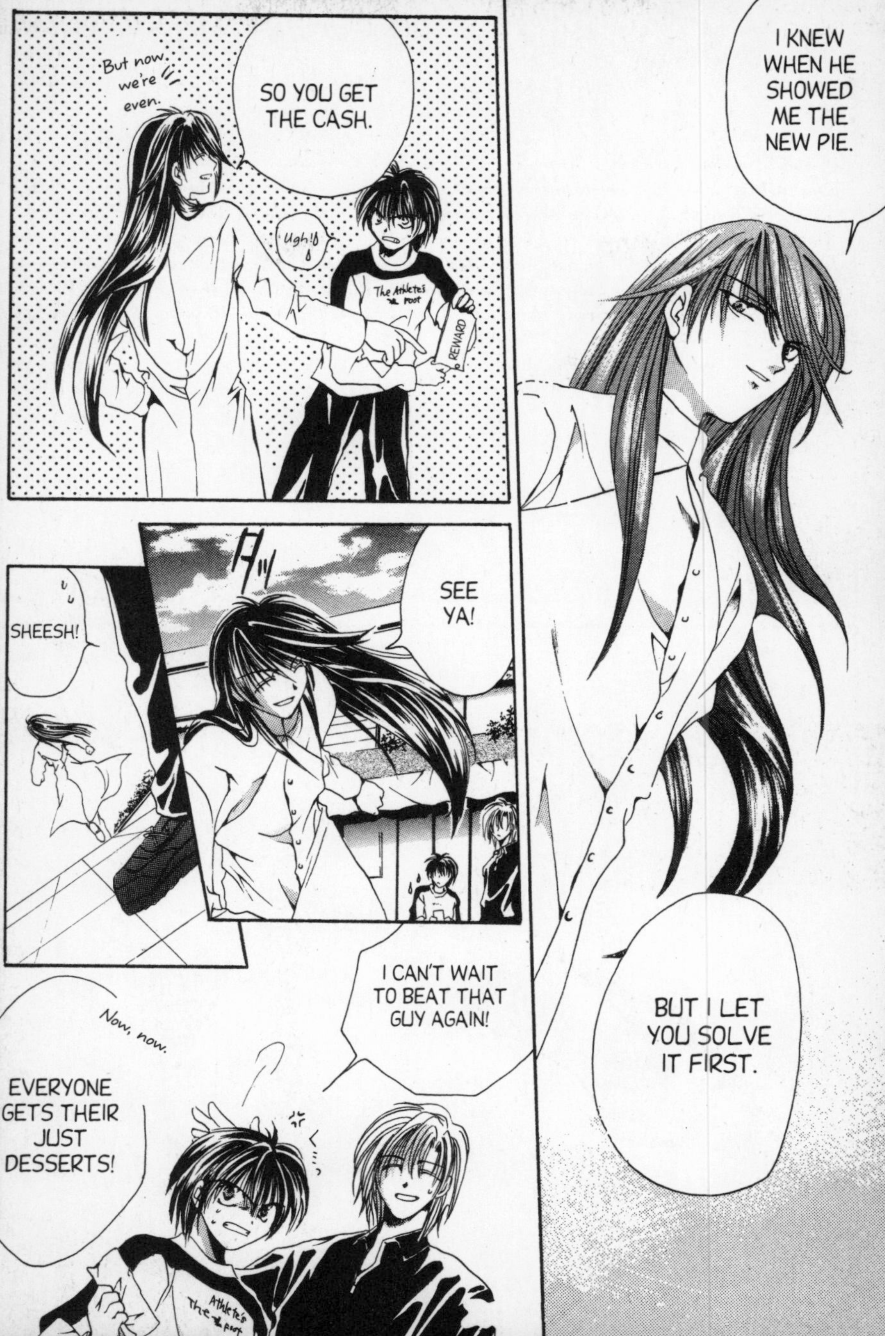
I KNEW WHEN HE SHOWED ME THE NEW PIE.
BUT I LET YOU SOLVE IT FIRST.
SO YOU GET THE CASH.
But now, we're even.
Ugh!!
The Athlete's Foot
REWARD
ダッ
SEE YA!
SHEESH!
I CAN'T WAIT TO BEAT THAT GUY AGAIN!
Now, now.
EVERYONE GETS THEIR JUST DESSERTS!
The Athlete's Foot

POSTSCRIPT

This is my postscript. It feels a little strange to see my first work turn into a book like this. It all started when my manager told me to write a story with two boys, and the first thing I imagined was this dramatic height difference, and that the little one was older. The whole story spun out of that. "Haunted by the Past" is my favorite episode. I got to draw my grandpa (laugh). I hope I was able to draw those old-fashioned styles okay. For "Impulse"--I don't know how many times I revised that story. I still don't like the way it turned out. In "Visitor" I was able to introduce the rival APP, so that's cool. I brought APP back in "The Cruelest Cut" because I wanted the two detectives to battle each other, but they ended up helping each other out, which bummed me out. About the characters...I've been asked many times by the readers about their profiles, so I'll spill my guts... Shima Yoshitsune: Born March 25. Type O blood. 159cm tall. 18 years old. Suruga Kaori (Kyo): Born November 2. Type A blood. 185cm tall. 16 years old. Hyuga Shuhei (APP): Type AB blood. 177cm tall. 20 years old. The End. All three characters' names are ancient Japanese regions. "Shima" and "Suruga" are Eastern Sea Lands. "Hyuga" is a Western Sea Land. So the original title of this series was "Yorozuya Tokaido Honpo." Many people comment that I draw too many guys in my works, but that's because I grew up reading mostly shonen manga more so than shojo manga. The next thing I know I'm drawing all guys... Is it too boring? I like to draw girls but I'm not good at it. I'll try harder...

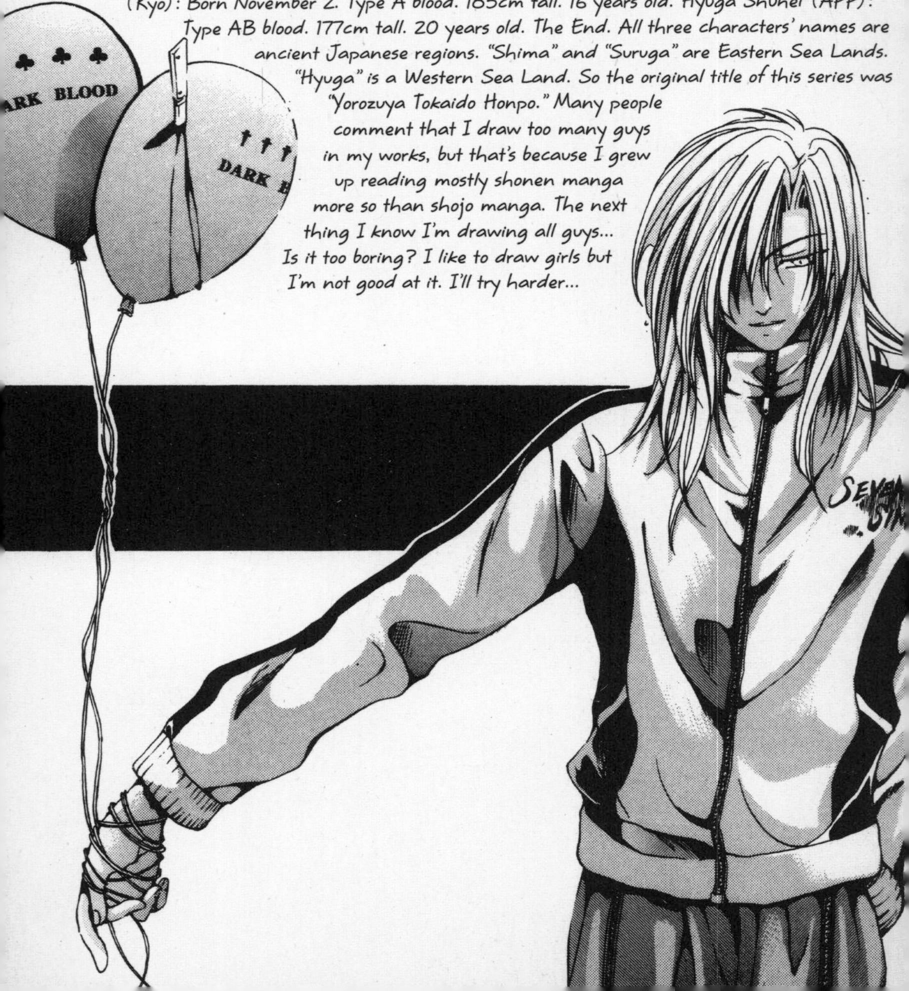
DARK BLOOD

LET'S TALK ABOUT YOUR FUTURE.

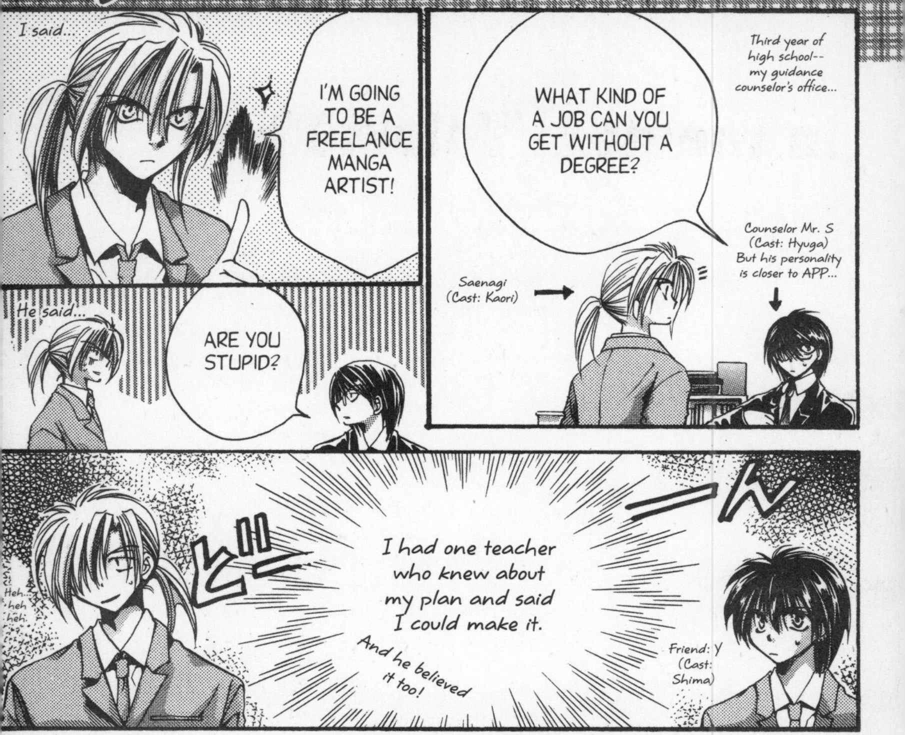
Third year of high school-- my guidance counselor's office...
WHAT KIND OF A JOB CAN YOU GET WITHOUT A DEGREE?
Counselor Mr. S (Cast: Hyuga) But his personality is closer to APP...
Saenagi (Cast: Kaori)
I said...
I'M GOING TO BE A FREELANCE MANGA ARTIST!
He said...
ARE YOU STUPID?
Friend: Y (Cast: Shima)
I had one teacher who knew about my plan and said I could make it.
And he believed it too!
Heh... heh heh.

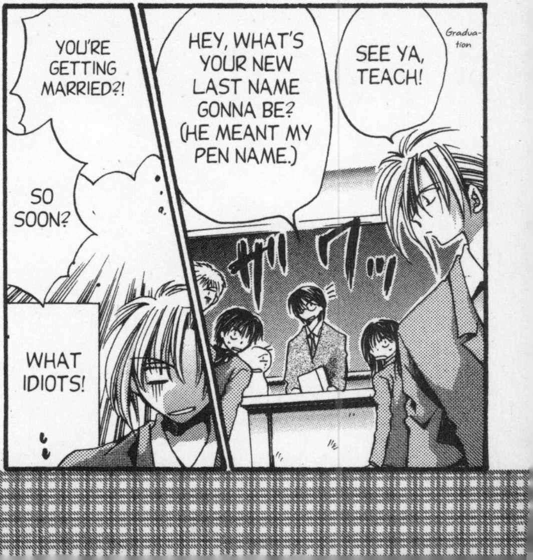
Gradua-tion
SEE YA, TEACH!
HEY, WHAT'S YOUR NEW LAST NAME GONNA BE? (HE MEANT MY PEN NAME.)
YOU'RE GETTING MARRIED?!
SO SOON?
WHAT IDIOTS!

Including that teacher, I have been supported by countless friends. I really rely on you guys! Since you've known me for the longest time, your criticisms are very straightforward! Please keep it up! I appreciate all my friends, family and helpers who help me with my work! I'm in debt to my manager... And of course to all of my readers out there: Thank you very much! (It's all I can say--but I mean it!!)

That's enough for now.
Saenagi was here!

In the next Volume of...

SATISFACTION GUARANTEED

We've got a brand new manga, never-been read, mint condition! What's in it, you ask? Why, blood-pumping tales of all-purpose handymen on the case to solve the world's biggest mysteries. This time super-sleuth Yoshitsune and handsome model Kaori face off against disgruntled amusement park employees and log cabin hooligans! Didn't get your heart racing? Well, just remember, with every purchase your satisfaction is guaranteed!